THE PRINCIPLES

OF THE

ADMINISTRATIVE LAW

GOVERNING THE RELATIONS OF

PUBLIC OFFICERS

BY

BRUCE WYMAN

OF THE FACULTY OF LAW IN HARVARD UNIVERSITY

With a New Introduction by
Kevin M. Stack
Professor of Law
Vanderbilt University Law School

THE LAWBOOK EXCHANGE, LTD.
Clark, New Jersey

ISBN 978-1-61619-426-0

Lawbook Exchange edition 2014

The quality of this reprint is equivalent to the quality of the original work.

THE LAWBOOK EXCHANGE, LTD.
33 Terminal Avenue
Clark, New Jersey 07066-1321

Please see our website for a selection of our other publications and fine facsimile reprints of classic works of legal history:
www.lawbookexchange.com

Library of Congress Cataloging-in-Publication Data

Wyman, Bruce, 1876-1926, author.
The principles of the administrative law governing the relations of public officers / by Bruce Wyman ; with a new introduction by Kevin M. Stack, Professor of Law, Vanderbilt University Law School.
pages cm.
Includes bibliographical references and index.
ISBN 978-1-61619-426-0 (hardcover : alk. paper)
1. Administrative law--United States. I. Stack, Kevin M. writer of introduction. II. Stack, Kevin M. Reclaiming "the real subject" of administrative law : a critical introduction to Bruce Wyman's The principles of the administrative law governing the relations of public officers (1903) III. Title.
KF5402.W9 2014
342.73'041--dc23

2014007872

Printed in the United States of America on acid-free paper

Reclaiming "the Real Subject" of Administrative Law

A Critical Introduction to Bruce Wyman's *The Principles of the Administrative Law Governing the Relations of Public Officers* (1903)

Kevin M. Stack*

Bruce Wyman's treatise on administrative law, *The Principles of the Administrative Law Governing the Relations of Public Officers* (1903),[1] provides the first development in American legal thought of the idea that the primary grounds of administrative legality are the internal practices and procedures that agencies adopt to structure their own exercise of discretion, as opposed to the standards and forms of judicial review. Wyman's conception was remarkable for its day. At the end of the nineteenth century, many scholars, including Wyman's colleagues at Harvard Law School, identified law with judicial decisions. But Wyman, writing a mere three years after his graduation from and subsequent appointment to the faculty of Harvard Law School, did not focus on "the external law of administration" imposed by courts, but rather mined "internal administrative law" created by agencies as the "real subject" of inquiry and source of administrative legality.[2]

---

* Professor of Law, Vanderbilt University Law School. I would like to thank Nicholas Bagley, Lisa Bressman, Edward Rubin, Daniel Sharfstein, and Ganesh Sitaraman for helpful comments on this introduction.

[1] First published by Keefe-Davison Co., St. Paul, Minn., 1903.

[2] BRUCE WYMAN, THE PRINCIPLES OF THE ADMINISTRATIVE LAW GOVERNING THE RELATIONS OF PUBLIC OFFICERS 12 (1903) [hereinafter

Wyman's conception did not, however, define the path of administrative law in the twentieth century. By the 1920s, administrative law scholarship had come to focus almost exclusively on judicial review of administrative action—its availability, standards, record for review, and remedies—and the signature intellectual contribution of Wyman's treatise fell almost completely out of view. We owe contemporary interest in Wyman's treatise to Jerry Mashaw who not only excavated it from near obscurity, but also illustrates the usefulness of Wyman's category of internal administrative law as a basis for reformation of administrative law.[3] "To the extent that we are interested in the reform of administrative law in the United States," Mashaw writes, "we might do better to operate on the internal law of administration than by ceaselessly tweaking the external law."[4] Wyman's treatise thus serves as a fount for this unfinished project devoted to internal administrative law.

The treatise contains many other insights that resonate in current debates. Indeed, in important ways, we can read Wyman as prescient: In terms strikingly familiar to our own, he defends broad legislative delegation to agencies, with agencies exercising their expert discretion to specify the requirements of the statute. He schematizes agency action as falling into executive, legislative, or adjudicative forms, offering an account of the unique processes and legal effects of each form. Wyman defends judicial deference to

---

Wyman, *Principles*]. Subsequent references to Wyman's treatise are in parenthesis to the pagination of the first publication retained in this republication.

[3] *See* JERRY L. MASHAW, CREATING THE ADMINISTRATIVE CONSTITUTION: THE LOST ONE HUNDRED YEARS OF AMERICAN ADMINISTRATIVE LAW (2012).

[4] Mashaw, *supra* note 3, at 313. For a helpful recent step in this direction, see Sidney Shapiro, Elizabeth Fisher & Wendy Wagner, *The Englightenment of Administrative Law: Looking Inside the Agency for Legitimacy*, 47 WAKE FOREST L. REV. 463 (2012).

administrative determinations in terms that parallel James Bradley Thayer's famous understanding of judicial deference to the constitutionality of legislation, a particularly striking position as "review" generally occurred at Wyman's time under common law forms of action against the officer individually. In these and other respects, Wyman presents a more comprehensive administrative jurisprudence than is commonly assumed to exist at the time of his writing. Wyman's treatise also provides a bracing reminder of other topics that fall within a broad definition of the field that have been carved out of it. Wyman, for instance, addresses police investigations and foreign affairs as part of the law of enforcement, and thus within the ambit of administration, prompting the contemporary reader to consider what has been lost from the isolation of these and other areas from the cognizance of the field.

For the student of American legal thought, Wyman's treatise offers many surprises. *The Principles of the Administrative Law* bucks the central trends of Wyman's period—and more particularly his milieu at Harvard Law School. In important respects, the treatise defies the legal formalism of the era and implicitly rejects *laissez faire* conceptions of the role of the state. Wyman saw a core and expanding regulatory mission for the state; he recognized that regulatory law will be concretized by agencies; and he understood that agencies make law by blending law and fact in a manner that makes it hard to separate law from politics.

With the hope of encouraging study of Wyman's treatise, the first section of this introductory essay provides a brief summary and reconstruction of the principal features of Wyman's vision of administrative law. The overview is selective; it is more a provocation and preview than a comprehensive restatement of Wyman's intricately organized book. The second section briefly describes the treatise's uneasy relationship with the dominant intellectual currents of the day and considers why the treatise was neglected for so long.

I. Overview of the Treatise

Wyman understands public law to have two coordinate branches, administrative law and constitutional law. (23) Constitutional law "prescribes the broad outlines of government;" with administrative law serving as it's "complement." (23) Administrative law consists of "that body of rules which defines the authority and the responsibility of that department of government which is charged with the enforcement of the law" (1), that is, "those rules which govern the executive department." (23) Administrative law, in turn, has two branches, the "external law" and the "internal law" of administration. (4) "Together, the external law and the internal law make up the law of administration." (4) This distinction, which appears to be original to Wyman, provides one of the foundational concepts in the treatise. The internal law of administration is Wyman's primary focus, and holds the most promise for reclamation. To understand Wyman's project for the internal law of administration, it makes sense to begin with Wyman's account of the external law.

The External Law of Administration

External administrative law concerns "the relations of the administration or of officers with citizens." (4) The external law is defined by common law forms of action that permitted suits against individual officers for damages, and thus is characterized by its enforceability in a judicial tribunal. At the time of Wyman's writing, there was no legislative authorization to sue the sovereign for injunctive relief or damages, as now provided by the Administrative Procedure

Act (APA) and the Federal Torts Claims Act, among other statutes. As Jerry Mashaw and Thomas Merrill have explained, "review" of an officer's action happened in the context of suits against individual officers on common law claims and under prerogative writs.[5] In a tort suit against the officer, the officer would offer the authorization by law as his defense; the court's evaluation of the defense provided review of the officer's authorization. This common "law of the land" (18) constituted, for Wyman, the external law of administration. We might identify this law as "external" in at least two senses. First, as to source, administrative functions played no role in constituting this common law; it is created by judges and exists independently from administrative powers. Second, this law is external to administration in the sense that it functions as monitoring by institutions outside of administrative bodies. (22) Today, the law establishing the grounds and standards of judicial review of agency action is external to administration in both of these senses.

Wyman does not provide a detailed discussion of the common law writs and forms of action; instead, he endeavors to provide a more general statement of this external law, as part of his effort to isolate "the first principles of the law of administration." (Preface) Wyman identifies the following as the "first rule" of external law: "that action in accordance with legal authorization is legal and the official so acting will always be justified; and that the action without warrant of law is illegal, and the official so acting will always be considered a private wrong-doer." (9–10) Wyman describes this rule, as "[w]ithout doubt," "the general rule of the common law

---

[5] Jerry L. Mashaw, *Reluctant Nationalists: Federal Administration and Administrative Law in the Republican Era, 1801–1829*, 116 YALE L.J. 1636, 1736 (2007); Thomas W. Merrill, *Article III, Agency Adjudication, and the Origins of the Appellate Review Model of Administrative Law*, 111 COLUM. L. REV. 939, 947–949 (2011).

governing the relations of officials with citizens." (10) This rule, as Wyman explains, has both a negative and positive element.

The negative element is that action without warrant in law, that is, without authorization or outside the grant of jurisdiction to the official, will always be illegal. This is the fundamental principle of *ultra vires*. As Wyman illustrates through *United States v. Lee*,[6] where the seizure of the claimant's property was without any legal authorization, even if ordered by the President, the seizure is unlawful and the claimant is entitled to relief: "All officers of the government from the highest to the lowest are creatures of the law and are bound to obey it." (11)

The positive side of this first principle of the external law has a broad sweep: "that all official action in pursuance of discretion vested in the officer by law is action in accordance with laws in whatever way that discretion may be exercised." (11) Wyman remarks that this positive side of the rule "is of great consequence; it is, indeed, the foundation of administrative law in a country subject to the common law system." (11) The scope of what it leaves unreviewable will be startling to the contemporary reader. Contemporary law under the APA makes arbitrariness review and review for abuse of discretion central grounds of judicial oversight of agencies. In contrast, as Wyman states the law of his time, "[t]he courts, therefore, in enforcing the external law of administration can only inquire whether the action has been in excess of power, never whether the action has been in abuse of power. In legal phrase, the question before the court is one of the jurisdiction; it is not one of the merits." (20)

Outside of this jurisdictional review, the only other mode of judicial review was for compliance with ministerial duties (those duties that require a "precise, definite act" such that

---

[6] 106 U.S. 196 (1882).

"all discretion is shut out by positive command of the law" (148))—the heartland of mandamus review. As famously illustrated by *Marbury v. Madison*,[7] mandamus provides enforcement of such duties; in Wyman's words, the performance of ministerial duties "will be commanded by the court." (149) Wyman thus describes a regime in which the presumption of reviewability for arbitrariness or abuse of discretion is reversed; judicial review is incident to common law forms of action, and as such, only available for the enforcement of ministerial duties and ensuring the officer did not act beyond his jurisdiction.

The sketch provided thus far would be consistent with reading Wyman as merely providing a restatement of the common law forms of action, untroubled by the delicate concerns implicated in the allocation of power between agencies and courts that characterize a mature administrative law. It might also be compatible with a formalist understanding of administration, in which most duties were understood as ministerial, and thus the unavailability of review for discretionary duties would be notable, but not a defining feature of the system.

Wyman's further exposition undermines both of these characterizations and reveals an understanding of the relation between courts and agencies that not only resonates today, but also illustrates the seeds of these ideas at the turn of the century. The conventional understanding of the standard of review in the context of a common law officer suit is *de novo*, with the court independently assessing whether the action fell within the scope of legal authorization.[8] Wyman, in contrast, endorses deference to the official's legal determinations and to the official's application of law to fact as it pertains to the agency's scope of power—and invokes a conception of

---

[7] 5 U.S. (1 Cranch) 137, 174 (1803).
[8] *See* Merrill, *supra* note 5, at 951.

legislative delegation to agencies that justifies why agencies are properly charged with specifying the content of the law.

Wyman's treatment of review of administrative regulations illustrates his embrace of deference to agency's legal determinations. To assess whether regulations issued by the Secretary of the Treasury fall within the scope of their authorizing statute, Wyman endorses the standard articulated in *Boske v. Comingore*:[9]

> In determining whether the regulations adopted by [the Secretary] are consistent with law, we must apply the rule of decision which controls when an act of Congress is assailed as not being within the powers conferred upon it by the Constitution; that is to say, a regulation should not be disregarded or annulled unless in the judge of the court it is plainly and palpably inconsistent with law. . . "Those who insist that such a regulation is invalid must make its invalidity so manifest that the court has no choice except to hold that the Secretary has exceeded his authority." (291; see also 69–70)

Here Wyman adopts James Bradley Thayer's deferential standard for constitutional review of legislation as the standard which should apply to review of the validity of administrative regulations, namely, that the violation be "so manifest as to leave no room for reasonable doubt."[10] Thayer had been Wyman's teacher and colleague for Wyman's first two years on the faculty before Thayer's death in 1902.[11] Thayer is credited with offering one of the first theories of

---

[9] 177 U.S. 459 (1900).

[10] James Bradley Thayer, *The Origin and Scope of American Doctrine of Constitutional Law*, 7 HARV. L. REV. 129, 140 (1893).

[11] CHARLES WARREN, HISTORY OF HARVARD LAW SCHOOL AND OF EARLY LEGAL CONDITIONS IN AMERICA, VOL. II, 472 (1908) (noting the "chief and saddest event of the year was the sudden death of Professor James Bradley Thayer on February 14, 1902").

judicial review of legislation grounded in the institutional balance between the judiciary and legislature. Wyman recognizes that balance is no less implicated in review of the validity of agency regulations. Indeed, the Thayarian standard Wyman embraces exceeds contemporary doctrine, identified with the *Chevron* decision,[12] as to the deference granted to the agency on determinations of law.

Wyman also saw a critical role for deference to an agency's application of law to fact, even where the application goes to the agency's jurisdiction (determinations later called "jurisdictional facts"). This view appears in Wyman's pointed criticism of Justice Holmes's resolution of the well-known nuisance case, *Miller v. Horton.*[13] In *Miller*, officers of the Board of Health killed the plaintiff's horse under an order from the Commissioners on Contagious Diseases in Animals because they determined the horse had glanders, an infectious disease. The trial court found that the horse did not in fact have glanders but denied plaintiff relief on the ground that the Board's action was justified. On appeal, the Supreme Judicial Court in Massachusetts reversed. Writing for the majority, Justice Holmes reasoned that "the authority and jurisdiction of the commissioners to condemn the plaintiff's horse under section 13 was conditional upon its actually having glanders."[14] Wyman would have dissented: "With all due respect to so eminent a judge, it seems that the solution of this case should be that the legislation had left the determination of the question of whether the animals were diseased or not to the fair discretion of the administration." (362) Wyman's critique of Justice Holmes's position foreshadows the development of

---

[12] Chevron U.S.A. Inc. v. Natural Res. Def. Council, Inc., 467 U.S. 837 (1984).
[13] 152 Mass. 540, 26 N.E. 100 (1891)
[14] 26 N.E. at 103.

deferential judicial review of agency factual determinations. Thus Wyman, far from providing a detached recounting of common law forms of action as merely *de novo*, embraces judicial deference to agency decisions, both on law and facts, within these common law forms—and reveals a keen awareness of the institutional balance between the judiciary and the executive. Scholars have typically not viewed these ideas as having much prominence in academic writing until the generation of scholars following Wyman.[15]

Just as intriguing and farsighted, Wyman offered a theory of delegation to justify the role of deference even within the narrow confines of the common law forms of action. His account so closely resembles contemporary understandings it is worth quoting in some length:

> Upon the whole the most of administration is with discretionary powers; and that is a desirable condition of things in government. The legislature will do well to pass its laws in general form and leave the executive to work out the details in enforcement. The methods and forms of administration are better decided upon by the department which is charged with enforcement of the law. As a matter of convenience, this should be the solution; since the executive department will be well versed in the difficulties that attend administration as well equipped with the means best equipped to carry a law into effect. . . . Accordingly, it seems that it will always be proper policy for the legislature to act upon to pass a general statute upon any subject matter and to leave the determination of the application of that statute to the executive. That is, again, that in the most of administration there should be discretion. (142–43)

---

[15] Merrill, *supra* note 5, at 951–952.

This short passage encapsulates a great deal of thought on legislative delegation and administration: Because the executive department will be "well versed" in the difficulties of carrying a law into effect, executive officers are in a better position to decide on the form and mode of administration (an early seed of the fundamental principle now associated with *Chenery II*[16]), and the legislature should delegate broadly. Indeed, Wyman is saying that the point of legislative delegation is to grant officers discretion. Putting this thought that most delegation will (and should be) vesting of discretion in agencies together with the unavailability of review of agencies exercise of discretion reveals the complete picture of the external law of judicial review: It operates largely on the margins, principally to check that agencies neither act as *ultra vires* nor neglect their nondiscretionary duties. But most of the work of administration, which involves the exercise of discretion, falls outside the cognizance of the external law of administration, and thus the cognizance of courts.[17]

Interestingly, for Wyman, the prohibition on judicial control over how an officer exercises discretion is not only grounded in executive expertise, but also in a strict conception of separation of powers. Wyman views the separation of powers as constituting each of the departments of government as "independent" and "co-ordinate," such that "the executive cannot be subordinated to either of the

---

[16] SEC v. Chenery Corp., 332, U.S. 194, 203 (1947) (agencies have wide discretion to choose the procedural form through which they act).

[17] For an account of nineteenth century review of administration, and critique of the current presumption of reviewability, see Nicholas Bagley, *The Puzzling Presumption of Reviewability*, 127 HARV. L. REV. 1285 (2014). Interestingly, this execution conception of administration is in some tension with his later reliance on the common law, administered by courts, as a primary source of substantive regulation of new forms of industrial organization, including of public utilities. *See* Bruce Wyman, *State Control of Public Utilities*, 24 HARV. L. REV. 624, 626, 633 (1911).

departments by any means." (62) In Wyman's view, the exclusion of judicial review of the exercise of discretion follows from this basic division and characterization of authority. In other words, once the exercise of discretion by officers is understood as an exercise of "executive" power, review by the judicial department is barred: "[T]he judicial department will not, therefore, be competent to review the evidence before the officer and revise his judgment."[18] (139) Indeed, Wyman advises, unless the prohibition on judicial review of executive discretion is established, "the administration can have no true independence in the enforcement of the law, since it will be without any real freedom of action." (135–136) Thus it makes sense that, for Wyman, "[u]pon the distinction between a discretionary duty from a ministerial duty everything turns." (137) That distinction marks the boundary of reviewable and unreviewable action. The external law of administration thus authorizes only a very narrow range of judicial review of the actions of public officers, leaving unreviewable the bulk of administration: how officials exercise power that involves discretionary duties.

---

[18] It is on these grounds that Wyman criticized the outcome in *United States v. Duell*, 172 U.S. 576 (1899), in which the Supreme Court upheld a statute permitting a court of appeals to review decisions of the Commissioner of Patents. *See* Wyman, *Principles*, at 82–85. Wyman protests, "How can there be a more flagrant example of the subordination of one of the great departments to another than is seen in this case, where a judicial court is put over an administrative office, where the action of an executive body is subject to revision by a judicial body. . . . And the end of a series of statutes might be to make the Chief Justice and the Associate Justices of the United States pass upon the propriety of every action of the President and Cabinet of the United States." (84)

The Internal Law of Administration

This narrow scope of judicial review does not, for Wyman, exhaust the contents of administrative law but rather defines the context in which its "real subject" operates—that is, the internal law of administration which addresses the constraints, practices and procedures developed by administrative bodies to structure how officials exercise administrative powers. Wyman's characterization of the internal law of administration is his most distinctive contribution.

Wyman conceives the internal law of administration as a law of collective action for bureaucracies. Wyman defines this internal law as concerning "the relations of officers with each other, or with the administration." (4, 14) Internal law addresses "the fact that many officers are bound together in action," and thus seeks to expose "the position of the officer in his organization and his function in its action." (14) The internal law thus concerns the allocation of authority among the many actors within the agency and the practices by which their individual actions constitute a collective action on behalf of the entity. Wyman acknowledges that this internal law is in part positive, something discernible as a social fact or institutional practice. The difficulty in studying administration, Wyman remarks, is "the problem is as often institutional as it is legal." (22) The "proper relations of the officials in the administration is the institutional problem." (23) But the internal law still has normative content; it is concerned with the "proper" relations of officials (23), "whether there has been proper or improper administration." (20) The internal law thus is the set of norms, procedures and practices that structure and unite activities of officers into proper collective action.

Wyman's conception of the internal law of administration, as Mashaw has forcefully argued, has not only been overlooked by contemporary administrative law scholarship, but provides a critical feature of administrative legality—whether in domestic administrative systems or for the project of global administrative law.[19] Given that oversight by elected officials is frequently politically motivated and review by courts comes sporadically and later in time, Mashaw argues, "[a] robust internal law of administration is always necessary to systemic legality and is often the most constant protector of private rights."[20] The suggestion that agency's own internal decisions on organization and procedure constitute a "law" does not make sense if we identify administrative law with external constraints on agency discretion.[21] But, as Mashaw explains, that understanding confuses the hierarchical position of a law within a legal system "with how to identify what counts as law."[22] Administrative practices, no less than judicial practices, may constitute law so long as those practices, like their judicial counterparts, have a normative element that recognizes their law-like character.[23] About these matters of jurisprudence, Wyman was not confused. Indeed, his treatise reflects an industrious effort to schematize the elements of internal administrative law.

A central element of this internal law is the organization of administration. As he writes, "[w]hen many officers are found in action together the law must provide for their inter-relation." (185) "It is the internal law of the administration to a large degree that deals with these complex matters of organization; it has to solve these intricate matters by theories of its own." (185) Centralized administrations, like the federal government (203), must "of necessity be a matter of

---

[19] Mashaw, *supra* note 3, at 281.
[20] *Id.* at 223.
[21] *Id.* at 280–281.
[22] *Id.* at 281.
[23] *Id.*

devolution of powers of superior upon inferior." (204) For Wyman, the distinction between discretionary and ministerial duties is the key to understanding the delegation of power internal to centralized administration, with discretionary duties by superiors eventually concretizing into ministerial duties of inferior offices. In the usual process of administration, for example, "the head of a department gives a general order to the chief of a bureau; the result is that it is the ministerial duty of the chief of bureau to act, but what action he shall take is within the discretionary power allowed to him by this general order." (215–16) This process recurs down the hierarchy until it ultimately reaches a lower-level official whose only duty is ministerial. (216) Wyman understands this allocation and reallocation of discretionary and ministerial duties to be the organizational basis for all methods of administration.[24] (261)

As part of the internal law, Wyman identifies "three processes of administration: First, administration by execution; second, administration by legislation; third, administration by adjudication." (262) These processes are structured by their own internal law. Perhaps of greatest interest among these three processes is Wyman's treatment of the administration by legislation, what we call rules or administrative regulations. Wyman sees the legislative functions of administration as having both written and unwritten elements. Wyman describes the function of written

---

[24] Not surprisingly, Max Weber's later conceptualization of bureaucracy also recognized the hierarchical structuring of the organization, through general orders as central to "modern public administration." *See* Max Weber, *Essays in Sociology*, *reprinted in* 58 GREAT BOOKS OF THE WESTERN WORLD 143–145 (Mortimer J. Adler ed.1990) (Chapter 8, Bureaucracy, I: Characteristics of Bureaucracy). For a contemporary account of the concepts of supervision and authorization in bureaucracy, see EDWARD L. RUBIN, BEYOND CAMELOT: RETHINKING POLITICS AND LAW FOR THE MODERN STATE 96–109 (2005).

regulations in terms sympathetic to contemporary understanding. Legislative regulations are necessary because "[w]hen the law is put in the statute book it is not specific enough for administration." (285) That is, the law "requires further elucidation. That is the office of the legislation which is done by administration." (285) With this essential function of specifying the law so it is in a shape for "convenient administration," Wyman already saw the seeds of the ubiquity of regulations as the operative source of legal obligations imposed by the government on the public:

> These regulations represent the exercise of a very considerable power on the part of public officers in their relation with the public. And they serve a purpose in the administration not commonly appreciated. There are innumerable instances of these regulations. The regulations, directions, circulars, instructions, forms, promulgated by the executive department confront the citizen in all his dealings with the government. (286)

So what, then, is the *unwritten* legislative function of administration? "To note an analogy," Wyman explains, "it may be said that the administration has statute law of its own—its regulations—and that administration has as well common law of its own—its customs." (294) The "rules" governing administration, Wyman writes, may be both written and unwritten, and "so long as administration proceeds by common consent in subjection with a body of rules, it makes no difference how many of those rules are written and how many of them are unwritten." (294) This unwritten law, a "national executive common law" (297), has a critical role. While executive officers are generally limited by statute, Wyman admonishes that it would reflect a foolish misunderstanding "[t]o attempt to regulate by law the minute movements of every part of the complicated machinery of government," (296)—an "unpardonable ignorance" that no doubt has claimed adherents in generations of students of administration. But even if it is foolhardy to specify in written law all operations of government, Wyman suggests that there must be some source of guidance and constraint. Wyman's answer is the "common law" of executive power. "Hence," Wyman writes, "usages have been established in every department of government which have become a kind of common law, and regulated the rights and duties of those who act within their respective limits." (296) The idea is that executive usage, or "construction of the statute in practice" when adhered to over a long period of years "must be regarded as absolutely conclusive in its effect." (299) Wyman thus sees executive gloss on a statutory power, when long maintained, as determining the meaning of the law and operating as a critical protector of legality in a fashion similar to the common law in courts:

> The theory of stare decisis as it is understood in the courts of law is thus to a certain extent the rule in offices of the executive departments. It would be unsatisfactory administration indeed where the determination of each question was as different as caprice might dictate. What is wished is an orderly administration, in which precedents are regarded, in which the principles involved in those precedents are respected, as the cases that are to govern future administration. That is the recognition of an unwritten body of law. No administration that does not proceed in that way can succeed. (303)

While the opinion giving function of the Office of Legal Counsel has received some attention as a source of law and precedent within the executive branch,[25] Wyman envisions a

---

[25]*See* Trevor W. Morrison, *Stare Decisis in the Office of Legal Counsel*, 110 COLUM. L. REV. 1448, 1492–1497 (2010) (defending a theory of stare decision for OLC); Dawn E. Johnsen, *Faithfully Executing the Laws:*

broader array of stable practices across the full scope of administration as constituting a set of rules that anchor agency decision making, a customary law of administration.[26] Here the legality of administration is more a matter of its own internal constraint than compliance with an external law. Wyman thus invites reconsideration of the place of agency practice in securing systemic legality within the administrative state, as opposed to naively trying to vanquish or micromanage that discretion from outside.

Wyman invites this consideration as to a much broader array of enforcement and executive entities than fit within the current gauge of administrative law. With the law governing public officers, Wyman includes powers associated with war, such as coercion and apprehension (266, 272), powers associated with police work, such as arrest and seizure (275, 278), and revenue collection (282). With a few exceptions, the executive's war powers and policing have fallen outside the occupation, even if not the definitions of, administrative law.[27]

Internal Legal Constraints on Executive Power, 54 UCLA L. REV. 1559 (2007) (examining OLC as a source of legal constraint on executive action); *see also* Curtis A. Bradley & Trevor W. Morrison, *Historical Gloss on the Separation of Powers*, 126 HARV. L. REV. 411, 417–424 (2012) (documenting reliance by courts on historical practice in determining the separation of powers).

[26] *See* John Gardner, *Some Types of Law*, in COMMON LAW THEORY 51, 6–74 (Douglas E. Edlin, ed. 2007) (distinguishing customary law *in foro*, of officials, from the Common Law). One prominent example is *FDA v. Brown & Williamson Tobacco Corp.*, 529 U.S.120, 145 (2000), in which the court relied on the agency's consistent construction of its statute as not authorizing the agency to regulate tobacco as a reason for prohibiting the agency from so regulating, despite solid textual arguments for its permissibility.

[27] For policing, the canonical exception is Kenneth Culp Davis. *See, e.g.*, POLICE DISCRETION (1975); for understanding prosecution as a mode of administration, *see, e.g.*, Rachel E. Barkow, *Administering Crime*, 52 UCLA L. REV. 715 (2005); Rachel E. Barkow, *Institutional Design and the Policing of Prosecutors: Lessons from Administrative Law*, 61 STAN.

II. Context and Consequence

The Principles of the Administrative Law is a remarkable book for its time and intellectual climate. At the broadest level of generality, Wyman's treatise could be viewed as consistent with the formalism often associated with Harvard Law School in the late nineteenth century. A core premise of Landgell's conception of law is that law is a science defined by a set of principles, few in number.[28] Wyman's treatise could be viewed as of a piece with this systematizing conception at least in the sense that he sets out to state "the first principles of the law of administration." Wyman's treatise manifests other formalist impulses as well, perhaps most clearly revealed in Wyman's categorical conception of the separation of powers.

But the general thrust of the treatise defies important tenets of Langdellian formalism. Perhaps most obviously and importantly, the focus of legal thought at the time was almost exclusively on judges. Indeed, the identification of courts with the law was conceptually thicker than today. As Robert W. Gordon writes, administrative materials, like statutes, could not be "accommodated by the methods of private-law science."[29] As a result, a strain of the Harvard faculty "did not even consider statutes and administrative decisions to be 'law' until and unless they were interpreted by a court."[30] Not

---

L. REV. 869 (2009). For consideration of war powers from an administrative perspective, *see, e.g.*, Curtis A. Bradley, Chevron *Deference and Foreign Affairs*, 86 VA. L. REV. 649 (2000); Ganesh Sitaraman, *Foreign Hard Look Review*, 66 ADMIN. L. REV. (forthcoming 2014).

[28] NEIL DUXBURY, PATTERNS OF AMERICAN JURISPRUDENCE 15 (1995); Thomas C. Grey, Langdell's Orthodoxy, 45 U. PITT. L. REV. 1, 13 (1983).

[29] Robert W. Gordon, *The Case for (and Against) Harvard*, 93 MICH. L. REV. 1231, 1244 (1994) (reviewing LOGIC AND EXPERIENCE: THE ORIGINS OF MODERN AMERICAN LEGAL EDUCATION by William P. LaPiana (1994)).

[30] *Id.*

so for Wyman. While judges play an important role on the periphery of administrative law, his treatise is largely devoted to providing a systematic description of administrative bodies, their membership, structures, and practices; all of these features exist independently from judicial cognizance.[31] Wyman's focus on the internal law of administration strikingly illustrates how far his thought was from the views of his Harvard colleagues John Beale, who was also Wyman's co-author, and John Chipman Gray that, as Neil Duxbury writes, "that judges always create the law and, accordingly, that nothing is law until declared to be so by the courts."[32]

Just as fundamentally, Wyman did not define law in opposition to discretion. As opposed to defying the category of law, the exercise of discretion is, for Wyman, part and parcel of the specification and elaboration of the law. He not only recognized that the administrative state is founded on vesting discretion—that "most administration will be discretionary powers"—but further acknowledges the overlap of administration and politics. "[I]n large matters," Wyman writes, "questions of administration cannot be separated from questions of politics." (196) Even if courts never fully embraced the purest versions of formalism which posited law as a scientific system, Wyman's embrace of discretion as a fount of law and its intermingling with politics, stands him closer to later pragmatic and realist writers than to his formalist colleagues. Indeed, for Wyman, the challenge for administrative law is to explain the constraints on discretion so that its exercise will be more than what "caprice would dictate," but not to deny the existence of discretion, or to try to "try to regulate by law the minute movements" of government. (303, 296) Discretion is a condition of

---

[31] In this respect, Wyman's treatise is closer to other early work on administrative bodies by Ernst Freund and Frank Goodnow.
[32] Duxbury, *supra* note 28, at 51.

administration, and eliminating it is not a precondition for administrative legitimacy.

Although *The Principles of the Administrative Law* is devoted to stating a trans-substantive law, not substantive regulation, Wyman's approach makes clear that he does not adopt *laissez faire* premises on the role of government. Prominent judicial decisions in the late nineteenth century embraced the idea, with strong echoes of Herbert Spencer, that "[p]rivate relations between economic actors were to be governed not by statutes, but by contractual rights and duties accepted by those actors."[33] The *laissez-faire* tenet that courts had a role in preserving an inviolable sphere of private contractual right from government regulation, a proposition commonly associated with *Lochner v. New York*[34] but with roots well before it,[35] finds no home in Wyman's treatise. Wyman's foundational law review article, *The Law of the Public Callings as a Solution to the Trust Problem*,[36] published one year after *The Principles of the Administrative Law*, makes this explicit. Defending public callings as a basis for regulating trusts, Wyman ends with an attack on *laissez faire* conceptions:

> The positive law of the public calling is the only protection that the public have in a situation such as this, where there is no competition among the sellers to operate in its favor. So much has our law been permeated with the theory of *laissez faire*, which was but lately so prominent in the policy of our state, that the admission has been made with much hesitation that state control is even necessary. But the modern conclusion, after some bitter experience, is that freedom can be allowed only where conditions of virtual

---

[33] Duxbury, *supra* note 28, at 30.
[34] 198 U.S. 45, 53 (1905).
[35] Duxbury, *supra* note 28, at 30.
[36] 17 HARV. L. REV. 156 (1904).

> competition prevail, for in conditions of virtual monopoly, without stern restrictions, there is always great mischief. . . [State control of public service companies] is based upon the conclusion that it is no inconsistency for the State to leave the generality of business free from restrictions, while controlling with a strict code such lines of industry as are affected with a public interest.[37]

Wyman thus rejects the idea that government had no role to play in regulating the market actors; the question is the balance and scope of that regulation. Wyman, moreover, saw the list of businesses falling within the ambit of public service regulation as likely to grow, including not only telephone service, but other utilities, ice plants, and "cotton factories of the South."[38] *The Principles of the Administrative Law* thus begins to see the logic for a growing administrative state prompted by the need for government regulation of the markets,[39] a core tenet of the emerging politics of the era.[40]

---

[37] 17 HARV. L. REV. at 172–173.

[38] Law of Public Service, Cambridge Tribune, vol. 36, No. 5, at 12 (Mar. 29, 1913).

[39] *See* William J. Novak, *Law and the Social Control of American Capitialism*, 60 EMORY L.J. 377, 393 (2010) (noting that Wyman, along with Freund and Goodnow, is a neglected architect of the emerging regulatory state); William J. Novak, *The Legal Origins of the Modern American State in* LOOKING BACK AT LAW'S CENTURY 249, 268-72 (Austin Sarat et al., eds. 2002) (providing account of administrative law in the fundamental rethinking of the American nation-state following the Civil War

[40] *See* JOHN WHITECLAY CHAMBERS II, THE TYRANNY OF CHANGE: AMERICA IN THE PROGRESSIVE ERA, 1890–1920 136–137 (1992 Second Edition) (describing the new interest in intervention in the markets prompted by mass immigration, rapid urbanization, industrialization, and the depression of the 1890s, among other forces); GABRIEL KOLKO, THE TRIUMPH OF CONSERVATISM: A REINTERPRETATION OF AMERICAN HISTORY, 1900–1916 (1963) (arguing business interest, with railroads in

The treatise was one of many works devoted to understanding the law applicable to regulated industry Wyman produced in his relatively short career as an academic. Wyman graduated from Harvard Law School in 1900 and was appointed to its faculty the same year, first as a Lecturer, teaching "a wholly new half course on Administrative Law" in the fall of 1900.[41] He continued as a Lecturer for two years, also teaching Surety and Mortgage, Property, Carriers and Conflicts of Law.[42] Wyman was appointed Assistant Professor in 1903, and in 1908, became Professor of Law, a title he held until his resignation in 1913. During that time he also taught Contracts and Public Service Companies.[43]

In addition to his administrative law treatise, Wyman published a torrent of material on public regulation, trade regulation and other regulated industries, including more than seven monographs and case books between 1902 and 1911,[44] as well as articles in periodicals such as the *Harvard Law Review*, *Yale Law Journal*, the *Columbia Law Review*, and the *Green Bag*. With the publication of his monograph, *Control of the Market: A Legal Solution to the Trust Problem* (1911), Wyman began to reach a popular audience. In 1912,

---

the lead, supported increased government involvement and regulation of the markets).

[41] Warren, *supra* note 11, at 471–472.

[42] THE CENTENNIAL HISTORY OF THE HARVARD LAW SCHOOL, 1817–1917, 287 (1917).

[43] *Id.*

[44] *See, e.g.*, CASES ON PUBLIC SERVICE COMPANIES: PUBLIC CARRIERS, PUBLIC WORKS, AND OTHER PUBLIC UTILITIES (1902), with his colleague Joseph Beale, CASES ON RESTRAINT OF TRADE (1903), with his colleague Jeremiah Smith, A SELECTION OF CASES ON MORTGAGES (1906), THE LAW OF RAILROAD REGULATION WITH SPECIAL REFERENCE TO AMERICAN LEGISLATION (1907), with Beale, CONTROL OF THE MARKET: A LEGAL SOLUTION TO THE TRUST PROBLEM (1911), THE SPECIAL LAW GOVERNING PUBLIC SERVICE CORPORATIONS AND ALL OTHERS ENGAGED IN PUBLIC EMPLOYMENT (1911).

the book received a glowing review in *The New York Times*. "It would be hard to find a better discussion" the review reported, of a more urgent issue.[45]

After a dozen years of ascent as an academic, Wyman's career at Harvard was cut short by a sequence of events resulting in this resignation in 1913. Wyman had lectured on numerous occasions taking a favorable stance to the powerful New York, New Haven & Hartford Railroad (the "New Haven") and the Boston & Maine Railroad without disclosing that he had been on retainer from the New Haven. When these facts came to light in December, 1913, Wyman immediately resigned from Harvard, stating that if he remained connected to the institution, he may cause the college and law school an injury "without regard to the innocence of my motives."[46] The nation's leading newspapers, including *The New York Times* and *The Boston Daily Globe* covered the resignation.[47] The New Haven operated on the wrong side of history. Louis Brandeis famously led investigations into the New Haven's business practices, ultimately resulting in convictions for political bribery, financing "independent" experts, filing misleading public reports, and misuse of funds.[48] Perhaps, as Arthur Sutherland opines in his history of Harvard Law School, Wyman's speeches on behalf of the railroads would have been beyond rebuke if he had merely pointed out his professional engagement.[49] "Half a century and more later,"

---

[45] *Regulating the Trusts, A Harvard Professor on the Leading Topic of the Day*, The New York Times BR 115 (Mar. 3, 1912).

[46] *Prof. Wyman Resigns: Harvard Instructor Admitted He Lectured For Pay*, The New York Times (Dec. 21, 1913).

[47] *Id.*; *Resignation Accepted*, Boston Daily Globe, p. 9 (Dec. 23, 1913).

[48] Edward C. Kirkland, Review of *The Fall of a Railroad Empire: Brandeis and the New Haven Merger Battle* by Henry Lee Stables and Alpheus T. Mason (1947), 14 LAW & CONTEMP. PROBS. 407, 408 (1949).

[49] ARTHUR E. SUTHERLAND, THE LAW AT HARVARD 217 (1967).

Sutherland muses, "one thinks of the episode with regret and sympathy."[50]

Following Wyman's unanticipated resignation from Harvard, Dean Ezra R. Thayer took over Wyman's "most important course," on Public Service Companies, his colleague Samuel Williston took over his contracts course, and his course on administrative law was taken over by N. Roscoe Pound.[51] Coincidently, members of the faculty at Harvard had previously been in contact with Felix Frankfurter, hoping to convince him to join the faculty.[52] As Justice Frankfurter later recounted, Wyman's abrupt resignation created a vacancy, which he ended up filling.[53]

After Wyman's departure from Harvard, he undertook a wide array of legal practice, serving as counsel to the New York, New Haven & Hartford Railroad, among other railroad lines and steamship companies. In his entry in the twentieth reunion notes of the Harvard Class of 1896, Wyman reproduced his publisher's praise for his forthcoming book, noting with some detachment, "[w]hen one has been as much before the public as I have, he becomes more or less indifferent to what is said in print, finding what is written as abuse and is meant as praise just about offset each other."[54]

Wyman continued to teach and write. He lectured at Chicago Law School, and in 1919 was one of the founding faculty members of the Portia Law School, charted "to furnish

---

[50] *Id.*

[51] *Harvard Reopens Its Doors*, The Cambridge Tribune, vol. 36, p. 3 (Sat. Jan. 10, 1914).

[52] FELIX FRANKFURTER, FELIX FRANKFURTER REMINISCES, RECORDED TALKS WITH DR. HARLAN B. PHILLIPS 78–80 (1960).

[53] *Id.* at 80.

[54] HARVARD COLLEGE CLASS OF 1896, SECRETARY'S FIFTH REPORT 299 (June 1916).

instruction in law to women only."[55] Wyman taught at Portia Law School, which today is New England Law School, until he died of heart trouble at the age of 50, on June 21, 1926. An obituary in *The New York Times* recognized him as "an international authority on transportation laws and public service utilities."[56]

One cannot help wonder how this sequence of events—the circumstances of Wyman's resignation, his relatively brief tenure at Harvard, and the prominence of Frankfurter as Wyman's successor—muted the reception of Wyman's work,[57] even of his administrative law treatise penned more than a decade before his resignation. Legal developments also contributed to the neglect of Wyman's treatise.[58] By the 1920s, administrative law was concerned primarily with judicial review of agency action, ultimately adopting what Thomas Merrill calls "the appellate review model" of judicial review.[59] Under this model, judicial review is based exclusively on the record before the agency, remands were issued if additional facts need to be developed, and the standard of review revolved around the law-fact distinction,

---

[55] An Act to incorporate the Portia Law School, Mass. Gen. Laws ch. 219 (June 27, 1919).

[56] *Bruce Wyman Dies; Rail Law Authority*, The New York Times (June 22, 1926).

[57] But nonetheless Wyman's impact on the public utility law was significant. *See, e g.*, Jim Rossi, *The Common Law "Duty to Serve" and Protection of Consumers in an Age of Competitive Retail Public Utility Restructing*, 51 VAND. L. REV. 1243–1266 (1989) (documenting Wyman's role in justifying a public utility duty to serve even when it is not profitable).

[58] Political developments no doubt contributed to his neglect as well. Professor Novak, for instance, argues that the achievements of Wyman, Freund, and Goodnow "have been obscured by a focus on the more visible and easily digestable achievements of muckraking and trustbusting progressives like Theodore Roosevelt." Novak, *supra* note 39, at 393.

[59] Merrill, *supra* note 5, at 941.

with the court exercising de novo review over questions of law and deferential review over questions of fact.[60] With the seeds of this model sprouting as early as 1906, as Merrill argues, Wyman's categories for external review of agency action was superseded in a matter of little over a decade. While it is possible to trace Wyman's influence on the development of a deferential standard of review of "jurisdictional" determinations,[61] and to make connections to other canonical principles, the fact remained that common law model of review Wyman explicated rapidly faded from prominence.[62] With the rapid rise of the appellate review

---

[60] *See id.* at 940.

[61] For instance, Wyman's criticism of *de novo* judicial review even of matters pertaining to the scope of the agency's jurisdiction found an eloquent and forceful expositor in John Dickinson. In Dickinson's important critique of *Crowell v. Benson*, 285 U.S. 22 (1932), for instance, Dickinson argued that if a court were to try de novo an agency's determination of a jurisdictional fact (such as whether individuals are "employees" within a labor act) the proceeding in the administrative tribunal "becomes infected with more than an appearance of futility." *See* John Dickinson, Crowell v. Benson: *Judicial Review of Administrative Determinations of Questions of "Constitutional" Fact*, 80 U. PA. L. REV. 1055, 1059–1062 (1932) (elaborating the challenge to *Crowell v. Benson*, with reference to *Miller v. Horton*). These ideas, so important to the independence of administrative action and adjudication, find footholds in Wyman's *The Principles of the Administrative Law*. In John Dickinson's earlier *Administrative Justice and the Supremacy of Law in the United States* (1927), Dickinson cites Wyman's treatise for exposition of the idea that every public officer is vested a certain "jurisdiction," such that "[w]ithin the boundaries of this area he can act freely according to his own discretion" *id.* at 41, and manifests an awareness that the *Miller v. Horton* rule, if not confined to nuisance and public health cases involving police regulation, could invite broad re-evaluation of the decisions of administrative tribunals. *See id.* 108–110. But by the time of Louis Jaffe's *Judicial Control of Administrative Action* (1965), Wyman had faded from recognition and acknowledgment.

[62] Merrill, *supra* note 5, at 964–998; Jerry L. Mashaw, *Rethinking Judicial Review of Administrative Action: A Nineteenth Century Perspective*, 32

model, Wyman's category of the internal law of administration faded from discussion, and with it, the most significant intellectual contribution of his treatise. The promise of Wyman's treatise for today is the recovery of this, the "real subject" of administrative law.

CARDOZO L. REV. 2241, 2245 (2011). The ascendance of the appellate review model, for better or worse, invited courts to substitute their judgment for the agency over a broader range of issues. Mashaw, *supra*, at 2249; Merrill, *supra* note 5, at 1002.

THE PRINCIPLES

OF THE

ADMINISTRATIVE LAW

GOVERNING THE RELATIONS OF

PUBLIC OFFICERS

BY

BRUCE WYMAN

OF THE FACULTY OF LAW IN HARVARD UNIVERSITY

ST. PAUL MINN.

KEEFE-DAVIDSON COMPANY

1903

PREFACE

This book is based upon an occasional course of lectures delivered in the Law School of Harvard University. No more is attempted than to deal with the elements of the administrative law which governs the relations of public officers. At the same time the matters brought out are specific, so that what is discussed may prove of service. The annotation is not exhaustive, but is intended to make reference to a variety of cases, valuable for the purpose of consultation, which bear upon the subjects discussed in the text. In the appendix are collected many statutes, regulations, orders, and forms which govern administrative practice before the principal executive departments, so that this book may be a manual for lawyers engaged in such matters. Upon the whole, this treatise deals with the first principles of the law of administration. To that end, the analysis of the subject is made upon the systematic basis that appears in the table of contents. It will then appear that the law upon administration is still in the making, because the phraseology employed had no accepted basis to found itself upon. So far as this law is developed this treatise purports to present it.

B. W.

TABLE OF CONTENTS

CHAPTER I.

THE LAW OF THE ADMINISTRATION.

CHAPTER II.

THE POSITION OF THE ADMINISTRATION.

CHAPTER III.

THE INDEPENDENCE OF THE ADMINISTRATION.

CHAPTER IV.

THE POWERS OF ADMINISTRATION.

CHAPTER V.

THE DUTIES OF THE ADMINISTRATION.

CHAPTER VI.

THE MEMBERSHIP IN THE ADMINISTRATION.

CHAPTER VII.

THE ORGANIZATION OF THE ADMINISTRATION.

CHAPTER VIII.

THE THEORY OF ADMINISTRATION.

CHAPTER IX.

THE AUTHORITY OF THE ADMINISTRATION.

CHAPTER X.

THE EXECUTION OF THE ADMINISTRATION.

CHAPTER XI.

THE LEGISLATION OF THE ADMINISTRATION.

CHAPTER XII.

THE REGULATION OF THE ADMINISTRATION.

CHAPTER XIII.

THE ADJUDICATION OF THE ADMINISTRATION

CHAPTER XIV.

THE PROCESSES OF THE ADMINISTRATION.

CHAPTER XV.

THE JURISDICTION OF THE ADMINISTRATION.

APPENDIX.

ADMINISTRATIVE LAW

CHAPTER I.

THE LAW OF THE ADMINISTRATION.

§ 1. Introduction.

It is intended in these lectures to deal with the law governing the execution of law by public officers so far as such a law has a place in our system of law. The attempt will be to discover the principal rules of law that govern in administration; the object of which is to arrive at some theory as to the nature of this administrative law which regulates the rights and duties of officials in their various relations. Administrative law, then, is that body of rules which defines the authority and the responsibility of that department of the government which is charged with the enforcement of the law. At all events, the experiment in these lectures will be to treat these problems of administration as matters of law.

Mr. Dicey in his admirable book The Law of the Constitution, which is already a classic among treatises upon political institutions, says in chapter 12: In many countries, servants of the state are in their official capacity to a great extent protected from the ordinary law of the land, exempted from the jurisdiction of ordinary tribunals, and subject to official law administered by official bodies. This scheme of so-called administrative law is opposed to all English ideas. The words Administrative Law are unknown to English judges and counsel, and are in themselves hardly intelligible without further explanation. This absence in our language is significant. It arises from non-recognition of the thing itself. In England and in the countries which like the United States derive their civilization from English sources, the system of administrative law and the very principles upon which it rests are in truth unknown. When the highest authority declares in so explicit a manner that administrative law is impossible under the common law system, at all events one thing can be promised in this course of lectures—novelty of subject.

It is the more remarkable that administrative law has not been conceived of as a department of our public law when it is part of the legal system of every country of continental Europe. *Droit administratif* is under every country of the civil law a well ascertained branch of public law. Indeed foreign writers cannot imagine orderly government without administrative law. They assume it as indispensable that the administration should have its own body of law to govern in all its legal relations. The character of these administrative laws, they say, must be different from the private laws which govern between individuals. For the interest of the state is a determining factor. All dealings, in short, in which the rights of an individual in reference to the state or to administrative officers come in question—as also the process whereby such rights and liabilities are to be enforced—come within the *contentieux administratifs.* And this is necessary, says M. VIVIEN in his Droit Administratif, Chapter 1: There are required different principles, different procedure, different training of judges, special knowledge and experience,—in fine, administrative justice can only be obtained by administrative law, and by the employment of the administrative process.

Now, political science is a universal science. However diverse in its manifestations, governmental power is the same in last analysis. Accordingly, there is no power exercised in any government which is not to be found in some form or other in every government. In every government there must be a department charged with the enforcement of the law. In the law of every state, therefore, there must be a body of rules in relation to the action of that department. In that sense at least, there must be an administrative law in the law of every state. In one state the administrative law may allow a large sphere of action to the executive department; in another state that law may allow a small sphere of action to that department. And that is indeed the fact; in the civil law system the law governing administration has a superior position to the law of the land; in the common law system the law governing administration has an inferior position to the law of the land. So wide is this distinction that it would be an impossible thing to import the civil law forms to classify the common law facts.

At the same time, since there is an administration which proceeds in accordance with a law in the common law system as well as in the civil law system, it ought to be obvious that administrative law has a place in the jurisprudence of every state. In this broad statement of the problem it is obvious that there is an administrative law in the United States. That law which governs the administration of law by public officers is the subject of these lectures.

§ 2. Law for administration.

In a discussion of administrative law there is a first distinction to be taken which may be marked by the phrases the external law and the internal law. External administrative law deals with the relations of the administration or of officers with citizens. Internal administrative law is concerned with the relations of officers with each other, or with the administration. And yet in a way both of these branches of this law are involved in any motion of the administration, since the administration cannot act upon an external matter without internal direction. Together, the external law and the internal law make up the law of administration.

To such extent is this interaction of the external law upon the internal law and of the internal law upon the external law the fact, that cases arise where there is an apparent conflict between these laws. Suppose the superior officer commands the inferior officer to do a certain act—it is the internal law that every order must be obeyed. But suppose that the external law directs the officer not to do that act—it is the external law that every law must be obeyed. Now, how can this inferior officer obey both the internal law and the external law when the one commands action, and the other requires inaction, as to the same subject matter? There must be some solution to allow the officer to escape from the horns of such a dilemma.

That is the question where the law of the land commands and the law of the administration demands—which? There are the two possibilities. As a first inquiry let it be asked whether in such a conflict the order of the superior officer will prevail. A case that involves that is Hendricks v. Gonzales, 67 Fed. 351 (1895). This was an action by a charterer of a vessel against the Collector of the Port of New York to recover damages for the detention of the steamer by refusal to give clearance papers. The facts brought to the attention of the collector were that the cargo consisted wholly of arms and munitions of war; and that she was bound to a port near the base of operations of the Venezuelan insurgents. Upon report to Washington, the Secretary of Treasury ordered the vessel to be held. The judge submitted to the jury the question of fact whether the defendant had reasonable cause to believe that the vessel was intended to be used in the hostilities; if he had, in fact, he was entitled to a verdict. Error was assigned because of the refusal of the trial judge to rule that the defendant was exonerated from liability for his acts by the instructions of the Secretary of Treasury.

WALLACE, the Circuit Judge, stated the judgment thus: The questions presented by the assignments of error seem free from doubt. The plaintiff having complied with the conditions entitling him to clearance, it was the duty of the defendant as collector of the port, to grant a clearance for the vessel and her cargo, unless he was justified in refusing to do so by some other statutory authority. Neither the Secretary of the Treasury nor the President could nullify the statute, and though the defendant may have thought himself bound to obey the instructions of the former, his mistaken sense of duty could not justify his refusal of the clearance, and these instructions afforded him no protection unless they were authorized in law.

One feels a conflict of rights and duties in this decision. On the one hand the collector is bound by the internal law of administration to obey his superior in the administration; on the other hand the collector is bound by the external law of the land to the shipmaster. And in that conflict the law of the land is held the superior law. This is an illustration of the supremacy of the law of the land; no test shows more how the law of the land dominates the situation in administration in countries under the common law. The order of the superior is no defense because it is not recognized as of any value when there is positive law of the land to the contrary. The law of the land—the external law—overrules the law of the administration—the internal law.

This solution is for the extreme case where the duty to be performed is purely ministerial. If in the duty to be performed something is left to discretion this solution is reversed. In any estimate of the situation a case like In re Fair, 100 Fed. 149 (1900), must be stated in order that any extreme doctrine may be qualified. One Morgan, a prisoner in a United States military prison, made his escape from the fort. Fair, a corporal, and Jockins, a private, who were on guard duty, were called upon to pursue the prisoner. The order as given was in substance as follows: Pursue the prisoner, if you sight him summon him twice; and if he does not halt fire upon him, and fire to hit him. About dusk they halted Morgan on a highway; he turned and ran across a field; they followed close after. Fair gave the order to fire and Morgan fell mortally wounded. For the killing of Morgan, Fair and Jockins were tried by court-martial, and found not guilty. Next they were indicted for manslaughter in the Nebraska Court.

MUNGER, the District Judge, ordered their release: The law is that an order given by an officer to his private, which does not expressly and clearly show on its face its illegality, the soldier is bound to obey; and such order is his full protection. The first duty of a soldier is obedience, and without this there can be neither discipline nor efficiency in an army. If every subordinate officer and soldier were at liberty to question the legality of the orders of the commander, and obey them or not as he may consider them valid or invalid, the precious moment for action would be wasted. Its law is that of obedience. No question can be left open of the right to command in the officer, or of duty of obedience in the soldier. While I do not say that the order given by Sergeant Simpson to the petitioners was in all particulars a lawful order, I do say that the illegality of the order, if illegal it was, was not so much so as to be apparent and palpable to the commonest understanding. If, then, the petitioners acted under such order in good faith, they are not liable to prosecution.

This decision certainly commends itself to common sense. The position of the soldier is so hard that it cannot be possible. Otherwise this often would be the alternative for the soldier: if he refused to obey a reasonable order—to be shot for disobedience; if he killed in pursuance of that order—to be hung for murder. It may be urged that this is always more or less the situation in all administration under the common law system, only the present case is more dramatic than the ordinary case. There is, however, distinction between this case and the former case. In the first case the officer exceeded the discretion vested in him in his action; in the second case the officer acted within the discretion vested in him. That makes the whole difference.

In crucial cases there will be this antinomy between conflicting duties. If it be granted that when there is a ministerial duty to perform a certain act the law of the land must be obeyed, in that case there is no conflict. And if it be granted that where there is a discretionary duty to perform a certain act the law of the administration should be obeyed, in that case also there is no conflict. That is the legal solution of this difficulty then. In the first case there was no place for the internal law left by the external law; in the second there was a scope for the internal law within the external law.[1]

[1] LAW FOR ADMINISTRATION.—Rogers v. Dutt, 13 Moo. P. C. 236; Raleigh v. Goschen [1898] 1 Ch. 73; Mitchell v. Harmony, 13 How. 115; United States v. Lee, 106 U. S. 196; Coblens v. Abel, Woolworth 293; Hendricks v. Gonzales, 67 Fed. 351; Eslava v. Jones, 83 Ala. 139; Lee v. Huff, 61 Ark. 494; Harpending v. Haight, 39 Cal. 189; Land Co. v. Routt, 17 Colo. 156; Raymond v. Fish, 51 Conn. 80; Dowling v. Bowden, 25 Fla. 712; State v. Bell, 9 Ga. 334; Strickfaden v. Zipprick, 49 Ill. 286; Governor v. Nelson, 6 Ind. 496; McCord v. High, 24 Ia. 336; State v. Francis, 23 Kan. 495; Lecourt v. Gas-

§ 3. External Law.

The external administrative law as defined deals with the relations of the administration, and of officials, with citizens. External administrative law is thus concerned with almost everything which the government asks of the citizens; and it is concerned with almost everything which citizens ask of the government. These subjects in the large, form the principal subject matter of these lectures. Since in this inquiry is involved the extent of the power of the administration, all the law as to the authority of officers is brought into the discussion. And since in the same inquiry is involved the limitation of the administration, all the law as to the responsibility of officers is brought in issue.

There is one fundamental question: Is the administration in its relations with citizens subject to the same rules of law as govern the relations of citizens among themselves? It has been remarked that under the foreign system of administrative law a special law governs relations with the administration, while in our system of administrative law it has been supposed that there is one law in the land which governs public officers and private citizens alike. It is very simple—this common law view—that action in accordance with legal authorization is legal and the official so acting will always be

ter, 50 La. Ann. 521; Harwood v. Siphers, 70 Me. 464; Magruder v. Swann, 25 Md. 173; Tellefsen v. Fee, 168 Mass. 188; Pawlowski v. Jenks, 115 Mich. 275; Hines v. Chambers, 29 Minn. 7; Newman v. Elam, 30 Miss. 507; Chouteau v. Rowse, 56 Mo. 65; State v. Kruttschnitt, 4 Nev. 178; Ela v. Shepard, 32 N. H. 277; Hann v. Lloyd, 50 N. J. Law, 1; Olmsted v. Dennis, 77 N. Y. 378; Board of Education v. Com'rs of Bladen, 113 N. C. 379; State v. Auditor, 43 Ohio St. 311; Williams v. Schmidt, 14 Ore. 470; Yealy v. Fink, 43 Pa. St. 212; Randall v. Wethersell, 2 R. I. 120; McKinney v. Robinson, 84 Tex. 489; Brown v. Mason, 40 Vt. 157; Board of Public Works v. Gannt, 76 Va. 455; Frazier v. Turner, 76 Wis. 562.

justified; and that action without warrant of law is illegal, and the official so acting will always be considered a private wrong-doer. Without doubt this is the general rule of the common law governing the relations of officials with citizens. This must be, therefore, the first rule of external administrative law.

A strong illustration of the effect of this rule that the circumstance that the act done purports to be under the authority of the government makes out no justification whatever is United States v. Lee, 106 U. S. 196 (1882). This was an action commenced by Lee against Kaufman and others for ejectment of the Arlington Estate. During the war the Lee family had been dispossessed by proceedings which the Lower Court held void. At that stage of the ejectment process the Attorney-General filed in the case a suggestion that these defendants held the premises as public officers acting under the direction of the President of the United States; and that the suit ought not to be maintained. The plaintiff demurred to this suggestion upon the ground that the action was against the defendants as private wrong-doers.

Mr. Justice MILLER delivered the opinion of the court: What is the right as established by the verdict of the jury in this case? It is the right to the possession of the homestead of the plaintiff. A right to recover that which has been taken from him by force and violence and detained by the strong hand. This right being clearly established we are told that the court can proceed no further because it appears that certain military officers acting under orders of the President have seized this estate and converted one part of it into a military fort, and another into a cemetery. It is not pretended as the case now stands that the President had any lawful authority to do this or that the legislative body could give him any such authority except upon the payment of just compensation. The defense stands here solely upon the absolute immunity from judicial inquiry of every one who asserts authority from the executive branch of the government, however clear it may be that the executive possessed no such power. No man in this country is so high that he is above the law. No officer of the law may set that law at defiance with impunity. All officers of the government from the highest to the lowest are creatures of the law and are bound to obey it.

This is the negative side of the rule, the responsibility of the administration to the external law of the land. The rule has a positive side, the authority of administration from the external law of the land. This depends upon the truism that all action by an officer in pursuance of law is legal; which has this further application, which is of the greatest importance: that all official action in pursuance of discretion vested in the officer by law is action in accordance with laws in whatever way that discretion may be exercised. In such action an officer cannot be in the position of a wrong-doer whatever it be. Without doubt this rule is of great consequence; it is, indeed, at the foundation of administrative law in a country subject to the common law system.

A strong illustration of this rule that the officer cannot be responsible for any action done in pursuance of discretion vested in him by law whatever that action may be is Seymour v. United States, 2 App. D. C. 240 (1894). This was an application for mandamus by the State against the Commissioner of Patents to compel the registration of a trade mark of the relator. It appeared that under its dispensary act that state was engaged in the manufacture and sale of intoxicating liquors. The commissioner found that the state had no authorized trade in liquors outside of its own limits and had not the use of a trade mark in interstate commerce, and that therefore the application should be denied. The state thereupon went to the courts for this mandamus, which was promptly refused it.

Mr. Justice SHEPARD said: To the judiciary department is intrusted the interpretation of the laws, the determination of rights, and the application of remedies, and in this regard it is sometimes difficult for the courts to properly appreciate the fact that the executive department is charged with perfectly independent duties which require the ascertainment of facts, involve the interpretation of laws, and in many respects call for the exercise of judgment and discretion; and this independence is so complete that no matter how gross an error may be committed in the execution of these duties, the courts are nevertheless powerless to interfere. Private interests may suffer in instances, and rights may sometimes be denied; but these alone do not authorize the interference of the courts with the duties of executive officers. Greater evils could not exist under our system of government than would follow the usurpation by the judiciary of powers not intrusted to them.

The position of internal administrative law under our system is to be found in some way within the law of the land. The exterior rules make the officers of the administration liable if anything is done by them without authority which can justify it, somewhere to be found in the law of the land itself. If proper administration cannot therefore exceed these limitations, how can any administration at all go on under such restrictions? Even at so early a stage of this inquiry it may be well to put forward the working hypothesis upon which these lectures are based. Cases must be put forward to establish it; other cases to develop it; others still to apply it.

In the usual conditions of administration in most jurisdictions there will be found an external law governing administration which both restricts and enables. In so far as it restricts, it must be respected; in so far as it enables, it must be observed. If there is one thing that is characteristic of the law of the land it is its rigidity; the external law, then, is from first to last a fixed obligation, the same in one case as in another, whatever the stress. And therein the external law differs from the internal law. If there is one thing that is characteristic of the law of administration it is its elasticity; the internal law, then, is from first to last an unfixed obligation, one way in one case, another in another, as expediency dictates.[2]

[2] External Law.—Mostyn v. Fabrigas, Cowp. 161; Gidley v. Palmerston, 3 Brod. & B. 275; Kearney v. Creelman, 16 N. S. 228; Baker v. Ranney, 12 Grant Ch. 228; Gaines v. Thompson, 7 Wall. 347; Noble v. Logging R. R., 147 U. S. 165; Decatur v. Paulding, 14 Pet. 497; Ex Parte Echols, 39 Ala. 698; McClure v. Hill, 36 Ark. 268; Ex Parte Tinkum, 54 Cal. 201; State v. Staub, 61 Conn. 553; Denver v. Dean, 10 Colo. 375; Seymour v. United States, 2 App. D. C. 240; State v. Drew, 17 Fla. 67; Collins v. McDaniel, 66 Ga. 203; People v. Kent, 160 Ill. 655; State v. Snodgrass, 98 Ind. 546; McCord v. High, 24 Ia. 336; Bridge Co. v. County Com'rs, 10 Kan. 326; Dickens v. Cemetery Co., 93 Ky. 385; State v. Wrotnowski, 17 La. Ann. 156; Davis v. County Com'rs, 63 Me. 396; Magruder v. Swann, 25 Md. 173; Nowell v. Wright, 3 Allen 166; People v. Governor, 29 Mich. 320; State v. Coon, 14 Minn. 456; Swan v. Gray, 44 Miss. 393; State v. McGrath, 91 Mo. 386; Merritt v. McNally, 14 Mont. 228;

§ 4. Internal Law.

Internal administrative law as defined deals with the relations of the officer in the administration to each other, and to the administration itself. The position of the officer in its organization and his function in its action is the object of this inquiry. This is the real subject. The administration is to be studied as an administration. What is the theory of administration—by what process does an administration act? What is the practice of administration—by what methods does an administration act? These are the questions to which these lectures are devoted the most of the time. In a word, the chief point in the administration that the internal law is concerned with is the fact that many officers are bound together in action.

The internal law governs the processes by which the laws in general are carried into execution by the officers of the administration. These processes are not all alike. The execution of law requires various methods at various stages of the enforcement. It may be well even at the outset to give some illustrations of the processes of the administration in order that the nature of the internal law that governs all of these methods may be seen. Administration seems to have three stages: first, the law is prepared; then the law is applied; then the law is enforced. It is, however, all one process.

The fundamental condition is that in administration

Miller v. Roby, 9 Neb. 471; Humboldt Co. v. County Com'rs, 6 Nev. 30; Orr v. Quimby, 54 N. H. 590; State v. Perrine, 34 N. J. Law, 254; People v. Chapin, 104 N. Y. 96; Holt v. McLean, 75 N. C. 347; State v. Moore, 42 Ohio St. 103; Commonwealth v. Martin, 170 Pa. St. 118; Mauran v. Smith, 8 R. I. 192; State v. County Com'rs, 28 S. C. 258; State v. Ruth, 9 S. D. 84; Meadows v. Nesbit, 12 Lea, 489; Chalk v. Darden, 47 Tex. 438; Richards v. Wheeler, 2 Aik. 369; McCullough v. Hunter, 90 Va. 699; State v. Doyle, 40 Wis. 204.

many officers are found together. The purpose of the law of administration is obvious, then; it is the science of common action. All the rules of the internal administrative law, then, have this basis in so far as there are rules that dictate the methods to be used in administration, this unifying principle—to bring order into the course of the execution of the law. All the processes of administration so far as they proceed according to the internal law of administration have this point of departure—common action. This is then the central point in these lectures to show this law of the administration—the totality of officers; that is the principal thing. Only by way of illustration is the law of officers—the single officer—brought into the discussion. Two cases may illustrate the object in view in these lectures. One significant case upon the processes of administration is Indian Regulations, 3 Compt. Dec. 218 (1896). The facts were these: Section 65 of the regulations promulgated by the Secretary of Interior for the Indian Office provided that all authorities to purchase in the open market expire at the end of the fiscal year. In this particular case a written authority to purchase flags in amount not exceeding $500, but without other limitation, was given by the Secretary of Interior to the Commissioner of Indian Affairs. Purchases were made under this authority after the fiscal year in which it was granted.

The then Comptroller, BOWERS, stated the internal law as to the methods of administration in this manner: To sustain these payments it is necessary to hold that the Secretary at the time of issuing the order determined to waive this regulation as not advisable in connection with the purchase of these flags. There can be no question of his authority to waive such a regulation, the same having been promulgated by him, and being at any time subject to his amendment, waiver, or abrogation. It is equally true that such a regulation may be waived by subsequent specific approval of a transaction by the Secretary of Interior. But in the absence of some action of the Secretary these formal printed regulations are binding upon all of the subordinate officers of his department.

This case is of a distinct importance in exposing the true nature of the internal law of administration. The regulation was internal law of the administration so that it would bind the inferior of the officer who made it. Yet it does not bind the officer that made it himself—why? Because the internal law is all based upon the discretion of a given officer; if he in his discretion promulgates a regulation he may in his discretion waive that regulation. The internal law of the administration is then no more than the usual order of the exercise of that discretion in the ordinary case; in the extraordinary case direct action can be taken notwithstanding.

A second case—a fundamental one—upon the methods in administration is Wilcox v. Jackson, 13 Pet. 498 (1839). This was an ejectment brought upon a patent for a tract of land in Cook County, Illinois, a fractional section embracing the military post called Fort Dearborn, at the time of the institution of the suit in the possession of the defendant as commanding officer. The land in question had been in fact reserved land held out from pre-emption by virtue of a provision of statute that land reserved from sale by order of the President should not be patented. In this particular case the plot had been reserved by the Commissioner of the Land Office under direction of the Secretary of War. The claimant therefore contended that the land was not in truth reserved at the time his patent issued from the Land Office, since there had been no order by the President himself.

Mr. Justice BARBOUR explained in his opinion the internal law as to action in the execution of the law: At the request of the Secretary of War, the Commissioner of the General Land Office in 1824 coloured and marked upon the map this very section, as reserved for military purposes, and directed it to be reserved from sale for those purposes. We consider this as having been done by authority of law; for amongst other provisions in the act of 1830 all lands are exempted from pre-emption which are reserved from sale by order of the President. Now although the immediate agent in requiring this reservation was the Secretary of War, yet we feel justified in presuming that it was done by approbation and direction of the President. The President speaks and acts through the several heads of departments in relation to the subjects which appertain to their several duties. Hence, we consider the act of the war department in requiring the reservation to be made as being in legal contemplation the act of the President, and consequently, that the reservation thus made was in legal effect a reservation made by order of the President within the terms of the act of Congress.

The ordinary rule, then, in execution is delegation. This case again shows the internal law of administration. A superior may give power to an inferior or he may withhold power from an inferior. If he commands, the inferior acts in his place and that act is his act; if he forbids, the inferior cannot do a valid act. So if a superior gives a general authority to an inferior to act in his place, the inferior may act in his place until the authority is revoked, as it may be at any time. That is the system in administration. The internal law of the administration is seen again to be no more than the usual order in the exercise of discretion. Such is administration.[3]

§ 5. Result for administration.

This is the administrative law. The external law and the internal law make up the law of administration. It must be plain why this distinction is of such importance. These are two concentric circles. The outer circle is the external law, that is the exterior boundary; the law of the land is rigid, that cannot be passed. The inner circle is the internal law, that is an interior boundary of a sort; for the law of administration is elastic, that law is the discretion of the officer that enforces it. This is not an academic distinction; it is in practical affairs of the greatest consequence. These will appear better by illustration. A case upon the remedy by the external law should be compared with a case upon the relief by the internal law.

[3] INTERNAL LAW.—Gidley v. Palmerston, 3 Brod. & B. 275; Reg. v. Secretary [1891] 2 Q. B. 326; Williams v. United States, 1 How. 290; Dinsman v. Wilkes, 12 How. 390; Ex Parte Selma R. R., 46 Ala. 423; McCreary v. Rogers, 35 Ark. 298; Jacobs v. Supervisors, 100 Cal. 121; Ely v. Parsons, 55 Conn. 100; United States v. Chandler, 13 D. C. 527; Towle v. State, 3 Fla. 202; State v. Thrasher, 77 Ga. 671; Whalin v. Macomb, 76 Ill. 49; State v. Snodgrass, 98 Ind. 546; Hildreth v. Crawford, 65 Ia. 339; State v. Robinson, 1 Kan. 188; State v. Dubuclet, 28 La. Ann. 85; Weston v. Dane, 51 Me. 461; Mayo v. County Com'rs, 141 Mass. 74; Albrecht v. Long, 27 Minn. 81; People v. Auditor General, 36 Mich. 271; Swan v. Gray, 44 Miss. 393; State v. McGrath, 91 Mo. 386; State v. Babcock, 18 Neb. 221; Commonwealth v. McLaughlin, 120 Pa. St. 518; Lane v. Schomp, 5 C. E. Green, 82; Phelps v. Hawley, 52 N. Y. 23; Morgan v. Pickard, 86 Tenn. 208; Sights v. Yarnalls, 12 Grat. 292.

The case in mind upon the remedy that the external law affords a claimant is Dunlap v. Black, 128 U. S. 40 (1888). This was an application by Oscar Dunlap, the relator to the Supreme Court of the District of Columbia for a writ of mandamus to be directed to the respondent Black as Commissioner of Pensions, commanding him to re-issue a pension. The relator said that whether he was entitled to a re-rating was a question of law; and that it did not lie in the discretionary power of the respondent, as Commissioner of Pensions to deny or otherwise abridge his rights under the statute.

Mr. Justice BRADLEY pointed out how limited was the power of the judiciary to give relief against the action of the executive: The courts will not interfere by mandamus with the executive officers of the government in the exercise of their ordinary official duties, even where those duties require an interpretation of the law, the court having no appellate power for that purpose; but when they refuse to act in any case at all, or when by special statute or otherwise a mere ministerial duty is imposed upon them, that is, a service which they are bound to perform without further question, then, if they refuse, a mandamus may be issued to compel them. Judged by this rule the present case presents no difficulty; the Commissioner of Pensions did not refuse to act or decide. He did act and decide. He adopted an interpretation of law adverse to the relator and his decision was confirmed by the Secretary of Interior, as evidenced by his signature of the certificate. Whether if the law were properly before us for consideration, we should be of the same opinion or of a different opinion, is of no consequence in the decision of this case. We have no appellate power over the Commissioner and no right to reverse his decision. That decision and his action taken thereon were made and done in the exercise of his official functions.

Decisions like this make up the external law of administration. It is well to appreciate their effect at the outset. The question before the judiciary is whether there has been legal administration or illegal administration, never whether there has been proper administration or improper administration. The courts, therefore, in enforcing the external law of the administration can only inquire whether the action has been in excess of power, never whether the action has been in abuse of power. In legal phrase the question before the court is one of the jurisdiction; it is not one of the merits. This puts the complainant at plain advantage. By the external law the claimant gets relief if there is error in law, never if there is error in fact in the decision of the officer of which he complains.

The case in mind upon the remedy that the internal law may afford the claimant is Morrison v. McKessock, 5 Land Dec. 245 (1886). One McKessock made a homestead entry in 1881. Six months after one Morrison filed an affidavit of contest alleging that the said McKessock had not resided continuously upon the land for six months but had abandoned it. The local land officers upon the contest rendered a decision in favor of McKessock, and dismissed the contest of Morrison. From this decision Morrison failed to appeal to the General Office within the time set by the regulations. However, the General Land Office took the case up at a later period upon the motion of Morrison. The decision then was in favor of Morrison. From this decision McKessock appealed to the Secretary of Interior upon the ground that the Commissioner was without jurisdiction in his action, no appeal having been taken to him within the time set.

Secretary LAMAR pointed out how extended was the power of an officer higher in the administration to give relief against the action of an officer lower in the administration under any circumstances whatever: The rule of practice applies to parties with reference to their rights as between themselves and does not operate as a restriction upon the power or authority of the Commissioner to reject or approve the finding of the local officers upon a question of fact or their decision upon the law applicable thereto. The action of the register and receiver is in no sense final as to the rights of the Government, but in all cases their decision either upon the law or facts is subject to the approval of the Commissioner whether directing the cancellation of an entry or approving it for patent. To give to rule 48 the effect contended for by the counsel for McKissock would require the Commissioner to approve the findings of the local officers not appealed from on all issues of fact although such finding might be contrary to his own judgment of what facts had been proven by the evidence submitted. The approval required of the Commissioner is not simply a ministerial act, but the decision of a tribunal especially charged with the duty of deciding from the evidence whether the law has been complied with, and in the discharge of this duty the whole record of the case should be considered by him as if it had been submitted to him originally for his decision thereon.

Decisions like this make up the internal law of administration. It is well to appreciate their effect at the outset. The question before the inferior is what is proper to be done, the question before his superior is whether what is done is fit. The superior thus takes the whole question up anew and decides himself what is just in the premises upon the merits. All of which is of plain advantage to the complainant. By the internal law the claimant gets relief upon any grounds that may appear. The internal law deals with the question between proper and improper administration, then—the inner circle; the external law is concerned with the question between legal administration and illegal administration—the outer circle. It must be obvious that in any controversy with the administration the first resort would be to the administration, the second resort to the judiciary.[4]

§ 6. Conclusion.

The difficulty is that in the study of administration the problem is as often institutional as it is legal. The administration may be considered as if a whole—the institutional problem; or as of various factors—the legal

[4] RESULT FOR ADMINISTRATION.—Marbury v. Madison, 1 Cranch, 169; United States v. Schurz, 102 U. S. 378; United States v. Raum, 135 U. S. 200; United States v. Black, 128 U. S. 40; Hall v. Steele, 82 Ala. 562; Pritchard v. Woodruff, 36 Ark. 196; Fowler v. Peirce, 2 Cal. 165; Land Co. v. Routt, 17 Colo. 156; State v. Staub, 61 Conn. 553; State v. Gamble, 13 Fla. 9; Barksdale v. Cobb, 16 Ga. 13; Bryan v. Cattell, 15 Ia. 538; Gill v. State, 72 Ind. 266; State v. Wrotnowski, 17 La. Ann. 156; Magruder v. Swann, 25 Md. 173; Deehan v. Johnson, 141 Mass. 23; People v. State Treasurer, 24 Mich. 468; McCulloch v. Stone, 64 Miss. 378; County Board v. State Board, 106 N. C. 83; Pfund v. Valley L. & T. Co., 52 Neb. 473; State v. Vanarsdale, 42 N. J. Law, 536; State v. Moore, 42 Oh. St. 103; Commonwealth v. Martin, 170 Pa. St. 118; Mauran v. Smith, 8 R. I. 192; State v. County Com'rs, 28 S. C. 258; Davis v. State, 35 Tex. 118; McCullough v. Hunter, 90 Va. 699; State v. Harvey, 11 Wis. 33.

problem. The proper relations of the officials in the administration is the institutional problem; the proper position of the officer towards the citizen is the legal problem. And yet both of these questions are involved in any business of the administration, which cannot move except as a whole, which cannot act except by its members. The problem in administration is then a complex one in every case. And it is necessary to have the whole law governing administration in mind to pass upon any question that may arise in regard to the execution of the law.

Administrative law is one of two co-ordinate branches of public law; constitutional law is the other. That is, administrative law is the complement to constitutional law; constitutional law prescribes the broad outlines of government—it describes the executive department of the government and fixes certain large limitations upon the functions of the administration. Administrative law organizes the administration—it prescribes in the minutest detail the rules which shall govern the executive department in administering the law. It is these rules which constitute the body of administrative law. Administrative law consists, as has been said, of those rules which govern the executive department in the administration of the law.

CHAPTER II.

THE POSITION OF THE ADMINISTRATION.

§ 7. Introduction.

In every government one condition is fundamental— that is the sovereignty of the state. Since law itself must be based ultimately upon the fiat of the state, it is the assent of that society that makes the law; no man, therefore, may question whether any action of the state is valid, since by the hypothesis it cannot but be legal. Even if it were possible to conceive of any wrong done by the state, the right would be of no value whatever to the individual wronged. For it is in the next place impossible to imagine that any suit could be brought against the state without its consent; since all the processes of justice proceed from the state itself. No act of the government as a government, therefore, ever can be questioned in any way. In that view no action of the administration as an administration is subject to the inquiry of the law; since the administration in the execution of its functions is conceived as the representative of the state with the immunities of the state itself. These immunities of the sovereign, not only from the imputation of wrong, but even from inquiry into its action, are without qualification; and the subjection of the individual to the state, its consequence, is also without exception. This, then, is one fundamental condition to be taken into the account in any consideration of the action of the administration.

On the other hand, there is another condition fundamental as this, and, in the actual conduct of administration, overshadowing. Wherever the common law prevails the doctrine of the supremacy of the law of the land is to be found. This doctrine, that before the law all persons must stand alike without regard to station, is in its consequences the most pervading principle in administrative law with us. No man may be seized, none of his goods may be distrained without the due process of the law. More than that, no man is above the law, but every man is subject to the ordinary law of the land and amenable to the jurisdiction of the ordinary tribunals. Before the law of the land, therefore, the public officer stands as a private person; and the result is startling: every act by every public officer may be subject of suit against the officer as an ordinary person. More than that, unless the officer can show an exact legal justification for the precise act which he has done, he has done nothing more nor less than a legal wrong by his interference, for which he must answer just as any private wrong-doer must answer for his wrongs. Such is the principal rule of the external law of administration in the common law system; and such is the working out of it into detail. In this view every action of the administration is subject to the law of the land; in that some officer of the administration must answer in his own person, if anything be done by it without the authority of positive law. This is the important condition upon administration under the common law system.

The problem to be worked out in these lectures is, therefore, the accommodation of these two principles upon which together the law relative to administration under our system depends. The whole situation is just this in brief: The administration, all of its officers together, is not responsible to the processes of the law, as the state is not; but the public officer, any one of the administration apart, is responsible to every suit, as a private individual may be. These are the conditions under which the administration must proceed in a country where the supremacy of the law is made the basis of political institutions. The attempt in this lecture will be to show by the conglomeration of many instances, how administration proceeds with us in conformity with both principles without ignoring either. It is therefore necessary to consider the precise extent to which the administration is free from liability; and the more indispensable to discover the exact point at which the liability of the officer begins. For it is evident that the business of government could not go on unless these rules were well established and well worked out into detail, with care to preserve the true rights and the true duties of all concerned; since no man of prudence and foresight would accept public office under liabilities which were undefined. The order of discussion will be therefore this: first, to inquire how far the administration is irresponsible; second, to discover how far the officer is responsible.

§ 8. Irresponsibility of the sovereign.

That the sovereign could not be sued in his own courts is found adjudicated in our earliest books; disposed of briefly even then, since in any time that must always be held a self-evident proposition. The case of the Abbot of Saint Searle to that effect is found reported as follows in Y. B. 30 Ed. I. 170 (1302): To a writ of right brought against the Abbot of Saint Searle it was answered that the tenements were seized into the King's hands by reason whereof the Abbot could not and ought not to answer. WESCOT.—Although the tenements are seized into his hands you are tenant of the freehold; judgment if you ought not to answer. BRUMPTON.—He ought to answer; but inasmuch as we cannot entertain the suit whilst the tenements are seized, I advise you who wish to sue for them to send to Court and purchase permission; for we will hold no such plea before we are commanded to do so.

The rule is as positive in the law of England today as ever it was. It is perhaps difficult to put a more extreme case than the actual case arising in the Goods of George III., Addams, 255 (1819). This was an application to the Prerogative Court of Canterbury for its process calling upon the Procurator General, proctor for and on behalf of the King George IV. as heir and successor of his late majesty King George III. to see the last will and testament of his late majesty propounded and proved in solemn form of law; promoted and brought by her highness Olive, daughter of the Duke of Cumberland, the only legatee named in the said will. This application the court refused to entertain utterly, as well it might.

Sir JOHN NICHOLL delivered the judgment; he said: To proceed by this sort of process against the King himself; to cite him personally; to put him in contempt; to do certain acts in pain of his contumacy—was too extravagant even to be attempted; and therefore the citation is prayed against the King's proctor. But here again exactly the same difficulty occurs both in principle and practice, either the King's proctor does or does not represent the sovereign. If virtute officii he represents His Majesty, he has the same privileges; nor can he be put in contempt, and proceeded against in poenam. If he does not officially quoad hoc and so as to be binding upon, represent the sovereign, this process is nugatory. Why is it to be supposed that the Legislature meant in future to submit the reigning successor to the ordinary jurisdiction to which no sovereign had ever before been subjected, and which would be a departure from and violation of the constitutional prerogatives of the crown? The King can do no wrong; he cannot constitutionally be supposed capable of injustice. If he is properly applied to in the forms prescribed by the constitution no doubt ought to exist that real justice will be done.[5]

[5] IRRESPONSIBILITY OF THE SOVEREIGN.—Goods of George III, Addams 255; Tobin v. Reg., 16 C. B. N. S. 310; Beers v. Arkansas, 20 How. 527; Russell v. United States, 182 U. S. 516; United States v. Surety Co., 74 Fed. 145; Comer v. Bankhead, 70 Ala. 493; Auditor v. Davies, 2 Ark. 494; Nougues v. Douglass, 7 Cal. 65; Mulnix v. Mutual Ins. Co., 23 Colo. 71; State v. Hartford, 50 Conn. 90; Mfg. Co. v. Taylor, 3 MacA. 4; Bloxham v. Florida R. R., 35 Fla. 625; Powers v. Bank, 18 Ga. 658; Holmes v. Mattoon, 111 Ill. 27; Crawfordsville v. Irwin, 46 Ind. 439; Metz v. Soule, 40 Ia. 236; Regents v. Hamilton, 28 Kan. 376; Tate v. Salmon, 79 Ky. 540; State v. Jumel, 38 La. Ann. 340; Weston v. Dane, 51 Me. 461; State v. Bank, 6 G. & J. 205; Railroad v. Commonwealth, 127 Mass. 43; Locke v. Speed, 62 Mich. 408; State v. Torinus, 22 Minn. 272; Edwards

§ 9. State action.

In the name of the King, the fountain of Justice, the King cannot by his own writ command himself. But the broader reason is, that it would be inconsistent with the very idea of supreme executive power, and would endanger the performance of the public duties of the sovereign, to subject him to repeated suits as a matter of right at the will of any citizen, and to submit to the judicial tribunals and control and disposition of his public property, his instruments and means of carrying on the government in peace and war, and the money in his treasury.

These principles go far; to such an extent that they must be taken into the account in everyday affairs in the commonest transactions. An instance in point is Lodor v. Baker, Arnold & Co., 39 New Jersey Law, 49 (1876). This was an attachment process against a non-resident debtor. The only property in New Jersey claimed for attachment was the sum of $1,000, in the hands of the Treasurer of the State alleged to be due from the state of New Jersey to the debtor. A motion was made to quash the writ on the ground that the claim which the defendant, the debtor, had against the state could not be attached. The argument made upon the motion was that this garnishment proceeding would in its working out involve a suit against the state of New Jersey. And

v. Lesueur, 132 Mo. 410; State v. Mayes, 6 Cush. (Miss.) 706; State v. Collins, 21 Mont. 448; People v. Butler, 2 Neb. 6; Torreyson v. Board, 7 Nev. 19; Sargent v. Gilford, 66 N. H. 543; Dock & Imp. Co. v. Trustees, 32 N. J. Eq. 434; O'Hara v. State, 112 N. Y. 146; Clodfelter v. State, 86 N. C. 51; State v. Board of Public Works, 36 Oh. St. 409; Schaffer v. Cadwallader, 36 Pa. St. 126; In Re State House Fund, 19 R. I. 393; Lowry v. Thompson, 25 S. C. 416; Moore v. Tate, 87 Tenn. 744; State v. Snyder, 66 Tex. 701; Board of Public Works v. Gannt, 76 Va. 461.

obviously, this was so; since the process must go against the state in order to enforce the payment of its claim against the state for the satisfaction of the creditor of the debtor.

The language of Mr. Justice VAN SYCKEL was emphatic: The state enjoys the immunity from suits as one of the essential attributes of sovereignty, it being an established principle of jurisprudence in all civilized nations that the sovereign cannot be sued in its own courts without its consent. New Jersey has never consented to surrender this prerogative right, and, therefore, if it can be shown that this proceeding will involve the garnishee in litigation, the attempt to interfere with funds in the treasurer's hands is unwarrantable. The law cannot be guilty of the inconsistency of inviting the suitor to attach funds of this nature, and at the same time deny him every remedy to enforce his lien. The right to attach must necessarily involve the right to compel the state to appear as party defendant at the suit of a private individual. This credit not being attachable, the writ is quashed.

These, then, are fundamental things. That the state cannot be sued seems at first a technical result; that the law has tied its own hands; and so has lost its supremacy. But does it not upon consideration seem an untechnical doctrine; for is it not brute force that dictates it rather than subtle logic? The state is sovereign not because it may be, but because it must be; the citizen is subject, not because it is law, but because it must be so. These things are not possible in theory; to have a state without a sovereign or a sovereign without subjects. However complex the state, somewhere there must reside sovereignty; whatever the form of the government, all must be subjects of that sovereign, however free they may be. These things must be so, in fact, because they are based upon the power somewhere, without which the whole system would be disintegrated. In last analysis these are reasons for the rule that the sovereign is irresponsible. Therefore, this is a rule without exceptions.

The gloss of this section, that the state is not responsible, as an elementary principle has many applications in the practical administration of the law. Whenever anything gets into the hands of the state, there it must remain, for no process of law can take it out. So well is this understood, that cases are few that discuss the issue when presented in so abstract a form. The state will return the property when it seems best to do it, no sooner. Claims against the state of other sorts have no better standing. The state seizes property for its uses; the state will pay therefor when it feels so inclined, no sooner. Since this also is well understood, claimants again are few who seek to get reparation by suit against the state. For the same reason there is no obligation which the state may not repudiate; debtors of the state are paid if the state wills, not otherwise. The consequence most noteworthy of all in this for administrative law must be apparent to any observer of these conditions. The administration has a free hand to work out its own devices; but the administrative officer has no freedom of action, except action within the law. Since the administration is irresponsible, the officer must be responsible.[6]

[6] STATE ACTION.—Tobin v. Reg., 16 C. B. (N. S.) 310; Raleigh

§ 10. Governmental.

The laws which subject the state to suit are few even at the present time. The United States is now subject to suit in the Court of Claims; and various of the states make some provision for adjudication of claims against them. Wherever such a law exists the extent of the submission of the state is statutory in the first instance. But, as in all questions of statutes, the common law must be employed in the construction of such enactments. This is the more necessary as such statutes are often general in form. It is plain that by such a statute the state should not be held to have held itself out as liable for every act done by every officer in the course of administration.

That is a question of much importance in our subject; whether if the state fail in its duty to carry out the laws by default of its governmental agencies, it shall be held liable for this as a wrong done by it to its citizens. A test case is Jones v. United States, 1 Ct. of Cl. 383 (1863). In this case it appeared that the claimants had entered into a contract with the Commissioner of Indian affairs for the survey of the districts described in the various treaties made between the United States and Indian tribes. An astronomer was appointed under the

v. Goschen [1898] 1 Ch. 73; Bowman v. Farnell, 8 N. S. W. 223; Beers v. Arkansas, 20 How. 527; The Siren, 7 Wall. 152; McMeekin v. State, 9 Ark. 553; Clinton v. Bacon, 56 Conn. 517; Brown v. Finley, 3 MacA. 77; O'Neill v. Sewell, 85 Ga. 481; Lightner v. Steinagel, 33 Ill. 510; Weston v. Dane, 51 Me. 461; Dewey v. Garvey, 130 Mass. 86; Brooks v. Mangan, 86 Mich. 576; Lodor v. Baker, etc., Co., 39 N. J. Law, 49; Agent of Prison v. Rikemam, 1 Denio, 279; State v. Godwin, 123 N. C. 697; Maddox v. Kennedy, 2 Rich. Law, 102; Moore v. Tate, 87 Tenn. 744; Board of Public Works v. Gannt, 76 Va. 455.

provisions of that contract to fix the initial points of the survey. When the parties were in the field the United States government withdrew the troops that had been employed in holding the Indian country; and thereby the contractors were long delayed in proceeding with their commission. The claimants, therefore, now insist as a matter of law that the United States could not withdraw their police forces from the Indian territory without incurring a liability to the contractors to make them compensation.

The judgment of the Court of Claims was delivered by Mr. Justice NOTT: This position cannot be sustained. The two characters which the government possesses as a contractor and as a sovereign cannot thus be fused; nor can the United States while sued in the one character be made liable in damages for acts done in the other. If the removal of troops from a district liable to invasion will give the claimant damages for unforeseen expenses against a private individual, as in any ordinary case it will not, then it will when the United States are defendants, but not otherwise. This distinction between the public acts and the private contracts of the government not always strictly insisted on in the earlier days of this court, frequently misapprehended in public bodies, and constantly lost sight of by suitors who come before us,—we now desire to make so broad and distinct that hereafter the two cannot be confounded; and we repeat as a principle applicable to all cases, that the United States as a contractor cannot be held liable directly or indirectly for the public acts of the United States as a sovereign.

All this is undoubted law; although the United States

may have submitted itself to suit by a general statute, the interpretation of that statute will not include a case like this where the government is sued as a government for a governmental act. The public acts of the sovereign are never to be conceived as done subject to private law; therefore, it will not be held possible that any private wrong is done thereby. Even when the government enters into contracts, it does not divest itself of its sovereign character; and the result often is that the administration acting in behalf of the state will interfere in the performance of a contract which the administration has entered into in some other capacity. Examples of this sort of thing may be found in many places and some of the cases put are hard indeed at first impression. But no harder than the necessity itself is upon which in last analysis the rule rests. The truth of the matter is that in administration there must be a possibility of unanswerable power; that in the meeting of emergencies which arise in the course of government there must be the right to break with every arrangement that has been entered into before and to do what the exigencies of the situation require.

In administrative action the situation may fairly be expressed by saying that the state is the principal and the officer is the agent. If, then, upon that description the analogy of the law of private principal and private agent is taken, for wrongs done by the officer in the course of administration the state would be liable. Let some case be taken to test this, for example, Gibbons v. United States, 8 Wall. 269 (1868), a leading authority. The wrong involved in that case at bottom was a false imprisonment with large consequential damages, although the petition, it is true, said nothing about any arrest, force, or duress. It was all an attempt under the assumption of an applied contract to make the government responsible for the unauthorized acts of its officers, those acts being in themselves torts.

Mr. Justice MILLER disposed of the case with his usual directness; he said: No government has ever held itself liable to individuals for the misfeasance, laches, or unauthorized exercise of power by its officers and agents. It does not undertake to guarantee to any person the fidelity of any of the officers whom it employs, since that would involve it in all its operations in endless embarrassments, and difficulties, and losses, which would be subversive of the public interests: the language of the statutes which confer jurisdiction upon the court of claims excludes by the strongest implication demands founded on torts. The general principle which we have already stated as applicable to all governments, forbids, on a policy imposed by necessity, that they should hold themselves liable for unauthorized wrongs inflicted by their officers on the citizens though occurring while engaged in the discharge of official duties.

No proposition of administrative law is so undisputed as this, that the government is not liable for torts in the course of governmental action; and no rule of administrative law is so without exception as this. As a matter of theory it is impossible to conceive of the state as a private principal subject to the liabilities of the law of private agency; the truth is that this is another realm, this is a public principal, the law of public agency governs; and according to that public law it is as impossible for the state to authorize wrong-doing, as it is inconceivable that the state should do wrong itself. But more than this, as a matter of policy the rule has every support. No government could hold itself out to answer for its shortcomings; that they are always present, it is evitable. A government is an imperfect machine at the best. Liable in various ways governments may make themselves; never in this. As this chapter goes on, this at least must be more evident with each case that is added: that no government could hold itself liable for all the wrongs that may arise in the course of administration, and long endure. Much remains to be explained in working out this principle; but this is the rule, once for all.[7]

§ 11. Administrative.

The chief obligation resting upon the administration in any government, great or small, is to see that the laws are faithfully executed. But suppose that the laws are not enforced, and because of this failure in administration some person suffers a special damage; is this a case for suit against the governmental body, or is it not? A dramatic case upon this special issue is Levy v. Mayor, 1 Sandford, 465 (1848). This was an action against the Mayor, Aldermen, and Commonalty of the City of New York for damages for the death of the plain-

[7] GOVERNMENTAL.—Russell v. Devon, 2 T. R. 667; Lee v. Munroe, 7 Cranch 366; Gibbons v. United States, 8 Wall. 269; Brown v. United States, 6 Ct. of Cl. 171; Jones v. United States, 1 Ct. of Cl. 383; Sherbourne v. Yuba Co., 21 Cal. 113; Stillman v. Isham, 11 Conn. 124; Marshall Co. Sup'rs v. Cook, 38 Ill. 44; McCaslin v. State, 99 Ind. 428; Fries v. Porch, 49 Ia. 351; Weston v. Dane, 51 Me. 461; Williams v. Adams, 3 Allen 171; Detroit v. Blackeby, 21 Mich. 84; Sooy v. State, 39 N. J. L. 135; Adams v. Wiscasset Bank, 1 Me. 361; Brown's Adm'r v. Guyandotte, 34 W. Va. 299.

tiff's son, an infant, who was killed in one of the public streets by swine which had run him down and trampled him to death. The City of New York had enacted an ordinance prohibiting swine from running at large in the streets, with a provision for the impounding of animals so found. Notwithstanding which, the plaintiff declared, the corporation of New York, being unmindful of its undertaking, did not keep the streets free and clear from swine straying therein; whereby some swine so suffered by the corporation to be so at large attacked, assaulted, fell upon, and mortally wounded said E. D. Levy.

Mr. Justice SANDFORD delivered an incisive opinion: The plaintiff's counsel well observed, that there was no precedent for such an action as this; and we are compelled to add, that there is no principle upon which it can be sustained. The corporation is undoubtedly vested with certain legislative powers, among which is the authority to restrain swine from running at large in the streets; and they have exercised it by enacting an ordinance to that effect. The idea, that because they may prohibit a nuisance, that therefore they must not only pass a prohibitory law, but must also enforce it, at the hazard of being subjected to all damages which may ensue from such nuisance, is certainly novel. The corporation of the city, in this respect, stands upon the same footing within its own jurisdiction, as the state government does in respect of the state at large. It is the duty of the government to protect and preserve the rights of the citizens of the state, both in person and property, and it should provide and enforce wholesome laws for that object. But injuries to both person and property will occur, which no legislation can prevent, and which no system of laws can adequately redress. The government does not guaranty its citizens against all the casualties incident to humanity or to civil society; and we believe it has never been called upon to make good, by way of damages, its inability to protect against such misfortunes. There would be no end to the claims against this city and state, if such an action as this is well founded. There are innumerable illustrations of the application of the principle. It suffices to say, that no government, whether national, state or municipal, ever assumed, or was subjected to a general liability of this description.

That the enforcement of law is a governmental act is perhaps the most fundamental proposition in this branch of this subject. The rule here is so plain a deduction from the general proposition as to the irresponsibility of the government that there is no conflict in the authorities. The cases are not many; and they are all to the same effect. The enforcement of law is a duty of government, to be sure, but it is a public duty; and as a public duty it is recognized only in public law. The result is that there is no liability to suit for a failure in administration, since administration is a most patent governmental duty.

Moreover, it is of course impossible that all of the law could always be enforced at once. Indeed, that is an elementary fact in administration, not often appreciated, that in administration it is always a question for the executive department what laws shall have enforcement, what laws shall not; or at least, to the enforcement of what laws shall the government direct its best efforts and first attention, and what laws shall by that process of procedure have a secondary enforcement. At all events the executive department should have a free hand in this matter, and it gets that freedom for the exercise of its discretion from this condition of the law.

Another instance of the application of this principle which appears from time to time in the reports may be represented by Wheeler v. Cincinnati, 19 Oh. St. 19 (1869), as well as by any other case. The plaintiff brought his action seeking to recover from the defendant the damages arising from the casual destruction of his house (situated within the limits of said city) by fire; on the ground that the defendant had failed and neglected to provide the necessary cisterns and suitable engines for extinguishing fires in that quarter of city in which his said house was situated, and that certain officers and agents of the fire department of said city had neglected and failed to perform their duties in regard to the extinguishing of said fire, by reason whereof said fire was not extinguished, as it otherwise might, and could have been. A demurrer to his petition, alleging these facts, was sustained by the court, and judgment rendered for the defendant, which was subsequently affirmed by the District Court, upon proceedings in error.

Upon this case the opinion of the COURT was this: The laws of this State have conferred upon its municipal corporations power to establish and organize fire companies, procure engines and other instruments necessary to extinguish fire, and preserve the buildings and property within their limits from conflagration, and to prescribe such by-laws and regulations for the government of said companies as may be deemed expedient. But the powers thus conferred are in their nature legislative and governmental; the extent and manner of their exercise, within the sphere prescribed by statute, are necessarily to be determined by the judgment and discretion of the proper municipal authorities, and for any defect in the execution of such powers, the corporation cannot be held liable to individuals. Nor is it liable for a neglect of duty on the part of fire companies, or their officers, charged with the duty of extinguishing fires. The power of the city over the subject is that of a delegated quasi sovereignty, which excludes responsibility to individuals for the neglect or nonfeasance of an officer or agent charged with the performance of duties. The case differs from that where the corporation is charged by law with the performance of a duty purely ministerial in its character. We know of no case in which an action like the present has been held to be maintainable.

Upon all the authorities this may be regarded as settled law, that for nonfeasance in matter of administration there is no liability upon the government. Why this must be so it is not difficult to see. It is obvious that the harm done is imputable to the state, incident to the unavoidable imperfections of a machinery so complicated as this system of administration. A government which should hold itself liable for all injuries consequent upon the failure of its administration to enforce the laws could not respond long to the damages in which it would be cast in innumerable suits. The truth of the matter is that we do not conceive of this liability to be enforced by the courts, but to be redressed at the ballot.[8]

[8] ADMINISTRATIVE.—Montreal v. Mulcair, 28 Can. Sup. 458; Delacauw v. Fosbery, 13 N. S. W. Wkly. Notes 49; Spalding v. Vilas, 161 U. S. 483; Workman v. New York, 179 U. S. 552; State v. Hill, 54 Ala. 67; Chope v. Eureka, 78 Cal. 588; Platt v. Waterbury, 72

§ 12. Responsibility of the officer.

The administration as an administration cannot be impleaded for an action done in the pursuance of the execution of the law. A late case which lays down the law with perfect discrimination is Raleigh v. Goschen [1898] 1 Ch. 73. This action was commenced against the Right Hon. George J. Goschen and five other persons described as the Lords Commissioners of the Admiralty, and Major E. Raban, described as the Director-General of Naval Works, the object of which was to establish against the Lords Commissioners and the Director-General that they were trespassers in entering upon certain land the property of Raleigh, the plaintiff, in the neighborhood of Dartmouth, to stake out ground for a naval college preliminary to process for compulsory purchase. By the defense it was submitted that the court had no jurisdiction to enter the action; that the defendants were agents of the crown; and that they were not liable to be sued in respect of acts done by them as part of the executive government on behalf of her majesty; and they submitted, as a matter of law, that the action could not be maintained.

Romer, J., said: I will state some principles of law which I conceive govern this class of cases. Now, in the first place, inasmuch as the plaintiffs could not sue

Conn. 531; Love v. Atlanta, 95 Ga. 129; Arms v. Knoxville, 32 Ill. App. 604; Summers v. Daviess Co. Com'rs, 103 Ind. 262; Ogg v. Lansing, 35 Ia. 495; Brown v. Vinalhaven, 65 Me. 402; Boehm v. Mayo, 61 Md. 259; Buttrick v. Lowell, 1 Allen 172; Edes v. Boardman, 58 N. H. 580; Wild v. Paterson, 47 N. J. Law, 406; Levy v. Mayor, 1 Sandf. 465; Springfield F. & M. Ins. Co. v. Keeseville, 148 N. Y. 46; Wheeler v. Cincinnati, 19 Oh. St. 19; McDade v. Chester, 117 Pa. St. 414; Wixon v. Newport, 13 R. I. 454; Horton v. Mayor, 4 Lea, 47; Mulcairns v. Janesville, 67 Wis. 24.

the crown for a past or threatened trespass, they could not in respect to any trespass, sue the defendants in the capacity of agents for or as respresenting the crown. On the other hand, the plaintiffs could sue any persons actually committing or threatening the trespass, even though those persons only acted on behalf of the Government. But in this case they could be sued not because, but in spite of the fact that they occupied official positions or acted as officials. In other words, to sum up shortly the result of the above by the use of convenient phraseology, the plaintiffs in respect of the matters they are now complaining of could sue any of the defendants individually for trespasses committed or threatened; but they could not sue the defendants officially or as an official body. I therefore order the present action dismissed.

It will be seen that the decision in this case covers the whole ground; it provides for the case where the administration is sued as an entity; it provides also for the case where the administration is brought into the courts as a collection of individuals. Suit may not be brought against an official body as an official body, since that is in last analysis a suit against the state; but suit may well enough be brought against the members of the body upon the basis of a single action against simple individuals. In the practical business of law it is worth note that an administrative body should never be made a defendant in its official capacity; the suit should always be brought against the persons composing the board as private parties. The theory that the administration cannot do a wrong act does not go so far in the protection of the administration as to the individuals composing the administration; no immunity can be invoked by them.

This same distinction may be taken in the case of a single public officer as well; he also may be conceived of in one view as an official, in another view as an individual. Gidley v. Palmerston, 3 Brod. & Bing. 275 (1835), is often cited to this effect. One Holland was a retired clerk upon a retiring allowance of £200 a year; he had become embarrassed in his pecuniary relations; and the Paymaster-General had suspended a part of his allowance to accrue as a fund for liquidating the claims of certain half-pay officers, widows and other persons upon the compassionate list, for whom Holland had acted as agent. The executor of Holland now sued Lord Palmerston, Paymaster-General, in assumpsit, alleging that Parliament had placed sufficient funds at his disposal to pay the allowance, whereupon it became his duty to pay it over in each year, wherefore he might be said to have promised to pay it over.

DALLAS, Chief Justice, took this difference: On these facts the question arises: whether, upon all or any of the counts in the declaration, the present action can be maintained; and we think that it cannot be maintained. It is not pretended that the defendant is to be charged in respect of any express undertaking or agreement between him and the testator, or in respect of any other character than his public and official character of Secretary at War. On principles of public policy, an action will not lie against persons acting in a public character and situation, which from their very nature would expose them to an infinite multiplicity of actions; that is to actions at the instance of any person who might suppose himself aggrieved; and though it is to be presumed that actions improperly brought would fail, and it may be said that actions properly brought should succeed; yet, the very liability to an unlimited multiplicity of suits, would, in all probability, prevent any proper or prudent person from accepting a public situation at the hazard of such peril to himself.

An official, therefore, cannot be sued in his official capacity, since that would involve a questioning of the validity of an official act, a thing inconceivable; but well enough an officer may be sued in his private capacity, since that involves the determination of the question whether his act was an official act done in pursuance of law or whether the action was without justification of law; for in the latter case the act is as much a private wrong as if done by any private person. That is the distinction taken in the cases cited at this point; it is stated absolutely here, since these are general principles of administrative law, it remains to work the law out in more detail when the law governing administration will be seen to be more complex.[9]

[9] RESPONSIBILITY OF THE OFFICER.—Rogers v. Dutt, 13 Moo. P. C. 236; Gidley v. Palmerston, 3 Brod. & B. 275; Raleigh v. Goschen [1898] 1 Ch. 73; Baker v. Ranney, 12 Grant Ch. 228; Kearney v. Creelman, 16 N. S. 228; Amy v. Supervisors, 11 Wall. 136; United States v. Lee, 106 U. S. 196; Coblens v. Abel, Woolworth 293; Eslava v. Jones, 83 Ala. 139; McClure v. Hill, 36 Ark. 268; Ex Parte Tinkum, 54 Cal. 201; Thames Mfg. Co. v. Lathrop, 7 Conn. 557; Denver v. Dean, 10 Colo. 375; Dowling v. Bowden, 25 Fla. 712; Collins v. McDaniel, 66 Ga. 203; Strickfaden v. Zipprick, 49 Ill. 286; Jarratt v. Gwathmey, 5 Blackf. 237; McCord v. High, 24 Ia. 336; Bridge Co. v. County Com'rs, 10 Kan. 326; Marksberry v. Beasley, 8 Ky. L. Rep. 534; State v. Mason, 43 La. Ann. 590; Hayes v. Porter, 22 Me. 371; Akin v. Denny, 37 Md. 81; Keenan v. Southworth, 110 Mass. 474; Raynsford v. Phelps, 43 Mich. 342; State v. Coon, 14 Minn. 456; Baugh v. Lamb, 40 Miss. 493; St. Joseph Ins. Co. v. Leland, 90 Mo. 177; Merritt v. McNally, 14 Mont. 228; Miller v. Roby, 9 Neb. 471; State v. Kruttschnitt, 4 Nev. 178; Orr v. Quimby, 54 N. H. 590; Bonnel v. Dunn, 28 N. J. L. 153; Hover v. Barkhoof, 44 N. Y. 113; Holt v. McLean, 75 N. C. 347; Murphy v.

§ 13. Public action.

Such, therefore, is the responsibility of the officer to the law of the land by the common law principle. It is a rule almost without exception that the officer may be impleaded for any wrong act done in the course of administration as a private wrongdoer may be. If this is the end of the matter the state in time of stress can never obtain vigorous enforcement of the law, it must be admitted. But may the state not protect its officers from suits based upon acts done in the course of administration by some special legislation, and thereby may not the situation be saved? This was the gist of Mitchell v. Clark, 110 U. S. 633. An officer of the United States forces during the rebellion had seized and withheld from the owners two store-houses in St. Louis, and this was a suit for the rent due for these three months. Among other defenses the defendant pleaded 12 United States Statutes, 755, Section 4, as follows: That any order of the President, or under his authority, made at any time during the existence of the present rebellion, shall be a defense in all courts to any action or prosecution, civil or criminal, pending or to be commenced, for any search, seizure, arrest or imprisonment, made, done or committed, or acts to be done under or by virtue of such order, or under color of any act of Congress, and such defense may be made by special plea or under the general issue. In pursuance of this statute, the officer made defendant introduced in evidence a military order issuing from Washington conveyed to him by the General in command of his department.

Holbrook, 20 Oh. St. 137; Work v. Hoofnagle, 1 Yeates 506; State v. Ruth, 9 S. Dak. 84; Alvord v. Barrett, 16 Wis. 175; Richmond v. Long's Adm'rs, 17 Grat. 375.

Mr. Justice MILLER, after reciting the facts in the foregoing language, continued: It is not at all difficult to discover the purpose of all this legislation. Throughout a large part of the theatre of the civil war the officers of the army as well as many civil officers were engaged in the discharge of very delicate duties among a class of people who, while asserting themselves to be citizens of the United States, were intensely hostile to the government, and were ready and anxious at all times, though professing to be noncombatants, to render every aid in their power to those engaged in active efforts to overthrow the government and destroy the union. Some special statutes were passed after delay of a general character, but it was soon seen that many acts had probably been done by these officers in defense of the life of the nation for which no authority of law could be found, though the purpose was good and the act a necessity. That an act passed after the event which in effect ratifies what has been done, and declares that no suit shall be sustained against the party acting under color of authority, is valid, so far as Congress could have conferred authority before, admits of no doubt. These are ordinary acts of indemnity passed by all governments when occasion requires it.

That is the gist of this case: These are ordinary acts of indemnity passed by all governments when occasion requires it. The inquiry at once presents itself, how can such an act stand as constitutional in the United States? Such a statute applied to matters between man and man could not be valid; it would deprive the party wronged of his fundamental rights. Yet it is allowed to be due process of law to protect an officer from the consequences of an act done in the course of administration, and properly so since this is the exercise of an indispensable governmental power in the last analysis. This can apply of course only to the ratification of such acts as there was constitutional power in Congress to have authorized if it had acted in advance. It must always happen that in a few cases for acts performed in good faith in the presence of an overpowering emergency there would be no constitutional power to make them good by subsequent legislation, since there would have been no power to authorize the seizure or the arrest by precedent legislation.

Another class of statutes for the exoneration of public officers is much more equitable for all concerned. An example of this sort is United States v. Sherman, 98 U. S. 565 (1878). This was an application for a mandamus to John Sherman, Secretary of the Treasury, commanding him to pay to Alexander McLeod, the relator, the sum of $4,279.94, with interest. It appeared that the relator had recovered judgment against one T. C. Callicott, a supervising special agent of the Treasury Department. The relator thereupon applied to the court for a certificate of probable cause under 12 United States Statutes, 741; he thereupon presented the certificate to the Treasury Department; where he was refused payment of full interest.

Mr. Justice STRONG refused the writ as prayed for: The twelfth section of the act of Congress of March 3, 1863, relative to suits against revenue officers, enacted that where a recovery shall be had in any such suit, and the court shall certify that there was probable cause for the act done by the collector or other officer, or that he acted under direction of the Secretary of the Treasury or other proper officer of the government, no execution shall issue against the collector or other officer, but the amount so recovered, shall upon final judgment be provided for and paid out of the treasury. When the certificate is thus given, the claim of the plaintiff in the suit is practically converted into a suit against the government, but not until then; thus interest runs from that time, not sooner.

In any usual conditions of government, this is a solution of the general problem that will commend itself. In those usual conditions it is only fair that the government itself should exonerate the officer from the consequences of an act done with probable cause in the course of administration; and in especial that seems the right of the matter when an act of a subordinate officer is in question which has been done in accordance with express orders of his superior officer. If there is no such general statute, the officer may hope with some confidence from a special statute for his special case, if it is clear that his act was done with probable cause in the course of the execution of the law. More than that, since this is also the view of the internal law of the administration that inferior officers ought act in obedience to their superiors, the administration will do its best to relieve its officers against the consequences of such proper obedience. One common practice is to put the forces of the office of the Department of Justice at the disposal of the officers to present his defense. And the disbursing side of the Treasury Department has been known to be so bold as to allow the costs of litigation to an officer as expense incurred in the course of duty.[10]

[10] PUBLIC ACTION.—Gidley v. Palmerston, 3 B. & B. 275; Grant

§ 14. Official.

The condition of the law governing administration being this, that the administration itself could not be sued, but any member of the administration might be, the attempt has often been made in appreciation of this situation to bring a suit against the individual officer, when in truth what is wished is to get relief against the state itself by force of the proceeding against the officer. A late case reviewing the failure of this attempt is the elaborate case of Pennoyer v. McConnaughy, 140 U. S. 1 (1891). This was an equitable suit against the Governor, Secretary of State, and Treasurer of Oregon, who comprised the Board of Land Commissioners, to restrain and enjoin them from selling and conveying a large tract of land to which plaintiff claimed title. An act of the Legislature of Oregon had required the Board of Commissioners to cancel such certificates as his, in pursuance of which the commissioners were acting. There was a demurrer to the bill on the ground that the suit was in substance against the state.

Mr. Justice LAMAR delivered the opinion of the court: The immunity of a state from suit is absolute and unqualified, and the constitutional provision securing it is not to be construed so as to place the state within the reach of the process of the court. Accordingly, it is equally well settled that a suit against the officers of

v. Secretary, 2 C. P. D. 445; Dinsman v. Wilkes, 12 How. 390; Mitchell v. Clark, 110 U. S. 633; United States v. Sherman, 98 U. S. 565; Bayard v. United States, 127 U. S. 246; Little Rock, etc., R. R. Co. v. Worthen, 46 Ark. 312; Sumner v. Beeler, 50 Ind. 341; State v. Burke, 33 La. Ann. 512; Warren v. Kelley, 80 Me. 512; Fisher v. McGirr, 1 Gray, 1; State v. Godwin, 123 N. C. 697; Williams v. Schmidt, 14 Ore. 470; Campbell v. Sherman, 35 Wis. 103.

a state to compel them to do acts which constitute a performance by it of its contracts, is, in effect, a suit against the state itself. In application of this latter principle two classes of cases have appeared in the decisions of this court, and it is in determining to which class a particular case belongs that differing views have been presented. The first class is where the suit is brought against the officers of the state as representing the state's action and liability, thus making it, though not a party to the record, the real party against which the judgment will so operate as to compel it specifically to perform its contracts. The other class is where a suit is brought against defendants who, claiming to act as officers of the state, and under the color of an unconstitutional statute, commit acts of wrong and injury to the rights and property of the plaintiff acquired under a contract with the state. Such suit whether brought to recover money or property in the hands of such defendants, unlawfully taken by them in behalf of the state, or for compensation in damages, or in a proper case where the remedy at law is inadequate for an injunction to prevent such wrong and injury, or for a mandamus in a like case to enforce upon the defendant the performance of a plain legal duty, purely ministerial—is not within the meaning of the eleventh amendment an action against the state. It cannot be said, therefore, that this is a suit against the state, within that amendment.

This general controversy has been of great historical importance in the constitutional history of the United States. Again and again, when some one or other of the states has attempted to stand upon its immunity as a state, suit after suit has been instituted against the officers of the state. In truth these officers in all of these suits were but obeying the orders of their governments, but that has not been always conceded in a straightforward manner; indeed the state has not always gotten its full immunity; there has been some success in this campaign to get at the state through suits against the officers of the state. The opinion just quoted is the outcome of long years, and such as it is, it represents the American view upon this problem of administrative law.

It may often be a difficult question to decide whether in any particular case the suit is in substance against the state or in truth simply against the officer. Belknap v. Schild, 161 U. S. 10 (1896) is hard to disentangle, since in part it is against the government and in part against the officer, as will appear. This bill for an injunction was filed by the owners of letters patent for an improvement in caisson gates, and alleged that the defendants infringed the patent by manufacturing and using such gates. In the defendants' plea to the whole bill, and in that of the Attorney-General on behalf of the United States, the single ground of each was that the only caisson gate that the defendants had any relation with was not made by them and was not used by them for their own benefit, but was made and used by the United States in a dry dock at a navy yard, and the defendants only operated it and used it as commandant, constructor, officer, servant and employee of the United States.

Mr. Justice GRAY treated the question with great consideration: The fact so pleaded and suggested could not consistently with previous decisions prevent the defendants from being held liable to the patentee for their own infringement of his patent. There was no error, therefore, in the overruling. But the Circuit Court erred in awarding an injunction against the defendants. In the present case, the caisson gate was a part of the dry-dock in a navy yard of the United States. The United States then had both the title and the possession of the property. Although this suit was not brought against the United States by name, but against their officers and agents only, nevertheless so far as the bill prayed for an injunction, the United States was the only real party, against whom alone in fact, the relief was asked, and against whom the decree would effectively operate; the plaintiff sought to control the defendants in their official capacity, and in the exercise of their official functions, as representatives and agents of the United States; and thereby to defeat the use by the United States of property owned and used by the United States for the common defense and general welfare; and therefore the United States was an indispensable party to enable the court, according to the rules which govern its procedure, to grant the relief sought; and the suit could not be maintained without violating the principles affirmed in a long series of decisions of this court.

This case opens a new field of inquiry. This is the end of immunity and the beginning of liability. It is important that suit against the administration in whatever form must always fail; and as was said in the preface to this chapter, that is a fundamental condition under which administration must go on under our system. But it is of overshadowing importance that of every act done in administration by any officer there may be judicial inquiry; and for every act done in the execution of law by any officer without justification of law there may be judgment against the officer. That is an elementary proposition in administrative law under our system—the responsibility of every public officer to the law of the land for every act done in administration.[11]

§ 15. Personal.

This, then, is a first principle in our administrative law: that the officer may always be impleaded as a private individual. A few cases from the mass of the authorities only need be recited for the principal doctrine. Mostyn v. Fabrigas, 1 Cowp. 161 (1774), has been often remarked. This was an action by Fabrigas against Mostyn brought in the English Common Pleas for false imprisonment for a period of eight months in the Island of Minorca. The defendant pleaded a special justification that he was at the time Governor of Minorca, and

[11] OFFICIAL.—Osborn v. Bank, 9 Wheat. 738; Louisiana v. Jumel, 107 U. S. 711; Poindexter v. Greenhow, 114 U. S. 270; In Re Ayers, 123 U. S. 443; Pennoyer v. McConnaughy, 140 U. S. 1; United States v. Clark, 31 Fed. 710; In Re Fair, 100 Fed. 149; Wolffe v. State, 79 Ala. 201; Lee v. Huff, 61 Ark. 494; Nougues v. Douglass, 7 Cal. 65; Sharps' Mfg. Co. v. Rowan, 34 Conn. 332; McCord v. High, 24 Ia. 336; Strickfaden v. Zipprick, 49 Ill. 286; Lecourt v. Gaster, 50 La. Ann. 521; Michigan Bank v. Hastings, 1 Doug. 241; Newman v. Elam, 30 Miss. 507; Beckham v. Nacke, 56 Mo. 546; Northern Pac. R. Co. v. Carland, 5 Mont. 146; State v. Kruttschnitt, 4 Nev. 178; Scudder v. Trenton, etc., Co., 1 N. J. Eq. 694; Woolley v. Baldwin, 101 N. Y. 688; Yealy v. Fink, 43 Pa. St. 212; Water Power Co. v. Electric Co., 43 S. C. 168; McKinney v. Robinson, 84 Tex. 489; Kerr v. Woolley, 3 Utah 456; Board of Public Works v. Gannt, 76 Va. 455.

that as such he ordered the arrest and imprisonment; wherefore, he prayed judgment. At the trial the jury gave a verdict for the plaintiff with £3,000 damages.

Lord MANSFIELD said: To lay down in an English court of justice such a monstrous proposition as that a governor acting by virtue of letters patent under the great seal is accountable only to God, and his own conscience; that he is absolutely despotic, and can spoil, plunder and affect his Majesty's subjects, both in their liberty and property, with immunity,—is a doctrine that cannot be maintained. Therefore, in every light in which I see the subject, I am of opinion that the action holds emphatically against the governor, if it did not hold in the case of any other person.

As a matter of constitutional history in England, this is the final and emphatic case which marks the assertion of the principal doctrine beyond any subsequent question. In this same last quarter of the eighteenth century the whole doctrine hung in the balance in the cases of the general warrants where the government openly demanded the immunity of its officers from judicial inquiry. Since those times it has been common knowledge that any officer may be sued. Indeed, suits against officers are of such every-day occurrence in the courts that it causes no comment whatever when a public officer is a party defendant. It is rather a thing contemplated in taking public office; for few can serve a term in any position of importance without being summoned into the courts again and again. Under so rigid a limitation as this, administration must proceed in a system like ours where the law of the land is supreme over all persons alike, of whatever station they may be.

That principle which makes any officer under any circumstances liable in damages for any act done in enforcement of the law which may prove to have been done without justification of law, when the matter is later examined, was not pushed to extreme cases without litigation. As important a state trial as one can find in the Supreme Court is Little v. Barreme, 2 Cr. 170 (1804). On the 2nd of December, 1799, the Danish brigantine Flying Fish, Barreme, owner, was captured near the island of Hispaniola by the American frigate Boston upon suspicion of violating the non-intercourse act. Captain Little, the Commander of the Boston, acted in strict accordance with orders of the President of the United States in making the seizure; it later appeared in proof that the Flying Fish had not in truth violated the statute; thereupon damages were assessed against Little.

Chief Justice MARSHALL delivered the opinion: I was at first strongly inclined to think that where in consequence of orders from legitimate authority a vessel is seized with pure intention the claim of the injured party for damages would be against that government from which the orders proceeded, and would be a proper subject for negotiation. But I have been convinced that I was mistaken and I have receded from this first opinion. I acquiesce in that of my brethren which is that the instructions cannot change the nature of the transaction or legalize an act which without those instructions would have been a plain trespass. It becomes then unnecessary to inquire whether probable cause exists; Captain Little, then, must be answerable in damages.

The great risks in accepting public office in this state of the law have been commented upon again and again. In brief, they are these: If any person imagine that he has been aggrieved by any public officer, if he believes any public officer to blame for any damages he may have suffered, he may bring a suit against the officer; even if successful in that litigation, the officer is put to the delays and expenses of litigation. More than that, if that officer, it may be proved, has deviated ever so little from his legal authority, if, with the best of intention or with the best of intelligence, he makes a mistake of law in interpreting his powers, or if he makes a mistake of fact applying the law to a particular case, he is by the principal doctrine, if applied to its logical conclusion, liable as a private wrong-doer, and responsible in such damages as may be proved.[12]

§ 16. Conclusion.

The necessary thing now is to accommodate these two doctrines. On the one hand is the law that in governmental action the officer is irresponsible; on the other hand is the law that in personal action the officer is responsible. The problem is to protect the officer from the crushing effect of these rules. This is done in this wise: If the officer does an act in the course of

[12] PERSONAL.—Ashby v. White, 2 Ld. Raym. 938; Entick v. Carrington, 2 Wils. 275; Amy v. Supervisors, 11 Wall. 136; Belknap v. Schild, 161 U. S. 10; Briggs v. Coleman, 51 Ala. 561; McClure v. Hill, 36 Ark. 268; Hartford Bank v. Waterman, 26 Conn. 324; Collins v. McDaniel, 66 Ga. 203; Porter v. Thomson, 22 Ia. 391; Lecourt v. Gaster, 50 La. Ann. 521; Nowell v. Wright, 3 Allen 166; Amperse v. Winslow, 75 Mich. 234; Merritt v. McNally, 14 Mont. 228; Bassett v. Fish, 75 N. Y. 303; Holt v. McLean, 75 N. C. 347; State v. Doyle, 40 Wis. 204.

administration it will be held a governmental act if it is within his authority. An act is within his authority if it is within his discretion. Therefore, if any officer act within the discretion, discretion which has been vested in him, he is irresponsible. Only if the duty of the officer left no discretion to him in the premises, can it be said with truth that what he does contrary to that duty is his personal act, for which he should be held liable as a private person. In this way an official gets protection in most of his action in the course of administration.

There is danger in too great insistence upon the negative doctrine applicable only to improper administration, that when there is no justification of law the officer will be liable. For the positive doctrine applicable to proper administration, that when there is justification of law the officer is not liable, may be for the moment forgotten. One such case is State v. Knoxville, 12 Lea, 146. This was an indictment for nuisance. In the proof it appeared that because of an epidemic of the smallpox the public authorities in the City of Knoxville had been driven to active measures to prevent the spread of the disease. Among the precautionary measures taken, the clothing, beds and bedsteads used by persons who had the disease at the pest house were regularly burned in pits upon the hospital grounds. The smoke and scent of these fires were at times offensive to people living in the immediate vicinity.

Upon these facts Mr. Justice FREEMAN delivered the only opinion possible: There are cases when it becomes necessary for the public authorities to interfere with the control by parties of their property, and even destroy it, where some controlling public necessity demands the interference or destruction. A strong instance of this description is where it becomes necessary to take or destroy the private property of individuals to prevent the spreading of a fire, the ravages of a pestilence, the advance of a hostile army, or any public calamity. The rule applicable to the present case is therefore that if the act was done by public authority or sanction, and in good faith and was done for the public safety and to prevent the spread of disease, and such means used as are usually resorted to and approved by medical science in such cases, and was done with reasonable care and regard for the safety of others, then the parties were justified in what they did.

Here the action by the public officers was justified, because the law is that under such circumstances the steps taken were proper. This principle in its innumerable applications is at the bottom of most of the body of administrative law which is the subject of this treatise. Indeed, the elaboration of this conception, that authority of the law must always be found for administrative action, is the real substance of any discussion of administrative law under our system. Whatever scope the administration may claim with us must be found inside the law upon justification there by authority shown, and not outside the law, for no defense exists. This whole doctrine from which the administration has its authority, and under which administration goes on, will receive the fullest treatment later and need not be anticipated.

On the other hand, a case like Mitchell v. Harmony, 13 How. 115 (1851), must be reckoned with. This other side is responsibility. When in the Mexican war Colonel Doniphan commenced his march for Chihuahua, Harmony, a trader, followed in the rear with a mule train and sold to the inhabitants, as opportunity offered. But after they had entered that province and were about to proceed in an attack against the city of that name, distant about three hundred miles, Harmony determined to proceed upon no such hazardous expedition. When this determination was made known to the commander he gave orders to Colonel Mitchell to compel him to remain; later in the battle of Sacramento his wagons, mules, and goods were used in the public service, and so when the Mexicans regained possession of the place all his property was lost.

Chief Justice TANEY considered the various aspects of the case at length: The instruction is objected to on the ground that it restricts the power of the officer within narrower limits than the law will justify. And that when troops are employed in an expedition into an enemy's country, where the dangers that meet them cannot always be foreseen and where they are cut off from aid from their own government, the commanding officer must necessarily be intrusted with some discretionary power as to the measure he should adopt; and, if he acts honestly, and to the best of his judgment, the law will protect. But it must be remembered that the question here is not as to the discretion he may exercise in his military operations, or in relation to those who are under his command. His distance from home and the duties in which he is engaged, cannot enlarge his power over the property of a citizen, nor give to him in that respect any authority which he would not, under similar circumstances, possess at home. And where the owner has done nothing to forfeit his rights every public officer is bound to respect them, whether he finds the property in a foreign or hostile country, or in his own. There are without doubt occasions in which private property may lawfully be impressed into the public service or taken for the public use. Unquestionably, in such cases, the government is bound to make full compensation to the owner; but the officer is not a trespasser. Every case must depend upon its own circumstances. It is the emergency that gives the right and the emergency must be shown to exist before the taking can be justified. In deciding upon this necessity, however, the state of the facts as they appeared to the officer at the time he acted must govern the decision. But it is not sufficient to show that he exercised an honest judgment and took the property to promote the public service; he must show by proof the nature and character of the emergency such as he had reasonable grounds to believe it to be, and it is then for a jury to say, whether it was so pressing as not to admit of delay. No case of peril or danger has been proved which would lay a foundation for taking possession of the goods of Harmony at San Elisario, on that ground, either as respects the state of the country or the force of the public enemy.

There is no privilege, therefore, for administration; that an act is done in the course of administration is in itself no defense. It is to be remarked that the action of the military officer in the case last discussed was done in entire good faith in the execution of an important commission. Proof positive, this is, that the fact that an act was done in the course of administration constitutes no justification; there is no privilege for the officer that he can plead as any mitigation. If no scope should be given an administration in the enforcement of the laws, the certain result would be inaction in execution, and a stoppage in the affairs of the government; for no officer would act promptly if he must always act at his peril. It must be found then, upon further examination into the rule that the officer is answerable, that there is some escape from it in some cases. Whenever an officer has discretion vested in him by the law he is irresponsible in every act that he may do within that discretion. In this way the doctrine of the responsibility of the officer is mitigated.

CHAPTER III.

THE INDEPENDENCE OF THE ADMINISTRATION.

§ 17. Introduction.

In every government constitutional in any sense there is a division into three departments: the legislative, the executive, and the judicial. Each of these departments is independent. Its independence is a condition to be taken into the account in any discussion of the position of the administration. As the departments are co-ordinate, the executive cannot be subordinated to either of the departments by any means. This is the legal consequence of the division of the departments.

The separation of powers in government must be taken into the same account. The usual distribution will follow the same division. There are three sorts of functions of government: legislative, executive, and judicial. The legislative department will in a normal case exercise all legislative functions; the executive department, all executive functions; the judiciary department, all judicial functions. Any other distribution would lead to a confusion of powers. This is the legal consequence of the separation of powers.

§ 18. Separation of departments.

In last analysis, as we have seen, all governmental power relates back to the sovereign. In any separation of departments, therefore, each department exercises sovereignty; each in its own sphere is beyond control even of the others. What division of powers there shall be between the departments is a high question of state beyond any rules, a division which may be made in one way in one nation, or in another way in another nation. Forms of government may differ. This essential unity back of it all in government as a whole gives political science its universal character. All exercise of governmental power through all the departments is upon the same basis then; and therefore it is not an abstract theory which makes the great departments of government co-ordinate, each beyond the control of the others in its action; it is rather a fundamental condition. As this discussion goes on, the precise values to be given to the various rules which make up the law upon the separation of powers will often prove to involve most subtle distinctions, it is feared.

This theory of the necessary separation of powers in government has been held from the beginning of speculation upon matters of state to be an elementary principle. In the ancient world ARISTOTLE in his Politics laid it down as accepted that in every form of government there are three departments,—these three, one is the part that deliberates, the second is that which has to do with public offices, and the third is the judicial part. At the beginning of the Rennaissance, these inquiries began anew; that most remarkable book the Defensor Pacis of MARSILLIO of PADUA, in intricate way, sets forth the essential division in the government between the giving of law, the enforcing of it, and the judging of it. Just before the French Revolution was a time of speculation in theories of government such as the world has never seen; in that time in his Esprit de Lois, MONTESQUIEU laid down the theory in final form: there are in each state three sorts of powers, the legislative power, the executive power, and the judicial power.

The direct effect of this theory of the separation of powers in determining the framework of governments in the United States can be proved by the express declarations of the makers of the original constitutions. No one with any acquaintance with the literature of that period can have any doubt that his theory of the separation of the departments is at the basis of our constitutional structure. It is so in form; in the typical constitution in the United States, one article is devoted to the construction of the legislature, another article to the erection of the judiciary, another to the creation of the executive. The suggestion that is in this is that the three departments have an equal origin in the constitution; it must therefore be a principle that they are co-ordinate.

A constitution which so divides the departments of government must be obeyed; legislation that contravenes such a constitution must be held void. An instance of the application of this rule is seen in Auditor v. Atchison, etc., R. R., 6 Kan. 506 (1870)—an important problem in view of the amount of legislation governing the administration of the matter of taxation. In this commonwealth a Board of Appraisers and Assessors was established by law to assess railroad preperty. The property of the railroad here in the litigation was assessed and the assessment was deposited with the Auditor of the State together with the full record of the proceedings. The auditor appealed from the assessment as too low to the Supreme Court of Kansas in accordance with the clause in the statutes providing such appeal. The appeal being filed, the railroad moved the court to dismiss it on ground of want of jurisdiction because of the unconstitutionality of the statute.

KINGMAN would not entertain the appeal: The legislature is restricted to the grant of appeals in their nature and essence judicial in their character. It would be absurd to claim that it is in the power of the legislature to clothe this court with authority to review acts purely executive in their character, by giving an appeal to this court. Many of the duties which the executive is called upon to perform require great care and judgment in deciding how to act. Yet, when the decision is made an appeal could not be given to this court for that would give to the court executive powers as well as judicial—a power as dangerous to good government as it is subversive of the constitution which has carefully kept separate the executive, legislative and judicial departments of the government. It certainly could not be so, or it would of necessity obliterate the lines by which the framers of that instrument sought to keep separate and distinct, the three branches of our government.

This principle of the independence of the administration must not be imposed too far, however, upon the conditions of constitutional government in the United States. It may be well to cite one remarkable claim of this sort, that made by the Comptroller, in Re Sugar Bounty, 2 Compt. Dec. 98 (1895). This was a claim of the Oxnard Beet Sugar Company for $11,782.50, bounty of 2 cents per pound on sugar produced within the United States, according to the provision in the act of July 31, 1894. The Auditor certified the case to the Comptroller; whereupon the Comptroller called upon the claimant to show why the Comptroller should not refuse payment of these bounties on the ground of the unconstitutionality of the appropriation.

And upon that basis BOWLER, the Comptroller, refused payment: The conclusion is irresistible that it is the duty of the executive officer to obey the law; that the constitution is the supreme law, and so are statutes passed in pursuance thereof; that statutes which do not conform to the constitution are not law, and therefore when a statute is in apparent conflict it becomes the duty of the executive officer to determine for himself as between the statute and the constitution whether the statute is the law. It is true that the statute is to be considered prima facie constitutional and that it should be followed unless clearly unconstitutional. It is true also that the officer acts at his peril if he does not execute a constitutional statute, but it is none the less true that he acts at his peril if he executes an unconstitutional statute. The comptroller has never claimed to be invested with any judicial power by virtue of which he is authorized to hold and treat an act as unconstitutional otherwise than is any superior executive officer charged with the responsibility of ascertaining what the law is in order to govern his actions.

As an abstraction this ruling is perfect in its logic. If you have three departments of government, each absolute in its independence granted, the next step is to say that the constitution addresses itself to each, so that each must decide the question of constitutionality of the acts of the other, and of its own acts in pursuance of any action of its own, since in that view it is impossible that any one of the departments should assume preponderance in any inquiry over the action of any of the others. All that is the logic of a constitution; so in France with a constitution which establishes the three departments of the government, the legislative, judicial, and the executive, the conclusion is reached that no one of these three departments can do wrong in the eye of the other. Whatever the legislature enacts must be regarded as constitutional, whatever the judiciary decides is final, whatever the executive does is well done. In France, therefore, the judiciary cannot doubt the validity of any statute passed by the legislature, nor question the propriety of any official action of the executive.

This is not so in the United States; we have another view of the function of the judiciary founded in our history and continued in our policy. Under our system the courts in last resort may inquire into the constitutionality of legislation and the validity of administration. Notwithstanding this, it would seem that the courts should give a certain weight to the separation of powers. Perhaps as much as this: the courts should recognize that the legislature is by the course of things first in the enactment of laws; that accordingly, unless the statute is unconstitutional beyond all doubt, it should be allowed. The same attitude should be taken toward the executive department; unless official action is squarely in conflict with law, it should be supported also, since that is the office of administration. It should only be in last resort that the judiciary should question executive action. Whenever there is doubt the administration, as an independent department, should at least be given the doubt.[13]

§ 19. Independence.

The proposition that each of the three departments of the government is co-ordinate involves the conclusion that no one of the departments can call the other to account in a direct proceeding brought against it. To a certain extent this is the fact; that neither of the oth-

[13] SEPARATION OF THE DEPARTMENTS.—Worcester v. Georgia, 6 Pet. 570; Mississippi v. Johnson, 4 Wall. 475; Fox v. McDonald, 101 Ala. 51; Ex parte Allen, 26 Ark. 9; Ex parte Shrader, 33 Cal. 279; Land Co. v. Routt, 17 Colo. 156; State v. Staub, 61 Conn. 568; In re Miller, 5 Mackey, 507; McWhorter v. Pensacola R. R., 24 Fla. 417; Hilliard v. Connelly, 7 Ga. 179; People v. Bissell, 19 Ill. 229; State v. Hyde, 121 Ind. 20; Brown v. Duffus, 66 Ia. 193; Auditor v. Atchison, etc., R. R., 6 Kan. 500; State v. Shakespeare, 41 La. Ann. 156; Dennett, Petitioner, 32 Me. 508; Baltimore v. State, 15 Md. 457; Supervisors of Election, 114 Mass. 247; People v. Hurlbut, 24 Mich. 63; State v. Dike, 20 Minn. 363; State v. Hathaway, 115 Mo. 36; Vicksburg & M. R. Co. v. Lowry, 61 Miss. 102; Miller v. Wheeler, 33 Neb. 765; Merrill v. Sherburne, 1 N. H. 199; In re Cleveland, 51 N. J. L. 311; In re New York Elevated R. Co., 70 N. Y. 327; State v. Chase, 5 Oh. St. 528; Gray v. Pentland, 2 S. & R. 23; Taylor v. Place, 4 R. I. 338; State v. McMillan, 52 S. C. 69; Turnpike Co. v. Brown, 8 Baxt. 490; Houston, etc., R. R. v. Randolph, 24 Tex. 317.

ers can have any position to command the other. Our first great state trial, United States v. Aaron Burr, Fed. Cas. No. 14,692 (1806), should have made this inherent lack of power in such an attempt plain once for all. In this was a motion for a subpoena duces tecum directed to the President of the United States.

Chief Justice MARSHALL granted the motion: The obligation to respond to process, he said, is a general one. The King in England, perhaps, may give his testimony. It is said to be incompatible with his dignity to appear under process of the court. But the President is altogether different from the King. By the constitution of Great Britain the crown is hereditary, and the monarch can never be a subject; by the constitution of the United States the President is elected from the people and returns to the mass of the people again. If upon any principle the President should be made an exception, it would be upon grounds of expediency, his office requiring his time; but that could be arranged for. So Marshall issued his subpoena; but Jefferson refused to obey it; and Marshall had no way to enforce it.

Once only has the possibility of directing the President been suggested in the Supreme Court of the United States, in Mississippi v. Johnson, 4 Wall. 475 (1866). This was a motion made on behalf of the state of Mississippi for leave to file a bill in the name of the state, praying this court to enjoin and restrain Andrew Johnson, a citizen of the state of Tennessee and President of the United States and his officers and agents for that purpose, and especially one Ord, military commander, from executing or in any manner carrying into effect two acts of Congress named in the bills commonly known as the Reconstruction Acts. The bill complained that scope of power so broad was never before vested in a military commander in any government, since it embraced all those subjects over which states have reserved the power of legislation for themselves. The bill further charged that in their opinion and belief the said Andrew Johnson, President, in violation of the sacred rights of the states and in violation of the constitution, would proceed, notwithstanding his veto, and as a mere ministerial duty, to the execution of the said acts as though they were the law of the land, which vetoes prove he would not do so if he had any discretion. The Attorney-General objected to the bill in limine as containing matter not fit to be heard; the issue therefore was upon the question of leave to file the bill.

Chief Justice CHASE was adequate to the situation; his opinion leaves nothing to be doubted: The simple point which requires consideration is this: can the President be restrained by injunction from carrying into effect an act of Congress alleged to be unconstitutional? It is assumed by the counsel for the state of Mississippi that the President in the execution of the Reconstruction Acts is required to perform a mere ministerial duty. In this assumption there is, we think, a confounding of the terms of ministerial and executive, which are by no means equivalent. The duty imposed upon the President by these Acts is in no just sense ministerial. It is purely executive and political. An attempt on the part of the judicial department of the government to enforce such duties by the President might justly be characterized in the language of Chief Justice Marshall, as absurd and excessive extravagance. It is true that in the instance before us the interposition of the court is not sought to enforce action by the executive under constitutional legislation, but to restrain such action under legislation alleged to be unconstitutional. But we are unable to perceive that this circumstance takes the case out of the general principles which forbid judicial interference in the exercise of executive discretion. Congress is a legislative department of the government; the President is the executive department. Neither can be restrained in its action by the judicial department, though the acts of both when performed are, in proper cases, subject to his cognizance. We are fully satisfied this court has no jurisdiction of a bill to enjoin the President in the performance of his official duties; and that no such bill ought to be received by us.

This case is without doubt one of the chief decisions in our administrative law, for it settles beyond question one of the fundamental principles. The President cannot be commanded by the courts, since the President himself is the executive department. As all of the departments are co-ordinate, all of the departments are independent. But suppose the judiciary should renounce this principle and should direct a mandamus for example against the President; who would enforce that decree? Not the United States Marshal, for he is an administrative subordinate of the President. The truth is that the execution of such an order is impossible, since all the powers of enforcement of law are in the hands of a President should he be advised to hold his ground. Such an impossibility makes any claim forever idle, it would seem.

These statements cannot be made without qualification, because the Governor of the state is not always treated like the President of the United States. There is a square conflict in the authorities upon this point; it may be best to defer discussion upon this point until a case upon each side is stated. On one side is People v. The Governor, 29 Mich. 320 (1874). This was an application for an order requiring the Governor to show cause why he had not issued a certificate of construction. It was claimed that whether he should issue it or not was a question for the judiciary to determine. The court upon a preliminary consideration of the petition declined to entertain the suit upon the ground of lack of jurisdiction in the judiciary to direct a mandamus to the Governor.

The whole issue was discussed by Judge COOLEY in one of the ablest of his constitutional opinions. His argument in substance was this: Our government is one whose powers have been carefully apportioned between three distinct departments which emanate alike from the people, have their powers alike limited and defined by the constitution, are of equal dignity, and within their respective spheres of action are of equal independence. One makes the laws, another applies the law in contested cases, while the third must see that the laws are executed. This division is accepted as a necessity in all free governments, and the very apportionment of power to one department is understood to be a prohibition of its exercise by either of the others. The executive is forbidden to exercise judicial power by the same implication which forbids the courts to take upon themselves his duties. As regards the question of immunity from coercion by the courts, the Governor of a state occupies a position analogous rather to the President of the United States, than to any inferior officers of the Executive Department. As to all authority therefore confided to the Governor, whether by the constitution or by statute, it will be presumed that the power belongs exclusively to the Executive Department and therefore it cannot be subject to coercion by judicial process.

The leading case on the other side of the controversy is State v. Chase, 5 Oh. St. 528 (1856). This, too, was an application for the allowance of a writ of peremptory mandamus. It was provided then in the law governing the incorporation of banks in Ohio, that the organization should be examined and certified to the Governor, who, should he be satisfied that the law had been in all respects complied with, issue his proclamation that the company was authorized to begin business. The relators alleged that in fact all the conditions precedent to incorporation had been fulfilled by them, notwithstanding which the Governor as yet had refused to issue the proclamation. The court would not listen to a plea of improper jurisdiction, but went into the merits of the matter.

In the opinion BARTLEY, the Chief Justice, discussed first this question: Whether the Governor can be controlled in his official action by the authority of a writ of mandamus from the Supreme Court. It is claimed on the part of the defense, he said, that inasmuch as the government by the constitution is divided into three separate and co-ordinate departments, the legislative, the executive and the judicial, it necessarily follows that each department must be supreme within the scope of the powers, and neither subject to the control of the others for the manner in which it performs or its failure to perform its legal or constitutional duties. This argument is founded on theory, rather than on reality. Under our system of government, no officer is placed above the restraining authority of the law; except in the exercise of a discretion vested by law no officer can claim exemption from judicial inquiry. It is not, therefore, by the person to whom the writ is directed, but the nature of the thing to be done that the propriety or impropriety of issuing a mandamus is to be determined. There is nothing in the nature of the chief executive office of this state which prevents the performance of duties merely ministerial being enjoined on the Governor.

The questions which arise in this section in truth test the balance of powers in our constitutional form of government. It involves the issue whether there is a true co-ordination of the departments of government. The executive himself is the executive department as truly as the judges are the court or the members are the legislative. Each in its sphere is supreme. In respect to the executive himself every act of his is of the same quality; the action of a governmental department with inherent constitutional powers. The chief executive in any state in all matters confided to him must be, it would seem, his own judge. Claims upon him for performance or non-performance should be remitted to the political forum for settlement; they should not be litigated in the courts.[14]

[14] INDEPENDENCE.—Mississippi v. Johnson, 4 Wall. 475; Green v.

§ 20. Co-ordination.

The rule which makes the department of the government independent limits governmental methods. It will be possible to put two departments at the same work if they are co-ordinated, each with its own function to perform; but it will not be possible to put two departments at the same businesses if one is subordinated to the other,—one superior, the other inferior. It is submitted that these must be the consequences of the rule for the division of the departments. There are two decisions in the Supreme Court of the United States about the middle of the century that test these propositions so thoroughly that it would seem that there could be no more to say upon this issue. These decisions are worth careful consideration, because the problem is a most important one in the actual conduct of the business of administration.

United States v. Ferreira, 13 How. 40 (1851), is the first case. This case arose in the matter of the Spanish claims in the Floridas. The determination of these claims in pursuance of the treaty of cession was referred to the jurisdiction of the judge of the territorial court in Florida. After the adjudication of such claims in this manner, it was provided that they should

Mills, 25 U. S. App. 383; Tennessee, etc., R. Co. v. Moore, 36 Ala. 371; Hawkins v. Governor, 1 Ark. 570; Middleton v. Low, 30 Cal. 596; Land Co. v. Routt, 17 Colo. 156; State v. Drew, 17 Fla. 67; State v. Towns, 8 Ga. 360; People v. Bissell, 19 Ill. 229; Gray v. State, 72 Ind. 567; State v. Warmoth, 22 La. Ann. 1; Magruder v. Swann, 25 Md. 173; Dennett, Petitioner, 32 Me. 508; People v. Governor, 29 Mich. 320; State v. Dike, 20 Minn. 363; State v. Stone, 120 Mo. 428; State v. Governor, 25 N. J. L. 331; Clark v. Miller, 54 N. Y. 528; State v. Chase, 5 Oh. St. 528; Mauran v. Smith, 8 R. I. 192; State v. Thorson, 9 S. D. 149; Houston, etc., R. Co. v. Randolph, 24 Tex. 317.

be reported to the Secretary of War at Washington, who, on being satisfied that they were just and equitable, should cause them to be paid. The principal case was an attempt to take an appeal from the judge to the Supreme Court of the United States. The only question determined in that court was whether there was any jurisdiction to determine the appeal; and, in order to decide that question, whether the nature of the proceedings before the district judge was judicial or administrative; since though a territorial judge might act as a commissioner, the Supreme Court could only act as a court.

Mr. Justice WAYNE examined the case with care, with the result that he found no jurisdiction to hear an appeal in the court: Congress has provided a special method of adjudication of these questions. When that tribunal was appointed it derived its whole authority from the law creating it, and not from the Treaty, and Congress had the right to regulate its proceedings, and limit its powers, and to subject its decisions to the control of an appellate tribunal if it appeared advisable to do so. If the tribunal acts at all, it acts under the authority of law and must obey the law. It is manifest that this power to decide upon the validity of these claims is not conferred on them, as a judicial function to be exercised in the ordinary limits of a court of justice. There is to be no suit, no parties in the legal sense, no process, no appearance for the United States, no obligatory summoning of witnesses. The proceeding is altogether ex parte. Again, the award is to be transmitted with the evidence to the Secretary of the Treasury, and the Secretary is to pay the claim if he judge it just and equitable. Such a tribunal is not a judicial one; the decision is not the judgment of a court of justice; it is the award of a commissioner. An appeal to this court from such a decision would be an anomaly in the history of jurisprudence. An appeal might as well have been taken from the awards of the board of commissioners under the Mexican treaty. We cannot see any ground for objection to the power of revision given to the Secretary. When the United States consent to submit the adjustment of claims to any tribunal, they have the right to make the approval of the award by the Secretary of the Treasury as one of the conditions upon which they will be liable. It is true that the powers conferred by these acts of Congress upon the judge as well as the Secretary are judicial in their nature when judgment and discretion must be exercised by both of them; but it is nothing more than the power ordinarily given by law to a commissioner appointed to adjust claims to lands or money under treaty, or special powers to inquire into or decide any other particular classes of controversies in which the public or individuals may be concerned. A power of this description may constitutionally be conferred on a secretary as well as on a commissioner, but it is not judicial in either case in the sense in which judicial power is granted by the constitution of the United States.

United States v. Ritchie, 17 How. 525 (1854), is an excellent second case for comparison with the case that has just been recited. These proceedings were originally commenced before the board of commissioners to settle private land claims in California under the act of March 3, 1851. The commission, after hearing the proofs filed by the claimant, ordered that the title be confirmed to Ritchie. The United States, in accordance with the process provided, filed a transcript of the proceedings in the district court of the United States, praying for a readjudication. Ritchie by his counsel raised the point of want of jurisdiction upon the ground that the procedure provided by the statute was against the constitution. If the case last recited represents a true rule, this present case cannot be within the jurisdiction of the Supreme Court; unless the process in the present case is upon a different foundation altogether.

Mr. Justice NELSON goes to that extent; he establishes the distinction: It is objected that the law prescribing an appeal to the district court from the decision of the board of commissioners is unconstitutional; as this board as organized is not a court under the constitution and cannot, therefore, be invested with any of the judicial powers conferred upon the general government. But the answer to the objection is that the suit in the district court is to be regarded as an original proceeding, the removal of the transcript, evidence, and papers into it from the board of commissioners, being but a mode of providing for the institution of the suit in that court. The transfer it is true is called an appeal; we must not, however, be misled by a name, but look to the substance and intent of the proceeding. The district court is not confined to a mere examination of the case as heard and decided by the board of commissioners, but hears the case de novo, upon the papers and testimony which have been used before the board, they being made evidence in the district court; and also upon such further evidence as either party may see fit to produce.

The general situation discussed in these cases involves the whole of the doctrine of the separation of powers. This must be premised: If there is some issue to be determined in the course of the business of administration the legislature may assign the adjudication upon that issue either to the executive department or to the judicial department. In some of the administration of law, indeed, it is almost impossible to distinguish between administration by adjudication and adjudication for administration. So indistinguishable in truth are these functions that if the legislature chose it may for example give over to the executive the determination of land grants or it may give over that inquiry to the judiciary; and in either case it cannot be said that the legislative has acted in an outrageous way in apportioning the power to either, so that their action cannot be attacked as against the constitutional rule requiring some degree of propriety in the distribution of the functions.

That first obstacle may therefore be circumvented; but there remains another bar, the rule requiring substantial independence for each of the departments in the exercise of any functions whatever that may be assigned to it. The two cases which have just been under consideration require that a distinction shall be taken in order that the truth may be told. One position of things is not possible in accordance with the rule forbidding subordination of one department to another. A matter cannot in the first place be given to the judiciary with in the second place an appeal to the executive; that would be an overt situation of superior and inferior which could not be borne. On the other hand another position is quite possible in accordance with the rule requiring co-ordination of the departments with each other. A matter may in the first place be given to the executive for decision, with a possibility for an adjudication by the judiciary in the second place, provided that the contest begins anew in the judicial department. Such a course as that in no way violates the rule against the independence of the departments; it is indeed founded upon that rule.[15]

§ 21. Subordination.

In the last paragraph a most satisfactory solution of this most difficult problem was found. If the two departments, the executive and the judiciary, were put in co-ordination, that was possible; but if the two departments were put in subordination, that was impossible. That is, the scheme of first one and second the other is well enough if the second takes up the matter as an original issue; but if the second takes up the matter as an appellate issue, that will not go. This, it would seem, is more than a formal requirement, it is substantial as well. The only difficulty is that two recent decisions in the Supreme Court of the United

[15] CO-ORDINATION.—United States v. Ferreira, 13 How. 40; United States v. Ritchie, 17 How. 525; Fremont v. United States, 17 How. 542; Avery v. Fox, 1 Abb. C. C. 246; Fox v. McDonald, 101 Ala. 51; Staude v. Election Com'rs, 61 Cal. 313; People v. Scott, 9 Colo. 422; Owners of Lands v. People, 113 Ill. 296; Flournoy v. Jeffersonville, 17 Ind. 169; Smith v. Gove, 70 Me. 551; Crane v. Meginnis, 1 Gill & J. 476; Turner v. Althaus, 6 Neb. 54; Thompson v. German Valley R. R., 22 N. J. Eq. 111; People v. Ulster, etc., R. R., 128 N. Y. 240; Brown v. Turner, 70 N. C. 102.

States do not observe this distinction which was laid down in those two earlier cases.

The first of these is United States v. Lies, 170 U. S. 628 (1898). This case came to the Supreme Court of the United States by virtue of a writ of certiorari issued to the Circuit Court of Appeals to determine why the government was not allowed to be heard in full in a customs proceeding there. The litigation arose out of a conflict of views between the Collector and the importers as to the manner of classification and the rate of duty to be imposed upon an importation of tobacco. The importers, dissatisfied, brought the case before the Board of General Appraisers; again dissatisfied, they brought the case into the Circuit Court—all in accordance with the Customs Administration Act of 1890. The government took no action to remove the case to judicial courts, so that the only protestants there were the importers; and subsequently the importers themselves withdrew their appeal.

At that stage the government itself claimed to be heard to contest that part of the decision of the General Appraisers brought up by the appeal that was unfavorable to it. Mr. Justice PECKHAM was of the opinion that the government had no standing left. He treated the whole transfer upon the basis of a formal appeal. The fact that one party appeals, he said, furnishes no reason for holding that the other can obtain all the benefits of an appeal himself without complying in any particular with the statute giving an appeal. There would be no reason or fairness in so providing, and we are of opinion the statute properly construed does not so provide. Although the Circuit Court has, upon application of the parties, power to take further testimony after the case is brought before it, and to that extent it may be regarded as something in the nature of a new proceeding, yet the proper procedure in deciding the appeal is in no way altered thereby. As the government in this case took no proceedings to review the decision of the Board of General Appraisers, it cannot be heard to object to an affirmance of such decision.

This judgment is proper enough. Clearly the government has no standing in the Circuit Court; if the proceedings are regarded as begun anew there, that seems the more conclusive; it is only the language that is objectionable, stating that to be a possible condition of affairs that the judiciary department is made appellate over a proceeding initiated in the executive department. In a decision in the next term that point came up squarely for decision. It became a direct issue in this next case whether an appeal could be taken from an executive office to an appellate court. Some expedition there may be in such a combined action of first executive as an inferior tribunal, and then the judiciary as a superior tribunal; but under our differentiation of public powers it seems hardly possible.

The second case is United States v. Duell, Commissioner of Patents, 172 U. S. 576 (1899). In an interference proceeding in the Patent Office between Bernadin and Northall, the Commissioner of Patents decided in favor of Bernadin; whereupon, Northall prosecuted an appeal to the Court of Appeals of the District of Columbia according to the provisions of the statutes. That court awarded Northall priority, reversing the decision of the

Commissioner; notwithstanding which Bernadin applied to the Commissioner to issue the patent to him; but the Commissioner refused to do this in view of the decision of the Court of Appeals, which had been certified to him. Bernadin then applied to the Supreme Court of the District of Columbia for a mandamus to compel the Commissioner to issue the patent in accordance with his prior decision on the ground that the statute providing for an appeal was unconstitutional.

Mr. Chief Justice FULLER delivered the opinion of the court: The contention is that Congress had no power to authorize the Court of Appeals to review the action of the Commissioner in an interference case on the theory that the Commissioner is an executive officer; that his action in determining which of two claimants is entitled to a patent is purely executive; and that, therefore, such action cannot be subjected to the revision of a judicial tribunal. However, the investigation of every claim presented involves the adjudication of disputed questions of fact upon scientific and legal principles, and is therefore essentially judicial in its character, and requires the intelligent judgment of a trained body of skilled officials, expert in the various branches of science and art, learned in the history of invention, and proceeding by fixed rules to systematic conclusions. We agree that it is of vital importance that the line of demarcation between the three great departments of government should be observed; and that each should be limited to the exercise of its appropriate powers; but in the matter of this appeal we find no such encroachment of one department upon the domain of another as to justify us in holding the act in question unconstitutional.

This case is a surprise—an unsatisfactory denouement. Every general principle stated in the case is sound. No better statement of the nature of the various rules requiring a separation of the departments and necessitating a proper distribution of functions can be found in so brief compass as in the last paragraph of this opinion. And yet it is submitted that the conclusion reached in this case is the direct opposite of its principles. It may well be asked with respect: How can there be a more flagrant example of the subordination of one of the great departments to another than is seen in this case, where a judicial court is put over an administrative office, where the action of an executive body is subjected to the revision of a judicial body; for what else can this process of appeal amount to? If this be allowed in this case it is difficult to see why it must not be permitted in every case. And the end of a series of statutes might be to make the Chief Justices and the Associate Justices of the United States pass upon the propriety of every action of the President and Cabinet of the United States—a reductio ad absurdum.

This is not an insistence upon an immaterial thing; it is a holding to the life principle in the rule of the separation of powers. If it be required that the judiciary shall never have more than external relations with the executive, that they may duly act in co-ordination so that each performs its own part and each judges for itself, well and good. But if it be permitted that the judiciary may interfere in the internal operations of the administration, that makes the executive act in subordination to the judiciary, which cannot be allowed. The importance of this distinction for the administration is this: Under the first supposition, the judiciary can only hold the administration in the wrong if there has been an excess of powers, if the administration has exceeded its jurisdiction, for example. But under the second supposition, the judiciary can revise action of the administration done in pursuance of its discretion, if there has been exercise of powers. In short, the administration may judge in one way in its discretion and the judiciary might now determine the matter in another way. This is contrary to the principle that the judiciary should have no business in the action of the administration; this is contrary to the balance of powers that the administration should be left without its own discretion in its own sphere. Although the judiciary may well entertain issues involving external administrative law, all questions involving internal administrative law should be decided upon by the administration itself, free from the review of any other department.[16]

§ 22. Division of functions.

In every government of the United States, then, we find these three departments, the legislative, the executive, and the judicial. Our concern is to separate the executive department from the others, to disentangle the functions of the administration from the others. In a general way the one follows upon the other: For the legislative department in a general way, all legislation

16 SUBORDINATION.—Ex parte Vallandigham, 1 Wall. 243; Gordon v. U. S., 7 Wall. 188; United States v. Lies, 170 U. S. 628; United States v. Duell, 172 U. S. 576; Langenberg v. Decker, 131 Ind. 471; People v. Auditor General, 38 Mich. 746; In re R. R. Commissioners, 15 Neb. 679.

—that is what it is most fit for, deliberation; for the judicial department in a general way, all adjudication —that, too, is what it is best formed for, judgment; and for the executive department in the same way, administration—that also is what it is adapted for, enforcement. Then does the legislative department alone lay down all rules; does the judiciary decide all issues; does the executive confine itself altogether to action?

That is the normal state of things at all events. An excellent statement of the scope of this rule of separation of powers is found in Ex parte Allis, 12 Ark. 101 (1870). One Allis presented a petition to this court representing that under and by virtue of an act for rebuilding the penitentiary the Board of Inspectors had entered into a contract with him for the construction. Petitioner then represented what progress he had made in the work he had undertaken. He then stated that he had called upon the Board of Inspectors to certify what work had been done to the Auditor of the State, but that the Inspectors refused to do so upon the ground that he had not complied with his contract; which the petitioner undertook to show was unjust to him by a detailed representation of what materials he had provided, money expended, and work performed by him during the quarter; and thereupon asked mandamus to the Inspectors to compel them to certify his first quarterly instalment.

Mr. Justice STRONG refused the mandamus; in his preliminary dicta he said: If this court has rightful jurisdiction in cases like this it must be found expressed in the Constitution or derived by a just and necessary implication from the expressions used in that instrument. Because it was by that instrument that the state government was instituted, the departments created, and the powers to be exercised by each defined and distributed. It is established by that instrument that the powers of government should be divided into the distinct departments. This is to be considered in connection with the known political truth that this is necessary no less for the security of public liberty than private rights —a truth that has been so proclaimed and enforced by some of the most wise and eminent men of this and other countries, and is besides in the full tide of successful experiment in all the sister states as well as the federal government.

A careful examination shows some exceptions to these usual conditions. It is hardly too much to say that in every American government the legislature by the forms of the constitution does something in an administrative way by its officials, at times may hold a trial in a judicial way. The judiciary also in accordance with permission of the constitution may in a few cases make rules for the conduct of its proceedings, and maintain direction over the execution of its decrees. The executive itself often has a part in the enactment of legislation, and certain questions are left to the adjudication of the administration. These exceptions are all of them unimportant. Nothing can be argued from the power of impeachment of the legislature, from the advisory opinions of the judges, from the veto of the executive. These are all avowed exceptions in the constitutional structure placed there in pursuance of a certain political doctrine —the theory of checks and balances. Whatever the positive provisions of a constitution may provide cannot be questioned; but neither can any qualification of the general theory of the division of functions be admitted that is not based so upon explicit constitutional provision. The truth of the matter is that the doctrine of the constitutional necessity of the distribution of the powers of government to the corresponding departments of the government is more than a principle of policy. It is a rule of law.

The most extreme instance of this rule against the confusion of powers may be imagined where an administrative body is given both legislative and judicial functions. An administrative body, then, will have legislative, judicial, and executive powers; that will be as contrary to the rule requiring separation of powers as can be. This is not a supposititious case; it is Western Union Tel. Company v. Myatt, 98 Fed. 335 (1899). By Chapter 28 of the Special Sessions Law of 1898, a special tribunal was established to pass upon all questions of rates of public service companies, to be denominated the Court of Visitation. One Maxwell tendered to the Western Union Company certain messages and a certain sum fixed by the Court at a previous sitting. Upon refusal of the complainant to perform the service at such rates, Maxwell filed a complaint with the state solicitor; and the latter filed an information thereon against the complainant in the Court of Visitation, caused citation to be issued upon it, and was proceeding to enforce the performance of the telegraphic service at the maximum rates prescribed. The complainant attacked the validity of said enactments of the legislature, and claimed that the enforcement thereof would operate to deprive it of its property without due process of law, and as a denial of the equal protection of the laws; and this suit was brought to enjoin further proceedings for the enforcement of the maximum rates complained of. The cause now arose on an application of complainant for a temporary injunction. The proofs on such application clearly showed that the rates prescribed by the law were not only not compensatory, but were materially less than the actual cost of the service It was not denied by defendants that sufficient proof had been made by complainant in this respect.

The opinion in this case was an elaborate one, citing many cases deciding upon the separation of powers. HOOK, District Judge, concluded: In the enactment of the law creating the Court of Visitation and defining its powers and jurisdiction, and of the subsequent law extending such powers and jurisdiction to telegraph companies, the legislature attempted to confer upon a single board or body important and substantial legislative, administrative, and judicial powers, to be exercised in the same proceeding, and as to the same subject-matter. It attempted to confer full power to regulate the operation of railroad and telegraph companies, and to prescribe schedules of rates and charges, which power is legislative or administrative in its character. It also attempted to confer upon the Court of Visitation the power to pass judicially upon its regulations, and the reasonableness of the rates fixed by it, to embody its determinations in decrees, which it was authorized to enforce by the appointment of receivers and the sequestration of the property of the companies. The distinction between legislative and judicial functions is a vital one, and it is not subject to change or impairment either by legislative act or by judicial decree, for such distinction inheres in the constitution itself, and is as much a part of it as though it were definitely defined therein. When the legislature has once acted, either by itself or through some subordinate board or agency, and has prescribed a tariff of rates and charges, then whether its action is violative of some constitutional safeguard or limitation is a judicial question, the determination of which involves the exercise of judicial functions. The question is then beyond the province of legislative jurisdiction.[17]

§ 23. Distribution.

How far these principles against confusion of powers would go came at once to the test when the earliest Congress began upon their work for the elaboration of the framework of the governmental system. One of the first missteps was in the enactment of the method of the grant of pensions. The Act of the 5th of April, 1791,

[17] DIVISION OF FUNCTIONS.—Murray's Lessee v. Hoboken Land Co., 18 How. 272; Stone v. Farmers' Trust Co., 116 U. S. 307; Andrews v. Hovey, 124 U. S. 717; Shoemaker v. U. S., 147 U. S. 282; Ex Parte Riebeling, 70 Fed. 310; Western Union Tel. Co. v. Myatt, 98 Fed. 335; Fox v. McDonald, 101 Ala. 51; Ex Parte Allis, 12 Ark. 101; Ex Parte Shrader, 33 Cal. 279; People v. Scott, 9 Colo. 422; State v. Staub, 61 Conn. 568; In Re Miller, 5 Mackey 507; McWhorter v. Pensacola R. R., 24 Fla. 417; People v. Harper, 91 Ill. 357; Langenberg v. Decker, 131 Ind. 471; Brown v. Duffus, 66 Ia. 193; Martin v. Ingham, 38 Kan. 654; State v. Shakespeare, 41 La. Ann. 156; Portland, etc., R. R. v. Grand Trunk R. R., 46 Me. 69; Baltimore v. State, 15 Md. 457; Supervisors of Election, 114 Mass. 247; People v. Hurlbut, 24 Mich. 63; State v. Hathaway, 115 Mo. 36; Thorp v. Woolman, 1 Mont. 168; Miller v. Wheeler, 33 Neb. 765; Sawyer v. Dooley, 21 Nev. 390; In Re Cleveland, 51 N. J. L. 311; Brown v. Turner, 70 N. C. 102; Taylor v. Place, 4 R. I. 338; Hoke v. Henderson, 4 Dev. 1.

provided that the petitions should be submitted to the judges of the United States who should certify their findings to the Secretary of War, who should then upon consideration of the whole matter grant or refuse the pension, as to him should seem fit. It is fortunate that we have some account of the rather obscure proceedings in the courts upon this statute in the report of Hayburn's Case, 2 Dallas, 409 (1792).

In the Circuit Court of the district of New York JAY proceeded, on the 5th of April, 1791, to take into consideration the Act of Congress entitled, "An Act to provide for the settlement of claims for petitions to be granted by the Secretary of War." And he was thereupon of opinion that by the constitution of the United States the government thereof is divided into three distinct and independent branches; that neither the legislative nor executive branch can constitutionally assign to the judiciary any duties but such as are appropriate thereto and to be performed in a judicial manner; that the duties assigned by this act make the decision of the court subject to the consideration and suspension of the Secretary of War and legislature,—whereas by the constitution neither the Secretary of War nor other executive officer is authorized to sit as a court of error upon the judicial opinions of this court. Such revision and control are deemed radically inconsistent with the independence of that judicial power which is vested in the court. The legislative, executive and judicial departments are each formed in a separate and independent manner, and the basis of each is the constitution, only within the limits of which each department can alone justify any act of authority; that as the objects of this act are exceedingly benevolent and do real honor to the humanity and justice of Congress, the judges will execute this act in the capacity of commissioners.

The Circuit Court for the district of Pennsylvania at the same time addressed a memorial to the President in which they say: Upon due consideration we have been unanimously of opinion that the court should not proceed. 1st: Because the business directed by this act is not of a judicial nature. 2nd: Because if upon this business the court had proceeded, its judgments might have been revised and controlled by the legislature, and by an officer in the executive department. Such revision and control we deem inconsistent with the independence of the department.

The Supreme Court, however, stood firm and it has been the law of that court ever since that the judiciary would not exercise powers, administrative in last analysis. The various decisions delivered in the course of the growth of the Court of Claims show how strictly the courts hold to this rule. Not until the Court of Claims had been made, in every essential, part of the judicial system would the Supreme Court of the United States entertain any appeal from it. How they stand now upon that position is shown by In Re Sanborn; 148 U. S. 222 (1893). One part of the functions of the Court of Claims was defined as follows: that when any claim or matter may be pending in any of the executive departments which involves controverted questions of law or fact, the head of such department, with the consent of the claimant, may transmit the same to the Court of Claims. When the facts and conclusions of law shall have been found the court shall report its findings to the department by which it was transmitted. In the present case the claim of Sanborn had been sent from the Department of Interior to the Court of Claims. The court decided that Sanborn was not entitled to recover. Thereupon, he made application to be allowed to appeal to the Supreme Court of the United States, which was denied.

This is not a judgment, said Mr. Justice SHIRAS: Such a finding is not made obligatory upon the department to which it was reported—certainly not so in terms —and so far as we think by any necessary implication. We regard the functions of the Court of Claims in such a case as advisory only. The finding or conclusion reached by that court is not enforceable by any process of execution issuing from the court, nor is it made by statute, the final indisputable basis of action either by the department or by Congress. The application for mandamus must accordingly be denied.

The doctrine at the bottom of these decisions is certainly of a fundamental importance in any conception of the proper distribution of the powers of government. In these particular instances of it the principles are these: the position given to the judiciary department to pass in first instance upon a matter which should later be passed upon in second instance by the executive department was contrary to the constitution in that this process involved the subordination of the judiciary department in this determination, whereas by the constitution all of the three departments must be co-ordinate. From another approach also this legislation was open to constitutional objection: the power of granting pensions was in its nature an administrative power, since it involved the execution of law; not a judicial power properly, since it did not involve litigation between man and man; it would be therefore contrary to the constitution to force powers not judicial upon the judiciary. Which comes to this: that under our constitution confusion of powers may not be permitted. If a principle like that is once admitted it must be of universal application.[18]

§ 24. Confusion.

The rule of distribution of functions will always be violated if in the apportionment of powers to an administrative body, powers belonging to any other department are given. For one instance, suppose that an administrative body is given legislative power. That is the case, it seems, in Ex parte Cox, 63 Cal. 21 (1883). The petitioner was convicted of a misdemeanor, the violation of a rule and regulation of a Board of State Agricultural Commissioners. The act establishing that commission declared it had power to enforce rules and regulations in the nature of quarantine to govern the manner of and prohibit the importation into the state of vines or cuttings infected or likely to cause infection. The prisoner had violated some regulation to which the board had attached a penalty. The court ordered his discharge;

18 DISTRIBUTION.—Hayburn's Case, 2 Dall. 409; Gordon v. U. S. 2 Wall. 561; U. S. v. Alire, 6 Wall. 573; In Re Sanborn, 148 U. S. 222; Hempstead v. Underhill's Heirs, 20 Ark. 337; Ex parte Allis, 12 Ark. 101; Ex parte Shrader, 33 Cal. 279; McWhorter v. Pensacola R. R., 24 Fla. 417; Chicago, etc., R. R. v. Jones, 149 Ill. 361; Portland, etc., R. R. v. Grand, etc., R. R., 46 Me. 69; Dow v. Wakefield, 103 Mass. 267; Andrews v. Judge of Probate, 74 Mich. 278; Pacific Exp. Co. v. Cornell, 59 Neb. 364; Atlantic, etc., Co. v. Wilmington, etc., R. R., 111 N. C. 463.

they said: For the purpose of local legislation, legislative functions may be delegated. But the legislature had not authority to confer upon the board the power of declaring what acts should constitute a misdemeanor. The legislative power is vested in the legislature; it cannot be attempted to confer that power upon any officers of the executive department.

As a second instance, suppose an administrative body is given a power which it is plain is judicial. Whether that can be is discussed in Interstate Commerce Commission v. Brimson, 154 U. S. 447 (1894). The petition in this case was based on the twelfth section of the act authorizing the Interstate Commerce Commission to invoke the aid of any court of the United States in requiring the attendance and testimony of witnesses, and the production of documents, books, and papers. The Circuit Court held the provision unconstitutional and void as involving a confusion of the powers of government, giving to an administrative commission the aid of judicial process, and forcing upon the judiciary functions not judicial. The question was whether this was forbidden by the constitution, without which obviously effective enforcement of the interstate commerce laws could not be effected.

Mr. Justice HARLAN recited the provisions of the interstate commerce law at great length; he continued: As the constitution extends the judicial power of the United States to all cases in law and equity, the fundamental inquiry upon this appeal is whether the present proceeding is a case or controversy within the meaning of the constitution. It was clearly competent for Congress to invest the commission with authority to require the attendance and testimony of witnesses, and the production of books, papers, tariffs, contracts, agreements, and documents relating to any matter committed to that body for investigation. We do not understand that any of these propositions are disputed in this case. The constitutionality of this provision, assuming it to be applicable to a matter that may legally be intrusted to an administrative body for investigation is, we repeat, not disputed, and is beyond dispute. They are issues between the United States and those who seek to obstruct the enforcement of its laws; it thus comes within the judicial power.

This preliminary view of the whole field cannot but establish as a working hypothesis this general rule against the confusion of powers as an elementary doctrine of constitutional law under our system. If this be proved true in entirety for every case that is fairly within its inhibition the consequence in administration will be of the first importance. It will result that the executive department must always be independent of the other departments in its proper sphere; more than that, that all administration must be handed over to the executive department. Of course, it must not be forgotten in the application of this principle that the business of government is a practical matter, not to be too much hampered by the application of some general principle where there is an unsubstantial departure involved in any case. Every scope must be given in the creation of governmental agencies and in the organization of them. The proper place for this principle, it is submitted, is in reserve, to be invoked whenever a substantial departure from the fundamental principle is involved. The cases discussed in this section indicate in a general way what may be done and what may not be done. What may not be enacted is overt confusion of powers—the giving of a legislative function to the administration. What may be provided is some co-operation between the departments—the lending to the administration of the process of the courts. This, it is suggested, is the solution of this problem in accordance with constitutional law under our system of government with its three departments—independence with inter-relation.[19]

§ 25. Conclusion.

In a previous discussion a rule was laid down for the position of the administration with two branches. That for action as an individual the officer might be impleaded in the courts as a private wrongdoer; but that for action as an official the officer might not be impleaded. The present discussion of the independence of the administration does not conflict with that. Action of an official as a representative of the executive department the judiciary department can take no cognizance of, still less can it enter upon review upon any appeal; but for individual action without authority of his position the officer may be proceeded against in the courts more or less as any wrongdoer. This is

19 CONFUSION.—La Abra Co. v. United States, 175 U. S. 423; Western Union Tel. Co. v. Henderson, 68 Fed. 588; Ex Parte Allen, 26 Ark. 9; Ex Parte Cox, 63 Cal. 21; State v. Johnson, 30 Fla. 499; People v. Kipley, 171 Ill. 44; Shoultz v. McPheeters, 79 Ind. 373; In Re Sims, 54 Kan. 1; Speed v. Crawford, 3 Metc. (Ky.) 207; Hartford Insurance Co. v. Raymond, 70 Mich. 485; State v. Hathaway, 115 Mo. 36; Thorp v. Woolman, 1 Mont. 168; Turner v. Althaus, 6 Neb. 54; Taylor v. Place, 4 R. I. 338; Gough v. Dorsey, 27 Wis. 119.

the solution in the administrative law of the United States again, the distinction between the two capacities of the official, as an officer and as a man. As an officer the official stands with his department and may claim its immunity; as a man he stands in the same place as other men. That is certainly, when all is said, the characteristic of the administrative law under our system, that these capacities are never in any material way to be confused. And the consequence is a free government, acting within its discretion, and a free people, protected in all their rights. This is the peculiar distinction of our system of administrative law.

CHAPTER IV.

THE POWERS OF ADMINISTRATION.

§ 26. Introduction.

The functions of the administration are of two sorts. To put the distinction in the more usual terms, these are: its executive functions and its administrative functions. The administration in truth has this double aspect; but these functions are in one sense interdependent. In the pursuance of its executive functions, the administration exercises inherent powers; while in its administrative functions, it performs derivative duties. In an extended discussion of this situation it may be said that the executive functions are powers, while the administrative functions are duties; but in truth in each case there is power and duty both.

Executive powers, then, are inherent, because the basis of them is the constitution itself. In the exercise of executive powers the executive is upon the same basis as the legislative or judiciary. The action of all of these alike is the expression of the will of the state. In such acts the executive is the head of the state; he conducts foreign negotiations; he leads armies; he grants amnesty; he promulgates proclamations. Executive powers are primary; in every such action the executive acts of his own motion, makes his own decisions, draws his own conclusions, enforces his own decrees. As it is this aspect of the administration that one is prone to think of when comparing the functions of this department with the legislative department and with the judiciary department, the department is in most discussion denominated the executive department.

Administrative duties are derivative. The direction of these functions is to the enforcement of the laws; the laws must therefore precede the exercise of these functions. There must be law for enforcement before there can be administration; the functions of the legislature, therefore, must be first exercised, these in turn creating duties for the administration to perform. Administrative functions, then, are secondary in a way, since the duty is to enforce a general law made and provided in a particular case. Enforcement of the law may then be conceived of as itself obedience to the command of the law. But the command of the law is not often absolute; it is in the usual case conditional, so that the officer has an independent position in his discretion.

Such is the distinction between executive powers and administrative duties which is proposed as the basis for discussion. And yet, after all, it may prove that the distinction between these two does not go to the bottom; at bottom they may be alike in essentials. In pursuance of administrative functions, the department may well require the position of an executive. More than this, in seeing the laws faithfully executed the head of the department may prove in truth an executive. At all events the administration in the exercise of executive and administrative powers together presents a certain unity to the observer, as if the business of the administration were all one, after all, however difficult it may be to explain this.

§ 27. Political powers.

One of the highest powers of the executive is seen in the determination of political questions. It may be well to give several instances of the exercise of such powers; since in no other line of cases is the position of the executive so well established. One of the earlier decisions upon this question is Foster v. Neilson, 2 Pet. 253 (1829). This case arose under the eighth article of the treaty between the United States and Spain in 1818, which provided for the determination of private rights. It was a suit brought to recover a tract of land to the east of the Mississippi, claiming upon a grant made by the Spanish government in 1804. The exception involved the defense that the grant was void; upon the ground that the territory in question at the time of the grant belonged to the United States, not to Spain. How should such an issue be determined?

The opinion in this case has weight in a constitutional discussion, as it is by Chief Justice MARSHALL. The question presented is, to whom did the country between the Iberville and Perdido rightfully belong when the title now asserted was acquired. The question has been repeatedly discussed by the government of the United States with that of Spain. In a controversy between two nations concerning national boundaries it is scarcely possible that the courts of either should refuse to abide by the measures adopted by its own government. The judiciary is not that department of the government to which the assertion of its interest against foreign powers is confided. Its duty is to decide upon individual rights according to those principles which the political departments of the nation have established. A question respecting the boundaries of nations is more a political than a legal question; and in its discussion the courts of other countries must respect the will of the political departments. Another decision would subvert those principles which govern the relations between the departments and mark the limits of each. The separation of powers, it is to be noted, is said to be at the bottom of this doctrine and the consequence is therefore established—the independence of the department.

An amplification of this doctrine is seen in such cases as Williams v. Suffolk Insurance Company, 13 Pet. 415 (1839). The schooner Harriet, insured for a sealing voyage, was ordered by the government at Buenos Ayres not to catch seal off the Falkland Islands. The master refused to abandon the enterprise in response to these threats upon the ground that the islands were not subject to the jurisdiction of that government. The result was that the vessels were captured and condemned by the Buenos Ayres authorities. When suit was later brought upon the policies, which covered any loss whatever, the underwriters tried to make out a defense based upon the circumstances detailed.

The court would not go into evidence to determine what state had sovereignty over the islands; it informed itself by inquiry what position the executive department had taken. Mr. Justice McLEAN upon this report stated the conclusion of the court; he said: The American government has insisted, through its regular executive authority, that the Falkland Islands do not constitute any part of the dominions within the sovereignty of the government of Buenos Ayres. There cannot be any doubt that when the executive branch of the government which is charged with our foreign relations shall in its correspondence with the foreign nations assume a fact in regard to the sovereignty of any island or country, it is conclusive on the judicial department. In this view it is not material to inquire, it is not the province of the court to determine, whether the executive be right or wrong; it is enough to know that in the exercise of his constitutional function he has decided the question. Having shown this under the responsibility which belongs to him, it is obligatory on the government; and we think in the present case, as the executive has viewed the jurisdiction, the fact must be taken and acted on by this court as thus asserted and maintained. The decision of the first point materially affects the second, which turns on the conduct of the master, who held that he was not appointed to decide but might lawfully stand on his right against all governments not having jurisdiction. The underwriters are therefore not discharged. This decision without doubt expresses the general law upon this whole question.[20]

[20] POLITICAL POWERS.—Nabob v. East India Co., 1 Ves. Jr. 375; Sullivan v. Earl Spencer, Ir. R. 6 C. L. 173; Foster v. Neilson, 2 Pet. 307; Luther v. Borden, 7 How. 39; Mississippi v. Johnson, 4 Wall. 500; Georgia v. Stanton, 6 Wall. 77; Jones v. United States, 137 U. S. 212; In Re Cooper, 143 U. S. 503; Quackenbush v. United

§ 28. Foreign.

The question of the recognition of the independence of states just decided must, it would seem, settle all questions as to the recognition of belligerency in states; since the greater must include the less. However, it may be well to cite one leading case in this matter of belligerency, since at times the problem has prominence. A case always mentioned at such times is United States v. Palmer, 3 Wheat. 610 (1818). This case was certified from the Circuit Court upon division of opinion as to the rights of belligerent cruisers of an unrecognized community; whether captures of the same constitute piracy. For, of course, unless the bare facts could be qualified by some doctrines of the law of war, the acts were acts of pirates.

In the course of the discussion of this case Chief Justice MARSHALL said: Questions which respect the rights of a part of a foreign empire which asserts and is contending for independence are generally rather political than legal in that character. They belong more properly to those who can declare what the law shall be, and who control the political designs of the nation. The proceedings in the court must depend upon

States, 177 U. S. 25; Taylor v. Beckham, 178 U. S. 578; Latham v. Clark, 25 Ark. 574; Haley v. Clark, 26 Ala. 439; In re Archy, 9 Cal. 147; Land Co. v. Routt, 17 Colo. 156; State v. Bulkeley, 61 Conn. 287; McWhorter v. Pensacola R. Co., 24 Fla. 417; Hilliard v. Connelly, 7 Ga. 179; People v. Supervisors, 100 Ill. 495; State v. Hyde, 121 Ind. 20; State v. Wagner, 61 Me. 178; Larcom v. Olin, 160 Mass. 102; Chamberlain v. Sibley, 4 Minn. 309; People v. Hurlbut, 24 Mich. 63; Morton v. Green, 2 Neb. 441; Thompson v. Canal Fund Com'rs, 2 Abb. Prac. 248; State v. Chase, 5 Oh. St. 528; Taylor v. Place, 4 R. I. 338; State v. McMillan, 52 S. C. 69; Druecker v. Salomon, 21 Wis. 621.

the course of the government, therefore the courts cannot condemn when the attitude of the government is declared. And so this is to be held no piracy. The courts of the Union must view any newly constituted government as it is viewed by the legislative and executive departments of the government of the United States. If the government remains neutral, the courts of the Union cannot consider as criminal those acts of hostility which the war authorizes.

Upon the same basis, the executive in all international negotiations must have entire independence. This is shown in the long litigation in regard to the La Abra award, in which again and again it was attempted to bring the action of the department under the review of the judiciary. The most important of the cases is United States v. Blaine, 139 U. S. 306 (1891). The act of June 18, 1878, subjected specifically the payment of the Weil and La Abra awards, under the Mexican Claims Commission, to the control of the President. One Boynton sought mandamus in the Supreme Court of the District of Columbia against Blaine, then Secretary of State, for a mandamus to compel him to pay the petitioner as assignee of the Weil claim. The Secretary set up the plea that the President had forbidden the payment; that he held it as agent of the President; that the matter fell exclusively within the powers and competency of the President; and that the Secretary as subordinate to him and subject to his direction and control, was in nowise subject to the jurisdiction and competency of the judicial department of the government of the United States. That as it would involve an interference by the said judicial department with a matter which was exclusively committed by the constitution to its co-ordinate, the executive, department, the court should therefore take no cognizance of the matter of the relator's petition.

Chief Justice FULLER disposed of the case in this wise: The writ of mandamus cannot issue in a case where its effect is to direct or control the head of an executive department in the discharge of an executive duty, involving the exercise of judgment or discretion. In view of these settled principles, could the relator be entitled to his writ? International arbitration must always proceed on the highest principles of national honor and integrity. Claims presented and evidence submitted to such an arbitration must necessarily bear the impress of entire good faith. No technical rules of pleading, as applied to judicial courts, ought ever to be allowed to stand in the way of national power to do what is right under all circumstances. Every citizen who asks the intervention of his own government against another must necessarily subject himself and his claim to these requirements of international comity. This is a consequence of the political trust with which every government is charged with respect to its own citizens. The act of Congress cannot undertake to set any new limits on the powers of the executive. From beginning to end it is in form, even, only a request from Congress to the executive. It is far from making the President for the time being a quasi tribunal. So long as the political branch of the government had not lost its control over the subject matters by final action, the claimant was not in position, as between himself and the government, to insist on the conclusiveness of the award as to him. On the contrary the control was expressly reserved and made the duty of the President. The writ of mandamus cannot issue in a case where its effect is to direct or control the head of an executive department in the discharge of an executive duty involving the exercise of judgment and discretion. The political department has no doubt of its power over the matter; and the intervention of the judicial department cannot now be invoked.

These diverse cases certainly are enough to establish that in governmental action the executive department can in no way be controlled. Certainly, these few cases are not enough to give any definite conception as to what the function of the executive in government is. However, it must be obvious by this time that the executive has a part in government that is its own. Under our constitutional system many of the highest matters of state are intrusted to the executive department. What these shall be in a broad way is a question for specification in the constitution. It cannot be said in how many ways the executive has governmental functions without reference to the constitution itself. But when an executive power is found the independence of it must be conceded.[21]

[21] FOREIGN.—Rose v. Himely, 4 Cranch 272; United States v. Arredondo, 6 Pet. 711; Williams v. Suffolk Insurance Co., 13 Pet. 420; Gelston v. Hoyt, 3 Wheaton 324; United States v. Palmer, 3 Wheaton 634; The Divina Pastora, 4 Wheaton 63; The Santissima Trinidad, 7 Wheaton 283; Kennett v. Chambers, 14 How. 50; Bayard v. White, 127 U. S. 246; Jones v. United States, 137 U. S. 212; Fong Yue Ting v. United States, 149 U. S. 712; Durand v. Hollins, 4 Blatchf. 454.

§ 29. Interior.

Adherence to this principle often leads to results which startle one. The case of In Re Cooper, 143 U. S. 472 (1892), illumines the discussion like a flash of lightning. This was an application to the Supreme Court by the owners of the Canadian schooner Sayward, for a writ of prohibition to the District Court for Alaska to restrain the enforcement of a sentence of forfeiture and condemnation against the vessel. At the time diplomatic correspondence was in progress between the United States and Great Britain as to the proper extent of the jurisdiction of the United States over the waters of Behring Sea. The Sayward had been seized by the United States revenue cutter Rush in latitude 44° 43′ north and longitude 167° 51′ west, fifty-nine miles from any land whatever. The schooner was engaged when captured in pelagic sealing, the indiscriminate shooting of fur seals at sea. The commanding officer of the Rush made the seizure in pursuance of express orders issuing from the Treasury Department at Washington, covering his action within these waters.

Mr. Chief Justice FULLER dealt with the problem in a large way: How did it happen that the officers received such orders? It must be admitted that they were given in assertion on the part of this government of territorial jurisdiction over Behring Sea to an extent exceeding fifty-nine miles from the shore of Alaska; that this territorial jurisdiction in the enforcement of the laws protecting seal fisheries was asserted by actual seizures during the seasons of 1886, 1887 and 1889 of a number of British vessels; that the government persistently maintains that such jurisdiction belongs to it;

and that negotiations are pending on the subject. It is conceded that in matters committed by the constitution and the laws of the United States either to Congress or the executive or to both, courts are clearly bound by the action of Congress or the executive or both, within the limits of the authority conferred. The executive power can alone speak so as to bind our courts in respect to the sovereignty of foreign territory, the changes in foreign governments, the existence of civil war in foreign countries, and the character of a foreign minister. The application calls upon the court to decide whether the government is right or wrong and to review the action of the political departments upon the question, contrary to the law upon that question.

In this connection a case that is worth careful discussion is Luther v. Borden, 7 How. 1 (1849), because of the relations between the nation and the states composing the Union that are involved. This litigation arose out of the Dorr Rebellion, so remembered, in Rhode Island in 1841. Rhode Island had kept on under her colonial charter, which provided no way of amendment. This led to a political revolt by a portion of the people, who held a convention, which submitted a constitution, and who thereupon held elections, declared their candidates elected. All this time the charter government held to its position. The consequence was that several encounters more or less violent took place. In the particular case, one of the constitutional side was arrested and his house searched; he thereupon sued an officer of the charter government. The defense was necessary acts performed by them as duly authorized acts of the state government during a state of military necessity.

The determination of such issues was indeed a delicate matter; and the caution with which Chief Justice TANEY proceeds is noticeable, in his desire that the judiciary may not seem to intrude into questions political in their nature: The question which the plaintiff raised has not been recognized as judicial in any of the state courts, but the courts uniformly held that the inquiry proposed to be made belonged to the political power and not to the judicial, though it rested with the political power to decide whether the charter government has been displaced or not, and when that decision was made the judicial department would be bound to take notice of it as the law of the state without the aid of oral evidence or the examination of witnesses. We do not see how the question could be judicially decided in a state court. Judicial power presupposes established government capable of enacting laws and enforcing their execution and of appointing judges to expound and administer them. Acceptance of the judicial office is recognition of the authority of the government from which it is derived. If it decides at all as a court, it necessarily affirms the existence and authority of the government under which it is exercising judicial powers. The constitution of the United States, as far as it has provided for an emergency of this kind, has treated the subject as political in nature and placed the power in the hands of that department. The judicial power is at that time bound to follow the decision of the political. It must be equally bound when the contest is over. The President recognizes the Governor under the charter as the executive power of the state. No court of the United States with knowledge of this decision could have been justified in recognizing the opposition party as the lawful Governor or not treated as wrongdoers or insurgents the officers of that present government. The court has been urged to express an opinion upon political rights and political questions. We decline doing so. This tribunal should be the last to overstep the boundaries that limit its jurisdiction. Whether a new government has been established or not is a question to be settled by the political power; and when that power has decided the courts are bound to take notice of the decision and to follow it.

In rough outline these cases cover the diplomatic field of political powers. The function of the executive department in determination of these matters is obviously of consequence; for these are high matters of state upon which great issues may depend. The recognition of the independence of an insurgent community may mean war for the state which presumes to recognize it. Even that lesser move, the recognition of belligerency, may be deemed an unfriendly act. The very statement of this situation shows that the questions involved are all political. The very description of political power shows that exercise of such functions must in any government be largely held by the executive department, as that branch of the government which must be so constituted to act with rapidity and to act with effect. It is for this that an executive department exists. Political power must in its nature be free from exterior influences so far as that may be permitted. There must be free activity for the conduct of the most consequential matters in a state, its political concerns.[22]

[22] INTERIOR.—Doe d. Clark v. Braden, 16 How. 657; United States v.

§ 30. Governmental powers.

It will be well to state for discussion a few definite examples of the sort of thing that governmental power is. The Emulous, 1 Gall. 563 (1813), will serve as a first case. This was a prize allegation, filed by the United States against five hundred and fifty tons of pine timber, part of the cargo of the ship Emulous, which was seized as property of the British enemy in the harbor of New Bedford. The seizure was objected to as not authorized by public authority; and if that were so, of course the action was void, since even in time of war private citizens cannot acquire to themselves a title to hostile property; if they depredate upon an enemy, they are at their peril.

STORY, J., stated his conclusion in this way: The question is, whether Congress have authorized the seizure of enemy's property afloat in our ports. The act of June 18th, 1812, is in very general terms, declaring war against Great Britain, and authorizing the President to employ the public forces to carry it into effect. Independent of such express authority, I think that, as the Executive of the nation, he must, as an incident to his office, have a right to employ all the usual and customary means acknowledged in war, to carry it into effect. It seems to follow that the Executive may authorize the capture of all enemy's property wherever

Lynde, 11 Wall. 643; In Re Baiz, 135 U. S. 403; Benson v. United States, 146 U. S. 331; Terlinden v. Ames, 184 U. S. 288; United States v. Blaine, 139 U. S. 306; Tennessee, etc., R. Co. v. Moore, 36 Ala. 371; Land Co. v. Routt, 17 Colo. 156; People v. Bissell, 19 Ill. 229; State v. Warmoth, 22 La. Ann. 1; Magruder v. Swann, 25 Md. 173; People v. Governor, 29 Mich. 320; State v. Chase, 5 Oh. St. 528; Mauran v. Smith, 8 R. I. 192.

by the law of nations it may be lawfully seized. It would be strange indeed, if the Executive could not authorize, or ratify a capture in our own ports, unless by granting a commission to a public or private ship. I am not bold enough to interpose a limitation, where Congress have not chosen to make one; and I hold, that by the act declaring war, the Executive may authorize all captures which, by the modern law of nations, are permitted and approved.

To repeat a fundamental conception, when the administration acts within its sphere its action is governmental action. It is not possible, therefore, for another co-ordinate department, as the judiciary, to enter upon any review of such action. One of the leading cases in the establishment of this as one of the principal rules of administrative law was Georgia v. Stanton, 6 Wall. 50 (1867). This was a bill in equity filed by one of the states to enjoin the Secretary of War, the General of the Army, and one Major General from carrying into execution the several provisions of the acts known as Reconstruction Acts of 2nd and 23rd March, 1867. Both of these acts had been passed despite the President's veto, upon the ground of their unconstitutionality. The ground was that such execution would annul and totally abolish the existing state government; and that, unless enjoined, the executive department would carry such acts into execution.

The bill was upon its filing vehemently opposed. The Supreme Court upon the argument dismissed the bill. A portion of the opinion of Mr. Justice CLIFFORD follows: It is urged that the matters involved and presented for adjudication are political and not judicial, and therefore not subject to judicial cognizance. This distinction results from the organization of the government in which are three great departments, executive, legislative and judicial; and from the assignment and limitation of the powers of each by the Constitution. The judicial power is vested in one Supreme Court and in such inferior courts as Congress may deign to establish. The political power of the government is in the other two departments. The distinction between judicial and political power is generally acknowledged in the jurisprudence both of England and this country. The propriety of such interposition by the courts may well be questioned. It savors too much of the exercise of political power to be within the province of the judicial department. We do not claim for this court the exercise of jurisdiction upon any matter properly falling under the denomination of political power that belongs to another branch of the government. The protection and enforcement of many rights secured by treaties most certainly do not belong to the judiciary. The prayers for relief call for the judgment of the court upon political questions and involve rights of political character. The substance of this opinion, it is clear, is that governmental matters should not be reviewed by the courts.[23]

[23] GOVERNMENTAL POWERS.—Musgrave v. Pulido, 5 App. Cas. 102; Mississippi v. Johnson, 4 Wall. 500; Georgia v. Stanton, 6 Wall. 77; Keim v. United States, 177 U. S. 292; Tennessee, etc., R. R. v. Moore, 36 Ala. 371; Hawkins v. Governor, 1 Ark. 570; Ex parte Shrader, 33 Cal. 279; Land Co. v. Routt, 17 Colo. 156; State v. Staub, 61 Conn. 568; McWhorter v. Pensacola R. R., 24 Fla. 417; People v. Secretary of State, 58 Ill. 90; Hovey v. State, 127 Ind. 588; Martin v. Ingham, 38 Kan. 641; State v. Fisher, 26 La. Ann. 537; Worthington v. Scribner, 109 Mass. 487; People v. Hurl-

§ 31. Domestic.

A further case in this doctrine is Martin v. Mott, 12 Wheat. 19 (1827). For in this case the very basis of executive functions is exposed. In March of 1814 the President called upon the militia of New York at a time of imminent danger of invasion. Mott refused to respond to the orders; he was at once tried and fined; later his goods were taken to satisfy the sentence; and now he seeks to recover in replevin. The justification of the officers who have taken the goods is public authority, and in particular, the orders issuing from the President. Mott claimed that the officer must show further justification in fact, as the event proved.

Mr. Justice STORY again delivered the opinion: By whom is the exigency to be judged of and decided? Is the President the sole and exclusive judge whether the exigency has arisen, or is it to be considered as an open question upon which every officer to whom the orders of the President are addressed may decide for himself, and equally open to be contested by every militia man who shall refuse to obey the orders of the President? We are all of opinion that the authority to decide whether the exigency has arisen belongs exclusively to the President, and that his decision is conclusive upon all other persons. The power itself is to be exercised upon sudden emergencies, upon great questions of state and under circumstances which may be vital to the existence of the Union. These powers must be so construed as to the modes of their exercise as not

but, 24 Mich. 63; Vicksburg R. R. v. Lowry, 61 Miss. 102; People v. Parker, 3 Neb. 409; Mauran v. Smith, 8 R. I. 192; Commonwealth v. Henry, 49 Pa. St. 530; Slack v. Jacob, 8 W. Va. 612.

to defeat the great end in view. It is not necessary in such a case that the particular exigency actually existed. It is sufficient that the President has actually determined it; and all other persons are bound by his decision.

A further illustration of the position of the executive in his executive powers is seen in Hartranft's Appeal, 85 Pa. St. 433 (1877). These proceedings followed upon the labor disturbances of 1877 in Pennsylvania. Portions of the National Guard of the state were sent by the Governor under the charge of their officers to protect the railroads in moving their trains. A collision took place between the soldiers and the strikers and during the progress of the riot a number on both sides were killed or wounded. The grand jury later took the matter up and in the course of the investigation subpoenas were issued to the Governor and to the high militia officers, all of whom refused to attend. The present motion was for the award of compulsory process to compel them to testify. The Attorney-General filed a paper setting forth that all the persons mentioned had acted throughout in their official character.

Whether that stopped such an inquiry as this is the question; Mr. Justice Gordon ruled that it did: In order to simplify matters we may treat this case just as though the process first and last were against the Governor alone; for if he is exempt from attachment because of this privilege, his immunity in such a matter protects his subordinates and agents. The general principle is that when the law vests any person with the power to do an act, at the same time constituting a judge of when the act may be done, and contemplating the employment of agents through whom the act is to be accomplished, such person is clothed with discretionary powers and quoad hoc is his judge. It follows that if the Governor as supreme executive and as Commander-in-Chief of the army of the Commonwealth is charged with the duty of suppressing domestic insurrections, he must be the judge of the necessity requiring the exercise of the powers with which he is clothed, and his subordinates who are employed to render these powers efficient and to produce the legitimate results of their exercise, can be accountable to none but him. We had better at the outset recognize the fact that the executive department is a co-ordinate branch of the government, with power to judge what should or should not be done within its own department, and what of its doings or communications should or should not be kept secret; and that with it in the exercise of these constitutional powers, the courts have no more right to interfere than has the executive, under like conditions, to interfere with the courts. This is an extreme opinion, it may be admitted; but upon the whole it does not overstate the case much.

The scope of this opinion is to be remarked. This is one of the cases rare by comparison where the place of executive power is exposed. It is not enough to say that in the exercise of executive powers the chief of the department has discretion within limits and that there can be no control of the exercise of that discretion. It is more than that; it is not too much to say that in the exercise of executive powers the head of the state has independence; and that therefore concerning the exercise of that power there can be no inquiry.

Whether the occasion was proper for the action cannot be judged by the judiciary; for the determination of the occasion was entirely without the scope of the judiciary, since it was within the sphere of a co-ordinate department. This irresponsibility is characteristic of executive power.[24]

§ 32. Colonial.

At the time of the present writing the American people have the highest interest in one special phase of government by the executive—colonial administration. A case much relied upon in current discussion is Cross v. Harrison, 16 How. 164 (1853). In 1846 in the war with Mexico the United States troops took military possession of all of Upper California, including the port of San Francisco. Early in 1847 the President, in his capacity of Commander-in-Chief of the army and navy, authorized the military and naval commanders of the United States forces in California, in the exercise of the belligerent rights of a conqueror, to form a civil and military government for the conquered territory, with powers therein to impose duties on imports and tonnage. A war tariff was accordingly promulgated and the duties under it were levied, until official notice was received by the Military Governor that a treaty of peace had been made with Mexico by which Upper California was ceded to the United States. Thereupon the Governor directed that the duties levied should be such

[24] DOMESTIC.—Faith v. Pearson, 6 Taunt. 439; Grisar v. McDowell, 6 Wall. 371; United States v. Blaine, 139 U. S. 306; The Orono, 1 Gall. 137; Benton v. Taylor, 46 Ala. 388; State v. Gleason, 12 Fla. 190; Parker v. State, 135 Ind. 534; State v. Cahen, 28 La. Ann. 645; Tyler v. Pomeroy, 8 Allen 480; Guthrie v. Hall, 1 Okl. 454; Commonwealth v. Henry, 49 Pa. St. 530; Slack v. Jacob, 8 W. Va. 612.

as were paid at other ports of entry according to the existing statutes.

The issue in the case was therefore as to the validity of these collections. The opinion was elaborate—one of the best of Mr. Justice WAYNE: Until California had been ceded in fact to the United States it was a conquered territory, within which the United States were exercising belligerent rights; and whatever sums were received for duties upon foreign merchandises, were paid under them thus. But after the ratification of the treaty California became a part of the United States, or a ceded, conquered territory. Our inquiry here is to be whether after the cession the duties could be collected. The existing government was continued by the definite instructions received from Washington in reference to the existing state of things in California. It was the government when the territory was ceded as a conquest; and it did not cease as a necessary consequence of the restoration of peace. Colonel Mason was fortunate in having his determination to continue the existing government sustained by the President of the United States and the Secretaries of his cabinet. It was said that the duties were illegally exacted because the laws of a ceded territory remain unchanged until the new sovereignty has changed them, and that this Congress had not done. But the acts of the executive are acts of the sovereign.

The questions in this last case in 1857 came up for discussion again in 1901, under circumstances almost exactly similar. This was an action begun by the firm of Dooley, Smith & Co., engaged in trade between Porto Rico and New York to recover certain duties exacted and paid under protest at the Port of San Juan, upon several consignments of merchandise imported into Porto Rico from New York between July 28th, 1898, and May 1st, 1900, under the following schedules: from July 26, 1898, to August 19, 1898, under the proclamation of General Miles, directing the exaction of the former Spanish and Porto Rican duties; from August 19, 1898, to May 1, 1900, under the customs tariffs for Porto Rico, proclaimed by order of the President. It further appeared that part of the duties were collected thus before the exchange of the ratifications of the treaty of cession on April 11, 1899, and in part afterwards. Thus by the facts the question in this case was as to the validity of these collections—Dooley v. United States, 182 U. S. 222 (1901).

Mr. Justice Brown delivered the opinion, which, because of the contrariety of view in the court, can hardly be called more than his own: There can be no doubt with respect to the exaction of duties under the war power, prior to the ratification of the treaty of peace. Upon the occupation of the country by the military forces of the United States, the authority of the Spanish government was superseded, but the necessity for a revenue did not cease. The government must be carried on, and there was no one left to administer its functions but the military forces of the United States. The most natural method was by the continuation of existing duties. In adopting this method General Miles was fully justified by the laws of war. Different considerations apply with respect to duties levied after the ratification of the treaty and the cession to the United States. We have no doubt, however, from the necessities of the case, the right to administer the government of Porto Rico, continued after the ratification of the treaty and until further action by Congress. At the same time, while the right to administer the government continued, the conclusion of the treaty of peace and the cession of the island to the United States were not without their significance. The spirit as well as the letter of tariff laws admit of duties being levied by a military commander only upon the importations from foreign countries, and while his power is necessarily despotic, this must be understood rather in an administrative than in a legislative sense. In our opinion the authority of the President as Commander-in-Chief to exact duties upon imports from the United States, ceased from the ratification of the treaty of peace.

These decisions represent about all the law that we have in our decisions upon this pressing problem of colonial administration; and these decisions were decided with reference to a transition from military occupation to civil government. Within the next few years we are certain to have many questions determined which are at present unsettled. The greatest constitutional problem of all in this matter is not decided beyond question by the Supreme Court of the United States. That is whether the guarantees of civil rights contained in the constitution apply in the government of colonies. A fair argument may be based upon various decisions as to the territories to the effect that these limitations in the constitution apply only to government by the United States within the United States themselves. But whether this is so cannot be known until this question is adjudicated once for all by some new decision of the Supreme Court of the United States. And until such a decision it cannot be certain that government of the colonies by the administration can be carried out. For example, if in every civil dispute there must be jury trial, government of these foreign peoples will be hampered; and if in every criminal proceeding there must be grand jury and petit jury, no effective police of these regions will be possible.

However, there should be no hasty action on the part of Congress in determining the form of our colonial government. If Congress has full power in the matter, the more cautious should be its exercise. And especially during this, which is called by the Hawaiian Court the transition stage, the firm government of the executive free from much interference by Congress is needed. It is only after some years of experience and after much discussion that we should determine our colonial policy and frame our colonial governments.

The political experience upon the subject has developed various types of colonial administration. If the wrong system is applied to the wrong situation, disaster follows. Note first that a colony may have a comparatively large number of inhabitants of the same race; or the colony may have inhabitants of an alien and inferior race. Again note that there are three principal forms of colonial administration: an almost complete independence, both legislative and administrative authorities being chosen locally; an almost complete dependence, both legislative and administrative authorities being appointed by the home state; a compromise between these two, the legislature being elected locally, the administrative authorities being appointed by the home state.

Let us see for a moment what has been the experience with these forms of colonial administration. Where the inhabitants are of the same race, a large measure of independence is given. Where the inhabitants are of an alien and inferior race, all powers are reserved to the governors and their councils appointed directly or indirectly by the home state. In some fewer instances there has been experiment with the combined type; but seldom with success, except in small units. Here have been the most conspicuous failures upon the whole.

If, then, so much depends upon applying the right type of colonial administration to the proper situation, let us face our new colonial problem at the outset squarely. For there is no such thing practical in colonial government as any one system of colonial administration. Each of our colonial problems must be met separately; and for each we must find our own solution. There are three such colonial problems: the Hawaiian Islands, the Philippine Islands, and Porto Rico.

The problem of the government of the Hawaiian Islands is a problem no longer. It is solved; and probably solved finally because it seems to be solved rightly. In Hawaii we have a compact American class large enough and strong enough in the end to dictate and maintain American government of the islands. This they had done before they came to us. They came to us a self-governing nation, and they were rightly incorporated into our American Empire as a self-governing unit—as of the first type of colonial government mentioned, rather than the third. Indeed, all that was done was to apply to the Hawaiian Islands the long established and well developed type of government which we had for a hundred years used in governing our territories. And in that type, although the administrative head, the Governor, is appointed from Washington, yet as a matter of fact, when applied to an American self-governing population, the control of Washington is very seldom felt, and so Hawaii cannot longer be cited as a colonial problem. Indeed, it is a proof of the capacity of the American in colonial administration.

In the Philippine Islands a proper beginning is being made. We are applying the proper type of colonial administration, the second type of direct administrative government from Washington, to the proper situation, alien and inferior inhabitants. The present civil government, executive for the most part, is well conceived. The instructions that come from Washington are among the ablest of American state papers. It would simply be an example of weak political sentimentality to give the Filipinos independence with nominal suzerainty of the United States. That a Filipino legislature should be set up against the American governor and his administration is not to be thought of, either. In governing the Philippines thus by administrative government, we are wise; we follow the ascertained result of political experience in governing tropical colonies peopled by an alien and inferior race.

But for Porto Rico the problem is different. We have an alien, but not inferior race to deal with. The plan begun, indeed, in the late legislation of Congress, is that of an appointed governor and an elected legislature. That is dangerous; it does not begin auspiciously. Already in the elections a strong anti-American party is appearing. It is to be feared that they will be led in the legislature by leaders who must make their political capital from criticisms of an administration which they themselves can never direct. These consequences will follow unless the fundamental principle is remembered: that the way to govern colonies—is to govern them.

Indeed, there is for alien colonies, as it seems, but one proper form of colonial government—complete administrative government: a governor with a properly organized administration, advised by proper administrative councils with legislative powers; all appointed directly or indirectly from Washington. For if the history of colonial administration teaches anything, it teaches the inherent dangers of the combined form of colonial administration. Doubtless it will be found expedient that the native inhabitants should be given all places in this administration and in these administrative councils possible. To that extent they should have a part in their own government. Such a form of government is secure. But this idea of pitting an alien legislature against an American administration is dividing the house against itself.[25]

§ 33. Conclusion.

Thus far in this discussion the executive department has been found in operation within the scope of its functions; many of the cases may have seemed extreme, but upon the whole nothing was found done that was

25 COLONIAL.—Loughborough v. Blake, 5 Wheat. 317; American Ins. Co. v. Canter, 1 Pet. 511; Benner v. Porter, 9 How. 235; Scott v. Sandford, 19 How. 393; Cross v. Harrison, 16 How. 164; Reynolds v. United States, 98 U. S. 145; Thompson v. Utah, 170 U. S. 343; De Lima v. Bidwell, 182 U. S. 1; Armstrong v. United States, 182 U. S. 243; Dooley v. United States, 183 U. S. 151; Fourteen Diamond Rings, 183 U. S. 176.

not within the power of the department. But it must have been obvious that many of these cases were close to a line; and that some limitation beyond which the executive department could not go must soon be laid down. Else the private rights would be at the disposal of the executive; and the head of the department would be in effect dictator; while under our constitutional government, of course, every power of government by whatever department exercised must be subject to various limitations. No person must be seized, none of his property may be taken, none of his rights may be abridged—without due process of law. This applies to the administration in the performance of executive functions. The President in his action as chief executive is not like the Czar in his action as chief executive; in every phase of our government the distinction between a constitutional system and an autocratic system must be observed.

An instance in point is seen in an opinion of the Attorney-General entitled The Diamonds of the Princess of Orange, 2 Opin. 452 (1831). It was represented to the executive department by the diplomatic representative of the Kingdom of Holland that a criminal had just entered the United States, a fugitive from Holland with diamonds in his possession stolen from the Princess of Orange. The request was that the diamonds be seized and returned and the man arrested and surrendered.

The opinion of TANEY reads as follows: I have the honor to state: 1st. That in my opinion, the President of the United States has not the power to order the delivery of the diamonds and precious stones referred to in the note of the Chevalier Huygens. The courts of justice alone have the power to decide upon the ownership of the property; and the court, upon proper proceedings, will award the possession to the party who may appear to be entitled. 2d. As there is no stipulation by treaty between the two governments for the mutual delivery of fugitives from justice, I think the President would not be justified in directing the surrender of the person upon whom a part of the stolen articles may have been found, in order that he may be brought to trial in the country where he is supposed to have committed the robbery.

This opinion at bottom involves the proposition that there is no international common law on the subject of extradition; therefore this consequence: that if the President should seize to surrender he would act without law. Exactly; this is now the view of the Supreme Court. In many governments the executive would have some power to act under, in answer to such requests of foreign governments, if it seemed fit, not in ours with the constitution in the way.

A most usual executive function is the power of pardon. As would be expected, the cases that involve the power of pardon grant to the executive entire independence in the exercise of that power. It is never possible to inquire into the reasons upon which the pardon was granted; since the grant of the pardon was wholly within the powers of the executive. This does not quite dispose of the whole question. The subject of pardons is divisible by two intersecting lines of cleavage; one divides fines or forfeitures due to an individual from those due to a government; the other divides con tempt proceedings from other proceedings. Thus there are four possible cases: Criminal convictions with a fine payable to the United States; criminal convictions with a fine payable to an individual; contempt commitments to vindicate the dignity of a court; and contempt proceedings in behalf of an individual. Under the constitutions the chief executive has usually the power to grant pardons and reprieves; and the lesser power to remit fines and forfeiture, if not expressed, will be implied.

This general analysis suggests the inquiry whether the power of pardon can be exercised in all cases consistently with our constitutional separation of powers. In (3) and (4) above, for instance, would not the executive by the pardon of a contempt interfere with the functions of the judiciary? This query was raised in a recent case, In Re Nevitt, 117 Fed. 448 (1902). Two county judges were ordered by mandamus from a circuit court to levy a tax for the payment of a judgment recovered against the county. The judges refused and were imprisoned for contempt. Thereupon, they filed a petition for habeas corpus; in the course of this proceeding they asked for a stay of proceedings in order to allow a petition to the President for a pardon. This application SANBORN, the Circuit Judge, refused; holding that the commitment was not in execution of the criminal laws of the nation, but was to secure a suitor in his rights in the course of a judicial proceeding. On that point he said in part: That in such a pardon the executive would go beyond his constitutional powers into matters confided in another department. In other words, has the executive the power, if he chooses to exercise it, of drawing to himself all the real judicial power of the nation which the constitution vested by express terms in the courts by means of his supreme control of the inherent and essential attribute of that power,—the authority to punish for disobedience to the orders of the courts? These questions seem to suggest their answers. The judicial power is granted to the courts in its entirety by means of the constitution, including the inherent and indispensable attribute of that power, the authority to punish for disobedience of their orders to the Federal Courts, free from the control or supervision of the executive department of the government, to the same extent that the entire executive power of the nation is vested in the President free from the supervision or control of the courts. This is a special case; but it seems sound—another example of the constitutional limitation upon the executive.

CHAPTER V.

THE DUTIES OF THE ADMINISTRATION.

§ 34. Introduction.

The execution of law involves a particular case. The law is a general rule; the administration of it is the application to a particular case of that general rule. That raises the next question: to what particular cases shall this law be applied? That sometimes is a matter requiring much judgment on the part of the administration; at other times it is a matter requiring little determination by the administration, which depends altogether upon the law and the fact. If the law is general the application requires much discretion; if the law is particular the application requires no discretion. Grant that the administration must obey the law; in the first case the command is conditional, it is within the discretion of the administration to determine whether the conditions exist; in the second case, since the command is absolute, the administration must obey without assertion. These distinctions are put forward at this stage as a working hypothesis.

The leading case in any discussion of this hypothesis must always be Marbury v. Madison, 1 Cranch, 137 (1803). This was a motion for mandamus against Madison, the Secretary of State, to compel him to deliver to Marbury his commission as Justice of the Peace for the District of Columbia. The commission had been made out by direction of Adams, the President outgoing; it had then been executed and sealed by the Secretary of State outgoing, but had not been delivered to the appointee. Under these circumstances the new Secretary upon his accession to office had withheld the commission, acting, it is believed, under the instructions of Jefferson, the President incoming. Thus the issue was raised for the first time in the national government whether the judiciary should give directions to the executive in matters pertaining to that department.

MARSHALL, the new Chief Justice, accepted the issue with the greatest pleasure. This opinion is elaborate: In the order in which the court has viewed this subject the following questions have been considered and decided: (1) Has the applicant a right to the commission he demands? (2) If he has the right, and that right has been violated, do the courts afford him a remedy? (3) If they do afford him a remedy, is it a mandamus issuing from this court?

(1) The President is to nominate, appoint and commission all officers of the United States. Appointment being the sole action of the President, it must be completely evidenced by every act to be performed by him, and this act has to be done by the President. His signature is the last act. Some point of time must be taken when the power of the executive over an officer

not removable at will must cease. That point of time must be when the constitutional power of appointment has been fully exercised and the last act performed.

(2) It is a settled and invariable principle of the laws that every right when withheld must have a remedy. The government of the United States has been emphatically termed a government of laws, not of men. Some acts are examinable and others not; there must, therefore, be some rule of law to guide the court in the exercise of its jurisdiction. By the constitution of the United States the President is vested with certain important political powers in the exercise of which he is to use his own discretion and is accountable only to his country in his political character and to his own conscience to aid him in the performance of these duties. He is authorized to appoint certain officers to act by his authority, and in conformity with his orders. In such cases their acts are his acts, and whatever opinion may be entertained of the manner in which executive discretion may be used, still there exists and can exist no power to control that discretion. The subjects are political. They respect the nation, not the individual rights, and being entrusted to the executive the decision of the executive is conclusive. The heads of departments are to conform precisely to the will of the President. He is the mere organ by whom that will is indicated. The acts of such an officer, as an officer, can never be examinable by the courts. When the legislature proceeds to impose upon that officer other duties, when he is directed peremptorily to perform certain acts, when the rights of individuals are dependent on the performance of these acts, he is, so far, the officer of the law, amenable

to the laws for his conduct. The conclusion is that whether heads of departments are the political or confidential agents of the executive merely to execute the will of the President, or whether they act in cases in which the executive possesses a constitutional or legal discretion, nothing can be more perfectly clear than that their acts are only politically examinable. Where a specific duty is assigned by law and individual rights depend upon the performance of that duty, it seems equally clear that the individual has a remedy in the laws. It is, then, the opinion of the court that it is the ministerial duty of Madison to deliver the commission to Marbury.

(3) It remains further to be inquired whether he is entitled to the remedy applied, for this depends on (a) the nature of the writ; (b) the power of the court. The writ of mandamus is to do a particular thing therein specified which appertains to the office of duty. The intimate political relation subsisting between President and heads of departments necessarily renders any legal investigation of the acts peculiarly irksome as well as delicate and excites some hesitation. The court cannot intrude into the cabinet or meddle with the prerogative of the executive. The province of the court is solely to decide upon the rights of individuals, not to inquire how the executive or executive officers performed duties in which they have a discretion. Questions in their nature political, or which are by the constitution and laws submitted to the executive, can never be made in this court; but this is not such a question. The office does not exempt the man from being sued for a political act where he is directed by law to do a certain act affecting the absolute rights of individuals. The performance

through the President cannot be lawfully forbidden, and, therefore, is never presumed to have been forbidden. In such cases of the legal doctrine mandamus may issue. But in this case no jurisdiction can be given this court. The authority given to the Supreme Court to issue writs of mandamus to officers, however, was not warranted by the constitution, and the rule must therefore be discharged.

No decision in the law of public officers is cited oftener than this. It is useless at this time to point out that all that is said as to the obligations of public officers is dicta; at the present day every rule stated in this opinion represents the law, as case upon case can be brought to demonstrate. It is too late to raise the question whether a decent regard for the independence of the executive ought not to exempt the high officers of state from the writ of mandamus; it is law everywhere in the United States that in certain of their functions they stand no better than the meanest public officer. That point certainly would bear an argument that in the case of the functions of high officers of state, no power can be conceived of without some discretion. But it is useless to argue along that line; for everywhere and for all public officers and in every state of things the principal case is accepted as the law.

The gist of the case is in the distinction taken between discretionary duties and ministerial duties. When an officer is ordered by law to do certain things, but the law is general in its phraseology, so that the application of it involves inquiry and decision, then it is said that the duty is a discretionary one. Since in such an instance the officer has the duty to decide, it is said with a correct conception of the issue he has the right to decide. And because this is so, it is said with a true appreciation of the situation this determination has been intrusted to the officer as in a co-ordinate department of the government—the executive—and therefore at this point there is no power in the co-ordinate department—the judiciary—to direct by any processes the way in which the officer shall decide. Such, it must be admitted, is the general rule for discretionary duties.

But as to ministerial duties it is said a difference exists. When an officer is ordered by law to do certain things, and the application of that law requires in the particular case under inquiry that a certain thing be done which is in some explicit way indicated, then it is said that the duty is a ministerial one. Since in such circumstances the officer has nothing to decide, it is said that he has no function but to act. If he fails to act, in his refusal he goes contrary to the law that commands him. Therefore, in our common law system he is a recreant person. When an officer refuses to do that which the law commands, it is just the office of the extraordinary writ of mandamus to force performance. This is the outline of the distinction taken between discretionary duties and ministerial duties. It remains to follow this rule out into its details.

§ 35. Discretionary duties.

The first branch of the rule under discussion was that the judicial courts would not interfere by their process to direct or control the action of any officer of the administration in any matter where that officer had discretion. Unless that proposition is established, the administration can have no true independence in the enforcement of the law, since it will be without any real freedom of action. There is no decision in the Supreme Court which is square upon the point until Decatur v. Paulding, 14 Peters, 497 (1840). On the 3rd of March, 1837, Congress passed on the same day a general naval pension law, within the benefit of which Mrs. Decatur would be, and a special pension law for her special benefit. The then Secretary of the Navy, Paulding, with whom the power to grant pensions was left, refused to pay her both pensions. Thereupon she applied to the proper court for a mandamus to order issuance of both pensions.

The opinion of Mr. Chief Justice TANEY against Mrs. Decatur was to this effect: In general the official duties of the heads of one of the executive departments imposed by act of Congress are not mere ministerial duties; the head of an executive department of the government in the administration of the various and important concerns of his office, is continually required to exercise judgment and discretion. He must exercise his judgment in expounding the laws and resolutions of Congress under which he is from time to time required to act. The court could not entertain an appeal from the decision of one of the Secretaries nor revise his judgment in any case where the law authorized him to exercise discretion and judgment. There is this distinction always between executive and ministerial acts. These resolutions of Congress required the exercise of judgment and investigation. We are satisfied that the performance of the ordinary duties of the executive department was never intended to be done by the courts. Questions which are given to the executive for construction and execution can seldom be litigated in this court.

An important case in this series of applications for mandamus against the heads of departments of the Federal administration is Carrick v. Lamar, 116 U. S. 423 (1886). This was an application for mandamus to the Secretary of Interior to cause a survey to be made of an island known as Arsenal Island in the Mississippi opposite St. Louis. The relator was one Carrick, who had made a settlement upon said island and wished the land surveyed and brought into the market. The Commissioner of the General Land Office rejected the application, but transmitted the papers to the Secretary of the Interior for his examination and instructions. The immediate predecessor of the present Secretary concurred with the Commissioner. The present Secretary declined to review the decision.

Mr. Justice FIELD delivered the opinion of the court: It is settled by many decisions of this court that in matters which require judgment and consideration to be exercised by an executive officer of the government, or which are dependent upon his discretion, no rule for a mandamus to control his actions will issue. It is only for ministerial acts in the performance of which no exercise of judgment or discretion is required that the rule will be granted. In the absence of any positive enactment the Secretary may therefore properly withhold any action tending to encourage a settlement there. This consideration alone is a sufficient answer to any rule for a mandamus.

Upon the distinction of a discretionary duty from a ministerial duty everything turns. Another case that confirms this is Burton v. Furman, 115 N. C. 166 (1894). The plaintiff was a claimant against a certain fund held by the state. His present action was to ascertain and declare the amount due and to procure a mandamus to the Auditor of the State compelling him to issue the warrant, and to the Treasurer of the State to compel him to pay the same. It was proved that under the existing state of the law it was the duty of the State Auditor to examine and to liquidate the claims of all persons against the state, and the duty of the Treasurer to pass and pay all claims against the state.

Upon the basis of the independence of these officers in the execution of their powers, the opinion of Mr. Justice MACRAE was founded: The purpose of this writ of mandamus is to require some officer to do some particular thing which pertains to his office or duty. This writ will not be granted to compel the performance of an act involving the exercise of judgment and discretion on the part of the officer to whom its performance is committed. Mandamus will lie only when the act required to be done is imposed by law, is merely ministerial. But it does not lie where judgment and discretion are to be exercised; nor to control the officer in the manner of conducting the general duties of his office. In the present case, therefore, no mandamus will be granted to compel the performance of action involving the exercise of judgment and discretion.[26]

[26] DISCRETIONARY DUTIES.—Gidley v. Palmerston, 3 Brod. & B. 275; Reg. v. Secretary [1891] 2 Q. B. 326; Marbury v. Madison, 1 Cranch, 169; United States v. Guthrie, 17 How. 284; United States v. Seaman, 17 How. 225; Commissioner v. Whiteley, 4 Wall. 522; Gaines v. Thompson, 7 Wall. 347; Decatur v. Paulding, 14 Pet. 497; Brashear v. Mason, 6 How. 92; Reeside v. Walker, 11 How. 272; Noble v. Logging R. R., 147 U. S. 165; United States v. Lamont, 155 U. S. 308; Ex parte Echols, 39 Ala. 698; Hawkins v. Governor, 1 Ark. 570; People v. Bell, 4 Cal. 177; State v. Staub, 61 Conn. 553; United

§ 36. General.

The rule in all of these cases is the same; that rule is, that in all matters that involve the exercise of discretion by a public officer, no processes of the court will go to control the exercise of that discretion. This must always be the case when the duty in question is one in the performance of which the officer must make an investigation and form a judgment. In such a case the power is a power in the executive department; the judicial department will not, therefore, be competent to review the evidence before the officer and revise his judgment. That would involve the subordination of a co-ordinate department, as has been set forth in a previous chapter; what may be done and what may not be done along those lines was there explained to some extent. This rule which invests the administration with independence in its action within the scope of discretion given to it is then a fundamental rule based upon elemental principles.

As much independence as this must be granted the

States v. Douglass, 19 D. C. 99; State v. Drew, 17 Fla. 67; State v. Thrasher, 77 Ga. 671; State v. Snodgrass, 98 Ind. 546; People v. Cullom, 100 Ill. 472; Hildreth v. Crawford, 65 Ia. 339; Dickens v. Cemetery Co., 93 Ky. 385; State v. Robinson, 1 Kan. 188; State v. Warmoth, 22 La. Ann. 1; Davis v. County Com'rs, 63 Me. 396; Miles v. Bradford, 22 Md. 170; Deehan v. Johnson, 141 Mass. 23; People v. Governor, 29 Mich. 320; State v. Somerset, 44 Minn. 549; Swan v. Gray, 44 Miss. 393; State v. McGrath, 91 Mo. 386; State v. Babcock, 18 Neb. 221; Sunapee School District v. Perkins, 49 N. H. 538; State v. Perrine, 5 Vroom. 254; People v. Chapin, 104 N. Y. 96; Raleigh, etc., R. R. v. Jenkins, 68 N. C. 499; State v. Moore, 42 Oh. St. 103; Carr v. Northern Liberties, 35 Pa. St. 324; Mauran v. Smith, 8 R. I. 192; Turnpike Co. v. Brown, 8 Baxt. 490; Chalk v. Darden, 47 Tex. 438; Richards v. Wheeler, 2 Aik. 369; McCullough v. Hunter, 90 Va. 699; State v. Harvey, 11 Wis. 33.

administration: that whenever a matter is left to the determination of a public officer his decision shall be final. The opinion in United States v. Windom, 137 U. S. 636 (1891), is a discriminating one. The petition was for a writ of mandamus against Windom, Secretary of the Treasury, by Redfield, the assignee of one Mitchell. Mitchell had furnished material and performed labor for the United States under a contract; when the work was done he presented his account to the proper officer for adjustment and settlement; the balance was found correct; but it was also found that through penalties and forfeitures that balance was liable to be reduced. The Treasury officers agreed with Mitchell that this account should be adjusted waiving the penalties and forfeitures, if he would consent that such indebtedness to sub-contractors should be paid out of the sum so allowed; he at first assented and a draft was prepared; then he refused to comply with these conditions.

Mr. Justice LAMAR said: The main assignment of error is that the court erred in not deciding that the duty of the Secretary to deliver the draft was purely a ministerial duty. The principles upon which persons holding public office may be compelled by writ of mandamus to perform duties imposed by the law have been distinctly defined and strictly adhered to in a great number and variety of cases before this court. That principle is that the writ of mandamus may issue where the duty which the court is asked to enforce is plainly ministerial, and when the right of the party applying for it is clear, and he is without any other adequate remedy; and it cannot issue in a case where its effect is to direct or control the head of an executive department in the discharge of an executive duty involving the exercise of judgment and discretion. In the extreme caution with which this remedy is applied by the courts, there are cases when the writ will not be issued to compel even the performance of a purely ministerial act. We repeat that upon the prima facie showing of the relator the case is clearly one of ministerial duty, but the facts, circumstances and conditions set forth in the report of the Secretary of the Treasury places the matter in another and quite a different light. It comes to this, that an officer who had discretion at the beginning, had discretion to the end.

This same principle, that whenever there is discretion vested in an officer the courts are incompetent to review his judgment, is laid down again and again in an unusual variety of cases, involving every grade of officer and every sort of administration. One illustration from the mass of these authorities may be added: People v. Adam, 3 Mich. 427 (1854). The facts in that case were these: The relator was the holder of a certificate of sale of lands sold at tax sale for delinquent taxes of the year 1844. On July 4th, 1848, he presented said certificate at the office of the Auditor-General, and demanded a deed of the premises described in the certificate, which was refused; and thereupon he made application to compel the conveyance of the premises to him by the Auditor-General, upon surrender of his certificate.

The opinion in that case was this: By the Court (MARTIN, J.): The act of 1843, under which the premises in question were sold, and the right of the relator accrued, authorizes the Auditor-General, if he shall discover before sale or conveyance of any lands, that on account of irregular assessments or for any other cause any of said lands ought not to be sold or conveyed, to forbear to sell, or to withhold a conveyance after sale, as the case may be. This act confers upon him judicial powers, and into the proper exercise of such powers we cannot inquire on proceedings of this nature. A mandamus will only be granted to compel the performance of a ministerial act, not dependent upon the exercise of judicial discretion, in the absence of an effectual legal remedy. Whether the deed in this case was properly withheld, therefore, is not a subject of inquiry. This court is clear: it will not intrude its processes into the jurisdiction of another department.

Upon the whole the most of administration is with discretionary powers; and that is a desirable condition of things in government. The legislature will do well to pass its laws in general form and leave the executive to work out the detail of its enforcement. The methods and forms of administration are better decided upon by the department which is charged with the enforcement of the law. As a matter of convenience, this should be the solution; since the executive department will be well versed in the difficulties that attend administration and well equipped with the means best adapted to carry a law into effect. The principle of the advantage of specialization in the conduct of any undertaking is employed in the matter of government with peculiar success. It is clear that the first separation between the legislature and the executive is upon just that basis; and if that is so, it is clear that the division should be observed so far as that is possible. Accordingly, it seems that it will always be a proper policy for the legislature to act upon to pass a general statute upon any subject matter and to leave the determination of the application of that statute to the executive. That is, again, that in the most of administration there should be discretion.[27]

§ 37. Directory.

This is true, that if a statute commands, the officer must obey; but it is well in the statement of such a rule to define its terms, since not all provisions of law are of the nature of command. French v. Edwards, 13 Wall. 506 (1871), is a case in point. This was an action for the possession of a tract of land situated in California. The land had been sold in pursuance of judicial proceedings. The issue before the court was whether the sheriff in making the sale had acted in accordance with law. There was a specific provision of law governing the way in which such a sale had been made. The only question was whether that was such law as must be obeyed. If not, why not?

Mr. Justice FIELD explains: There are undoubtedly

[27] GENERAL.—United States v. Commissioner, 5 Wall. 563; United States v. Seaman, 17 How. 225; Mason v. Rollins, 2 Biss. 99; Ex parte Selma R. R., 46 Ala. 423; McCreary v. Rogers, 35 Ark. 298; Freeman v. Selectmen, 34 Conn. 406; United States v. Chandler, 13 D. C. 527; Towle v. State, 3 Fla. 202; People v. Knickerbocker, 114 Ill. 539; Hightower v. Overhaulser, 65 Ia. 347; Louisiana College v. State Treasurer, 2 La. 394; Weston v. Dane, 51 Me. 461; Mayo v. County Com'rs, 141 Mass. 74; Green v. Purnell, 12 Md. 329; People v. Auditor General, 36 Mich. 271; Board of Police v. Grant, 17 Miss. 77; State v. Fletcher, 39 Mo. 388; State v. Scott, 18 Neb. 597; County Board v. State Board, 106 N. C. 83; Commonwealth v. McLaughlin, 120 Pa. St. 518.

many statutory requisitions intended for the guide of officers in the conduct of business devolved upon them which do not limit their power or render its exercise in disregard of the requisitions ineffectual. Such, generally, are regulations designed to secure order, system, and dispatch in proceedings and by disregard of which the rights of parties cannot be seriously affected. Provisions of this character are not usually regarded as mandatory unless accompanied by negative words importing that the acts required shall not be done in any other manner or time than that designated; but when the negative is prescribed, they are intended for the protection of the citizen and to prevent a sacrifice of his property, and by disregard of which his rights might be and generally would be injuriously affected; these are not directory but mandatory. They must be followed or the acts done will be invalid. The power of the officer in all such cases is limited by the manner and conditions prescribed for its exercise.

All comes back to the positive rule that the officer must enforce a law which commands. A case which throws a light upon this principle from another angle is United States v. Randall, 1 Sprague, 546 (1853). This was an information for a penalty filed by the District-Attorney for Massachusetts against the master of the brig Nitheroy for not making a report of the arrival of his vessel to the Deputy Collector of the port of Holmes' Hok in accordance with the customs act. The excuse of the master was that the collector had in effect waived that provision. Upon that point indeed there was not much weight placed; and yet it was necessary to dispose of it. If this were a matter of private law between man and man the defense would be good; but this was a case of public law, between the state and the citizen.

This defense was disposed of by SPRAGUE, the District Judge, in one line, which is well worth preservation: An officer of the customs has no dispensing power, and cannot excuse a party from duties required by statute. This proposition, again, is so elementary that few cases are to be found which discuss it; and when found it is needless to recite them. As an officer must enforce the law, it is obvious that he cannot dispense with its enforcement. But caution, that all of the cases discussed in the section before the last which bear upon discretionary power must be taken into account in any discussion of the limitations upon the functions of the administration, since in a discretionary power the discretion may be so wide as to include the right to decide what cases the law shall be enforced, in what cases the law shall not be enforced. The general principle remains true that whenever the law lays a command upon an officer he must enforce that law. That is the limitation that is always about administration—the law.[28]

§ 38. Ministerial duties.

The second branch of the general rule of administra-

[28] DIRECTORY.—Postmaster General v. Trigg, 11 Pet. 172; Mason v. Fearson, 9 How. 248; Carlisle v. United States, 7 App. D. C. 517; Jacobs v. Supervisors, 100 Cal. 121; Gallup v. Smith, 59 Conn. 357; Whalin v. Macomb, 76 Ill. 49; Abney v. Clark, 87 Ia. 727; Kansas R. R. v. Reynolds, 8 Kan. 628; State v. Dubuclet, 28 La. Ann. 85; Shober v. Cochrane, 53 Md. 544; People v. Auditor General, 38 Mich. 746; Swan v. Gray, 44 Miss. 393; State v. Bishop, 42 Mo. 504; Phelps v. Hawley, 52 N. Y. 23; Springfield, etc., Co. v. Lane Co., 5 Ore. 265; Morgan v. Pickard, 86 Tenn. 208; Sights v. Yarnalls, 12 Grat. 292.

tive functions was that the judicial courts would interfere by their processes to direct the action of any officer of the administration in any matter where the duty of that officer was ministerial. An early instance of the exercise of this power against a high public officer was Kendall v. United States, 12 Peters, 524 (1838). One Stokes brought this mandamus against Kendall, the Postmaster-General, upon the following case: When the Postmaster-General took office he examined the contracts entered into by his predecessor, and directed that certain allowances and credits should be withdrawn. Congress thereupon passed an act for relief, by which the Solicitor of the Treasury was authorized and directed to settle and adjust the claims of the relators, to inquire into and determine the equity of such claims, to make relators such allowances thereupon as, upon full examination of the evidence, might seem right according to the principles of equity; and the Postmaster-General was thereby authorized to credit the relators with such amount when the said solicitor should communicate his views of award to Postmaster-General. When all had been done thereunder the Postmaster-General had refused to act altogether.

The opinion in this case was an elaborate one, as its importance deserved. In the course of the discussion Mr. Chief Justice TANEY said in part: We do not think the grant of mandamus in this case interferes in any respect whatever with the rights and duties of the executive as it does not seek to direct or control the Postmaster-General in the discharge of any official duty partaking in any respect of an executive character. The theory of the constitution undoubtedly is that the powers of government are divided into separate departments, and so far as these powers are derived from the constitution the departments must be regarded as independent of each other; but beyond that all are subject to regulations by law touching the discharge of duties required to be performed. The executive power is vested in a President, and so far as his powers are derived from the constitution he is beyond the reach of any other department; but it by no means follows that every officer in every branch of the department is under the exclusive direction of the President. There are certain political duties imposed upon many officers of the executive department the discharge of which is under the direction of the President; but it would be an alarming doctrine that Congress cannot impose upon any executive officer any duty they may think proper. In such cases the duty and responsibility grow out of and are subject to the control of the law. Under this law the Postmaster-General is vested with no discretion or control over the decisions of the Solicitor, nor is any appeal or review of that decision provided for by the act. The terms of the submission were matters resting entirely in the discretion of Congress, and if they thought proper to vest such a power in any one, although an officer of the government, it did not rest with the Postmaster-General to control Congress or the Solicitor in that affair. To contend that the obligations imposed on the President to see the law faithfully executed subjects the Postmaster-General and the whole administration to the direction and control of the President, and implies a power to forbid their execution, would be a novel construction of the constitution. The act required by law was a precise, definite act, purely ministerial. It was not an official one in any other sense than being the transaction of the department where the books and accounts were kept. All discretion is shut out by the positive command of the law.

These are extreme cases in which a high officer of the administration is held in no better position before the courts than the meanest officer. It may be well to state another celebrated case of this sort, United States v. Schurz, 102 U. S. 378 (1880). This petition for mandamus alleged that the relator McBride was possessed of all the qualifications necessary to entitle him to pre-empt one hundred and sixty acres of the public lands of the United States; that he had acted in compliance with the land laws in respect to occupation of such appropriation; that his proof had been filed in the public land office and there adjudicated; that afterwards the patent had been duly countersigned and recorded; but that delivery of the deed at the local land office had been refused by special order from the Secretary of the Interior.

The opinion in this case is excellent, one of Mr. Justice MILLER'S, at his best: The constitution of the United States declares that Congress shall have power to dispose of and make all needful rules and regulations respecting the territory and other property belonging to the United States. Under this provision the sale of the public lands was placed under the control of the Secretary of the Interior. To aid him in the performance of this duty a bureau was created, at the head of which is the Commissioner of the General Land Office, with many subordinates. To them, as a special tribunal, Congress confided the execution of the laws which regulate the surveying, the selling, and the general care of these lands. Congress has also enacted a system of laws by which rights to these lands may be acquired, and the title of the government conveyed to the citizen. The court has with a strong hand upheld the doctrine that so long as the legal title to these lands remained in the United States and the proceedings were yet in fieri, the courts would not interfere to control the exercise of the power thus vested in that tribunal. To that doctrine we still adhere. We are of opinion that when upon the decision of the proper office the citizen has become entitled to a patent and such a patent has been made out in that office and signed by the President, sealed with the seal of the General Land Office, countersigned by the Recorder of the Land Office, and duly recorded in the Record Book, it becomes a solemn public act of the government of the United States. But no further authority to consider the patentees' case remains in the Land Office. Their power is functus officio. There remains simply the ministerial duty to deliver the patent, a duty which can be enforced by mandamus and which will open the portals of the courts to a performance of their order.

The position of the courts as to ministerial duties is therefore square. Whenever a duty is directed by law, it will be commanded by the court. If the law is not carried out by the administration of its own motion, it will be enforced by the motion of the court. All this is in consequence of our fundamental idea of the supremacy of law. The officer must act in accordance with law, just as every person must act in accordance with law. The officer will be forced to act in accordance with law if the law so provides, just as every person must act in accordance with legal process when forced to act, if the law so provides. It comes to this, then: the distinction between discretionary powers and ministerial duties is in last analysis the question what the law is in any particular case.[29]

§ 39. Specific.

So far as this discussion has gone, this distinction has been insisted upon: either that the duty was ministerial, as in these latter cases, in which cases the rule was positive that a full mandamus would issue, or that the duty was discretionary, as in those former decisions, in which cases the rule was positive again that no

[29] MINISTERIAL DUTIES.—Reg. v. Income Commissioners, 21 Q. B. D. 313; Marbury v. Madison, 1 Cranch 169; Kendall v. United States, 12 Pet. 524; United States v. Schurz, 102 U. S. 378; United States v. Black, 128 U. S. 40; Smith v. Strobach, 50 Ala. 462; Ex parte Selma R. R., 46 Ala. 423; Danley v. Whiteley, 14 Ark. 687; Harpending v. Haight, 39 Cal. 189; Land Co. v. Routt, 17 Colo. 156; State v. Staub, 61 Conn. 553; State v. Gamble, 13 Fla. 9; Barksdale v. Cobb, 16 Ga. 13; People v. Kent, 160 Ill. 655; Governor v. Nelson, 6 Ind. 496; Bryan v. Cattell, 15 Ia. 538; State v. Francis, 23 Kan. 495; State v. Wrotnowski, 17 La. Ann. 156; Baker v. Johnson, 41 Me. 15; Magruder v. Swann, 25 Md. 173; Deehan v. Johnson, 141 Mass. 23; People v. State Auditors, 42 Mich. 422; Chamberlain v. Sibley, 4 Minn. 309; McCulloch v. Stone, 64 Miss. 378; State v. Lesueur, 136 Mo. 452; Humboldt Co. v. County Com'rs, 6 Nev. 30; Kimball v. Lamprey, 19 N. H. 215; State v. Vanarsdale, 42 N. J. L. 536; People v. Collins, 7 Johns. 549; Raleigh, etc., R. R. v. Jenkins, 68 N. C. 499; State v. Auditor, 43 Oh. St. 311; Commonwealth v. Martin, 170 Pa. St. 118; Randall v. Wetherell, 2 R. I. 120; State v. County Com'rs, 28 S. C. 258; Meadows v. Nesbit, 12 Lea 486; Bledsoe v. International Ry., 40 Tex. 537; Sights v. Yarnalls, 12 Grat. 292; State v. Hastings, 15 Wis. 83.

mandamus would issue. Upon this statement the question arises: why may not a duty be ministerial at first and later on discretionary; and what then? Let it be supposed for an example that it is the duty of a State Auditor to allow claims against the state, but that in a particular case he refuses to pass upon a claim. Why may it not be said that it is his ministerial duty to take action in the matter, but that it is within his discretionary power to allow or disallow? Such a rule would meet many difficulties that arise in administration.

The case just supposed is People v. The Auditor, 2 Colo. 97 (1873). In this decision BELFORD, Justice, took that distinction: Where an officer is charged with the performance of a fairly ministerial duty, and he fails to perform it, a writ will issue; but where it appears that the officer, as in this case, is called upon to audit and examine claims, and in so doing is invested with judicial powers, a court, while it may compel him to take action, will never dictate what his decision shall be, and this is the exact thing which the plaintiffs in error asked. If a party were to present a claim against the territory, and the auditor should refuse to examine it, the court would issue a writ commanding him to do so. But this case is not of that character. We are asked to compel the auditor not to audit the claim, but to allow and pay it, and this, too, when he believes the same to be excessive and fraudulent. The discrimination made in this case is a useful one; and it is often employed.

The principal rule remains, when a duty is ministerial in all respects, a court will direct its performance upon that allegation made out. One of the leading cases upon that rule at the present time is Roberts v. United States, 176 U. S. 221 (1900). The facts upon which this controversy arose were uncontradicted, as follows: One Evans had done a large amount of work for the District of Columbia in laying concrete and brick pavements in the City of Washington, for which two certificates were issued to him. After the issue of these certificates, long delays followed before the claimant could get them into his possession, because he was in default. In the meantime various acts of Congress had been passed applicable to his case. At last he presented his claim to the Treasurer of the United States, Roberts, the defendant in this case. The Treasurer thereupon refused to pay interest upon this claim, taking a view of the effect of the various statutes in the case which the Supreme Court of the United States held to be unwarrantable. His final defense is that mandamus should not go against him, error or no error, since the making of payments was part of his official function.

The Supreme Court—Mr. Justice PECKHAM writing the opinion—disposed of this position: The remaining and most important objection is that this is not a case in which the writ of mandamus can properly be issued to one of the executive officers of the government. The law relating to mandamus against a public officer is well settled in the abstract; the only doubt which arises, being whether the facts regarding any particular case bring it within the law which permits the writ to issue where a mere ministerial duty is imposed upon an executive officer, which duty he is bound to perform without any further question. If he refuses under such circumstances, mandamus will lie to compel him to perform his duty. In this case there is but one act of Congress to be examined. We think its construction quite plain and unmistakable. It directs the Treasurer to pay interest on the certificates redeemed by him; and the only question is whether they had been redeemed by him within the meaning of the act. That they were, we have already attempted to show; and the duty of the Treasurer seems to us to be at once plain, imperative, and entirely ministerial, and he should have paid the interest as directed in the statute.

Unless the writ of mandamus is to become practically valueless, and is to be refused even where a public officer is commanded to do a particular act by virtue of a particular statute, this writ should be granted. Every statute to some extent requires construction by the public officer whose duties may be defined therein. Such officer must read the law; and he must therefore in a certain sense construe it, in order to form a judgment from the language what duty he is directed by the statute to perform. But that does not necessarily and in all cases make the duty of the officer anything other than a ministerial one. If the law direct him to perform an act in regard to which no discretion is committed to him, and which upon the facts existing he is bound to perform, then that act is ministerial, although depending upon a statute which requires, in some degree, a construction of its language by the officer. Unless this be so, the value of the writ is very greatly impaired.[30]

[30] SPECIFIC.—Hall v. Steele, 82 Ala. 562; Pritchard v. Woodruff,

§ 40. Mandatory.

That is the beginning and the end of the administrative function—the law. The function of the administration is to enforce the law; in a case where there is explicit law to enforce, there is no scope for any function of the administration. The law is the authority for administration; the law is also the limitation upon the administration. This appears by an examination of both sides of the statement that the law is at the beginning and the end of the administrative function. This involves two propositions, one negative, one positive; if there is no law there can be no sort of government; if there is law there may be any sort of administration. All this is statement and restatement of an abstract proposition. It will be well to proceed at once to more definite discussion.

The negative proposition, that if there be no law there can be no administration, must be evident; since if there is no law to enforce there cannot be any law to carry out. There is a brief case in one of the books of administrative cases to that effect—McElfatrick, 5 Pen. Dec. 278 (1892). This was a claim for a pension as the dependent sister. It appeared by construction of the pension law that no pension was provided by law for a dependent brother or sister until after the termination of the prior

36 Ark. 196; Fowler v. Peirce, 2 Cal. 165; Land Co. v. Routt, 17 Colo. 156; Bryan v. Cattell, 15 Ia. 538; Gill v. State, 72 Ind. 266; Martin v. Ingham, 38 Kan. 641; State v. Board of Liquidation, 42 La. Ann. 647; Chase v. Canal Co., 10 Pick. 244; People v. State Treasurer, 24 Mich. 468; Swann v. Buck, 40 Miss. 268; State v. Hoblitzelle, 85 Mo. 620; State v. Milne, 36 Neb. 301; Humboldt Co. v. County Com'rs, 6 Nev. 32; School Directors v. Anderson, 45 Pa. St. 388; Lane v. Schomp, 5 C. E. Green, 82; Citizens' Bank v. Wright, 6 Oh. St. 318; Cotten v. Ellis, 7 Jones L. 545.

right to pension of the dependent mother and father, and at that date the alleged dependent brother or sister was under sixteen years of age. As at that date this dependent had long since passed the age of sixteen, the department rejected the claim.

This paragraph in the opinion of Assistant Secretary BUSSEY must be fundamental in all discussion of the function of the administration: The department has no right, authority, or power to grant a pension to any person for whom the law does not provide a pension, no matter what may be the circumstances of the case, nor how much it may appeal to the sympathies. The only relief for the appellant must be sought at the hands of Congress, whose power to grant pensions is unlimited. The rejection of this claim by the bureau was strictly in accordance with law, was undoubtedly correct, and is affirmed accordingly. A brief statement like this clarifies matters. It is of course obvious. It is nevertheless indispensable from time to time in any discussion to recur to first principles.

There is one class of cases which upon analysis require nothing else than this elementary rule for their solution. Davis v. Porter, 66 Cal. 658 (1885), may represent this class as well as any other case. This was a petition for mandamus to compel the treasurer of the City of Sacramento to pay to the petitioner the amount due upon certain coupons, together with interest upon the same from the date of maturity. A motion was made to strike from the directions the clause requiring the payment of interest, upon the ground that there was no provision of law which authorized the payment of such interest. This case was made out to the court, which found accordingly that, upon all the statute law upon the subject, there was no such duty. What must be the result of such a finding upon the issuance of the mandamus?

There could only be one result, as Mr. Justice THORNTON points out: Is the petitioner entitled to the writ with the command as claimed by him? This writ is issued to enforce the performance of an act especially enjoined by law, as a duty resulting from an office, trust or station. No court in this state can command a person to perform an act beyond that enjoined by law upon him as a duty pertaining to his office or position. If then such command in the writ of mandate to be issued would impose upon the respondent, as treasurer of the city as aforesaid, the performance of an act beyond what was required of him by law in the discharge of the duties of his office, such command should not be inserted in the writ.

All of which amounts to this: that if there is no law to execute there is no duty to perform—which must be an axiom in the law governing administration. All of the cases discussed in the last paragraph which bear upon ministerial duties are in point in this matter in a negative way, for it is only if the duty is directed by some exact law that the courts will command the performance.[31]

[31] MANDATORY.—Supervisors v. United States, 4 Wall. 435; United States v. Windom, 137 U. S. 643; Ex parte Banks, 28 Ala. 28; Middleton v. Low, 30 Cal. 596; Freeman v. Selectmen, 34 Conn. 406; Howell v. Cooper, 2 Colo. App. 531; State v. Barker, 4 Kan. 379; Logansport v. Wright, 25 Ind. 512; Brown v. Crego, 32 Ia. 498; Thomas v. Owens, 4 Md. 189; People v. Supervisors, 3 Mich. 475; State v. Francis, 95 Mo. 44; State v. Roderick, 23 Neb. 505; State v. Blasdel, 4 Nev. 241; State v. Titus, 47 N. J. L. 89; Raleigh, etc.,

§ 41. Conclusion.

It is hoped that nothing that has been said in this chapter is inconsistent with what has been said in the previous discussion or with what is said in the subsequent discussion. This is a comprehensive chapter in a way; for the whole doctrine of administrative law is involved. This chapter deals with the functions of the administration as a whole. In one view it shows how far these functions go; how that in most of its functions the methods and means of administration are within the discretion of the department; and that therefore in the exercise of this discretion the department is independent, so that no other department can inquire what has been done within the scope of these functions. In another view it shows how soon these functions are limited; how that in all actions the administration is subject to the supremacy of the law of the land, so that if an officer of the administration is ever found without law to justify his action he is liable to any process the courts may send against him. This is the whole of administrative law in general outline; it remains to fill in the detail.

According to the obvious distribution of the functions of government, it is the legislature which makes the laws; it is the executive which enforces the laws; it is the judiciary that adjudicates upon the laws. Without doubt this enforcement of the laws is the principal business of the administration. Without enforcement of the laws, government would come to its end; the

R. R. v. Jenkins, 68 N. C. 502; State v. Chase, 5 Oh. St. 528; Commonwealth v. Lyter, 162 Pa. St. 50; Peters v. Auditor, 33 Grat. 368.

administration is the life of the government. It is now recognized at last that it is in its administration that a government succeeds or fails; no advance can be made unless the administration takes up the work. To get at the real business of government, therefore, it is necessary to make a careful study of the working of the administration. And that requires an insight into the nature of the function of the administration. Administrative duties may then be defined as those functions which are directed to the enforcement of the laws. That the executive shall see that the laws are faithfully executed is the common phrase of the constitutions. The aim of this discussion is to arrive at some idea of the nature of the duties of the administration.

CHAPTER VI.

THE MEMBERSHIP IN THE ADMINISTRATION.

§ 42. Introduction.

One of the most particular parts of the law governing administration is that which is concerned with membership in the administration. One of the elements of the situation is the officer himself, considered apart. What is the selection of the officer—election or appointment? What is the term of the officer—term or pleasure? How is the removal of the officer—arbitrary or judicial? Upon all of these questions concerning the officer as a member of the association there is an elaborate law. It is to be outlined but briefly in this discussion.

§ 43. Classification of officials.

The first question in the organization of the administration is concerning its component parts. These are the office and the employment; the principal agencies of the administration are its officers, the minor agencies are its employees. The emphasis of this distinction is upon status rather than upon function. Office is a conception of public law, employment is a conception of private law; the officer is the public agent, the employee is the private agent. That the officer has the principal role in administration is as obvious as that the employee has the minor part. In abstract theory alone it is possible that the administration should contract for the services of a Secretary of State; in any administration that has been known, that position has always been filled by an officer.

Upon this distinction between office and employment the leading case seems to be United States v. Maurice, 2 Brock. 96 (1823). This was an action upon a bond running to the United States given for the faithful discharge of the duties appertaining to his office by an agent of fortifications and his sureties. The defendants insisted that the bond was void, it being taken for the performance of duties of an office, which office had no legal existence, and consequently no legal duties; for no violation of duty, it was urged, could take place where no duty existed. Moreover, it was argued, since the appointment was not given to the Secretary of War by statute, this officer so appointed could be no officer in any case.

Chief Justice Marshall, then upon circuit, held: Is the agent of fortifications an officer of the United States? An office is defined to be a public charge or employment, and he who performs the duty of an office is an officer. Although an office is an employment, it does not follow that every employment is an office. A man may certainly be employed under a contract express or implied to do an act or to perform a service without becoming an officer. But if the duty be a continuing one, which is defined by rules prescribed by the government, and not by contract, which an individual is appointed by the government to perform, who enters on the duties appertaining to his station without any contract defining them, if those duties continue although the person be changed, it seems very difficult to distinguish such a charge or employment from an office, or the person who performs the duties from an officer. The official bond given in this case by this agent of fortifications, whose appointment was irregular but whose office was established by law, is binding on his sureties.

In this last case the office was found, but no proper appointment to it. That raises the question between officers de jure and officers de facto. The former is a normal case. An officer is de facto where the duties of the office are exercised: Without known appointment or election, but under such circumstances of reputation that acquiescence is calculated to induce people to submit to or invoke his action supposing him to be the officer he assumed to be; under color of a known and valid appointment or election, but where the officer had failed to conform to some precedent requirement or condition; because the officer was not eligible or because there was want of power in the electing or appointing body, or under color of an election or appointment pursuant to an unconstitutional law before the same was adjudged such. Although the acts of such an officer are not those of a lawful officer, the law will hold them valid so far as the interests of all persons concerned are affected.

An excellent discussion of these principles is to be found in a ruling on Additional Compensation, 4 Compt. Dec. 696 (1898). Revised Statutes, section 1765, provided that no officer in any branch of the public service should receive any additional compensation for any other service whatever. One Dickinson was a disbursing agent for the World's Columbian Commission; he at the same time acted as Secretary. The question was whether this provision of the statutes applied to him. And it was held that it did not; since neither of these positions was an office.

Comptroller TRACEWELL wrote, in substance, on this point: The essential characteristic of an office is the exercise of some function of the government. An employe is one who is employed under a contract to perform a service. A public employment is distinguished from a public office by the fact that in the one case the authority to perform a public service is derived from a contract, while in the other it is derived from the law. An office is a public station. The term embraces the ideas of tenure, duration, emolument, and duties. If there is a contract with another person to perform some portion of the service, the persons thus employed are known as agents or employees.[32]

[32] CLASSIFICATION OF OFFICERS.—United States v. Hartwell, 6 Wall. 393; State v. Gardner, 43 Ala. 234; Humphry v. Sadler, 40 Ark. 100; Patton v. Board of Health, 127 Cal. 388; Ogden v. Raymond, 22 Conn. 379; In re House Bill, 9 Colo. 628; State v. Hocker, 39 Fla. 477; Polk v. James, 68 Ga. 128; Matter of Notaries Public, 8 Hawaii, 561; People v. Kipley, 171 Ill. 44; Foltz v. Kerlin, 105 Ind. 221; State v. Spaulding, 102 Ia. 639; State v. Cobb, 2 Kan. 33; Perkins v. Auditor, 79 Ky. 306; Opinion of Justices, 3 Me. 481; County Com'rs

§ 44. Officer.

A public office, then, is the right, authority and duty conferred by law by which for a given period, either fixed by law or through the pleasure of the creating power of government, an individual is invested with some portion of the sovereign functions of the government to be exercised by him for the benefit of the public. The warrant to exercise powers is conferred, not by a contract, but by the law. It finds its source and limitation in some act of expression of governmental power. Oath, salary, operation, scope of duties, are signs of the official status; but no one is essential. The essential thing is that in some way or other the officer is identified with the government.

The position of the officer is well set forth in Byers v. United States, 22 Ct. of Cl. 59 (1887). The Consul-General at Rome was paid at the rate of $2,000 a year; he claimed that the salary was $3,000; and this suit is brought for the difference. For the year during which he held office the Diplomatic Appropriation Act appropriated $2,000, of which the Secretary of State notified him when his appointment was made. His predecessor in office had, indeed, been paid at the rate of $3,000 per annum by disposition of the executive, but in the

v. Duvall, 54 Md. 350; Brown v. Russell, 166 Mass. 14; People v. Langdon, 40 Mich. 673; County Com'rs v. Jones, 18 Minn. 199; State v. Bus, 135 Mo. 325; Shelby v. Alcorn, 36 Miss. 273; State v. Moores, 52 Neb. 770; State v. Broome, 61 N. J. L. 115; Whitehouse v. Langdon, 10 N. H. 331; People v. Vilas, 36 N. Y. 459; Eliason v. Coleman, 86 N. C. 237; State v. Jennings, 57 Oh. St. 415; Hamlin v. Kassafer, 15 Ore. 456; Commonwealth v. Evans, 74 Pa. St. 124; Gray v. Granger, 17 R. I. 201; Alexander v. McKenzie, 2 S. C. 81; Beard v. Decatur, 64 Tex. 11; McCornick v. Thatcher, 8 Utah, 294; Leigh's Case, 1 Munf. 468; Matter of Mosness, 39 Wis. 509.

present case it was plain that the present appointment was upon the $2,000 basis.

The case is of interest for the analysis of the situation. RICHARDSON, the Chief Justice, said in one part: It has been claimed by the executive that by the constitution to the executive alone is granted the power to appoint diplomatic agents of any rank or title at any time and at any place; and upon the exercise of this power Congress can place no extension or limitation by undertaking either to create, abolish or change the character, title or rank of officers. On the other hand, to the legislative branch of the government alone is granted the power to provide for the compensation of those as well as all other public servants. During part of the terms of the early presidents, Congress annually appropriated a sum in gross for the expenses of intercourse with foreign nations, leaving it to the executive to fix the salaries of its several appointees. In some cases appropriations have been made for particular officers, not to exceed the sums named, still leaving the executive all discretion to determine the amount to be paid. When Congress, by inadvertence or otherwise, has used language in legislative enactments which appear to encroach upon the constitutional prerogative claimed by the executive in the establishment of diplomatic agents abroad, it has been met with dignified expressions of exception.

This distinction between an officer and an agent is seen again in Ogden v. Raymond, 22 Conn. 379 (1853). This was an action of assumpsit to recover for services for teaching school by the plaintiff. The defense of the defendant was that the services in question were rendered to a school district in consequence of a contract made by the defendant as trustee of the school district. Is a school trustee an officer or an agent then? That is the issue.

ELLSWORTH held on that point in substance: The defendant was a public agent and is therefore to be presumed to have acted in a public capacity. We apprehend that the defendant, deriving his power from a general law in an election by the people, is a public agent as much as an officer of the state, county, town or district is. Wherein is the difference? All derive their power from the same source. All such are officers, not agents. The determining thing is that the person is constituted a representative of the government.[33]

§ 45. Employe.

An elementary case upon this distinction between office and employment is Daily v. Freeholders of Essex, 58 N. J. L. 319 (1895). An act to reorganize the boards of chosen freeholders, etc., passed in 1894, provided in one clause that the terms of office of all officers now holding office shall expire and all such offices shall become vacant. Did that law apply to the plain-

[33] OFFICER.—United States v. Hartwell, 6 Wall. 393; Comer v. Bankhead, 70 Ala. 493; Humphry v. Sadler, 40 Ark. 100; People v. Woodbury, 14 Cal. 43; Castle v. Lawlor, 47 Conn. 340; Kennedy v. School Dist., 48 Ia. 189; State v. Cobb, 2 Kan. 33; Snapp v. Commonwealth, 82 Ky. 173; McManus v. Weston, 164 Mass. 263; People v. Langdon, 40 Mich. 675; State v. May, 106 Mo. 488; People v. Pinckney, 32 N. Y. 377; Kenny v. Hudspeth, 30 Vroom. 320; Doyle v. Alderman of Raleigh, 89 N. C. 133; State v. Jennings, 57 Oh. St. 415; In re Newport Charter, 14 R. I. 655; Alexander v. McKenzie, 2 S. C. 81; United States v. Hatch, 1 Pin. 182.

tiff in this case, a janitor of the court-house—was he an officer or was he an employee?

LIPPINCOTT, J., said as to that: It is clear from the provisions of this section of the act that the prosecutor, a janitor of the court-house, was protected from removal unless for cause and upon notice and a hearing. There exists no justification for the suggestion that he held a public office. He was holding a position. He was no more a public officer of the county by virtue of his appointment as janitor, than is the janitor of an insurance building an officer of the insurance company that occupies it. This is too clear, indeed, for further discussion.

The relation between officer and employee it seems may be stated in as brief a form as this: The officer may employ agents when necessary in the course of administration—Power of Appointment, 4 Opin. 248 (1843). The questions propounded concerned, first, whether the executive could appoint an agent or commissioner to make certain investigations; second, whether such agent or commissioner could be paid under a general appropriation law. It was intimated in the request that the urgency was pressing, and that the Secretary of War felt that the best interests of the country called for this particular appointment at this particular time. Employment of agents, it was claimed, was a method of administration.

The opinion of Attorney-General NELSON was brief, but it was to the point: The power of appointment of agents results from the obligation of the executive department of the government to take care that the laws be faithfully executed; an obligation imposed by the constitution and from the authority of which no mere act of legislation may operate as a dispensation. Congress may, however, indirectly limit the exercise of this power by refusing the appropriations to sustain it, and thus hamper a function which it is not competent to destroy. The authority to requite such services cannot safely be implied from the general terms of an appropriation law in view of the qualifying enactments.

This special power to employ agents is a general inference from the constitution and from the constant practice in all administration. The administration has certain executive functions and certain large administrative functions. It is obvious that the President, in whom these powers are vested, must perform them largely through agents. Hence, he must have incidentally the power to appoint officers and employ employees for these purposes if Congress do not furnish them or if Congress do not furnish such as he wishes. The same applies to his principal subordinates. The check is that these agents cannot be paid unless there be general or special appropriation by Congress that is applicable.[34]

§ 46. Selection of officials.

There are two methods of selection for office: first, by election; second, by appointment. In every admin-

[34] EMPLOYE.—United States v. Mouat, 124 U. S. 303; Auffmordt v. Hedden, 30 Fed. 360; State v. Gardner, 43 Ala. 234; McDaniel v. Yuba Co., 14 Cal. 444; Perkins v. New Haven, 53 Conn. 215; State v. Spaulding, 102 Ia. 639; Maxwell v. McIlvoy, 2 Bibb 211; Farwell v. Rockland, 62 Me. 296; Trainor v. Board, 89 Mich. 162; Lindsey v. Attorney-General, 33 Miss. 508; Whitehouse v. Langdon, 10 N. H. 331; State v. Broome, 61 N. J. L. 115; Eliason v. Coleman, 86 N. C. 237; State v. Anderson, 57 Oh. St. 429; Sawyer v. Corse, 17 Grat. 230; Matter of Janitor, 35 Wis. 410.

istration, both methods are found, the officers are in part elected; in part, appointed. Whether election or appointment preponderates is the question. In one way or another it all comes back to the people. In the case of election the selection of the people is direct; each officer is designated by the electorate. In the case of appointment, the highest officer is elected by the people, and that officer designates the others. In the case of election it comes from the people directly; in the case of appointment, indirectly; but all is derived from the sovereignty of the people in either case.

If it becomes necessary to draw a distinction between election and appointment, from the very nature of the case the distinction between election and appointment becomes one of degree. This test may help: when an officer appointed is an inferior, the action will be appointment. Election is a designation by the people putting someone over them; appointment is the designation by an officer putting someone under him.

This distinction between appointment and election is, perhaps, the most consequential in the law of administration. It is the question between centralization and decentralization. Whatever bonds there are between officers experience proves are determined by the question of origin. The theory of the law is that the responsibility of the official is to the electorate; that is, the responsibility of an elected official is political only. The responsibility of an appointed official to a superior may be fairly called, for distinction, administrative. Unity in administration cannot exist when an inferior can plead against the order of a superior his common designation by popular will. Every officer who is elected by the people is upon equal terms with every other officer.[35]

§ 47. Election.

The first method, then, is election. The law of election is an external law to the administration. The election of a governor and of a judge are conducted according to the same law. The official becomes a subject of administrative law strictly only when the election is finished, when he comes with his valid credential. The officer, then, is taken into the administration. What follows is law of the administration. What precedes is not. Whether there was a nomination in legal form; whether voters were qualified; whether there was a proper election; whether a fair count—these are questions of the complex law of elections which governs these matters.

The right to office is not a natural right. It is limited in various ways, although, broadly speaking, it is the principle of our law that the right to office is coextensive with the right of suffrage. There are few positive

35 CREATION OF OFFICERS.—Quackenbush v. United States, 177 U. S. 27; Ex parte Lambert, 52 Ala. 79; State v. Askew, 48 Ark. 82; Conger v. Gilmer, 32 Cal. 75; People v. Osborne, 7 Colo. 605; State v. Barbour, 53 Conn. 76; Matter of Executive Communication, 25 Fla. 426; Bradford v. Justices, 33 Ga. 332; People v. Dutcher, 56 Ill. 144; Cleveland, etc., R. R. v. Backus, 133 Ind. 513; Whittam v. Zahorik, 91 Ia. 23; Taylor v. Commonwealth, 3 J. J. Marsh. 401; State v. Abbott, 41 La. Ann. 1096; Silver v. Magruder, 32 Md. 387; Speed v. Crawford, 3 Met. (Ky.) 207; Lawrence v. Hanley, 84 Mich. 399; State v. Lovell, 70 Miss. 309; Wilson v. Lucas, 43 Mo. 290; Prather v. Hart, 17 Neb. 598; State v. Hadley, 64 N. H. 473; Ransom v. Black, 54 N. J. L. 446; People v. Bull, 46 N. Y. 57; State v. Constantine, 42 Oh. St. 437; State v. Briggs, 15 R. I. 425; Kottman v. Ayer, 3 Strob. 92; Brewer v. Davis, 9 Humph. 208; Pearson v. Supervisors, 91 Va. 322.

qualifications for office. There are some expedient negative limits. The usual qualifications for office concern citizenship, age, sex, or property. The usual disqualifications are, in addition, the holding of another office and criminal practices. The question of the qualifications and disqualifications for office are largely bound up in the question of appointment or election. The tendency of the law is to reduce the qualifications for election to a minimum and increase the qualifications for appointment to a maximum.

When an office is an appointive one there cannot be election to it. A case that recites the elementary principle is State v. Hyde, 121 Ind. 20 (1889). The legislature of Indiana established a division of mineral oils in the department of geology, and the office of inspector of mineral oils was established. The same act which constituted this department provided that the general assembly, immediately after the taking effect of it, should elect a head of the department, who should appoint a chief of division. The constitutionality of this act was attacked by these proceedings upon the ground that this was an encroachment by the legislature upon the executive.

Mr. Justice BERKSHIRE held that it was: The powers of government under our constitution are divided into three separate departments—the legislative, the executive, and the judicial. That the power to appoint to office is not a legislative function it seems there can be no question. Is it an executive function? That the power to appoint to office is intrinsically an executive function has been decided over and over again. Therefore the legislature cannot do what it has attempted in this case: take upon itself the appointment of a head of a department, as the appointment to office is an executive function.

The other side of this question is seen in Shoemaker v. United States, 147 U. S. 282 (1893). Congress in legislating for the creation of a commission for a park provided that three of the members of it should be appointed by the President by and with the consent of the Senate, and that two of its members should be two existing officers of the United States, already so appointed. The question was whether such organization of such a commission was constitutional.

Mr. Justice HARLAN disposed of this point in this manner: It is pointed to as invalidating the act that while Congress may create an office, it cannot appoint the officer. As, however, the two persons whose eligibility is questioned, were at the time of the passage of the act and of their action under it, already officers of the United States who had been heretofore appointed by the President and confirmed by the Senate, we do not think that because additional duties, germane to the offices already held by them, were devolved upon them by the act, it was necessary that they should be again appointed by the President and confirmed by the Senate. It cannot be doubted and it has frequently been the case, that Congress may increase the power and duty of an existing office without thereby rendering it necessary that the incumbent should be again nominated and appointed.[36]

[36] ELECTION.—Blake v. United States, 103 U. S. 232; Ex parte Lusk, 82 Ala. 519; Wickersham v. Brittan, 93 Cal. 37; State v. Peelle, 124 Ind. 515; Baltimore v. State, 15 Md. 376; Webber v.

§ 48. Appointment.

The second method, then, is appointment. Certain divisions of the subject must be made at the outset. The appointing power vested in the administration may be distinguished as primary and secondary. The one is the power of original appointment; the other is the power of appointment to fill a vacancy. Primary appointment is the ordinary case; secondary appointment, the extraordinary case. A power to appoint to an office includes theoretically the power to make the appointment in case of vacancy. Expediency has given to the executive in practice an exceptionally broad power of secondary appointment to fill the vacancies in offices which were originally filled by election. This is very common in our public law. We continually find the power to fill vacancies for a limited period or for the rest of the term in offices falling vacant in which the executive had no power of original appointment. A great deal of public law has grown up about the word "vacancies" and the term "appoint"; and these have received various shades of interpretation.

Again, the power of appointment may be either absolute or conditional. If the choice requires nothing more than the commission of the appointing power to make it perfect, the appointment may be called absolute. If there is confirmation or consent of some other body required previous to a commission of the appointing power, it may be termed conditional. Example of the former is the power of the President to appoint to inferior office; and of the latter is the constitutional re-

Davis, 5 Allen, 393; Thomas v. Burrus, 23 Miss. 550; People v. Thomas, 33 Barb. 287; Haight v. Love, 10 Vroom. 14; Territory v. Ashenfelter, 4 N. M. 93; State v. McCollister, 11 Oh. 46; State v. Barber, 4 Wyo. 409.

quirement of the advice and consent of the Senate in the larger executive appointments.

Of whatever sort, appointment is an executive function. It may be defined as the act of designation by the executive of a person to an office in the administration. In such appointment the executive has an inherent power. As the function is executive, it is independent; no dictation to the department can be made without violation of the rule of separation of powers. Qualifications upon the eligibility of officers may be made, but directions as to the choice of officers may not be made. Since appointment is an executive function, these results follow.

The primary rule is that of the previous case: that the executive must have the right to appoint to an office. The limitation upon that is in the last case: that the legislature may prescribe as to the office itself. The result of the interaction of these two principles upon each other is that the one may prevail, which results in a discretionary system, or the other may prevail, which results in a civil service system. In the one case the appointing officer may designate whom he pleases upon any basis of preference. In the other case the appointing officer is limited in his choice to a certain number of men certified to him upon some basis of merit.

The constitutional limitations must be observed in any case. The power of appointment conferred by the constitution is a substantial and not merely a nominal function, and the judgment and will of the constitutional depository of that power should alone be exercised or have legal operation in filling offices created by law. The right of the legislature to prescribe qualifications for office is limited by the necessity of leaving scope for the judgment and will of the person or body in whom the constitution vests the power of appointment. The legislature cannot vest such appointment elsewhere directly or indirectly. Accordingly, an act requiring the executive to appoint to office the persons designated by an examining board as the fittest would be at variance with the constitution, inasmuch as it would virtually place the power of appointment in that board. But, although the result of an examination before such a board cannot be made legally conclusive upon the appointing power, against its own judgment and will, yet it may be resorted to in order to inform that power. And notwithstanding that the appointing power alone can designate an individual for an office, still, either the legislature by direct legislation, or the executive by authority derived from the legislature, can prescribe qualifications, and require that the designation shall be out of a class of persons ascertained by proper tests to bear those qualifications.

A provision invalid according to these limitations is seen in People v. Roberts, 148 N. Y. 360 (1896). The relator was appointed clerk to the collector of canal statistics by the Superintendent of Public Works upon his own motion. When he applied for his salary the Comptroller of the state refused to audit the same. The ground of refusal was that the relator was appointed to the position without having taken the civil service examination, and, of course, therefore without certification of his name by the Civil Service Commission.

O'Brien, for the majority judges, held: It is quite clear that the civil service statutes constitute a general system of statute law applicable to appointments in every department of the civil service of the state. It is therefore apparent that a new principle, far reaching in its scope and effect, has been firmly imbedded in the constitution. That this must, if fairly and honestly administered, go far to suppress very grave evils and abuses that have become peculiarly rife and acute in our political system, no intelligent person who has given the matter much attention can doubt. Our conclusion is that, as the commission had not certified to this relator, his appointment is invalid.

A provision invalid according to these limitations is seen in Brown v. Russell, 166 Mass. 14 (1896). This was a petition for mandamus to the Civil Service Commissioners of Massachusetts praying that they be required to restore the petitioner to the highest place upon the list of candidates eligible for certification and appointment to a position on the district police for the commonwealth, a preference for certification and appointment having been given to one Bean in conformity with a statute of 1895 which required that a veteran of the civil war, who should make application, should be certified first to the Governor, which had the effect of requiring the Governor to appoint him if he appointed anybody.

The Chief Justice, FIELD, gave the decision upon the grounds: We think that it is inconsistent with the nature of our government and particularly with our constitution that the appointing power should be compelled by legislation to appoint to public offices persons of a certain class in preference to all others without the exercise on its part of any discretion, and without the favorable judgment of some legally constituted board designated by law to inquire and determine whether the persons to be appointed are actually qualified to perform the duties which pertain to the offices. In our form of government it is fundamental that public offices are a public trust; and that the persons to be appointed should be selected solely with a view to the public welfare.

This is a period of distrust in the free discretion of the executive in appointment. The alternative is this civil service system. The civil service reform has fought its way to recognition. It has passed through the stages of, first, pass examinations; second, limited competitive examinations; and third, present form of open competitive examinations. Among those few thus qualified the executive must now choose most officers, except the highest. Far from perfect as the system is, it is, on the whole, the best that has been devised. Administration will be better than it ever has been, because it will be a permanent provision; but in the process the administration may become a bureauocracy. At all events, something of the old will be gone that was of advantage together with all that was of disadvantage.[37]

§ 49. Removal of officials.

As the selection for office is different in appointment and in election, removal from office is different in the

[37] APPOINTMENT.—United States v. Perkins, 116 U. S. 483; State v. Askew, 48 Ark. 82; Wickersham v. Brittan, 93 Cal. 34; State v. Dillon, 32 Fla. 545; Franklin v. Kaufman, 65 Ga. 260; Kreitz v. Behrensmeyer, 149 Ill. 496; Boone Co. Com'rs v. State, 61 Ind. 379; Miner v. Olin, 159 Mass. 487; Attorney General v. May, 99 Mich. 538; State v. Squire, 39 Oh. St. 197; DeWalt v. Bartley, 146 Pa. St. 529; Flatan v. State, 56 Tex. 98; Bean v. Territory, 3 Wash. Ter. 129.

case of officers that have been appointed and in the case of officers that have been elected. If there is one single principle in the whole question it is this: that the power of selection and the power of removal are correlative things. The power that selects may remove. An officer who has appointed may dismiss by this rule. This is the normal case; there are some few abnormal cases. So the people who elect may alone dispose by the same rule. This is the normal case; there are some few abnormal cases. Upon the whole, the principle stands that the power to select involves the power to remove.

There are two sorts of removal: first, arbitrary, and second, judicial. The first sort is the ordinary case in centralized administration. The power of appointment and the power of dismissal are both inherent powers in an executive department of the centralized type, like the administration of the United States. Both the power to appoint at will and to remove at will are involved in the conception of the centralized administration. On the other hand, in a decentralized administration, like that of the states, as each of the different officers has his own place by election, any removal from that position by other officers will be an extraordinary case. When such a process is provided it will always be by some quasi judicial method for due cause shown.

This fundamental difference between the removal of appointive officers by the mere motion of the executive and the removal of elective officers by solemn adjudication of the administration, if at all, is seen in an opinion on the Removal of Officers, 16 Pa. Co. Ct. 305 (1895). One Curley held the elective office of Recorder of Deeds for the City of Philadelphia. He held that office by interim appointment from the Governor. The question was whether the Governor could remove him at pleasure and appoint another in his place. It all turned upon whether he was an elective officer or an appointive officer.

The Attorney-General, McCormick, advised the Governor: The officers provided by the constitution and the laws are either appointive or elective. As to the former—except those specifically excepted—there can be no doubt of the Governor's power to remove; as to the latter—except those as to whom specific provision is made—they can be removed only by impeachment. Does the present incumbent become an appointed officer within the meaning of the constitution, because he was appointed to fill a vacancy in an executive office? I am of the opinion that the provision of the constitution giving the power to remove appointed officers means officers holding offices that are appointive in their character and not elective. Otherwise there would be possibilities not contemplated by the constitution.

Of these two forms of removal, arbitrary motion is the characteristic form in centralized administration; judicial amotion is the characteristic form in decentralized administration. Instant dismissal without the obligation to give reasons is the necessary situation in centralized administration; the arbitrary form of dismissal prevails there because upon the whole it is experience that in no other way can an administration be maintained in a high state of efficiency. What is indispensable in centralized administration is instant obedience, which can be enforced only by this power of instant removal. On the other hand, in a decentralized administration, removal for cause only prevails. It is only necessary that good behavior should be shown by each separate officer. There is no obedience required other than this. The quasi judicial form meets that situation well enough.[38]

§ 50. Arbitrary.

That in a centralized administration the power of removal is involved was shown at the beginning of the working out of the details of the Federal administration in a debate on the Power of Removal, 1 Ann. Cong. 350 (1789), in the first session of the first Congress that met after the adoption of the Constitution. This arose upon the propriety of inserting in the statute establishing the department of foreign affairs this clause: To be removable by the President. Upon this question there was a difference of opinion in the House of Repre-

[38] REMOVAL OF OFFICERS.—Osgood v. Nelson, L. R. 5 H. L. 636; Hill v. Reg., 8 Moo. P. C. 138; Grant v. Secretary, 2 C. P. D. 445; Hammond v. McLay, 28 U. C. Q. B. 463; Stuart v. Gould, 16 N. S. Wales, 132; Ex parte Hennen, 13 Pet. 230; United States v. Avery, Deady 204; Ledbetter v. State, 10 Ala. 241; Kaufman v. Stone, 25 Ark. 336; Sponogle v. Curnow, 136 Cal. 580; Trimble v. People, 19 Colo. 187; Fairfield Co. Bar v. Taylor, 60 Conn. 11; Territory v. Cox, 6 Dak. 501; State v. Johnson, 30 Fla. 433; State v. Frazier, 48 Ga. 137; Wilcox v. People, 90 Ill. 186; Carr v. State, 111 Ind. 109; Brown v. Duffus, 66 Ia. 193; Lynch v. Chase, 55 Kan. 367; South v. Commissioners, 86 Ky. 186; Andrews v. King, 77 Me. 224; State v. Register, 59 Md. 283; Williams v. Gloucester, 148 Mass. 256; Attorney-General v. Detroit Common Council, 112 Mich. 145; State v. Peterson, 50 Minn. 239; Newsom v. Cocke, 44 Miss. 352; State v. Police Com'rs, 88 Mo. 144; Quinn v. Portsmouth, 64 N. H. 324; Stewart v. Freeholders, 61 N. J. L. 117; People v. Dalton, 158 N. Y. 204; State v. Hawkins, 44 Oh. St. 98; Brower v. Kantner, 190 Pa. St. 182; Johnson v. Hacker, 4 Cold. 431; Collins v. Tracy, 36 Tex. 547; Richards v. Clarksburg, 30 W. Va. 491; State v. Seavey, 7 Wash. 564.

sentatives; and later in the Senate there was one of the closest of divisions, the Vice-President casting the deciding vote. In the end the bill passed without the enabling clause upon the understanding that such a clause was unnecessary because the power belonged to the executive without it.

In this great debate Mr. MADISON is reported to have said: It is absolutely necessary that the President should have the power of removing from offices; it will make him in a peculiar manner responsible for their conduct, and subject him to impeachment himself if he suffers them to perpetrate with impunity high crimes or misdemeanors against the United States, or neglects to superintend their conduct so as to check their excesses. Of the same opinion were other members of the convention that framed the Constitution. No higher evidence can be had.

For three-quarters of a century Congress acquiesced in this arbitrary power of removal by the executive. Then in 1867 the Tenure of Office Act was passed over the veto of the President. The effect of that act is seen in the opinion concerning Rollins, 12 Opin. 444 (1868). An officer, within the Tenure of Civil Office Act, tendered in writing to the President the resignation of his office, to take effect upon the qualification of his successor, nominated by the President and confirmed by the Senate. When his tenure of the office could be regarded as relinquished, was the question. Upon the event named in his communication, was his contention; but the President wished to remove him at once.

EVARTS, his Attorney-General, advised that he could not; the purpose of the Tenure of Office Act was to change the doctrine and practice of the government, by which removal from office at the mere discretion of the President had been established as a proper, and, as had been thought, a necessary attendant of the executive duty and responsibility under the constitution to maintain the efficiency and fidelity of the public service in fulfilling the manifold and incessant obligations in administration and in execution of the laws. Mr. Rollins, then, at the date of his letter to the President was entitled to hold the office of Commissioner of Internal Revenue until a successor should have been appointed by and with the advice and consent of the Senate and should have qualified.

Later the Tenure of Office Act was in effect repealed. Just how the matter stands in our constitutional law today is seen in Parsons v. United States, 167 U. S. 324 (1897). In 1892 one Parsons was appointed by the President and Senate, District Attorney for Alabama for four years. In 1893, he was removed from office by the President without explanation. In 1894, he sued for the balance of his salary in the Court of Claims. His contention was that his commission gave him his office for four full years; and that the President had therefore no power to remove him.

Mr. Justice PECKHAM said in substance: 'It would seem to be a sound and necessary rule to consider the power of removal as incident to the power of appointment. The executive power which by the Constitution is vested in the President over all officers appointed by him makes their tenure no more stable than his pleasure. We are satisfied that the intention of Congress was to concede to the President the power of removal, and to enable him to remove an officer when in his discretion he regards it for the public good, although the term of office be fixed. Upon the whole this opinion is strong enough to be authority against any tenure-of-office legislation henceforth.[39]

§ 51. Judicial.

The extent to which the rule goes that requires judicial action in removal from office is seen in People v. Treasurer, 36 Mich. 416 (1877). The Board of Supervisors of a county passed a resolution to remove the Overseers of the Poor. The statute fixed the terms of these overseers at three years, which time had not half run out in this case. And the provision for making removal by the supervisors prescribed certain grounds, which were not present in this case. The supervisors had selected these overseers at the outset, however. It was claimed, therefore, that the supervisors might at any time remove the overseers by virtue of that situation.

The court—GRAVES, J.—laid down an important limitation upon the rule that a power to appoint involves a power to remove: Our state system favors appointments for fixed periods, and almost entirely rejects the policy of removals at will, and this rule of action should

[39] ARBITRARY.—Eckloff v. District, 135 U. S. 241; Patton v. Vaughan, 39 Ark. 211; Sponogle v. Curnow, 136 Cal. 580; Carter v. Durango, 16 Colo. 534; State v. Johnson, 30 Fla. 433; State v. Mitchell, 50 Kan. 289; Sanborn v. Kimball, 64 Me. 140; Field v. Malster, 88 Md. 691; Williams v. Gloucester, 148 Mass. 256; People v. Stuart, 74 Mich. 411; Parish v. St. Paul, 84 Minn. 426; State v. Cooper, 53 Miss. 615; State v. Board of Lands, 7 Neb. 42; Weidman v. Board, 7 N. Y. Supp. 309; State v. Owen, 125 N. C. 212; Field v. Commonwealth, 32 Pa. St. 478; Maroney v. City Council, 19 R. I. 3; Keenan v. Perry, 24 Tex. 253; State v. Prince, 45 Wis. 610.

be observed in this case. We have not found any case where an officer who was appointed for a fixed term—and when the power of removal was not expressed and declared by law to be discretionary—has been held to be removable except for cause; and whenever cause must be assigned for the removal of an officer he is entitled to notice and to a chance to defend. Every officer appointed for a fixed term should be entitled to hold his office until the expiration of such period unless removed therefrom for cause upon a fair trial. This is the general argument that is made in the states where the administration is decentralized.

Where the power of removal is judicial the principal issue is whether there are sound reasons or not. A representative case on that is Todd v. Dunlap, 99 Ky. 449 (1896). The Board of Public Safety and the Board of Public Works, executive boards of the government of the City of Louisville, instituted these actions in equity in which it was alleged that the Mayor and the Board of Aldermen were about to remove the members constituting the two boards from office without cause, and the sole question in each case was: Had the Mayor the power, with the approval of the Board of Aldermen, to remove these officials without notice and trial and without assigning any cause for their action? The statute law upon the subject was to the effect that the Mayor, giving his reasons, might remove with the approval of the Aldermen.

Chief Justice PRYOR held against the Mayor: These officials having been appointed by the Mayor, it is urged in his behalf that any reason satisfactory to himself and approved by the Board of Aldermen is a compliance with the statute, and that no limitation on this power of removal exists when applied to those officers holding under his appointment, and, however competent and faithful they may be in the discharge of their duties, their positions are held at the mere will of the Chief Executive. But we think that when the power to remove is for reasons given, the legislative meaning was a removal for cause—for legal reasons based upon a sufficient cause—and when removed for reasons given or for cause, the parties are entitled to a hearing and to be proceeded against in due form upon charges, notice, and opportunity to be heard.[40]

§ 52. Conclusion.

The results of the conditions related in this chapter go far. An administration in which membership is given by appointment and taken away at discretion is one type. An administration in which membership is acquired by election and lost only by a judicial process is another type. The result in the first type is centralized administration; while in the second type the result is decentralized administration. As will appear as the discussion advances, the processes of centralized administration are of one sort; the processes of decentralized administration are of another sort. Indeed, these two types are opposites.

[40] JUDICIAL.—Marbury v. Madison, 1 Cranch, 137; State v. Hixon, 27 Ark. 402; People v. Mizner, 7 Cal. 519; Trimble v. People, 19 Colo. 187; State v. Barbour, 53 Conn. 76; Queen v. Atlanta, 59 Ga. 318; State v. Chatburn, 63 Ia. 659; Todd v. Dunlap, 99 Ky. 449; Duboc v. Voss, 19 La. Ann. 210; Townsend v. Kurtz, 83 Md. 331; Andrews v. King, 77 Me. 224; Hallgren v. Campbell, 82 Mich. 255; State v. Peterson, 50 Minn. 239; State v. Smith, 35 Neb. 13; State v. Trenton, 50 N. J. L. 338; Territory v. Ashenfelter, 4 N. M. 95; People v. Roosevelt, 168 N. Y. 488; State v. Mitchell, 115 N. C. 190; State v. Archibald, 5 N. D. 359; Keenan v. Perry, 24 Tex. 253.

CHAPTER VII.

THE ORGANIZATION OF THE ADMINISTRATION.

§ 53. Introduction.

When many officers are found in action together the law must provide for their inter-relation. Some officers act in co-ordination with each other—how shall their functions be divided? Other officers act in subordination one to another—how shall their duties be ranked? It is the internal law of the administration to a large degree that deals with these complex matters of organization; and it has to solve these intricate matters by theories of its own. These questions require full discussion, which will be had later on. Administrative law has much to do with these questions; for it is obvious that administration could not proceed without rules of law of some sort. And without a properly balanced organization an administration could not go on.

What external divisions between administrations themselves there shall be is a question of constitutional law; while what internal divisions there shall be in an administration is the question in administrative law. At the same time no description of the position of the administration in the United States can be given unless the general divisions between the various administrations is exposed as the basis of the general schemation of the administration. These, then, are the principal divisions of the problem of the organization of the administration. The first concerns the external division between administrations; while the second concerns the internal sub-divisions of the respective administrations.

§ 54. External sub-divisions.

In the United States the number of independent administrations is the greatest in the world. In no other nation is there such division of powers between the various governments, and the disorganization of the administrations is the consequence of this. In the first place there is that entire division between the government of the United States and the government of the states. This inevitably results in an entire division between the federal administration and the state administrations. This entire division between the administrations is a necessity as a practical matter if the theory of the founders of the federal nation is to be preserved and the relative independence of the state and nation is to be maintained.

But within the administrations of the states themselves there is the same disorganization. The central administration in the state has seldom any administrative relations with the local administrations in the state. The central administration and the local administration are in the usual case both elected by the people. Each, therefore, is independent of the others in its position. The central administration cannot remove the officers of the local administration in any normal case. Altogether no such decentralism is known in any other nation as is found in the United States throughout.

There is but one external division in the federal administration—that one that divides it from the administrations of the states. Within itself the federal administration is a single administration. All of its subdivisions are internal ones, as is the case in any centralized administration; while in any decentralized administration like that of the states the organization is based upon external division. That is the fundamental difference between the law of the federal administration, which is based upon administrative relations, and the administrations of the state, which are based upon legal relations. Thus the divisions of the federal administration are internal, while those of the state administration are external.[41]

§ 55. Federal.

The national administration in the United States constitutes a complete system, separate altogether from the state administration. This is not indispensable in a federal government. In some such governments the

[41] EXTERNAL SUBDIVISIONS.—Tennessee v. Davis, 100 U. S. 257; Ex parte Siebold, 100 U. S. 371; In re Neagle, 135 U. S. 1; Ohio v. Thomas, 173 U. S. 284; In re Beine, 42 Fed. 546; Campbell v. Waite, 88 Fed. 106; Ex parte Wiley, 54 Ala. 226; Hathcote v. State, 55 Ark. 183; People v. Whitman, 10 Cal. 38; People v. Curley, 5 Colo. 412; State v. Hocker, 39 Fla. 477; Mehringer v. State, 20 Ind. 103; State v. Waite, 101 Ia. 380; State v. Lamantia, 33 La. Ann. 446; Melcher v. Boston, 9 Met. 75; Fuller v. Ellis, 98 Mich. 96; State v. Kiichli, 53 Minn. 147; People v. Hurlbut, 24 Mich. 44; Oliver v. Jersey City, 63 N. J. L. 96; State v. Clarke, 3 Nev. 566; De Turk v. Commonwealth, 129 Pa. St. 151; In re Corliss, 11 R. I. 638; State v. Buttz, 9 S. C. 156; McGregor v. Balch, 14 Vt. 428.

officers of the states do work for the federation. There is no such situation in the United States; indeed, no officer of the state as an officer of the state has functions to perform for the United States by virtue of that position, so separate are these administrations in point of law.

One case will be enough to show that division—Judge Handlin, 11 Opin. 116 (1864). The gist of the complaint of this Judge Handlin was that Governor Hahn of Louisiana had treated him unjustly in removing him from office without cause. In his letter to the President of the United States he said: Governor Hahn had no power to take the step he did; he could have no power then, except he derived it from you, the President. The President asked the Attorney-General whether he had any power to interfere in the controversy.

Attorney-General BATES said: I do not perceive that the President has any power to interfere between the conflicting officials of the same state government. He is not the judge of the officers of the state. If, as Mr. Handlin affirms, the Governor had no power under the state constitution to remove him from office and vacate his commission, the state judiciary alone has power to hear and determine the question of right; and if they find the Governor in the wrong, and the judge in the right, they will doubtless be able to protect the judge in the enjoyment of his office, and in the legal exercise of his legitimate functions. I think it is a matter which belongs entirely to the state of Louisiana, and that the President has no legal authority in the premises.

The division between the two administrations is more than a matter of law, however; it is a matter of fact, as well. Not only have the state officers as officers no function in the national administration, but the state officers as persons are as a matter of universal practice not made officers of the national administration. This depends largely upon the executive order in the national administration which declares in effect that acceptance by a national officer of an office under a state will in usual cases be considered a resignation by such officer of his appointment in the service of the United States. The effect of this is discussed in the Incompatibility Case, 4 Lawrence, 486 (1883).

In his general discussion of this matter LAWRENCE, the Comptroller, said: Such acceptance does not ipso facto divest the national officer of the title to his office under the United States, but subjects such officer to removal in the discretion of the proper authority. Each state can prescribe the qualifications of its own officers, but not those of national officers. Congress can prescribe the qualifications generally of national officers, but not of state officers. On principles of constitutional law inherent in the structure of the dual system of national and state governments in the United States, and without any express provision on the subject, it is possible that there may be incompatibility in law, however. It will be seen, therefore, that as a matter of fact the division between the administration of the United States and the administrations of the states is complete.[42]

[42] FEDERAL.—Dobbins v. Erie Co. Com'rs, 16 Pet. 435; Collector v. Day, 11 Wall. 113; In re Lee, 46 Fed. 61; Wood v. Drake, 70 Fed. 881; In re Strawbridge, 39 Ala. 387; Hollingsworth v. State, 111 Ind. 289; Melcher v. Boston, 9 Met. 75; Fuller v. Ellis, 98 Mich. 96; Oliver v. Jersey City, 63 N. J. L. 96; In re Treasurers' Appointment,

§ 56. State.

In each state of the United States there are three grades of administration. The administration of the state, the administration of the county, and the administration of the local body—these three. This is so because the governmental organization of necessity determines the external division of the administrative organization. These three degrees of government, each in action independent of the other, make up a condition of disorganization in government unknown elsewhere. What is back of this is the institutional theory held by the majority of people in the United States. Local self-government is not a legal principle, it is true; but it is an accepted policy, at all events.

The state administration is not central, in truth, for it has no administrative relations with the county administration; the county administration is not the superior of the local administration in any proper sense, for it has no control over it. Hence, the only relations that there may be between the administrations in the states are legal, not administrative. After all, these external divisions depend upon the general constitutional structure within the state. Although this leads the discussion outside of our topic, it is perhaps necessary to sketch these divisions.

In the central administration, a Governor is found as the chief executive in all the states; in a few instances there is an executive council to advise the Governor. Next in grade are the heads of the executive department; these are in part single-headed, in part headed

5 Kulp. 98; State v. Buttz, 9 S. C. 156; Calloway v. Sturm, 1 Heisk. 764; McGregor v. Balch, 14 Vt. 428.

by boards. Next are various officers scattered about the state who exercise functions by direct commission from the state. Altogether, the number of officers thus in the service of the state administration is not infrequently the lowest. That is because the work done by the state in the normal case is least. The central administration plays the smallest part in the government, as it touches the ordinary citizen seldom.

Local organization in the United States may be divided into three classes, which division turns upon whether the county or the town is given the most prominence in government. The division was largely historical, and this matter still remains a local question, therefore. In New England the township system gives the preponderance to the locality. In the south the county system gives most of the functions of the government over to the county. In the middle states there is a system which dates to the Duke of York between these two extremes. In the west there is no regular system, all of the three just mentioned being found. In every system of local government both the county and the locality exist.

Whatever the type of organization, the administrations are independent, as they consist always of separate elective officers. There is some qualification of this statement necessary in dealing with the relations between the township and the county. If the county officers are elected directly by the people without reference to the township, we have the commissioner system. And if the township organization is represented in the county organization by some officers from it, we have the supervisor system. The commissioner system prevails in most states; under that there is direct election of the county officers by the voters of the county. The supervisor system is, however, spreading; for the intimate connection between the local governments under this system has been well liked. The usual form of this organization is that the chief executive officer of the local body is a member of the county board.

In local administration the variety is so great as to defy an accurate statement in brief form. An obvious distinction, indeed, may be made between the rural localities which are unincorporated, and the civic localities which are incorporated. That difference, of much importance in law, is of the same importance in the actual business of administration. In truth the real distinction is that in rural administration the work is so small that almost any arrangement will meet with moderate success; while in civic administration the work is so large that not even the best organization of the administration has proved to be a conspicuous success.[43]

§ 57. Internal sub-divisions.

The proper questions of the law governing administration begin with the problems as to the inner organization. An explanation of this highly complex organism

[43] STATE.—Baker v. Grice, 169 U. S. 284; Ex parte Wiley, 54 Ala. 226; People v. Whitman, 10 Cal. 38; People v. Curley, 5 Colo. 412; Perkins v. New Haven, 53 Conn. 215; State v. Hocker, 39 Fla. 477; Foltz v. Kerlin, 105 Ind. 221; State v. Waite, 101 Ia. 380; State v. Gilmore, 20 Kan. 551; State v. Lamantia, 33 La. Ann. 446; People v. Hurlbut, 24 Mich. 44; Lindsey v. Attorney-General, 33 Miss. 508; State v. Dillon, 90 Mo. 229; State v. Clarke, 21 Nev. 333; Taggart v. Commonwealth, 102 Pa. St. 354; State v. Glenn, 7 Heisk. 472; Day L. & C. Co. v. State, 68 Tex. 526; McGregor v. Balch, 14 Vt. 429; Burch v. Hardwicke, 30 Grat. 24.

may be helped by a biological analogy. In any government its organs correspond in some degree to the functions required of it. Indeed, the differentiation therein is no more than a matter of functional adaptation. Such specialization results in efficiency. At bottom it seems that the division in the agencies of administration is dictated by law inherent in all growth; as it is an internal reflection of external environment. In other words, make this the first question: what has the administration to do; that will answer the second question: what departments of government are there?

The principle in organization is system. Organization requires system in the proper co-ordination of officers. For this all officers upon the same grade must be so assigned that some are at one work, others at another work. Organization requires system also in the proper subordination of officers for direction. To make this out to its full extent each officer should be under his chief, their chiefs under another chief, this chief under the head of the chief executive himself. In any administration these forms will be preserved to a greater or to a lesser extent. For, indeed, some such arrangement is involved in any organization whatsoever.

In usual organization there is thus built up this articulated body. The object of this organism is to produce definite action. To this end there is specialization in the separate officers, so that there may be equipment for action. To this end, also, there is this organization of these officers into a whole, so that there may be direction in action. The purpose in administration is the enforcement of the law; and this can only be accomplished through the process of an administration that is organized upon definite lines to that end. All this is said in a clear exposition of The Duties of the Attorney-General, 6 Opin. 346 (1854).

Attorney-General CUSHING said in part: The organization of the executive departments of the administration implies order, correspondence, and combination of parts, classification of duties—in a word, system; otherwise there is waste and loss of power, or conflict of power, either of which is contrary to the public service, which has a regard of so much work to be done by such persons at a given cost of either time or money. Besides which, in a political relation, want of due arrangement of public functionaries and their functions is want of due responsibility to society and to law. Accordingly, it has been the general purpose of Congress, at all times, both as to the great subdivision of departments and the arrangements of the duties of each, to classify and systematize.[44]

§ 58. Department.

An administration is a hierarchy. In the typical administration the department is the largest division. How many departments there shall be is a question; in some governments there are more, in some less. It is all as the need is in any case. As the amount of things done by a government increases, the number of its principal departments will increase by division of

[44] INTERNAL SUBDIVISIONS.—Fox v. McDonald, 101 Ala. 51; Ex parte Allis, 12 Ark. 101; People v. Turner, 20 Cal. 142; Bunn v. People, 45 Ill. 397; State v. Board of Liquidation, 42 La. Ann. 647; Thomas v. Owens, 4 Md. 189; Lindsey v. Attorney-General, 4 George, 508; Cotton v. Phillips, 56 N. H. 220; People v. Schoonmaker, 13 N. Y. 238; State v. Weston, 4 Neb. 234; State v. Brown, 5 R. I. 1; State v. Hastings, 10 Wis. 525.

the business of one old department between two new departments. Moreover, if wholly new powers are assigned to a government a new department will be required. Organization, as has been remarked before, is a reflection of the activities of a government.

The growth of the departments can be traced with great ease in some such public document as the Report of the Dockery Commission, 53 Cong. 2nd Sess. House Rep. 49 (1893). The first thing to be noted in that report is the original organization of the executive departments. There were four at first: the Department of State for political and foreign affairs; the Department of War for military and naval affairs; the Department of Treasury for collection and disbursement; and the Department of Justice for legal and judicial matters. The next step was the separation of a Department of Navy; the next the creation of a Department of Interior; the next the promotion of the office of Postmaster-General; the next the invention of a Department of Agriculture; the last the provision for a Department of Commerce. All this is a growth upon the lines indicated.

This is not quite the whole story. These nine departments do not include every officer of the United States; there are some few unattached officers. This situation becomes of some importance at times. For example, it came to light in the opinion on the Civil Service Commission, 22 Opin. 62 (1898). This was a request for an opinion upon the question whether an act which required all clerks in all executive departments to work not less than seven hours applied to the clerks of the Civil Service Commission. It must be obvious that, in an exceptional office with exceptional duties pertaining to all the departments, it would be best if it need not be placed within the regular organization.

Attorney-General GRIGGS advised that the case did not apply: No board, commission, bureau, or office which is not expressly or by implication under the control of one of the chief executive departments can be considered as belonging to an executive department. There is nothing in the act constituting the Civil Service Commission which makes it subject to any regulation or control except that of the President himself. It follows therefore that when an act of Congress refers to the executive department it does not embrace and cannot properly be applied to any branch office or bureau which is not under the control of one of the executive departments presided over by a cabinet officer.

The departments, then, are those offices which are headed by the cabinet officers. In the American system of government the high political officers are also the actual working heads of the administrative department. Modern constitutional government has found by experience that whenever a gap exists between the chief officers of the state and the heads of the administrative departments that the administration suffers by this lapse. Because, after all, in the larger matters, questions of administration cannot be separated from questions of politics.[45]

[45] DEPARTMENT.—Attorney-General, 6 Opin. 346; Civil Service Commission, 22 Opin. 62; State v. Hutt, 2 Ark. 282; Love v. Baehr, 47 Cal. 364; In re House Bill, 21 Colo. 32; State v. Keena, 64 Conn. 215; State v. Bloxham, 26 Fla. 407; Julian v. State, 122 Ind. 68; Bryan v. Cattell, 15 Ia. 538; State v. Nield, 4 Kan. App. 626; State v. Mason, 43 La. Ann. 590; Scharf v. Tasker, 73 Md. 378; In re

§ 59. Bureau.

In the typical administration the next largest division is the bureau. How many bureaus there shall be is again a question of how many things that department is assigned to do. The designation of the work to each bureau on the whole goes upon the lines of specialization. In a large way this question of the determination of the organization, as has been pointed out, is a legislative question, not an administrative question.

One case is enough to show that situation—Militia Bureau, 10 Opin. 11 (1861). The question submitted to the Attorney-General was as to the propriety of a proposed order detailing Lieutenant Ellsworth of the first dragoons for special duty as inspector general of militia for the United States, charging him with the transaction, under the direction of the Secretary of War, of all business pertaining to the militia, to be conducted as a separate bureau, of which it was proposed to make Lieutenant Ellsworth the chief. There had been no legislation upon this bureau, which it was proposed to establish by an executive order.

The advice of Attorney-General BATES was: It proposes the establishment of a bureau heretofore unknown in the organization of the War Department. That department is divided into a number of subordinate divisions, as the quarter-masters, the commissariat, the pay-masters, the ordnance, the engineers, and the medical, all of which are created and their respective duties defined by legislative enactment. Some of them are called bureaus and in some the duties are subdivided

State House Commission, 19 R. I. 390; Territory v. Stokes, 2 N. M. 63; State v. Hastings, 10 Wis. 525.

into divisions; but all are established to perform duties especially authorized by law. The same remark is true of the bureaus in the other departments of the government, as will be seen by reference to the acts creating them. In view of these precedents, I cannot avoid the conclusion that the creation of a bureau in the War Department can only be authorized by an act of Congress designating its chief, defining his duties, and providing for the appointment of the necessary clerical force.

The situation will be made clear by a few illustrations taken at random of this subdivision of the department into bureaus. A recent public document entitled Executive Departments at Washington (1893), is the authority. Bureaus are not always so denominated; sometimes the name is office, sometimes commission. But in any administration organized upon any systematic arrangement there must be these increasing subdivisions, each included in the one above it, each including the ones below it. The nomenclature is unimportant.

Thus, in the Treasury Department the next subdivision in order is into: first, mint; second, inspector of vessels; third, statistics; fourth, life saving service; fifth, lighthouse board; sixth, supervising architects; seventh, comptroller; eighth, currency; ninth, commissioner of customs; tenth, auditor; eleventh, treasurer; twelfth, register; thirteenth, internal revenue; fourteenth, navigation; fifteenth, coast survey; sixteenth, engraving. This is a long list. And yet the possibilities for orderly administration must be apparent even upon a cursory examination.

Again in the Department of the Interior the bureaus

are: first, land office; second, Indian affairs; third, pensions; fourth, patents; fifth, education; sixth, railroad; seventh, geological survey; eighth, census. These interests, after all, may well enough fall within the Department of the Interior, since they are internal affairs. And yet obviously so diverse are they that it will be impossible to expect proper administration if they were undistributed. It is only by division that administration is possible.[46]

§ 60. Division.

In the typical administration the last principal unit is the division. The administration is divided into departments; the departments are divided into bureaus; the bureaus are divided into divisions; and the divisions are usually made up of single officers. This is the whole scheme of the construction of an administration from top to bottom. To repeat, an administration is a hierarchy.

At about this stage the conditions are such that the administration may take a part in the organization. This is seen in the Employment of Clerks, 2 Compt. Dec. 173 (1895). This was an application for a construction of that portion of the act of March 2nd, 1895, providing for the preparation, printing and publication of bulletins for farmers. The question was whether the statutory roll of employee in the seed division of the Agricultural Department might be employed in mailing and

[46] BUREAU.—Masters' Clerk's Case, 1 Phillips, 650; Hydrometer Case, 6 Lawrence 128; Woods v. Gary, 25 Wash. L. R. 591; People v. Auditor, 2 Colo. 97; Baker v. Kirk, 33 Ind. 517; People v. Woodruff, 32 N. Y. 355.

addressing these bulletins; and whether the chief of that division might be legally so employed.

The Comptroller, BOWLER, ruled that this might be done: The appropriation contained in the act provides for a chief and certain clerks and employees of the division of seeds, a sufficient sum being appropriated to pay their salaries. Under this appropriation the appointment and retention of this chief and these clerks and employees is authorized for the current fiscal year. And the method of their employment rests wholly within your executive discretion.

When this stage in administration is reached the principle upon which organization shall be based is not so apparent. If there is a variety of work to be done the organization proceeds as before along the most useful line of co-operation for that case—specialization. If, however, there is much work to be done of the same sort, the organization proceeds along the most useful lines of co-operation for that case—division. An example of each of these forms of the separation of division in a bureau will make this situation plain.

The most extreme form of organization upon the basis of specialization is seen in the Patent Office. The divisions there by their numbers are as follows: 1, Tillage; 2, farm; 3, metallurgy; 4, engineering; 5, finance; 6, chemistry; 7, games; 8, furniture; 9, hydraulics; 10, wagons; 11, boots; 12, mechanics; 13, arms; 14, apparatus; 15, paper; 16, telegraph; 17, printing; 18, steam; 19, furnaces; 20, hardware; 21, textiles; 22, navigation; 23 instruments; 24, machine; 25, mills; 26, electricity; 27, brushes; 28, pneumatics; 29, turning; 30, lamps; 31, gas; 32, advertising. The purpose in this organization is apparent.

On the other hand, the most extreme form of the organization for division upon the basis of simple distribution is seen in the adjudicating offices of the Pension Bureau. There the division is outright according to the locality from which the applications come. The different states in the United States are distributed into four classes: 1, Eastern; 2, Middle; 3, Western; 4, Southern. The necessity of this is obvious. There is so much work of the same sort to do that it can be disposed of only by simple division. The principal reason in the creation of these separate divisions is so that there may be more immediate superintendence.[47]

§ 61. Conclusion.

The object in the construction of so elaborate a hierarchy must be plain. It is to create the possibility for precise action by the officers detailed to do the final act. This is brought about by the two methods of division upon the lines of specialization. And it is to create the conditions for effective superintendence that chiefs are put over chiefs in this way. In fine, both co-ordination of officers upon the same plane and subordination of officers upon different grades are the chief principles in the law governing the organization of the administration.

[47] DIVISION.—Departmental Clerks, 21 Opin. 355; Departmental Clerks, 1 Comp. Dec. 4; State v. Feibleman, 28 Ark. 424; Denver v. Dean, 10 Colo. 375; State v. Mayne, 68 Ind. 285; State v. Bloxham, 33 Fla. 482; Lewis v. Wall, 70 Ga. 646; Abry v. Gray, 58 Kan. 149; Newman v. Elam, 30 Miss. 507.

CHAPTER VIII.

THE THEORY OF ADMINISTRATION.

§ 62. Introduction.

There are two systems of administration: first, centralized administration, and second, decentralized administration. In centralized administration there is central direction; in decentralized administration there is no central direction; while in centralized administration there is one head, in decentralized administration there are various heads. Indeed, in centralized administration all the functions of administration are conceived of as in the head of the administration and everything is held to be done under his direction; so that in a centralized system every officer is inferior to some officer and superior to some other officer in turn. Whereas, in a decentralized administration the conception is that each officer has his own functions vested in him, and that in consequence everything is held to be done of his own motion. It results that in a decentralized system all officers are equal and in the exercise of their functions each is independent. Interdependence is the theory of centralism, on the other hand.

This statement is too much of an abstraction, perhaps, to meet actual conditions in government. No administration exists which is complete in its centralism, still less is any administration known which is absolute in its decentralism. It is plain that no administration could act which was so integrated that there was no discretion in any of its members; it is equally clear that no administration could act which was so disintegrated that every officer had unregulated discretion. In the actual business of government, order carried to the extreme of rigidity and disorder carried to the extreme of confusion would alike stop administration. There must not therefore be too much insistence upon logic in the use of either theory; either system has good effect when qualified to a certain extent by the employment of the other. Therefore, the effort should be to discover in a particular governmental unit what form of administration is best adapted, and to make that the principal form. In the working out of that system, however, much use should be made of the alternative form to fill in the detail. As in most theories of government the best results often will be obtained by a compromise position.

Examples of the two divergent principal types of administration may be found in the United States in two positions of equal prominence in the government; since the Federal government has centralized administration, and the state governments have decentralized administration. Examples, too, of the qualification of one type used as principal, and the other type used as auxiliary, may be found in all governments of the United States.

In the Federal administration, that is true,—the administration is centralized with the President as the head; and yet throughout various functions its officers have discretion. In the state administrations, that is true, also,—the administration is decentralized, the Governor has certain functions, so has each head of each department, so that the Governor is not the head, but there are these various heads; and yet throughout, within the various departments themselves, there is centralized organization. With this preface the attempt in this chapter will be to show the processes of administration in the centralized Federal administration, and by contrast in the decentralized state administrations; and at the same time to expose the decentralism in the one and the centralism in the other.

§ 63. Centralized administration.

It has been pointed out in the introductory paragraph that in a centralized administration the conception is that all powers of administration have been vested in the head of the executive department and that all officers act under his direction. At the outset it must be admitted that the President could not perform in person all this function. Neither could any head of department perform in person all that the President intrusts to him of the business of execution. Centralized administration must of necessity be a matter of devolution of powers of superior upon inferior. The legal question involved in this preliminary inquiry is how far powers which have been vested in a superior may be delegated to an inferior. One recognizes that this is a fundamental question, that the discussion of centralized administration cannot proceed until this is determined.

This was the issue in Runkle v. United States, 122 U. S. 543 (1887). In a suit brought in the Court of Claims by Major Runkle for back pay, the decision turned upon this: whether he had been dismissed from the army by due sentence of court martial, which was the defense of the United States. The conviction, findings, and sentence of the court martial were offered in proof; thereupon the objection was made that no action by the President confirming the sentence had been shown, as was required by the 65th Article of War; after which it was shown that the Secretary of War had approved the findings.

Mr. Chief Justice FULLER put a strict construction upon this article: As the sentence under consideration involved the dismissal of Runkle from the army, it could not become operative until approved by the President, after the whole proceedings had been laid before him. The important question is therefore whether that approval has been positively shown. There can be no doubt that the President, in the exercise of his executive powers under the constitution, may act through the head of the appropriate executive department. The heads of the departments are his authorized assistants in the performance of his executive duties, and their official acts, promulgated in the regular course of business, are presumptively his acts. That has been many times decided by the court. Here, however, the action required of the President is judicial in its character, not administrative. As Commander-in-Chief of the army, he has been made by law the person whose duty it is to review the proceedings of courts martial in cases of this kind. This implies that he is himself to consider the proceedings laid before him, and decide personally whether they ought to be carried into effect. Such a power he cannot delegate. His personal judgment is required—as much so as it would have been in passing upon the case, if he had been one of the members of the court martial itself. He may call others to his assistance in making his examination, and in informing himself what ought to be done, but his judgment when pronounced must be his own judgment and not that of another.

That this case is sound in its special facts, it cannot be doubted; and yet, obviously, the rule of this case must be of very limited application. The most of administration must go on by delegation, and this opinion, read with attention, if a proper discrimination is made, is not in the way of that need.

Whether this ruling represents the general law governing administration may well be doubted. At all events it cannot be used to contradict or to qualify the leading case—Williams v. United States, 1 How. 290 (1843). This was an action by the United States against the sureties of a marshal in which certain defaults by the marshal were set forth, among them failure to account for money advanced him by the United States. It appeared in the report that the money was advanced at a time when a statute was in force which prohibited the advance of public money in any case whatsoever to the disbursing officers of government except under special direction by the President. It was proved that the money was advanced in this case under special warrant from the Secretary of the Treasury, who had been authorized in writing by the President to make such advances from time to time to various classes of the disbursing officers of the government as should be found necessary to the prompt discharge of their respective duties. The contention for the sureties upon these facts were that the advances were not made in accordance with law.

The opinion of Mr. Justice DANIELL shows a full appreciation of the problem: It is insisted upon as the correct interpretation of this statute that the power thereby vested to make advances for the public service is not one appertaining to the office of President, but is an authority strictly personal and ministerial, to be exercised in every instance only by the individual himself, by his own hand, and never in any respect to be delegated. Such an interpretation of the law this court can by no means admit; it would render the government an absolutely impracticable machine. The President's duty in general requires his superintendence of the administration; yet this duty cannot require of him to become the administrative officer of every department and bureau, or to perform in person the numerous details incident to services, which, nevertheless, he is in a correct sense by the constitution and laws required and expected to perform. This cannot be, because if it were practicable, it would be to absorb the duties and responsibilities of the various departments of the government in the personal action of one chief executive officer. It cannot be for the stronger reason that it is impracticable; nay, impossible.

In most matters of administration, then, delegation must be the rule of action. An extreme case of this is that of the assistant to the head of a department. It is well decided that he may act in the stead of his chief in matters of administration with all powers that the chief would have. A brief ruling to this effect is Hisey v. Peters, 1896, Pat. Dec. 22 (1895). Hisey's appeal from the primary examiner in the Patent Office denying his motion to dissolve the above-entitled interference was assigned by the Commissioner to the Assistant Commissioner for hearing and determination, and upon such hearing both parties appeared before the Assistant Commissioner and were heard. On the 26th day of January, 1895, the Assistant Commissioner rendered his decision, dismissing the appeal upon the ground that the question thereby raised was a question touching the merits, and upon which the appeal lay in the first instance to the Board of Examiners in Chief. Thereupon by a motion the authority of the Assistant Commissioner to hear and determine any quasi judicial question was challenged. It was claimed that the Commissioner could not assign to the Assistant Commissioner duties of that character.

But SEYMOUR, the Commissioner, ruled: That the Assistant Commissioner, under such an assignment, had authority to hear and determine the said appeal; and that his determination was therefore the legal determination thereof. So that the motion to rehear the appeal was denied. And, indeed, no other decision would be possible; it would be a singular doctrine and subversive of the purposes for which these offices of Assistants have been created, if their acts were to be held of no force until ratified by the head. It is to relieve the overburdened principal of performance in person of a part of his duties that this office is established. If no virtue attached to the acts of this assistant until approved by the head, any inferior clerk would answer the purpose as well. It is not intended to deny that the assistant is the subordinate of the chief; can be ordered to do or not to do particular things; and can be reversed or set aside. But until so revoked or disapproved the action of the assistant stands as action of the chief.

The converse of this last case would be that no inferior can exercise by delegation any power that his superior could not exercise himself. It must be self-evident in this class of cases; so obvious, that it is all but impossible to discern a case for it. An obscure circular is all that is at hand that is in point—Power of Officers to Administer Oaths, Treas. Dec. No. 8741 (1888). It appears from this that the Solicitor of the Treasury gave an opinion under date of February 9, 1888, that an auditor or clerk in the Customs Service appointed as Deputy Collector could administer only such oaths as the Collector himself had authority to administer; and that as the Collector had no authority by law to administer oaths generally, the auditor in his position of Deputy Collector could assume no authority to administer oaths generally in matters of the Customs Service. All of which is axiomatic; but it is well at times to return to first principles. And surely these are the elements of administration by devolution of powers that the superior acts by his inferior, and the inferior acts from his superior—no more, no less, in either case. This is the first situation to ascertain and determine in any study of centralized administration.[48]

[48] CENTRALIZED ADMINISTRATION.—Martin v. Mott, 12 Wheat. 31; Williams v. United States, 1 How. 290; Runkle v. United States, 122 U. S. 543; Cheatham v. Phillips, 23 Ark. 80; Joyce v. Joyce, 5 Cal. 449; Ely v. Parsons, 55 Conn. 83; Young v. Blackhawk Co., 66 Ia. 460; Jackson Co. Sup'rs v. Brush, 77 Ill. 59; Triplett v. Gill, 7 J. J.

§ 64. Interdependence.

Much light is thrown upon devolution by an opinion upon the Relation of the President to the Executive Departments, 7 Opin. 453 (1855). The President asked the opinion of the Attorney-General upon the following question: Are instructions issued by the heads of department to officers, civil and military, within their respective jurisdictions, valid and lawful without containing express reference to the direction of the President; and is or not such authority implied in any order issued by the competent department? The Attorney-General, CUSHING, returned a long statement; in the course of it he set forth with elaboration the relation of the President to the heads of the departments. This is the first full discussion of the centralism which is the characteristic of the federal administration:

By the explicit language of the constitution the executive power is vested in the President of the United States. In perception, however, of the fact that the actual administration of all executive power cannot be performed personally by one man—that this would be impossible, and that if it were attempted by the President, the utmost ability of that one man would be consumed in official details, instead of being left free to the duty of general direction and supervision,—in perception, I say, of this fact, the constitution provides for the sub-divi-

Marsh. 432; State v. Shaw, 64 Me. 263; Watson v. Watson, 58 Md. 442; Commonwealth v. Smith, 143 Mass. 169; Hall v. Collins, 117 Mich. 617; Monette v. Cratt, 7 Minn. 234; Neill v. Gates, 152 Mo. 588; Pfund v. Valley L. & T. Co., 52 Neb. 473; State v. Paterson, 34 N. J. L. 163; Birdsall v. Clark, 73 N. Y. 73; Covington v. Rockingham, 93 N. C. 134; Anderson's Lessee v. Brown, 9 Ohio 151; Coffee v Tucker, 7 Humph. 49; Caldwell v. Bush, 6 Wyo. 352.

sion of the executive powers vested in the President among administrative departments. In the organization of each department in turn it was provided that the head thereof should discharge his administrative duties in such manner as the President should direct, being in effect the executors of the will of the President. It could not as a general rule be otherwise because in the President is the executive power vested by the constitution, and also because the constitution commands that he shall take care that the laws be faithfully executed; thus making him not only the depository of the executive power, but the sole responsible executive minister of the United States. In a word, there is a general solidarity of responsibility for public measures as between the President and the heads of departments of direction to the President and of execution to the heads of department.

Another brief opinion that is the complement of this last opinion is Decisions of Heads of Departments Binding upon Subordinates, 5 Opin. 87 (1849), which reads as follows: The opinion of the Secretary of Interior, directing the claim of H. Lassell for two thousand two hundred and twenty-four dollars and ninety-five cents, against the Miami nation of Indians, to be paid, is, in my judgment, binding upon all the subordinate officers by whom the account is to be audited and passed. This has been the practice of the government from its origin and is well authorized by the laws organizing the departments as it is absolutely necessary to the proper operation of the government. I deem the point so clear that I feel it to be unnecessary to refer to opinions upon the question given at different times by this office. This completes the description of centralism in the federal administration—it is the rule throughout.

As a matter of practical government the performance of centralized administration seems prodigious. The secret of the success is system. System—in the subordination of officers inferior to superior; system—in the co-ordination of officers of the same grade for division of labor. The subordination is necessary so that all may be overseen from step to step. The result in administration is the possibility of immediate action. Whatever any superior wishes done, he may command it done with definiteness by the most remote inferior. Matters of routine are done at the bottom; only where they involve extraordinary action are they referred to the top; and yet in each case the theory is preserved that all action proceeds from the top. The matters of routine are done by every officer of the same grade in co-ordination. The principle is well understood that ten men properly co-ordinated upon lines of exact specialization or precise division can do the work of fifty acting as separate individuals. The effectiveness of a centralized administration is therefore no untested theory; it is a demonstrated fact.[49]

§ 65. Superior.

Centralism granted, various consequences follow. It is worth while now to look into the processes of admin-

[49] INTERDEPENDENCE.—Snyder v. Sickles, 98 U. S. 211; Catholic Bishop v. Gibbon, 158 U. S. 167; Parsons v. Venzke, 164 U. S. 89; Carter v. Ruddy, 166 U. S. 493; Dart's Case, 11 Opin. 109; Hooper v. Ferguson, 2 Land Dec. 712; In re Hull, 1869 Pat. Dec. 68; In re Hamilton, 2 Pen. Dec. 217; Fees of Clerks of Courts, 7 Comp. Dec. 814; Proceedings in rem, etc., Treas. Dec. No. 11,942; Real Estate, 3 Int. Rev. Rec. 37.

istration to see what these consequences are. The matter of the pension of one Miller produced two most instructive cases. The first is Miller v. Black, 128 U. S. 50 (1888). Miller, the relator, having made an unsuccessful application to the Commissioner of Pensions for an increase of his pension, finally appealed to the Secretary of Interior; it was decided that Miller came within the laws granting a special rating to those persons who require special aid and attendance; and accordingly the Secretary sent down a memorandum overruling the decision of the Commissioner. The petition for mandamus complained that the Commissioner refused to perform his duty in the premises to carry into effect the official decision of the Secretary.

Mr. Justice BRADLEY gave this opinion upon this case: If, as the petition suggests, the Commissioner of Pensions refuses to carry out the decision of his superior officer, there would seem to be prima facie ground for at least calling upon him to show cause why a mandamus should not issue. This is all that the petitioner asked, and this the court below refused. As a general rule, when a superior tribunal has rendered a decision binding upon an inferior, it becomes the ministerial duty of the latter to obey it and carry it out. So far as respects the matters decided, there is no discretion or exercise of judgment left. The appellate tribunal in the present case is the Secretary of the Interior, who has no power to enforce his decision by mandamus, or by any process of like nature; and, therefore, a resort to a judicial tribunal would seem to be necessary in order to afford a remedy to the party by the refusal of the Commissioner to carry out his decision. But it is suggested that a removal of the contumacious subordinate from office or a civil suit brought against him for damages would be effectual remedies. We do not concur in this view. We think that the case suggested is one in which it would be proper for the court to interfere on mandamus.

The second case is United States v. Raum, 135 U. S. 200 (1890). In pursuance of this decision in Miller v. Black, the rule was granted to show cause why the mandamus should not issue. The Commissioner thereupon filed an answer, by which he claimed, among other things, that his official action in the rating of pensions is not subject to review by the courts, since the determination of that question has been left to his discretion; that there is no specific provision in any statute providing any set rate of pension, in case of disability such as that of the plaintiff; that he has carried out the decision of the Secretary of Interior rendered in his case by placing the petitioner within the class designated by that decision; but that he has fixed the rate in accordance with his own practice in such cases.

Mr. Justice Bradley again delivered the opinion: Without assuming to decide whether the construction given by the Commissioner to the act was right or wrong, the question which we are to consider is whether, in adopting the construction he did and acting upon it, he disregarded and disobeyed the decision of the Secretary of the Interior. In Miller v. Black, 128 U. S. 50, it is held that when a subordinate officer is overruled by his superior having appellate jurisdiction over him, his duty to obey the decision of such superior is a ministerial duty, which he can be compelled by mandamus to perform. In that case the relator was the same person as in the present; but the record was very meagre, and did not set forth all the facts. With the additional facts before us, which are now presented by these documents, in connection with the answer of the Commissioner, we are satisfied that there was no failure to comply with or to carry out the decision of the Secretary. Whatever may have been the ground upon which the Commissioner based his conclusion, it is clear that the decision of the Secretary left the matter open; that he only decided that the relator came under the meaning of the law granting pensions to those who require regular aid and attendance; and that the Commissioner acquiesced in this decision and rated the pension at $50 upon that basis.

These two decisions taken together show what the law of administration is in a very striking manner. In these decisions the course of things in administration is described in a very exact manner. Where a superior officer has a discretionary power, any action by him in pursuance of that power may create a duty for his inferior officer of such nature as he may designate in his order. If by this process a superior officer lays an explicit command upon his inferior officer, the result is that the inferior officer is now under a ministerial duty which he must perform according to the tenor of the command. This in a simple case is the working out of administration. The usual processes of administration are more complicated, because one such step is added to another such step For example, the head of a department gives a general order to the chief of a bureau; the result is that it is the ministerial duty of the chief of bureau to act, but what action he shall take is within the discretionary power allowed to him by this general order. He in turn gives a special order to the chief of some division; the same process recurs; it is the ministerial duty of the chief of division to act, but what directions he shall give are within his discretion. The last step is the designation of the chief of division of some special clerk to do some special act; here at last the duty is ministerial, the clerk must do that act. In brief, this is the process of administration, the continuous process of the action of a superior creating duties for an inferior.[50]

§ 66. Inferior.

If this description is correct, anything that is contrary to this in principle cannot stand in any administration which is constructed upon the theory of centralism. The opposite of all this would be to conceive of a state of the law where the action of some inferior with some discretion concluded matters and created thereby ministerial duties for the superior to perfect that action. This would be an inversion indeed. And yet this is no supposititious case. Again and again, it has been urged in various cases upon various facts that the action of some subordinate had made the matter res adjudicata. It is well, therefore, to be prepared for such a contention.

A leading case in this phase of the question is Orchard v. Alexander, 157 U. S. 372 (1895). This case arose out of a competition for a tract of government land in Washington State. The plaintiff was first in the field; on December 20, 1880, he filed his declaratory statement

[50] SUPERIOR.—United States v. Black, 128 U. S. 40; United States v. Raum, 135 U. S. 200; Las Animas Grant, 15 Opin. 94; Fowler v. Dodge, 1898 Pat. Dec. 257; Law & Prac. of Reimbursement, 6 Pen. Dec. 297; Revision of Accounts, 4 Comp. Dec. 723; Pueblo Case, 5 Land Dec. 483.

as required by the Land Laws, and on March 12, 1883, he made his final proof to the register and receiver of the Local Land Office, together with his payment, all of which was duly approved by the local officials in accordance with law. The defendant came into the controversy at this stage; on August 7, 1883, he filed in the office of the Commissioner of the General Land Office his corroborated affidavit, in which he alleged that the plaintiff had at no time taken up residence upon the land, so that all his entry was void; the Land Bureau, upon due proceedings had upon the merits of this contested case, gave decision for the defendant. Thereupon the plaintiff brought this ejectment in the state courts upon the ground that his right had vested by the decision of the local officers at the outset; and that therefore it was beyond the power of the department.

Mr. Justice BREWER delivered an able opinion: All powers of the local officers ceased to be final when the general power of review and supervision of all executive duty concerning the survey and sales of lands was vested in the higher officials of the Land Department at Washington. Stress is laid upon the words "executive duties" as though the approval of the evidence of settlement and improvement was not an executive duty but a purely judicial act. This is a mistake. True, it involves the weighing of testimony and the exercise of judgment, but equally so do many administrative acts. The approval of the evidence offered in respect to settlement and improvement is only quasi judicial. It is as much an administrative as a judicial act. It is only one step in the procedure by which through an executive department the title to public land is obtained by an individual. Great inequalities in the administration of the Land Department of the United States would inevitably ensue if the final determination of matters connected with the sale and disposal of the public lands were left to a multitude of local land officers. Obviously, in order that equal justice might be administered, it was necessary that there should be a superintendence of all the actions of the local land officers and all the proceedings in the local land offices.

The most perspicuous thing that is said in this last opinion is that unless the supremacy of the head is admitted in all matters of administration there will not be uniform administration. The further down in administration one goes, the more obvious it is that this must be. The case of Hull v. Commissioner, 2 MacArthur, 90 (1875), was a motion for mandamus commanding the Commissioner of Patents to issue a patent to the relator, Hull. In the Patent Office there are three grades: the Primary Examiners, the Examiners-in-Chief, and the Commissioner. The application of Hull was rejected by the primary examiner but allowed by the Examiners-in-Chief. At the issue of the patent the Commissioner interfered. Hull claimed that it was the ministerial duty of the Commissioner to issue the patent.

The court was to the contrary: A favorable decision of the Board of Examiners in Chief in the Patent Office upon an application is not conclusive upon the Commissioner of Patents, and it does not follow that thereupon he has only the ministerial duty to perform of countersigning and sealing the patent; the interpretation contended for would turn the head of the office into the tail. I think all rights of appeal are omitted because it was unnecessary to confer it; for the Commissioner's supervisory powers over all acts of all subordinates in his office is such as to preclude any heed for such specification. The essential fact is that the grant of the patent is at last the act of the Commissioner, and he may refuse to grant it.

The perspicacity of these cases is to be remarked again. In each of these cases a duty is assigned by law to an inferior in a department, but it is assigned to him as an inferior in a department. Whatever power is given to an inferior under a superior is given as to an inferior under a superior. No action of an inferior in a centralized administration can be independent of a superior. Still less can any action of an inferior create a duty which a superior must perform. These things are contrary to centralized administration.

A consistent account of centralized administration can be made if it is said that every act of every officer is done under some other officer and every act of that officer under some other officer and so up from the many officers at the bottom to the one officer at the top. This is the hierarchy in a centralized administration which results from the systematic organization. And this is the process of administration in a centralized administration. At the top the powers of the chief should be regarded as all discretionary; at the bottom the duties of the officers should be regarded as all ministerial; in the grades between these the officer will have ministerial duties in his relations to his superior and discretionary powers in his relations to his inferiors.

It is by the interaction of these powers and duties that administration goes on.[51]

§ 67. Decentralized administration.

In centralized administration things run all one way, in decentralized administration things run all the other way. Decentralized administration is an inversion of centralized administration. As an abstract statement, in centralized administration no officer in the administration has independent powers, in decentralized administration every officer in the administration has independent powers; in centralized administration every officer is subordinate to some other officer, in decentralized administration no officer is subordinate to any other. These statements in themselves are enough to show that such a thing as an absolute decentralized administration would be unworkable. And in fact it does not anywhere exist in such an absolute form.

When it is said in the governments of the American states the administration is decentralized, it is meant that the characteristic thing in those administrations is decentralism. And so it is. In the state governments themselves, there is a governor, and there are the Secretary of State, the State Treasurer, and the others. These are separately elected by the people; the heads of departments do not owe their position to the Governor in any way, therefore. The result is in the state ad-

51 INFERIOR.—Knight v. Land Ass'n, 142 U. S. 161; Orchard v. Alexander, 157 U. S. 372; Hull v. Commissioner, 2 MacArthur 90; Mississippi v. Durham, 4 Mackey 238; Relation of President to Executive Dept., 7 Opin. 453; In re Day, 3 Pen. Dec. 76; Advance Decisions, 5 Comp. Dec. 49: Power of Officers, Treas. Dec. No. 8,741; Mott of Coffman. 19 Land Dec. 106; In re Jones, 1874 Pat. Dec. 53.

ministration that the powers of the heads of the departments are their own, subject to the direction of no one else; the duties of the heads of the departments are their own subject to the direction of no one else. It is an inaccuracy to speak of the Governor of the state as the Chief of the Administration; the administration of the states has many heads.

There is no administrative relation between the Governor and the heads of the departments, therefore. If the Governor commands, the head of the department is under no obligation to obey whatever. Not only is this so in theory, it often is shown true in fact. There is, however, a legal relation between the Governor and the heads of the departments. Every officer in the state has by law certain rights and certain duties. That is true of the Governor; that is true of the head of the department. And this further is true: that there may be some legal interrelation between these rights and these duties. It may be that the exercise of some power by the Governor may, when the act is done, furnish the occasion for the performance of some duty by the head of the department. If that is so, that is a legal relation which the judicial courts may deal with.

It comes to this in a court of law: was the action of the Governor discretionary, and is the action required of the head thereby ministerial? If such be the case the propriety of the issue of mandamus by the courts appears in a most clear manner. State v. Wrotnowski, 17 La. Ann. 156 (1865). This was an application for a mandate ordering Wrotnowski, Secretary of State, to affix his official signature and the seal of his office to a commission signed by Wells, Governor of the State.

The Secretary in his return to the petition set forth that he refused to issue the commission because he regarded the action of the Governor illegal and void. The reason was that the office was then held by one Shaw, whose commission did not expire until the next regular election; and therefore he maintained that the Governor was without any authority to supersede the said Shaw. Matters thus at a deadlock, the court undertook to decide.

The opinion of ILSLEY is interesting reading: Divested of all extraneous, superfluous, and irrelevant surroundings, what is the real question to be solved? We apprehend it to be this: Is the Secretary of State a mere ministerial officer as regards the authorization by him of official acts; or is he, under the constitution and laws, vested with a discretionary and supervisory power which enables him, before executing the functions imposed upon him in this particular, to judge for himself whether such official acts as need his ministry are constitutional or not constitutional, legal or illegal, and to affix or withhold from such acts, at his option according to his discretion, his official signature, and the impress of the great seal of the state? It seems to us that the Secretary of State is not to suspend his action to inquire why and wherefore any appointment by the Governor is made. His duty is plain; he is not directed, but ordered by law to perform it. When commissions from the Governor need authentication he shall affix his official signature and the public seal of the state, for these are official acts of another which must be effectuated. Were this right of supervision, which is almost equivalent to a veto power, in the Secretary of State, as it is seriously contended that it is, it would indeed produce most startling consequences. The Secretary of State could paralyze at will all such constitutional action of the Governor. There is no argument why the Secretary of State should attempt to exercise discretionary powers where the law confers none on him, but on the contrary imperatively orders him to do the act required of him.

A case to the same effect well worth insertion here because of the clearness of its view is State v. Crawford, 28 Fla. 441 (1891). This case is remarkable at the outset in its parties, since the Governor of Florida was the relator and the Secretary of State was the defendant. The Governor had appointed one Davidson United States Senator as an interim appointment, and the Secretary of State had refused to seal and countersign the commission. The Governor prayed the writ to carry into effect his executive act by a direction of the court to the Secretary to countersign the same. Here there is an unusual situation of things, the executive as executive obliged to proceed to the courts to get his acts performed—a situation possible only in a decentralized administration; for as will be shown in a later chapter, in a centralized administration there would be administrative process to compel.

The opinion of RANEY, then Chief Justice, leaves nothing to doubt: That the writ of mandamus lies to require the performance of a clear official duty involving discretion, by any one of the administrative officers of the executive department of this state is a settled proposition of the law. To hold that the mere fact of these officers belonging to the executive department of the government should exempt them from this judicial process as to a plain ministerial duty or where they are given no official discretion, would be irreconcilable antagonism to a consistent line of judgments. The writ effectually secures the performance of public official duty and the establishment of public right. It is the character of the duty, and not of the nature of the office, which must, as long as the law is regarded, always control a court in deciding whether or not it will issue a mandamus against the defendant. The duty devolved upon the Secretary in this case before us is purely ministerial; and it involves no discretion.

This legal relation enforced by the courts makes decentralized administration possible, for it imposes a certain order upon the course of action in administration without which there would be such disorder that the business of administration would come to a stop often. It is a rougher method than the administrative relation enforced by the executive, but it is tolerable. The same solution governs in what relations the departments must have each with the other. There is no central administrative control to accommodate their differences, but there is the legal control of the courts to break any deadlock which might result if such stood upon its inherent independence in its relations toward the other.

Within the departments themselves the centralized system is almost invariable. Administration in general may go on with a decentralized administration; but administration in particular is not possible with any effect except by centralized administration. There are within most of the departments in state administration centralized organizations. And in municipal government the present fashion in the charters based upon the experience of failure of the decentralized forms, is to make the administration centralized throughout, as the only hope for proper enforcement of the law.[52]

§ 68. Independence.

In the last paragraph examples of centralism in decentralism were seen. In the present paragraph examples of decentralism in centralism will be seen. The case supposed is that an officer in a centralized administration has a power vested in him by law, in the exercise of which he has discretion by the external law of administration. Has he, therefore, independence by the internal law governing administration? This is the issue between centralism and decentralism in a most difficult form. For the independence of the inferior officer it may be said that this duty has been vested in him by the assignment of the legislature; it is his duty, therefore the discretion must be his; it is his discretion, therefore no other officer can control in it. For the dependence of the inferior officer it may be said that every one of his duties he must perform under the direction of his superior; since he is an inferior officer, he is subordinate in whatever may be given to him to do; and as an inferior he must in all matters obey his superior. To choose between these balanced arguments will require a careful investigation.

Butterworth v. Hoe, 112 U. S. 50 (1884), is one of

[52] DECENTRALIZED ADMINISTRATION.—State v. Crawford, 28 Fla. 441; Shaw v. Macon, 21 Ga. 280; State v. Welsh, 109 Ia. 19; McMaster v. Herald, 56 Kan. 231; State v. Wrotnowski, 17 La. Ann. 156; Albrecht v. Long, 27 Minn. 81; Minkler v. State, 14 Neb. 181; People v. Mace, 84 Hun, 344; Davis v. State, 35 Tex. 118; State v. McCarty, 65 Wis. 163.

the most perplexing cases in American administrative law. The facts upon which this controversy arose are shown by the record to have been as follows: In 1881, Gill, one of the relators, made application to the Commissioner of Patents, the defendant, for letters patent. An interference was declared with an unexpired patent of one Scott. The Examiner of Interferences decided in favor of Scott; Gill appealed to the Examiners-in-Chief, but the decision was affirmed; Gill then appealed to the Commissioner of Patents, who adjudged that the patent showed issue; and thereupon an appeal was taken by Scott to the Secretary of Interior; and at that last stage the decision was for Scott. Gill now asked for a mandamus to the Commissioner of Patents to compel him to issue the patent in pursuance with his own decision. The Secretary in his return based his refusal solely upon the reversal of that decision by his superior, the Secretary of Interior, whom he felt bound to obey.

In a case of such moment, it is well to examine the opinion with the care which the occasion deserves. Mr. Justice MATTHEWS said: Mandamus evidently will not lie to compel an officer to do a thing which his superior in authority has lawfully ordered him not to do. The direct and immediate question then is whether the Secretary of Interior had power by law to revise and reverse the action of the Commissioner of Patents in awarding to Gill priority of invention, and adjudging him entitled to a patent. The authority and power claimed for the Secretary of Interior are asserted and maintained upon these general grounds: that he is the head of the department of which the Patent Office is a bureau; that the Secretary is by various statutes charged with supervision over the commissioner; that this general relation of official subordination, with the accompanying powers of supervision and direction, extends to all the official acts of the commissioner, without regard to any distinction between those which are merely ministerial and those which are judicial in their nature.

Such supervision and direction may be exerted at any stage of a proceeding in the discretion of the Secretary, whether in advance, or during its progress, or after its termination, and embraces, therefore, the mode of appeal, though no appeal in express terms is actually given. If the Secretary is charged by law with judicial supervision, he is bound to fulfill it. It is imperative, not discretionary. He cannot discharge it in a manner either arbitrary or perfunctory. He cannot satisfy it by rules or directions for superintendence and general oversight to secure conformity only. It is a maxim of the law, admitting few, if any exceptions, that every duty laid upon a public officer, for the benefit of a private person, is enforceable by judicial process. Thus in the Patent Office there is claimed equal right of all parties to obtain his review of the acts of the Commissioner, not only in final judgment but upon all interlocutory questions.

Congress has on the contrary provided four tribunals for hearing applications for patents, with three successful appeals in which the Secretary of the Interior is not included, giving jurisdiction in appeals from the Commissioner to a judicial body. The conclusion cannot be resisted that to whatever else supervision and direction on the part of the head of a department may extend, they do not extend to a review of the acts of a Commissioner of Patents in those things in which, by law, he is bound to exercise his discretion judicially. It is not consistent with the idea of judicial action that it should be subject to the direction of a superior in the sense that authority is conferred upon the head of an executive department in reference to his subordinates. Such objection takes from it the quality of a judicial act. That it was intended that the Commissioner of Patents in issuing or withholding patents, in re-issues, interferences and extensions, should exercise quasi judicial functions, is apparent from the nature of the examinations and decisions he is required to make and the mode provided by law, according to which exclusively they may be reviewed. We think further that mandamus will lie, and it is properly directed to the Commissioner of Patents. We have adjudged that it belongs exclusively to the Commissioner to decide the question for himself whether a patent ought to be issued.

An accurate presentation of what is in effect decided by this last case is to be found in Houston v. Barker et al., 1888, Pat. Dec. 173 (1888). It appeared that in the course of a trial in the Patent Office of an interference proceeding in the case of Houston v. Barker v. Bannister v. Eastman, a motion was made by counsel for Eastman and Bannister to suppress or strike out the deposition of one of Barker's witnesses on the alleged ground that said witness, while testifying, had, under the advice or instruction of Barker's counsel, refused to answer certain questions propounded to him on cross-examination. The Commissioner granted the motion; and it is from his action in so doing that Barker appealed to the Secretary. The respondent at the outset denied the appellate jurisdiction of the Secretary.

An Assistant Attorney General, MONTGOMERY, advised the Secretary of Interior as follows upon the question of the appellate jurisdiction of the Secretary over the Commissioner of Patents: The Commissioner of Patents has two classes of duties to perform, to wit: Duties imposed by Congressional legislation, and duties imposed by Departmental rules and regulations emanating from or authorized by the Secretary of Interior as the head of the department of which the Patent Office is a part. When performing that class of judicial or quasi judicial duties which by an act of Congress have been imposed upon the Commissioner of Patents it seems to be well settled that no appeal lies from the Commissioner of Patents to the Secretary of Interior. But where it is not Congress but the Secretary of Interior who in the exercise of his legitimate authority as the head of the department prescribes rules and regulations for the government of the Commissioner of Patents and his subordinates, I think there can be no question but that he has jurisdiction to review and reverse the action of the said Commissioner whenever the latter disregards or violates any of the rules thus legally prescribed by the Secretary for his government. In the present case the action was judicial and therefore no appeal lies.

It must be admitted that this is the law of the administration of patents. The situation is that of a decentralized bureau in a department which in other respects is centralized. The position of things is made altogether abnormal by the provision that there shall be a direct appeal from the bureau to the courts of the District of Columbia. This subordination of the administration to the judiciary in this instance is altogether contrary to the rule requiring separation of powers, as was pointed out in this very situation in a previous chapter. The result is this monster in the administration. This situation in the bureau of the Department of Interior is altogether an exception. It is discussed here so that the full force of the argument that the inferior officer should be independent when a power is given him by law may be seen at the outset.[53]

§ 69. Lower.

As a matter of argument there is about as much to be said for the position that when a power is vested in an inferior officer he has entire independence in its exercise as there is to be said for the position that when a power is vested in an inferior officer by a statute his superior may direct him in its exercise. And yet that former view discussed in the last paragraph is the rule for only a few bureaux; in the federal administration as a whole the rule of the present paragraph governs. The truth is that the solution of this problem has been by events rather than by arguments, by power rather than logic. In an administration which is centralized by its organization it is not possible for the head of a single department to stand out against the chief

[53] INDEPENDENCE.—Marbury v. Madison, 1 Cranch 169; Butterworth v. United States, 112 U. S. 50; State v. Hixon, 27 Ark. 402; People v. Mizner, 7 Cal. 519; Trimble v. People, 19 Colo. 187; Queen v. Atlanta, 59 Ga. 318; Todd v. Dunlap, 99 Ky. 449; Dubuc v. Voss, 10 La. Ann. 210; Andrews v. King, 77 Me. 224; People v. Roosevelt, 168 N. Y. 488; Keenan v. Perry, 24 Tex. 253.

executive, and argue for his independence to a certain extent upon certain matters for certain reasons. Right or wrong, in a presidential administration the head of the department, must obey if it comes to a square issue, from which neither will retreat in whatever matter of administration the issue may arise.

It never did come to such an issue until the reign of Jackson. At that epoch the first announcement of the doctrine of centralism in its entirety was set forth in an obscure opinion upon an unimportant matter—The Jewels of the Princess of Orange, 2 Opin. 482 (1831). These jewels, as has been related before, were stolen from the Princess by one Polari, and were seized by the officers of the United States Customs in the hands of the thief. Representations were made to the President of the United States by the Minister of the Netherlands of the facts in the matter, which were followed by request for return of the jewels. In the meantime the District Attorney was prosecuting condemnation proceedings in behalf of the United States which he showed no disposition to abandon. The President felt himself in a dilemma, whether if it was by statute the duty of the District Attorney to prosecute or not, the President could interfere and direct whether to proceed or not.

The opinion was written by TANEY, then Attorney-General; it is full of pertinent illustrations as to the necessity in an administration of full power in the chief executive as the concomitant of his full responsibility. It concludes: If it should be said that, the District Attorney having the power to discontinue the prosecution, there is no necessity for inferring a right in the

President to direct him to exercise it—I answer that the direction of the President is not required to communicate any new authority to the District Attorney, but to direct him in the execution of a power he is admitted to possess. The most valuable and proper measure may often be for the President to order the District Attorney to discontinue prosecution. The District Attorney might refuse to obey the President's order; and if he did refuse, the prosecution, while he remained in office, would still go on; because the President himself could give no order to the court or to the clerk to make any particular entry. He could only act through his subordinate officer the District Attorney, who is responsible to him and who holds his office at his pleasure. And if that officer still continue a prosecution which the President is satisfied ought not to continue, the removal of the disobedient officer and the substitution of one more worthy in his place would enable the President through him faithfully to execute the law. And it is for this among other reasons that the power of removing the District Attorney resides in the President. This opinion shows a comprehension of the general problem seldom equalled in any discussion of the nature of administration.

Moreover this opinion came at the psychological moment. President Jackson had just begun his war upon the United States Bank. As the law then stood the Secretary of the Treasury had the management of the funds of the government under the direction of Congress. Congress had just resolved that the deposits might with safety be continued in the Bank of the United States; Duane, the then Secretary of the Treasury, had informed the President that as he was unable to share the President's view he must continue the deposits upon his own responsibility. President Jackson immediately returned the letter to him as unbecoming in one of his position, curtly refused all further discussion, and asked him for a decisive answer to the question whether he would obey. Duane refused; whereupon Jackson sent him his dismissal. On the very same day, Jackson appointed Taney to be Secretary of the Treasury; and Taney gave the necessary order for the removal of the deposits without delay. Before the next Congress, Taney justified his action as within discretion vested in him by law, and his obedience as the duty owed by him to the President as the chief executive.

This account of these events is worth a hundred cases from the law reports. The President it appears has the power in all matters whatsoever to force any officer whatsoever to do any act which the officer has power to do. He can dictate in all matters, because he has the power of instant dismissal without giving reasons therefor, and thereupon the right of immediate appointment without limitation therein. And this is true to a greater or to a lesser extent of the power of every superior over every inferior at every step in the hierarchy of a centralized administration. Might makes right. Whatever the superior commands will be done by the inferior because of this sanction. An administration which is centralized in its organization will always prove to be centralized in its action. It cannot work out otherwise.[54]

[54] LOWER.—Smith v. Strobach, 50 Ala. 462; Danley v. Whiteley,

§ 70. Higher.

Since that day when Jackson removed the Secretary of the Treasury in order to effect the withdrawal of the deposits by the appointment of a new Secretary of the Treasury, no one has doubted but that the federal administration was centralized to every intent and purpose. But the argument that all that was done was in accordance with a proper theory of administration was not developed in a complete form until much later. Indeed, even today it is difficult to find precise cases in point which discuss the consequences of centralized administration.

The opinion upon the Memorial of Captain Meigs, 9 Opin. 462 (1860), marks a distinctive advance in the discussion. Congress in 1860 passed an appropriation act containing among other clauses an appropriation for the completion of the Washington aqueduct of five hundred thousand dollars, to be expended according to the plans and estimates of Captain Meigs, and under his superintendence. Captain Meigs in his memorial set forth that this appropriation was granted by Congress upon his assurance of its sufficiency and upon the express condition that it should be expended under his supervision. He added that the purpose of the grant was only on condition that its expenditure should be made under his effective control, guided by his experience, a high compliment to his ability. He then complained that by assignment of another officer to take an

14 Ark. 687; Turner v. Melony, 13 Cal. 621; State v. Gamble, 13 Fla. 9; Shaw v. Macon, 21 Ga. 280; State v. Lawrence, 3 Kan. 95; State v. Bourgeois, 47 La. Ann. 184; Magruder v. Swann, 25 Md. 173; State v. Secretary of State, 33 Mo. 293; People v. Schuyler, 79 N. Y. 189; Davis v. State, 35 Tex. 118.

important part in the superintendence of the work the War Department had permitted a clear evasion of the law, and a violation of the condition of the appropriation. Altogether this is a rather extraordinary document, as one sees.

The advice of Attorney General BLACK is without hesitation: As Commander-in-Chief of the army, it is your right to decide according to your own judgment what officers shall perform any particular duty, and as the supreme executive magistrate, you have power of appointment. Congress could not if it would take away from the President or in any way diminish the authority conferred upon him by the Constitution. This clause of the appropriation bill was not intended to appoint Captain Meigs as Chief Engineer of the aqueduct nor was it meant to interfere with your authority over him or any other of your military subordinates. But Captain Meigs now asserts that this which you believe to be a recommendation was in fact a condition, a most important part of the law itself. He thinks at all events that you must either let the appropriation be expended by him according to his own plan of operation, or else let the work stand still. But this is a manifest error. If Congress had really intended to make him independent of you, that purpose could not be accomplished in this indirect manner any more than if it were attempted directly. Congress is vested with legislative power; the authority of the President is executive. Neither has a right to interfere with the functions of the other. Indeed, this must be so; otherwise there would be two administrations: the administration of the President, and the administration of the Captain.

Another opinion, more useful because more definite, is that in the Las Animas Grant, 15 Opin. 94 (1876). One Colonel Craig applied to the President for an order directing the Surveyor General of Colorado to issue to him a parcel of land included in the Las Animas grant in accordance with the decision of the Register and Receiver General of the Land District of that territory. The question whether the executive should take any action upon this application was referred to the Attorney General, who found that Colonel Craig was entitled according to his petition. The only question left was whether the President had any function to interfere in such a case, even under these circumstances.

Attorney General PIERREPONT advised that the President had a certain function in all such appeals. This he defined in these terms: The case may be regarded as an appeal from a decision of the head of the Interior Department touching the authority of a subordinate officer in that Department; and the point now to be considered is, can the President entertain this appeal? After much reflection I am of opinion that the appeal is one which may be entertained by the President. It presents a question concerning the authority of a subordinate executive officer over a particular subject. The President in the exercise of his general superintendence may interfere to restrain an officer from assuming an authority which does not belong to him, as he unquestionably may to compel the officer to perform a duty which does belong to him. The functions of the President, viewed with reference to such superintendence, seem to me to include as well the power of requiring various officers of the executive department of the government to keep within the proper limits of their authority, as the power of requiring them to discharge the public trust imposed upon them.

The law on this point is somewhat elaborate; but it represents without doubt the present rule of administrative law upon this vexed subject. Without such a superintendence in the head of the administration there would be no centralism. At the same time, without order in the process by which the President is reached, all the business of administration might be thrown upon the President in first instance. The precise rule, then, in centralized administration is that if appeal is allowed it must go through the regular order of advancement from inferior to superior at every step in the administrative hierarchy.[55]

§ 71. Conclusion.

Centralism and decentralism are but modes of administration, after all. The methods used in administration are about the same in any administration of any sort. It is to these methods of administration to which attention is directed henceforward. It is without doubt impossible to make perfect distinctions in the varieties of administrative action; but the attempt will not be without advantage in gaining a near view of the administration at its work. Upon such a near view the methods are various. What arrests attention in such an examination is that the administration seems at one time or another to act as a complete governmental body in the enforcement of the law.

[55] HIGHER.—Chisholm v. McGehee, 41 Ala. 192; Hawkins v. Governor, 1 Ark. 570; Fremont v. Crippen, 10 Cal. 212; State v. Crawford, 28 Fla. 441; State v. Welsh, 109 Ia. 19; State v. Wrotnowski, 17 La. Ann. 156; People v. McClay, 2 Neb. 7; People v. Roosevelt, 168 N. Y. 488; State v. Staley, 38 Oh. St. 259; Commonwealth v. Perkins, 7 Pa. St. 42.

CHAPTER IX.

THE AUTHORITY OF THE ADMINISTRATION.

§ 72. Introduction.

The one central fact in the law governing administration is that the officer is an agent. That is the general situation. The state may be regarded as the principal in behalf of which the agent acts. The officer may be regarded, then, as the agent when he acts as an officer. To a certain extent, then, the law of agency is applicable to the processes of the administration. That indeed was remarked in the discussion of the theory of the administration. It is true, that this public agency is different from private agency; but in so far as there is a difference, it exists because of the policy in the situation.

§ 73. The state as principal.

In the eye of the law, when the officer acts in behalf of the state he is an official; when an officer acts in his own behalf, he is a person. In so far as an officer exercises public functions, the theory is he does so by order of the state as the agent of the state; in so far as the officer purports to exercise public functions, the theory is he does nothing unless he has the explicit authority of the state to fall back upon. That is, it is all a question of actual authority. If an officer has authority he acts in behalf of the state, not otherwise; if he has no authority he subjects the state to no liability.

The rule in private agency is that the agent may bind his principal within the scope of his authority—express or implied. Whether the whole of that rule is applicable to public agency is the question. It is in the nature of things that if an officer has express authority the state will be bound as his principal. But how if the officer has in fact no express authority? Can the parties who have dealt with him show that what he did seemed to be within his authority? This is not clear; there is a policy here for the protection of the state against liabilities which it has not expressly submitted itself to. This policy to a certain extent abrogates the rule of implied authority that is found in private agency. The problem for discussion in this chapter is how far the state will be made liable by the action of its officers. That involves an examination of the position of the state as a principal in relation to the position of the officer as an agent.[56]

[56] THE STATE AS PRINCIPAL.—Musgrave v. Pulido, 5 App. Cas. 102; O'Brien v. Reg., 4 Can. Sup. Ct. 529; Lee v. Munroe, 7 Cranch 366; Hawkins v. United States, 96 U. S. 691; Comer v. Bankhead, 70 Ala. 493; Fluty v. School District, 49 Ark. 94; Butler v. Bates, 7 Cal 136; State v. Hartford, 50 Conn. 89; Koones v. District of Columbia,

§ 74. Limitation.

The principle of law governing in public agencies that one is confronted with at this stage is somewhat startling. In Baltimore v. Eschbach, 18 Md. 276 (1861), that special rule is laid down in its most extreme form. Under the ordinances of the city of Baltimore the City Commissioner could make contracts for grading and paving and assess taxes therefor in two classes of cases: First upon the application of a majority of front feet where the street had been condemned; second upon the like application of all of the front feet where the street had not been condemned. A contractor made a contract with the City Commissioner for grading and paving a certain street. As a matter of fact the street had not been condemned, and only a majority of the front feet had applied. The city, upon that defense, now refused to pay for the work that had been done upon that contract.

The court by COCHRAN held the city not liable: The fact that the contract made, related to a subject within the scope of the powers of the Commissioner does

4 Mackey 339; Hawkins v. Mitchell, 34 Fla. 405; Penitentiary Co. v. Gordon, 85 Ga. 160; Van Dusen v. People, 78 Ill. 645; McCaslin v. State, 99 Ind. 428; Clark v. Des Moines, 19 Ia. 199; Commissioners v. Smith, 50 Kan. 350; Baltimore v. Eschbach, 18 Md. 276; Klein v. Pipes, 43 La. Ann. 359; Hubbard v. Woodsum, 87 Me. 88; Thomas v. Owens, 4 Md. 189; Vose v. Deane, 7 Mass. 280; Benalleck v. People, 31 Mich. 200; Sanborn v. Neal, 4 Minn. 126; State v. Hays, 52 Mo. 578; State v. Weston, 6 Neb. 16; Sargent v. Gilford, 66 N. H. 543; Dock Co. v. Trustees, 32 N. J. Eq. 434; McDonald v. New York, 68 N. Y. 23; Clodfelter v. State, 86 N. C. 51; State v. Hancock Co. Com'rs, 11 Oh. St. 183; Snow v. Deerfield, 78 Pa. St. 181; In re State House Fund, 19 R. I. 393; Morton v. Comptroller General, 4 S. C. 430; State v. Strickland, 3 Head, 644; Silliman v. Fredericksburg R. R., 27 Grat. 119; Boyers v. Crane, 1 W. Va. 176; State v. Hastings, 10 Wis. 525.

not make it obligatory upon the city, if there was want of specific power to make it. Although a private agent acting in violation of specific instructions, yet within the scope of general authority, may bind his principal, the rule as to the like act of a public agent is otherwise. The City Commissioner, upon whose determination to grade and pave, the contract was made, was the public agent of a municipal corporation clothed with powers and duties especially defined and limited by ordinances bearing the character and effect of public laws, ignorance of which can be presumed in favor of no one dealing with him. As this contract was entered into by the Commissioner on behalf of the city under circumstances which gave him no power to bind it, we think it cannot be held liable in any action.

This rule is stated repeatedly in this extreme form. No government can be estopped from denying the validity of unauthorized acts of its officers. Again, officers cannot dispense with a requirement of law by any waiver. Every person, it is the theory, is bound at his peril to know the extent of the authority of public officers. Contracts thus made without the authority of law are no more than void; and such void agreement is ineffectual to fix any liability upon the government. Just as much as a contract made by an officer in direct violation of a law is void, so a contract that is made in a way not authorized by law is held void. To a certain extent this is the law governing the authority of public officers—that they only have in effect such authority as they may show in fact. Another instance is Koones v. District of Columbia, 4 Mackey, 339 (1886). The appellant averred that on a certain day he paid the taxes which were due by him to the District of Columbia in a check for four hundred and ninety dollars on a bank in Washington, which bank was open on the day the check was delivered and on the next day. The third day, however, it suspended payment; and the Collector of Taxes, not having presented the check, it was claimed, therefore, by the complainant, that he should be credited with the amount of the check by reason of the default of the Collector in not presenting the check in due season, according to the mercantile law, for payment at that bank.

In disposing of this contention Mr. Justice MERRICK said: The doctrine which expands an agency by reason of the acts and dealings of the parties from time to time has no application whatsoever to the official acts of a public officer. Everybody knows the public law or is charged with knowledge of it; the extent of the powers of that officer and his superior officers so to speak cannot qualify except so far as the law has delegated to them a power to control or modify or expand his legal obligations. Hence, there can be no such thing as a presumption of agency growing out of the dealings of a public officer in respect to his public duties; because whatever presumption might arise in favor of a delegated authority from an outward act of dealing, so far as the public officer is concerned that presumption is repelled by the known law of the land, which known law of the land limits, defines and bounds his power, and qualifies and corrects any presumption of agency which might otherwise arise out of those facts and dealings. This is so because the authority of a public officer must be derived directly or indirectly from some law or other.[57]

§ 75. Implication.

In any question of interpretation, general legal notions must be used. The determination whether a certain action is or is not within the authority of a public agent depends to a large extent, therefore, upon the ordinary legal conception of the scope of a defined authority. The general principles of agency are of much use here because the problem in the large is the same both for public agencies and for private agencies. The difference of importance at this point between the law governing public agency and the law governing private agency is the one that was insisted upon at the outset. No implication can give an officer power to bind the state, but implication may give an agent power to bind his principal. However, the question as to the extent to which an express authority goes is a question of construction which is the same for both cases.

A distinction is to be taken at this point which is well brought out in Thompson's Case, 9 Ct. of Cl. 187 (1873). During the winter of 1864 the Quarter-Master's Department at Nashville, Tennessee, did not ad-

[57] LIMITATION.—Floyd Acceptances, 7 Wall. 666; Coler v. Cleburne, 131 U. S. 173; Fluty v. School District, 49 Ark. 94; Sutro v. Pettit, 74 Cal. 332; Mulnix v. Ins. Co., 23 Colo. 71; Koones v. District of Columbia, 4 Mackey, 339; Penitentiary Co. v. Gordon, 85 Ga. 160; Hull v. Marshall Co., 12 Ia. 142; Van Dusen v. People, 78 Ill. 645; Clark v. Des Moines, 19 Ia. 199; Baltimore v. Eschbach, 18 Md. 276; Murray v. Carothers, 1 Met. (Ky.) 71; Mitchell v. County Com'rs, 24 Minn. 459; State v. Hays, 52 Mo. 578; Lebscher v. Custer Co. Com'rs, 9 Mont. 315; Brumfield v. Douglas Co. Com'rs, 2 Nev. 65; Backman v. Charlestown, 42 N. H. 125; McDonald v. New York, 68 N. Y. 23; Sooy v. State, 39 N. J. L. 135; Day L. & C. Co. v. State, 68 Tex. 526.

vertise for proposals, but bought mules in the open market. The Chief Quarter-Master was in constant communication with the Commanding General, but no formal order was ever issued declaring that an emergency existed. According to statute then in force, there must be held a public letting of all contracts except in the case of actual exigency. The Quarter-Master's Department in this case had contracted for one thousand mules, of which two hundred had been delivered when the war came to an end. Thereupon, the United States refused to take the other eight hundred mules.

NOTT, Judge of the Court of Claims, held the United States liable: A contractor dealing with the government is chargeable with notice of all limitations of authority which the statutes place upon the powers of public officers. But there is a difference between those powers which are expressly defined by statute and those which rest upon the discretion confided by law to an officer. The distinction should be made between the case where a statute expressly defines the powers,—there it is notice to all the world; but where a statute confides a discretion to an officer, a party dealing with him in good faith may assume that the discretion is properly exercised. And if the discretion is vested in a superior officer, while the transaction is with his subordinate, the contractor may assume that the discretion in like manner has been properly exercised, and that the subordinate is acting in accordance with his superior's orders and carrying out the exercise of the superior's discretion.

An obvious case along this line is Myerle v. United States, 33 Ct. of Cl. 1 (1897). The claimant had entered into a contract with the Secretary of the Navy to do important work of construction. There were various modifications and changes from time to time. In the end, the part of the appropriation that had been assigned by the department to this part of the naval construction ran out. The contractor acted in good faith from first to last under the assumption that the Secretary of the Navy had due authorization of the law and without knowledge of any deficiency that had resulted from the changes in the appropriation. The issue was whether the United States was liable for the work that had been done, which could only be if the Secretary had authority.

The judgment of the Court of Claims was given by DAVIS: It appears that the contract, whether authorized at its inception or not, had been brought repeatedly to the attention of Congress; that that body had authorized payments to be made upon the contract, and that the Navy Department had made payments from time to time upon it. The work was done. The contract we hold was made by competent authority and was binding upon the parties. The services performed by this contractor were under general appropriations covering several vessels; he was not therefore chargeable with knowledge as to the Secretary's apportionment of the appropriation between him and other contractors for other vessels built from the same fund. It has been heretofore decided that persons contracting with the government for partial service under general appropriations are not bound to know the condition of the appropriation account at the treasury.

The extent of the authority of an officer then depends

upon the law which defines his authority. This law may be general or specific. If general, the authority of the officer is general; if special, the authority of the officer is special. That is, this law may give the officer discretionary powers, or it may impose upon the officer ministerial duties. If discretionary, the officer has actual authority to do in behalf of the state anything that is within the scope of that authority; if ministerial, the officer has no authority to do anything not within the scope of the authority. There is no difference in the law here. It is only a difference in fact. The whole problem, then, is the application by construction of the law giving the authority in any particular course of action.[58]

§ 76. Liability.

For the reasons discussed before, the government is not liable for torts done by officers in the course of employment. No government today, as has been shown, holds itself liable for the misfeasance of officers in the course of administration. It would be the ruin of the state if it held itself liable for failure in administration of any sort. A case which shows the extent to which this principle will go is Maxmilian v. The Mayor, 62 N. Y. 169 (1875). The plaintiff while attempting to enter a street car in the city of New York was struck and killed by an ambulance which was driven by an

[58] IMPLICATION.—Myerle v. United States, 33 Ct. of Cl. 1; Thompson's Case, 9 Ct. of Cl. 187; Barton v. Swepston, 44 Ark. 437; Harris v. Gibbins, 114 Cal. 418; Wright v. Nagle, 48 Ga. 367; State v. Haworth, 122 Ind. 467; Commissioners v. Smith, 50 Kan. 350; Backman v. Charlestown, 42 N. H. 125; Richmond Co. Sup'rs v. Ellis, 509 N. Y. 620; Silliman v. Fredericksburg R. R., 27 Grat. 119.

employee of the Commissioners of Public Charity. The evidence showed that the accident was caused by the negligence of the driver of the ambulance who was at the time engaged in the performance of his duties. The city denied liability, since the acts were all done in the execution of governmental functions.

Mr. Justice FOLGER held the city not liable,—he said in part: There are two kinds of duties which are imposed upon a municipal corporation; one is that kind which arises from a grant of a special power, in the exercise of which the municipality is a legal individual; the other is of that kind which arises or is implied from the use of political rights under the general law, in the exercise of which it is sovereign. The former power is private and is used for private purposes; the latter is public and is used for public services. The former is not held by the municipality as one of the political divisions of the state. The latter is. In the exercise of the former power and under the duty to the public which the acceptance and the use of the power involved, a municipality is like a private corporation, and is liable for a failure to use its power well, or for any injury caused by using it badly. But where the power is intrusted to it as one of the political divisions of the state and is conferred not for the immediate benefit of the municipality but as a means to the exercise of the sovereign power, the corporation is not liable for non-user nor for mis-user toward the public.

At all events the law upon the governmental side is plain. No matter how apparent the negligence of the public officer may be in the course of his duties, the government is in no way responsible. That is true, although in a general way it may be said that there is no objection if a municipal corporation is impleaded. Liable a municipal corporation may be, but it cannot be sued for negligence in the course of the administration of its governmental functions. Governments of whatever degree can protect themselves by the principle that no tort done by a public officer can by possibility have been authorized by a valid law.

The rule of this section, indeed, goes to the furthest extent. So that if a public officer commits a positive tort in the course of executing the law, the governmental ing peaceably upon a sidewalk in the city of Lowell 1 Allen, 172 (1861). While the plaintiff was standing peaceably upon a sidewalk in the City of Lowell two police officers ordered him off; and upon his refusal to go they assaulted, arrested and imprisoned him, claiming that by so doing they were only performing their official duty. The court held that this was a false arrest, and assault and battery. The plaintiff now brings the present action against the city to recover his damages for this imprisonment.

Mr. Justice BIGELOW disposed of the case in this way: Police officers can in no sense be regarded as agents or servants of the city. Their duties are of a public nature. Their appointment devolved on cities and towns by the legislature as a convenient method of exercising the function of government; but this does not render them liable for their unlawful or negligent acts. For the mode in which they exercise their powers and duties the city or town cannot be held liable. The enforcement of the laws and other similar powers and duties with which police officers are intrusted are derived from the law.[59]

§ 77. Relation.

The reason in all this is that public policy which must shape the law in every system of government. That public policy it is which relieves the state of responsibility for acts done in the course of administration without authority. A leading case in this rule is Dunlop v. Munroe, 7 Cranch, 242 (1812). This was a suit against the Postmaster, the superior officer, for the loss of a letter by the neglect of a carrier, the inferior officer. In the declaration the person who had lost the letter charged that it was lost by the negligence of the Postmaster.

Upon that point Mr. Justice JOHNSON said: The third exception is intended to raise the question how far the Postmaster is liable for the neglect of his assistants; but connected with the pleading it presents another and very different question, to-wit, whether when the suit is taken upon the neglect of the Postmaster himself, it is competent to give in evidence the

59 LIABILITY.—O'Brien v. Reg., 4 Can. Sup. Ct. 529; Gibbons v. United States, 8 Wall. 269; Whiteside v. United States, 93 U. S. 247; Workman v. New York, 179 U. S. 552; State v. Hill, 54 Ala. 67; Perry v. Hyde, 10 Conn. 329; Love v. Atlanta, 95 Ga. 129; Marshall Co. Sup'rs v. Cook, 38 Ill. 44; Summers v. Daviess Co. Com'rs, 103 Ind. 262; Ogg v. Lansing, 35 Ia. 495; Brown v. Vinalhaven, 65 Me. 402; Boehm v. Baltimore, 61 Md. 259; Buttrick v. Lowell, 1 Allen, 172; Miller v. Minneapolis, 75 Minn. 131; Hale v. Woods, 10 N. H. 470; Wild v. Paterson, 47 N. J. L. 406; Maxmilian v. New York, 62 N. Y. 169; Wheeler v. Cincinnati, 19 Oh. St. 19; State v. Bevers, 86 N. C. 588; McDade v. Chester, 117 Pa. St. 414; Wixon v. Newport, 13 R. I. 454; Horton v. Nashville, 4 Lea, 47; Mulcairns v. Janesville, 67 Wis. 24.

neglect of the assistants acting under him. Now, the distinction between the relation of the Postmaster to his sworn assistants acting under him and between master and servant generally, has long been settled; and although the latter relation might sanction the admission of such evidence, we are unanimously of opinion, that, if it is intended to charge a Postmaster for the negligence of his assistants, the pleadings must be made up according to the case; and his liability then, will only result from his own neglect in not properly superintending the discharge of the duties of his office by them.

A late case to the same effect is Robertson v. Sichel, 127 U. S. 507 (1888). The object of this suit was to recover damages for the loss of the contents of a trunk. The trunk was detained by a customs officer for appraisal. During the period of custody it was kept on the pier instead of being sent to the public store; so that when the pier was burned by an accidental fire the trunk was destroyed. The owner sued the Collector of the Port of New York for this negligence. At the close of the case for the plaintiff, the defendant asked the court to direct a verdict for him upon the ground that the only negligence shown was that of subordinate officers, which ought not to be imputed to the superior officers.

Mr. Justice BLATCHFORD reviewed the authorities: The defendant was not liable for the wrong, if any, committed by his subordinates. There is nothing in the evidence to connect the defendant personally with such wrong. No evidence was given that the officers in question were not competent or were not properly selected for their respective positions. A public officer is not responsible for the misfeasances or positive wrongs or for the nonfeasances or omissions of duty of the sub-agents or other officers properly employed by or under him in the discharge of his official duty. Competent persons could not be found to fill positions of the kind if they knew they would be held liable for all the torts and wrongs committed by a large body of subordinates in the discharge of duties which it would be utterly impossible for the superior officer to discharge in person.[60]

§ 78. The officer as agent.

It must be obvious now that office is not quite like agency. The private agent may subject his principal to liability in contract or in tort by any act which may be said to be within the scope of his employment; while the public agent cannot submit his principal to liability in contract or in tort by any act which may not be said to be in law within the scope of his authority. That is, while in private agency all turns upon the inference of the scope of the employment, in public agency all turns upon the construction of the authority.

The principal distinction is the same in this topic as in every question of the law governing administration. This distinction between discretionary powers and ministerial duties it must be obvious is the principal distinction in this problem of the application of the law.

[60] RELATION.—Raleigh v. Goschen [1898] 1 Ch. 73; Dunlop v. Munroe, 7 Cranch 242; Robertson v. Sichel, 127 U. S. 507; Ely v. Parsons, 55 Conn. 100; Huey v. Richardson, 2 Harr. 206; Scott Co. v. Fluke, 34 Ia. 317; Anne Arundel Co. Com'rs v. Duvall, 54 Md. 350; McKenna v. Kimball, 145 Mass. 555; Donovan v. McAlpin, 85 N. Y. 185; Sawyer v. Corse, 17 Grat. 230; Murphy v. Holbrook, 20 Oh. St. 137; Tracy v. Cloyd, 10 W. Va. 19.

If the duty is ministerial, all that there is to be done in the administration of the law is to do what the law directs; but if the power is discretionary, it is a question of the application of a conditional law upon the determination of existent facts. The scope of the function of an officer in the administration of the law, then, depends upon the extent to which discretion had been vested in it.[61]

§ 79. Authorization.

If, then, the case for the application of the law be one where the officer has discretion, he has the power to determine in what condition of affairs the law shall be applied. To confide such a power to a public officer seems to intrust him with an arbitrary power. State v. Yopp, 97 N. C. 478 (1887), is the real answer to that. In this case every person had been forbidden by a statute to use upon a certain highway any vehicle not drawn by horses without the permission of the Superintendent of the road. This was a police regulation and as such not much argument could be made against it. The chief contention against the law was that it left an arbitrary power to the Superintendent to admit some and exclude others at his whim.

[61] The Officer as Agent.—Musgrave v. Pulido, 5 App. Cas. 102; Board of Liquidation v. McComb, 92 U. S. 531; Harbin v. Stewart, 4 Port. 370; Woodward v. Campbell, 39 Ark. 580; Bateman v. Colgan, 111 Cal. 587; State v. Staub, 61 Conn. 553; United States v. Douglass, 19 D. C. 99; State v. Drew, 17 Fla. 67; State v. Thrasher, 77 Ga. 671; People v. Knickerbocker, 114 Ill. 539; Clark v. Des Moines, 19 Ia. 199; Mayo v. Commissioners, 141 Mass. 74; Baltimore v. Reynolds, 20 Md. 1; People v. Auditor General, 36 Mich. 271; Swan v. Gray, 44 Miss. 393; State v. Bank, 45 Mo. 528; State v. Scott, 18 Neb. 597; Phelps v. Hawley, 52 N. Y. 23; State v. Yopp, 97 N. C. 478; Ex parte Black, 1 Oh. St. 30; Commonwealth v. McLaughlin, 120 Pa. St. 518.

The court—MERRIAM—answered: This is a misapprehension of the true import of the provision cited. The discretion vested in the Superintendent is not arbitrary. He is the agent of the law, and he is bound to exercise discretion vested in him honestly and fairly, reasonably and without prejudice, for the just purpose of effectuating the intention of the statute. It not infrequently happens that statutes require particular things to be done that must be made to depend upon the judgment—discretion—of a designated officer, and the discretion in such cases is not arbitrary, it is lawful and it must be lawfully executed. In our case the purpose of the statute is obviously a lawful one—a proper regulation of the use of property—and the designation of the agent and the discretionary power conferred upon him are for the lawful purpose of effectuating the just intent of the statute; and he is amenable for any abuse of that discretion.

United States v. Douglass, 19 D. C. 99 (1890), is to this same effect. This was a petition for a writ of mandamus commanding the Commissioners of the District of Columbia to approve and issue a retail liquor license to the relator. He states in his petition his proceedings in applying for the license now in question, and alleges that the Commissioners rejected his application in consequence of an adverse report made to them by an incompetent officer, Lieutenant Amiss, which report he further declared to be false. The issue thus became whether the court would go into the matter; for if they would a case for reversal seemed to have been made out.

As in the case before decided, this power was held discretionary. On that point the court by Mr. Justice JAMES said: The meaning of the term "discretionary," when granted by the law either expressly or by implication, in connection with the exercise of official duty, is that the discretionary decision shall be the outcome of examination and consideration. In other words, that it shall constitute the discharge of official duty and not be a mere expression of personal will. Thus, where discretionary power is granted to approve or disapprove a license, an arbitrary disapproval without examination of relative facts, and expressing nothing but the mood of the officer, would not be in exercise of discretionary powers within the legal meaning of that term. In exercising their discretionary power to grant or refuse licenses, the mode of inquiry by which the Commissioners may satisfy their judgment is not subject to the rules which apply to the judicial ascertainment of disputed private rights; no mode of inquiry is prescribed by the statutes, and they are therefore by implication authorized to adopt any that may reasonably be used in attaining the end in view. In every system of executive discretion, the executive head may act upon mere information received from accountable superiors.

All of these cases are in truth to the same effect. In the application of law the requisite thing is judgment. The application of a general law to a particular case involves the determination in a particular case whether the general law is applicable. There is a certain science in administration, but it all turns about this one point, the application of a general law to a particular case; and that all depends upon one thing, the determination in a particular case of the application of that general law. In a sense the first is a question of law, the second is a question of fact. That is, all administration is a mixed question of law and fact. To reduce it to two phrases, administration involves interpretation of law and determination of fact; or, in a word, the application of law.[62]

§ 80. Interpretation.

To continue along the same line of thought as in the preceding section, what is the extent of the express authority depends upon interpretation in each case for itself. A case for illustration is McCormick, Ct. of Cl. o. s. No. 199 (1856). This opinion is as follows: This award, as has been said, is the foundation of this suit, and is the only evidence offered to prove the amount claimed against the government. Commodore Jones, it is true, was acting as an agent of the government with respect to this mill. Whether his authority was limited to having the mill built for the use of the government, or whether his authority in regard to the mill was that of a general agent, is not deemed material. We consider the law to be that such an agent of the government as the Commodore was, cannot without being especially authorized to do so, bind the government by submission of matters in dispute in arbitration. It fol-

62 AUTHORIZATION.—Reg. v. Secretary [1891] 2 Q. B. 326; Marbury v. Madison, 1 Cranch, 169; Harbin v. Stewart, 4 Port. 370; Woodward v. Campbell, 39 Ark. 580; Freeman v. Selectmen, 34 Conn. 406; United States v. Chandler, 13 D. C. 527; Towle v. State, 3 Fla. 202; Dart v. Hercules, 57 Ill. 449; Louisiana College v. State Treasurer, 2 La. 394; Weston v. Dane, 51 Me. 461; Waite v. Delesdernier, 15 Me. 144; Mayo v. Commissioners, 141 Mass. 74; Stevens v. Lake George R. R., 82 Mich. 426; Swan v. Gray, 44 Miss. 393; State v. Walbridge, 69 Mo. App. 657; Bucher v. Thompson, 7 N. M. 115; Danolds v. State, 89 N. Y. 36; Carr v. Northern Liberties, 35 Pa. St. 324; Turnpike Co. v. Brown, 8 Baxt. 490.

lows that the contract of the 7th of April, 1849, with Parker, which provides for a submission to arbitration, is void for want of authority in the Commodore to make it; and of course the award must therefore be void.

This opinion may with profit be compared with the opinion of the Compromises, 22 Opin. 491 (1899). The drift of that opinion may be seen from the following quotation: Unless express provision of law is in a specific case to the contrary the powers of the Attorney-General are plenary upon these matters. The primary broad and general control of the Attorney-General of suits in which the United States is interested conferred by statutes, fully authorized such disposition of pending litigation as seems to him meet and proper. He exercises general supervision over proceedings instituted for the benefit of the United States; and to him is necessarily intrusted, in the exercise of his professional discretion and because of the nature of the subject, the determination of many questions of expediency and propriety affecting the continuance or dismissal of legal proceedings. He may absolutely dismiss suit; a fortiori he may terminate at any stage by way of compromise or settlement.

The parallel between these last two decisions is illuminating. Why is the power to leave to arbitration not within the authority of the Commodore; and why is the power to compromise in litigation within the authority of an Attorney-General? In neither case is the power given explicitly; why, then, is it held to be within the scope of the authority of the first, and not within the scope of the authority of the second? The answer must be that authority is deduced from the nature of the office; what is incident to one office will not be incident to another office. That is, a law which grants the power to a public officer is rightly construed with reference to the object to be attained. If the subject matter of the office is general, the wider will be the radius of the authority of the officer; if the object of the office is a special one, the narrower will be the scope of the authority of the officer. Viewed in this light, the implication of authority depends upon the facts found in each case.[63]

§ 81. Responsibility.

In private agency, if there is an unauthorized contract made by an agent with a third person on behalf of a principal, if it prove that the agent did not have authority to bind the principal as he purported to do, the agent is himself liable to the third party. That situation is canvassed in the case of Macbeath v. Haldimand, 1 T. R. 172 (1786). The Governor of the Province of Quebec appointed one Sinclair to be Governor of a post, directing him to procure supplies and to draw bills therefor upon the government as the practice was. Later the Treasury disavowed these requisitions. The question was then whether the Governor himself was liable.

ASHHURST said: In great questions of policy we cannot argue from the nature of private agreements. But even in these cases the question must be, what was the

[63] INTERPRETATION.—Thompson's Case, 9 Ct. of Cl. 187; Myerle v. United States, 33 Ct. of Cl. 1; Haynes v. Butler, 30 Ark. 69; Bateman v. Colgan, 111 Cal. 587; Huey v. Richardson, 2 Harr. 206; State v. Haworth, 122 Ind. 462; Vose v. Deane, 7 Mass. 280; Lynch v. Donnell, 104 Mo. 519; Armstrong v. Ft. Edward, 159 N. Y. 315; State v. Hudson, 44 Oh. St. 137.

meaning of the parties at the time of entering into the contract. In the present case, the government was made the debtor. Great inconvenience would result from considering a Governor as personally responsible in such cases as the present. For no person would accept of any office of trust under a government upon such conditions. And, indeed, it has been frequently determined that no individual officer is answerable for any engagement which he enters into in behalf of the government.

This law that the public agent is not to be held to warrant his authority as the private agent must, has been worked out in an exact manner of late in the case of Dunn v. MacDonald [1897] 1 Q. B. 555 (1897). The plaintiff alleged in his statement of claim that the defendant, who was her majesty's Commissioner for the Niger Protectorate in Africa, had engaged him to serve for a term of three years in his own service; alternately the plaintiff alleged that the defendant warranted that he was authorized to engage the plaintiff for three years in her majesty's service.

The judgment of Lord Justice LOPES was as follows: The liabilities of public agents on contracts made by them in their public capacity are on a different footing from the liabilities of ordinary agents on their contract. In the former case, unless there is something special which would evidence an intention to be personally liable, an agent acting in behalf of a government is not liable for the breach of a contract made in his public capacity, even though he would under the same circumstances of contract be bound if it were an agency of a private nature. That is the short answer to the plaintiff's case.[64]

[64] RESPONSIBILITY.—Macbeath v. Haldimand, 1 T. R. 172; Dunn

§ 82. Subjection.

The result of all of these cases, it would seem, is plain. The public agent cannot act to the prejudice of his principal as the private agent often may. A test case upon that is United States v. Kirkpatrick, 9 Wheaton, 720 (1824). This was a suit against the sureties of a Collector of Taxes. The defense of the sureties was that whereas the law required periodical accounts and settlement of them, the Collector had been left by his superiors in default, and that no summary measures had been taken to compel a settlement. In brief the defense against the government was based upon the laches of its officers.

Mr. Justice Story delivered the opinion of the court: The general principle is that laches is not imputable to the government; and this maxim is founded not upon the notion of extraordinary prerogative but upon a great public policy. The government can transact its business only through its agents; and its fiscal operations are so various and its agencies so numerous and scattered that the utmost vigilance would not save the public from the most serious losses if the doctrine of laches

v. MacDonald [1897] 1 Q. B. 555: Hodgson v. Dexter, 1 Cranch, 345; Davis v. Garland, 5 Cranch, C. C. 570; Peck v. Robinson, 4 New Br. 687; Comer v. Bankhead, 70 Ala. 493; Anderson v. Pearce, 36 Ark. 293; Dwinelle v. Henriquez, 1 Cal. 387; Ogden v. Raymond, 22 Conn. 379; Samuel's Ex'r v. McDowell, 1 Harr. 108; Tucker v. Shorter, 17 Ga. 621; Mann v. Richardson, 66 Ill. 481; Newman v. Sylvester, 42 Ind. 106; White v. Jones, 67 Ia. 241; Murray v. Carothers, 1 Metc. (Ky.) 71; Noyes v. Loring, 55 Me. 408; Cutler v. Ashland, 121 Mass. 588; Sanborn v. Neal, 4 Minn. 126; Copes v. Matthews, 10 Sm. & M. 398; Tutt v. Hobbs, 17 Mo. 486; Delano v. Goodwin, 48 N. H. 203; Paulding v. Cooper, 74 N. Y. 619; Providence v. Miller, 11 R. I. 272; Robinson v. Howard, 84 N. C. 151; Miller v. Ford, 4 Rich. L. 376; Syme v. Butler, 1 Call, 105.

were applied to its transactions. It would in effect work a repeal of all securities.

A much more extreme case is German Bank v. United States, 26 Ct. of Cl. 198 (1891). United States bonds belonging to a trust estate were in terms payable to one Cockran, executor. He died, and an administrator with the will annexed was appointed, who filed copies of his letters at the Treasury Department. He delivered the bonds to the German Bank to sell, which forwarded them to the Chemical Bank for sale. The Register of the Treasury, upon inquiry by this last bank, replied: There is on file in this office satisfactory power in favor of your bank to transfer the bonds. The bonds were sold and the proceeds paid over to the administrator, who absconded. The cestuis of the original trust brought suit against the bank and recovered. Has the first bank now any action against the United States?

The Chief Justice, RICHARDSON, held not: The government is not responsible for erroneous opinions concerning the right of an administrator to transfer United States bonds, although an innocent party made the transfer on the faith of the opinion. To give advice and assistance in the transfer of bonds is an excess of authority by a public officer, and to transfer them without authority is a wrongful act, and for neither is the government responsible. The government is not responsible for the laches or wrongful acts of its officers. The scope of authority of the Register is to transfer only on proper authority the ownership of registered bonds from one person to another. It can go no further.[65]

[65] SUBJECTION.—Dox v. Postmaster-General, 1 Pet. 318; United States v. Kirkpatrick, 9 Wheat. 720; Sharon v. Salisbury, 29 Conn. 113; German Bank v. United States, 26 Ct. of Cl. 198; State v. Has-

§ 83. Conclusion.

In last analysis, then, this question of the authority of the officer is reduced to the distinction between discretionary powers and ministerial duties. If an officer has discretion he may do any act within that discretion; and all that he does will be held to have been done by express authorization of law. On the other hand, if the duty of the officer is ministerial only, that very act which he had been directed to do can be held to have been done with authorization of law. Therefore, if he acts beyond this express authorization, his acts will be held to be void. Every method of administration of every sort that may be found may be reduced in the last analysis to this distinction between discretionary powers and ministerial duties. Whatever form these may take, it is all administration.

kell, 20 Ia. 276; Holten v. Lake Co. Com'rs, 55 Ind. 194; Mitchell v. Rockland, 41 Me. 363; People v. St. Clair Co. Sup'rs, 30 Mich. 388; State v. Olson, 55 Minn. 118; State v. James, 1 Cush. (Miss.) 300; Blackmore v. Boardman, 28 Mo. 420; McKecknie v. Ward, 58 N. Y. 541; Pittsburg R. R. v. Shaeffer, 59 Pa. St. 350; Commissioners v. Rose, 1 Desaus. 461; Crawn v. Commonwealth, 84 Va. 282.

CHAPTER X.

THE EXECUTION OF THE ADMINISTRATION.

§ 84. Introduction.

In the discussion of the methods of administration, it will be useful to make certain discriminations. Upon examination there appear to be three processes of administration: First, administration by execution; second, administration by legislation; third, administration by adjudication. All of these three are manifestations of the process of administration. By the first, the administration enforces the law; by the second, the administration is reduced to rule; by the third, the controversies that arise in administration are decided. In perfected administration all of these three processes will be found. To each of these methods of administration a chapter will now be devoted. These, after all, are the chief problems in administration, the invention of methods whereby the laws may be carried into effect. To a certain extent these are questions which the administration must decide for itself; to a certain extent they are decided for it. That is, a part of the law governing the methods of administration is internal, a part is external.

§ 85. Extraordinary process.

Execution requires no elucidation. The need for enforcement of law arises when there is opposition; and then, if there is resistance, force must be met with force. There are such and such laws in the books. The officer takes such and such steps to carry them into execution. To a certain extent the force employed is a question, the necessity of which the administration must determine for itself. A government which does not succeed in the maintenance of its laws against opposition stands a confessed failure before the world.

This enforcement of the law often approaches to an exterior limit. That is the same limitation which is present in all governmental action—due process of law. That a man shall not be seized nor his goods taken except by due process of law has been the law of the land from the earliest day; therefore, as to what is due process in government there is some agreement. It is plain that much action by an administration that is summary may yet be due process of law; on the other hand, it is plain that some action by the administration in the execution of the law is too arbitrary to be due process. The attempt in this chapter will be to draw that line.[66]

[66] EXTRAORDINARY PROCESS.—Sullivan v. Earl Spencer, Ir. R. 6 C. L. 173; In re Neagle, 135 U. S. 1; In re Debs, 158 U. S. 579; Johnson v. Jones, 44 Ill. 157; Langenberg v. Decker, 131 Ind. 482; Mitchell v. Rockland, 41 Me. 363; Nichols v. Boston, 98 Mass. 39; Burroughs v. Eastman, 101 Mich. 426; Cochran v. Toher, 14 Minn.

§ 86. Enforcement.

That nation which does not make its coercive force felt throughout the length and breadth of the land is in a state of disintegration. The example of this that will never be forgotten in the United States was the fatal failure to attempt to maintain the federal law throughout the United States in the winter of 1860 and 1861. Late in 1860 the secession began. The President did nothing. The valuable property of the United States was seized by disorganized forces. The President still did nothing. The customs houses fell into the hands of the state governments. At last the President did something; he asked the advice of the Attorney-General. He received in reply such an opinion as he wished—The Power of the President, 9 Opin. 516 (1860).

This was the advice of Attorney-General BLACK: To the Chief Executive Magistrate of the Union is confided the solemn duty of seeing the laws faithfully executed. That he may be able to meet this duty the forces of the United States are under his orders as their Commander-in-Chief. But his power is to be used only in the manner prescribed by the legislative department. He cannot accomplish a legal purpose by illegal means. I now come to the point in your letter which is probably of the greatest practical importance. By various acts the land and naval forces of the United States and the militia of the several states may be called forth by you whenever the laws of the United States shall be opposed or the execution thereof obstructed in any state. These

385; McLaughlin v. Green, 50 Miss. 466; Taylor v. Place, 4 R. I. 338; State v. McMillan, 52 S. C. 69; Martin v. Snowden, 18 Grat. 142.

existing laws put and keep the Federal Government on the defensive strictly. You can use force only to repel an assault on a public property and to aid the courts in the performance of their duty. If the means given you to collect the revenue and enforce the other laws be insufficient for that purpose, Congress may extend and make them more effectual to those ends.

Within a few months a new President came into office and began war. He had no hesitation as to the power of the President in executing the laws. He found the laws of the United States opposed in the Southern States; he called out the militia of the Northern States. He found the forces of the Union confronted with the forces of the Confederacy; he declared a blockade of all the states in secession, and this, with or without action of Congress,—it did not seem to matter to him much. All this he did upon the basis that the President had the coercive forces of the nation at his disposal to enforce the laws whenever those laws were opposed. And in the end Congress ratified what he did as proper at the time; the Supreme Court of the United States declared what he did was within his power; and history has set its high approval upon this administration of Lincoln.

One of these opinions of the Supreme Court just referred to is the Prize Cases, 2 Black, 634 (1862). A part of the opinion of Mr. Justice GRIER follows: Had the President a right to institute a blockade of ports in the possession of persons in armed rebellion against the government? By the Constitution Congress alone has the power to declare a national or foreign war. It cannot declare a war against the state or any number of the states by virtue of any clause of the Constitution.

The Constitution confers on the President the whole executive power. He is bound to take care that the laws be faithfully executed. He is Commander-in-Chief of the Army and Navy of the United States. He is not authorized, but bound to resist force with force. He does not initiate war, but is bound to accept the challenge without waiting for special legislative authority.[67]

§ 87. Apprehension.

In many ways the civil war enlarged the conception of the functions of government but in no particular more than in the appreciation of the extent of the powers of the executive. Indeed the test of this principle that the executive is subject to distinct limitations in the enforcement of the law will come in time of war. For a most important part of any state or martial law is the making of arrests of civilians charged with various offenses. So, to arrest and hold is in effect to suspend the writ of habeas corpus; for, indeed, no military government can be practical if the writ of habeas corpus is enforced. This is recognized in one provision of the Constitution which contemplates the suspension of the writ of habeas corpus in time of military necessity, without, however, designating in whom the power to suspend the writ shall be vested.

This was the situation at the outbreak of the War of the Rebellion when a case came before the Chief Jus-

[67] ENFORCEMENT.—Whiteside v. United States, 93 U. S. 247; In re Snow, 120 U. S. 286; Tennessee & C. R. Co. v. Moore, 36 Ala. 371; Hawkins v. Governor, 1 Ark. 570; Ex parte Shrader, 33 Cal. 279; McWhorter v. Pensacola R. R., 24 Fla. 417; Johnson v. Jones, 44 Ill. 157; Langenberg v. Decker, 131 Ind. 482; Mitchell v. Rockland, 41 Me. 363; Nichols v. Boston, 98 Mass. 39; McLaughlin v. Green, 50 Miss. 466; Sooy v. State, 39 N. J. L. 135; Mauran v. Smith, 8 R. I. 192.

tice of the United States which raised this very question —Ex parte Merryman, Taney, 246 (1861). The petition for the habeas corpus recited that on the 25th of May, 1861, the petitioner, a citizen of Baltimore, was arrested by order of a Major-General of the United States, and committed to Fort McHenry, within the District of Maryland. A writ of habeas corpus was issued by the Chief Justice, then sitting in chambers, to the Commandant of the fort, directing him to bring the prisoner to the court. The Commandant refused to produce the prisoner upon the ground that the arrest was made by the military arm, while the prisoner was in an overt act of treason, and upon the further ground that the Commandant was duly authorized by the President of the United States in such cases to refuse the writ of habeas corpus. Chief Justice TANEY, in high indignation, ordered attachment to issue. The officer proceeded to Fort McHenry for the purpose of serving the writ. Stopped at the outer gate, he sent in his name; after a time the messenger returned with the reply that there was no answer to his card. In view of the superior force at the disposal of the Commandant, the Chief Justice excused the marshal from taking any further proceedings.

On the next day this memorandum was placed on file for an opinion: I ordered the attachment yesterday because upon the face of the return the detention of the prisoner was unlawful upon the grounds: 1. That the President under the Constitution of the United States cannot suspend the privilege of the writ of habeas corpus nor authorize a military officer to do it. 2. A military officer has no right to arrest and detain a person not subject to the rules and articles of war, for an offense against the laws of the United States; and if a party be arrested by the military it is the duty of the officer to deliver him over immediately to the civil authority to be dealt with according to law.

The result of this collision was that the executive held its man. That must always be the result; and, indeed, the humiliation of the Chief Justice was merited. The truth of the matter is that effective execution in time of war requires that, when necessity arises, the writ of habeas corpus shall be suspended at once. The President is charged with the faithful execution of the laws, and by consequence empowered to use every possible means that may be given him by implication. The executive power of the government must suppress rebellion and repel invasion. It is first in the field, best acquainted with the extent of the danger, and well qualified to judge of the circumstances. As a present question in constitutional law, it is hardly too much to claim that the executive might today suspend the writ.

But to allow the suspension of the writ is one thing, and to allow conviction by a court martial is quite another thing; one cannot be founded upon the other. The leading case in this whole subject is Ex parte Milligan, 4 Wall. 2 (1866). The case made for the petitioner was this: He was a civilian, he had been arrested by the military, he had been tried before a military commission, he had been sentenced to be hanged; and the question certified to the Supreme Court of the United States was: Whether such a military commission had power to try a civilian in the state of Indiana in 1864.

Mr. Justice Davis delivered an impressive opinion:

The importance of the main question presented by this record cannot be overstated; for it involves the very framework of the government and the fundamental principles of American liberty. No graver question was ever considered by the court, nor one which more nearly concerns the rights of the whole people; for it is the birthright of every American citizen when charged with crime to be tried and punished according to law. No doctrine involving more pernicious consequences was ever invented by the wit of man than that any provisions of the Constitution can be suspended during the exigencies of government. It is difficult to see how the safety of the country required any such martial law in Indiana in 1864. If any of her citizens were plotting treason the military had the power of arrest until the government was prepared for their trial. The courts were ready and open to try them. Milligan will therefore be discharged. Martial law is created only by a necessity.[68]

§ 88. Command.

These coercive forces in government in time of need are well set forth in Durand v. Hollins, 4 Blatch. 451 (1860). This was an action of trespass for the destruction of property of the plaintiff at Greytown, Nicaragua, by order of the defendant. The defendant pleaded that he was a commander in the navy of the United States; that by virtue of order of the President, he directed the

[68] APPREHENSION.—Hardy v. Murphy, 1 Esp. 294; Booth v. Hanley, 2 C. & P. 288; Martin v. State, 89 Ala. 115; State v. Brown, 5 Harr. 505; Vandeveer v. Mattocks, 3 Ind. 479; Boutte v. Emmer, 43 La. Ann. 980; Commonwealth v. Wright, 158 Mass. 149; Quinn v. Heisel, 40 Mich. 576; State v. Dierberger, 96 Mo. 666; Burns v. Erben, 40 N. Y. 463; Neal v. Joyner, 89 N. C. 287; Douglass v. Barber, 18 R. I. 459.

bombardment of Greytown, which resulted in the destruction complained of; and that the bombardment was justified by the failure of the authorities of Greytown to give redress for acts of violence perpetrated upon inhabitants of the United States.

Mr. Justice NELSON upon circuit held: The executive power under the constitution is vested in the President of the United States. He is Commander-in-Chief of the Army and Navy, and has imposed upon him the duty to take care that the laws be faithfully executed. As the executive head of the nation the President is made the only legitimate organ of the general government to open and carry on negotiations with foreign nations. Now, as it respects the interposition of the executive abroad for the protection of the lives and property of the citizen the duty must of necessity rest in the discretion of the President. The great object and duty of government is the protection of the lives, liberty, and property of the persons composing it, whether at home or abroad, and any government failing in the accomplishment of that duty is not worth preserving. It is quite clear that in all cases where a public act or order rests in executive discretion neither he nor his authorized agent is civilly responsible for the consequences.

This conception is seen in a late assertion of the plenary papers of the executive in the opinion on the Foreign Cables, 22 Opin. 13 (1898). On May 4, 1897, the French ambassador submitted to the Secretary of State the application of the French Company Telegraphic Cables for permission to land a cable supplementary to that which it had between Brest and Cape Cod, upon the same terms and conditions as the main cable. The State

Department answered that the present executive did not regard himself as clothed with authority to authorize the landing of submarine cables without legislation of Congress. This note was forwarded to the company through the ambassador; but the work of landing the cable had been completed by the company in the meantime. The opinion of the Attorney-General was asked as to what could be done under those circumstances.

RICHARDS, the acting Attorney-General, returned a vigorous opinion: The preservation of our territorial integrity and the protection of our foreign interest are intrusted in the first instance to the President. In the protection of these fundamental rights, which are based upon the Constitution and grow out of the jurisdiction of this nation over its own territory as a distinct sovereignty, the President is not limited to the enforcement of specific acts of Congress. I am of opinion, therefore, that the President has the power in the absence of legislative enactment to control the landing of foreign submarine cables. He may either prevent the landing if the rights intrusted to his care so demand, or permit it on conditions which will protect the interests of the government and its citizens. And if a landing has been effected without the consent or against the protests of this government, respect for its rights and compliance with its terms may be enforced by applying the prohibition to the operation of the line unless the necessary conditions are observed, and this may be done by force.

This certainly is an elementary power of the administration—the power to command. The right to direct what shall be done is the right of the chief executive in all governments. In this aspect the administration is the government in action. Instant obedience must be the requirement in certain contingencies. The power to give orders and the duty to obey such orders is the characteristic situation in administration.[69]

§ 89. **Coercion.**

This power in the administration may go to any extent that is necessary—even to killing. The leading case for that is In re Neagle, 135 U. S. 1 (1890). David Neagle, a deputy marshal of the United States, was brought into the United States court from the custody of a California court upon his averment that he was held in imprisonment for an act done in execution of the laws of the United States. Neagle had killed a former judge, Terry, who had made an attack upon Mr. Justice Field of the Supreme Court of the United States. An order was entered discharging Neagle from custody upon a finding that he was held in custody for an act done in pursuance of a law of the United States.

Mr. Justice MILLER, after stating the case as above, said: In the view we take of the Constitution of the United States, any obligation fairly and properly inferable from that instrument, or any duty of the Marshal to be derived from the general scope of his duties, is law. It would seem that the argument might close here. If the duty of the United States to protect its officers from violence even to death in discharge of duties

69 COMMAND.—United States v. Klein, 13 Wall. 137; Mitchell v. Harmony, 13 How. 115; Hawkins v. Nelson, 40 Ala. 553; Worthy v. Kinamon, 44 Ga. 297; La Salle County v. Simmons, 10 Ill. 513; Logansport v. Justice, 74 Ind. 378; Terrill v. Rankin, 2 Bush, 453; Ford v. Surget, 46 Miss. 130; Drehman v. Stifel, 41 Mo. 184; Branner v. Felkner, 1 Heisk. 228; Koonce v. Davis, 72 N. C. 218.

which the law has laid upon them be established, and Congress has made the writ of habeas corpus one of the means by which this protection is efficient, and if the facts show that the prisoner in this case was thus acting in accordance with his duty—no murder can be conceived of as committed. The prisoner should be discharged by this writ of habeas corpus, because he was not liable to answer in the courts of California for the part he had in that transaction.

The present principle may then be stated in as extreme a form as this: Whenever it is necessary for the enforcement of a law that a certain thing should be done by an officer in order to carry it into execution, that thing may be done. This is found laid down at the time of the fugitive slave law in an opinion on the Extradition of Fugitives, 6 Opin. 466 (1854). It appeared that on the 2nd of June, 1851, a warrant was issued from the Commissioner of the United States in the city of Chicago for the apprehension of a fugitive slave under which the Marshal had arrested the negro. Thereupon, a rescue being threatened, the Commissioner and the Marshal deemed it necessary and proper to call to their assistance a party of men, police and militia, as a guard. For the subsistence of this guard the Marshal provided. He now claims allowance for their compensation.

In a learned opinion CUSHING, then Attorney-General, upheld the legality of this method of executing the law; in substance, he said: A Marshal of the United States, when opposed in the execution of his duties by unlawful combinations, has authority to summon the entire force of his precinct as a posse comitatus. This ancient power exists today. This authority comprehends not only bystanders and citizens generally, but any and all organized armed forces, whether militia of the state or forces of the United States. If the object of resistance to the Marshal be to obstruct and to defeat the execution of the provision of an act of Congress, the expenses of such posse comitatus are properly chargeable to the United States.[70]

§ 90. Ordinary process.

The basis of all administration is found in the law itself. If the law is absolute, what is commanded must be done; if the law is specific, that must be performed that is directed—to the extent that a duty is ministerial, mechanical execution is required. This is not a question in such a case of the better method; that method which is indicated must be followed. This is by means uncommon that the law should be explicit even to the extent of prescribing methods of administration. Even administrative statutes arranging a whole course of administration are sometimes enacted. An example of this is the United States Customs Administrative Act of 1890.

On the other hand, the law may not be absolute, but conditional; in which case the officer must decide in what way the law is to be enforced. That is, to the extent to which a duty is discretionary, the officer has the

[70] COERCION.—Rex v. Pinney, 5 C. & P. 254; Lamar v. Browne, 92 U. S. 194; In re Neagle, 135 U. S. 1; Logan v. United States, 144 U. S. 295; In re Debs, 158 U. S. 579; Holmes v. Sheridan, 1 Dillon, 351; United States v. Mullin, 71 Fed. 686; Parham v. Justices, 9 Ga. 341; Highway Com'rs v. Ely, 54 Mich. 175; Hogue v. Penn, 3 Bush, 663; McLaughlin v. Green, 50 Miss. 453; Bryan v. Walker, 64 N. C. 141.

power to decide upon the method to be used in administration. Upon the whole, this is the more usual. The law usually leaves the method of execution to the administration. This is the right of the matter in theory, since it observes the separation of powers in leaving to the administration its proper function. It is expedient also, since it gives over the methods of administration to those that understand it.[71]

§ 91. Arrest.

These cases where force must be met with force involve the authority of peace officers more often than the power of higher officers of the administration. These public officers are at all times confronted with the necessity to determine on the instant whether they will use force or not and how much force they must use. Upon these questions of the law governing execution there is much law; and upon all these points the law is very exacting of the officer. He must not use force at all unless there is breach of the peace; more than that, if he must use force he may not use more force than is absolutely necessary.

For example, upon the question of the authority of an officer to arrest without warrant there is much special

[71] ORDINARY PROCESS.—Beckwith v. Philby, 6 B. & C. 635; Murray's Lessee v. Hoboken L. & I. Co., 18 How. 272; Lawton v. Steele, 152 U. S. 133; The Bolina, 1 Gall. 75; Knot v. Gay, 1 Root 66; Long v. State, 12 Ga. 293; Commissioners v. Reeves, 148 Ind. 472; McMillen v. Anderson, 27 La. Ann. 19; Kellar v. Savage, 20 Me. 199; Tellefsen v. Fee, 168 Mass. 188; Burroughs v. Eastman, 101 Mich. 426; Nelson Lumber Co. v. McKinnon, 61 Minn. 222; Ela v. Shepard, 32 N. H. 277; McMahon v. Palmer, 102 N. Y. 176; State v. Wilson, 121 N. C. 454; Cleveland v. Tripp, 13 R. I. 64; Musser v. Adair, 55 Oh. St. 472; State v. Sponaugle, 45 W. Va. 430.

law. A simple case in point is Boyleston v. Kerr, 2 Daly, 220 (1867)—an action for false imprisonment against a policeman. The testimony was to the effect that Boylston had gone into the cafe of Kerr and had ordered a luncheon. Boylston was given a check for forty cents, the amount to which he had eaten; but at the counter he substituted a check for fifteen cents, which he had obtained. After he had reached the street Kerr called out for a policeman. The policeman arrested Boylston, which is the imprisonment complained of.

DALY, the presiding Justice, disposed of the case briefly: As the arrest was made without a warrant, the defendant, as a party assisting in making an unlawful arrest, was liable to an action by the person arrested. There was no breach of the peace to authorize an arrest without a warrant. The only rule in the matter is that the police officer virtute officii may arrest a person for a breach of the peace committed in his presence. The arrest of the plaintiff was therefore unlawful. This is a strict, but a necessary rule for the protection of the citizen.

There is a mitigation of this strict rule in favor of the public officer—a rule of administrative law, therefore, in the strictest sense of that term. That is well stated in Beckwith v. Philby, 6 B. & C. 635 (1827). This was an action for assaulting, beating, handcuffing and imprisoning the plaintiff; and keeping and detaining him, handcuffed and imprisoned, for forty-eight hours upon a false charge that he had been apprehended in the course of a felony. The officer pleaded that he had reasonable and probable cause in making the arrest.

Lord TENTERDEN said: The only question of law in

the case is whether a constable having reasonable cause to suspect that a person has committed a felony may detain such a person until he can be brought before a justice of the peace to have his conduct investigated. There is this distinction between a private individual and a constable: In order to justify the former in causing the imprisonment of a person, he must not only make out a reasonable ground of suspicion, but he must prove that a felony has actually been committed; whereas a constable having reasonable ground to suspect that a felony has been committed is authorized to detain the party suspected until inquiry can be made by the proper authorities.

The cases are all in accord with these general doctrines. It will be too hard for the officer if there be not some mitigation in his position. So harsh a rule of law had to give way somewhat to an administrative rule for his protection based upon that policy. The law of the land which protects the individual is in logic as much violated in one case as in the other. In a similar way from a similar policy officers who institute prosecution are protected even if it prove in the outcome that the party prosecuted was innocent, if at the time the officer acted upon probable cause. And upon the same basis, whatever acts an officer does in reasonable compliance with process fair upon its face may be justified by him. All these are true rules of administrative law of the foreign sort. In our domestic law these are exceptions.[72]

[72] ARREST.—Beckwith v. Philby, 6 B. & C. 635; Howard v. Clarke, 20 Q. B. D. 558; Kurtz v. Moffitt, 115 U. S. 487; Knot v. Gay, 1 Root, 66; Long v. State, 12 Ga. 293; Kindred v. Stitt, 51 Ill. 401; Scircle v. Neeves, 47 Ind. 289; Leddy v. Crossman, 108 Mass. 237; Bur-

§ 92. Seizure.

The summary power of the administration is seen in the Bolina, 1 Gall. 75 (1812). An information of seizure was filed against the Bolina and her cargo for not unlading her cargo. The Collector of Customs upon her refusal had directed the Surveyor to take possession of the schooner as forfeited; which he accordingly did, and gave information of the seizure on the evening of the same day to the claimant, the owner. A variety of grounds of defense was presented. Most of these exceptions related to the course of proceedings followed by the Collector; indeed, the validity of the principal statute was admitted.

The opinion was by Mr. Justice STORY: It is further contended that the Collector had no authority to make a seizure in this case, it not being within the express purview of any statute giving him authority that he shall have power to seize. At common law any officer might seize uncustomed goods to the use of the King. This doctrine is supported by Lord Hale and better authority could not be. On general principles, therefore, the objection would be without foundation. The conclusion is that the seizure was lawfully made. Since there is implied authority in officers of the customs to pursue by seizure the powers which the law intrusts to them, it is of importance that the Executive should have this power in the enforcement of the law.

One noteworthy case along this line of discussion is

roughs v. Eastman, 101 Mich. 426; Wahl v. Walton, 30 Minn. 506; Angle v. Runyon, 9 Vroom. 403; Boyleston v. Kerr, 2 Daly, 220; Yount v. Carney, 91 Ia. 559; McCarthy v. De Armit, 99 Pa. 63; Eanes v. State, 6 Humph. 53; Johnston v. Moorman, 80 Va. 131.

Lawton v. Steele, 152 U. S. 133 (1894). This case involved the constitutionality of an act of the Legislature of the State of New York which forbade the taking of fish in Lake Ontario by any device other than a hook and line; providing that any net or pound maintained or found within those waters should be held a public nuisance; directing that it should be the duty of each and every game constable to seize and forthwith destroy the same; enacting that no action of damages should lie or be maintained for or on account of any such seizure or destruction. The facts in this case were undisputed. Certain nets had been set by the plaintiff, a fisherman, within the prohibited waters, which had been destroyed by the defendant, a fish warden.

Mr. Justice BROWN delivered the opinion, which follows: The extent and limits of what is known as the police power has been a fruitful subject of discussion in the Appellate Court of every state in the Union. It is universally conceded to justify the destruction or abatement by summary proceedings of what may be regarded as a public nuisance. It is not easy to draw the line between the cases where the property illegally used may be destroyed summarily, and where judicial proceedings are necessary for its condemnation. If the property were of great value, as for instance, if it were a vessel employed for smuggling, it would be putting a dangerous power in the hands of a customs officer to permit him to sell or destroy it as a public nuisance, and the owner would have good cause to complain of such act as depriving him of his property without due process of law. But where the property is of trifling value and its destruction is necessary to effect the object of a certain statute, we think it is within the power of the Legislature to order its summary abatement. The value of the nets in question was but $15 apiece. Upon the whole, we agree in holding this act constitutional.[73]

§ 93. **Demand.**

These cases give a large conception of what due process of law is, and what is not due process of law. Much force may be used in administration and yet all that is done be due process. So that whether it is due process or not depends, it would seem, in a practical case, upon what has been the practice in government. Proprieties and improprieties in government are for the most part matters of usages and conventions.

The leading case on this whole question is Murray's Lessee v. Hoboken Company, 18 How. 272 (1855). The lands in question in this case had first been levied upon by virtue of what is denominated a distress warrant issued by the Solicitor of the Treasury upon his own motion. The Collector was in default to the Government in this case and his lands had been levied upon in accordance with an act of Congress, which authorized this warrant. The question certified was whether the effect of the proceeding authorized by the act in question was to deprive the party against whom the warrant issued from the Treasury Department of his liberty and property without due process of law.

[73] SEIZURE.—Lawton v. Steele, 152 U. S. 133; The Bolina, 1 Gall. 75; People v. Simon, 176 Ill. 171; Colon v. Lisk, 153 N. Y. 196; Kellar v. Savage, 20 M. E. 199; Osborn v. Charlevoix Cir. Judge, 114 Mich. 665; Hines v. Chambers, 29 Minn. 7; Tellefsen v. Fee, 168 Mass. 188; Ela v. Shepard, 32 N. H. 277; Ex parte Keeler, 45 S. C. 544; Martin v. Snowden, 18 Grat. 142; State v. Sponaugle, 45 W. Va. 430; Houston v. State, 98 Wis. 486.

The court, by Mr. Justice CURTIS, held that the law was constitutional: It is due process of law. It was a settled usage and order of proceedings of the common statutory law of England that summary process should be used for the recovery of debts to the crown, especially those due from receivers of revenue. The power to collect and disburse revenue and to make all laws which will be necessary and proper for carrying that power into effect includes all known appropriate means of effectually collecting and disbursing that revenue unless some such means should be forbidden by the Constitution. The recovery of public duties by this summary process of distress issued by some public officer authorized by the law is an instance of redress of a particular kind of public wrong by a special process. The action of the executive power upon matters committed to its determination by constitutional law is conclusive.

This point is worth repetition—Weimer v. Bunbury, 30 Mich. 201 (1874), is a like case. A City Treasurer was in default to a County Treasurer for taxes given over to him to collect for the county. Thereupon the County Treasurer, under a statute, issued a warrant directed to the Sheriff to levy upon all properties of the City Treasurer. The Sheriff seized, advertised and sold certain property as directed in the statute. This was the trespass charged in the declaration.

The opinion was by Mr. Justice COOLEY; it is one of the best discussions upon the law governing administration that there is in our books: It is claimed that such summary process as gives the party whose property is seized no opportunity to contest the claim set up against him cannot be due process of law. There is nothing in these words, however, that necessarily implies that due process of law must be judicial process. Much of the process by means of which government is carried on and the order of society is maintained is purely executive or administrative. Deprivations of liberty or property must often take place through the action of ministerial or executive officers or functionaries where it would never be supposed that the common law would afford a redress. While a day in court is a matter of right in judicial proceedings, in administrative proceedings it is otherwise, since they rest upon different principles. Summary process to enforce payment by delinquent or defaulting tax collector was usual and known at the time of the adoption of our Constitution; it was, therefore, due process of law.[74]

§ 94. Distraint.

These summary powers in administration are most obvious in matters affecting the collection of taxes from tax payers. State National Bank v. Morrison, 1 McCrary, 204 (1874), is one case from the mass of cases upon that subject. This was an action brought against a Deputy Collector of Internal Revenue to recover the amount seized by him in satisfaction of the tax upon the earnings of the bank. The bank, it appeared, had refused to make any return of its condition. But a tax had been assessed against it. Thereupon, a warrant was issued by the Collector to the Deputy Collector commanding

[74] DEMAND.—Murray's Lessee v. Hoboken L. & I. Co., 18 How. 272; Springer v. United States, 102 U. S. 594; Baltimore v. Hopkins Hospital, 56 Md. 46; Nelson Lumber Co. v. McKinnon, 61 Minn. 222; Weimer v. Bunbury, 30 Mich. 201; Wilson v. Salem, 24 Ore. 509; Musser v. Adair, 55 Oh. St. 472; State v. Allison, 8 Heisk. 3.

him to distrain upon the goods and chattels of the bank. This was done. The bank now brings suit upon the basis that all that has been done was illegal and void.

NELSON, the District Judge, held the officer entitled to judgment: The act of Congress imposed the tax upon the income of the bank. These taxes the bank refused to pay after due notice and demand, and the Collector very properly under authority vested in him by the act of Congress proceeded to distrain for the same. The proceedings for the levy of public revenue, indeed, almost universally are conducted without judicial forms. Where such action is not required, the proceedings are regarded as purely administrative, and any hearing allowed parties in their process is but as a means of enlightening the Revenue Officers upon the facts which should govern their action. This has been so from time immemorial; and it has never been supposed that the tax payer had a constitutional right to resist the tax because he never had a judgment against him on a judicial hearing to fix the amount.

A case that is always prominent in any discussion of these problems is McMillen v. Anderson, 95 U. S. 37 (1877). The defendant, a tax collector of the State of Louisiana, seized property of the plaintiff and was about to sell it for the payment of a license tax for which the plaintiff was liable; in accordance with the laws of Louisiana the plaintiff brought an action of trespass on account of the sale. The defendant pleaded that the seizure was for taxes due, and that his duty as collector required him to make it. On full hearing the state courts sustained his defense. This was a writ of error upon the ground that his proceedings did not give due process of law.

Mr. Justice MILLER on that point said: Looking at the Louisiana statute here assailed we feel bound to say that if it is void upon the ground assumed, the revenue laws of nearly all of the states are void for the same reason. The mode of assessing taxes by all governments is necessarily summary, that it may be speedy and effectual. By summary is not meant arbitrary or illegal or unequal. It must under our constitution be lawfully done. But that does not mean, nor does the phrase due process of law mean, by a judicial proceeding. The nation from whom we inherit the phrase due process of law has never relied upon the courts of justice for the collection of her taxes. We need not go here into the literature of that constitutional provision, because in any view that can be taken of it the statute here does not violate it, as it gives an opportunity to be heard.[75]

§ 95. Conclusion.

These cases in this discussion point to a central principle. The question is, what is due process of law for the administration?—not, what would be due process of law for the judiciary? It is a necessity that the processes of administration should be summary. Outright enforcement is the characteristic thing in the action of the administration. The executive must dominate the situation or its administration will prove a failure. The law concedes this. Much that is done by the administration in a summary way is yet held not to violate the rule which requires due process of law.

[75] DISTRAINT.—Davidson v. New Orleans, 96 U. S. 105; Palmer v. McMahon, 133 U. S., 669; Winona, etc., Land Co. v. Minnesota, 159 U. S. 537; Commissioners v. Reeves, 148 Ind. 472; McMillen v. Anderson, 27 La. Ann. 19; Eames v. Savage, 77 Me. 222; McMahon v. Palmer, 102 N. Y. 176; Gibson v. Mason, 5 Nev. 302; State v. Wilson, 121 N. C. 454; Cleveland v. Tripp, 13 R. I. 64; State v. Sponaugle, 45 W. Va. 422; Violett v. Alexandria, 92 Va. 561.

CHAPTER XI.

THE LEGISLATION OF THE ADMINISTRATION.

§ 96. Introduction.

As has been remarked, the whole of administration is governed to a greater or a lesser extent by fixed rules. These rules are made by the executive itself in the course of administration to facilitate the enforcement of the law. In part these rules are written, then they are called regulations; in part they are unwritten, then they are called usages. The general result is a definiteness in usual administration. The situation that is found is this: When the law is put upon the statute book it is not specific enough for administration. It requires further elucidation. This is the office of the legislation which is done by the administration. That is, the administration first of all puts the law in shape for convenient administration. The force of these regulations that thus accompany the statute is the legal problem. The general conception is that these regulations have the force which any governmental action has. This is usually summed up in the ordinary decision by the statement that these regulations have the force of law.

The position of such regulations is seen in a long series of decisions. An early case that settled the matter is the United States v. Eliason, 16 Pet. 291 (1842). This was assumpsit against Eliason for a balance against him on the books of the government brought by the United States. An agreed case was made up from which it appeared that the point in issue was the force that should be attached to certain army regulations under which the defendant had acted.

The opinion of the court was by Mr. Justice DANIEL: The power of the executive to establish rules and regulations for the government of the army is undoubted. The Secretary of War is the regular constitutional organ of the President to promulgate such rule. Such regulation cannot be questioned or defined because they may be thought unwise or mistaken. The right of so considering and treating the authority of the executive, vested, as it is, with the command of the military and naval forces, would be a complete disorganization of both the army and the navy. A regulation has the force of law within the sphere of its legal operation.

The regulations upon examination of the situation will be found to be as multifarious as the statutes upon which they depend. These regulations represent the exercise of a very considerable power on the part of public officers in their relation with the public. And they serve a purpose in the administration not commonly appreciated. There are innumerable instances of these regulations. The regulations, directions, circulars, instructions, forms, promulgated by the executive department confront the citizen in all his dealings with the government. So far as these are all put forth in due course of administration the citizen must conform to them. This is the chief office, indeed, of the regulation to reduce administration to a regular system for the ordinary case that arises in administration.

§ 97. **Written rules.**

That is the general doctrine, then, that the regulations of the executive department under certain circumstances are enforced as law. The next point in the discussion must be the determination of these circumstances. The case of In re Smith, 23 Ct. of Cl. 455 (1888), is encyclopaedic in its treatment of this question. The only formal issue in that case was whether the Secretary should order the stoppage of the pay of a paymaster for a payment made by him in good faith without other authority for his protection than the army regulation. This involved an inquiry into the position of such regulation before the law.

Upon this point Mr. Justice NOTT said: Congress has the power to make rules for the government of the military forces. Congress has, however, from an early day proceeded upon the theory that the power might be delegated to the President. It is well settled that with or without action of Congress regulations have the force of law when founded upon, first, the President's constitutional powers as Commander-in-Chief of the army, or second, the administration of statutes by the President which have been enacted by Congress in reference to the military forces. All of these regulations have the same validity.[76]

[76] WRITTEN RULES.—United States v. Eliason, 16 Pet. 291; United States v. Symonds, 120 U. S. 46; Maddux v. United States, 20 Ct. of Cl. 193; In re Smith, 23 Ct. of Cl. 455; United States v. Ormsbee.

§ 98. Scope.

The extent of the scope of the regulation is seen in the case of Manning, 6 Lawrence, 13 (1885). July 21, 1884, Eliza Mauran, as administratrix de bonis non of Suchet Mauran, second, deceased, recovered judgment against the United States in the Courts of Commissioners of Alabama Claims for $91,500.96, on a petition filed in said court, January 4, 1883. Said judgment was rendered on a claim arising out of the capture of the ship "Marshall," by the Confederate cruisers, "V. H. Ivy" and "Music." The transcript of the judgments of said court certified by the clerk thereof to the Secretary of State, and transmitted by him to the Secretary of the Treasury, in pursuance of the act of June 3, 1884, shows that C. T. and T. H. Russell of Boston were the attorneys of record for the plaintiff in the above mentioned judgment. Said claim was adjusted by the Fifth Auditor, and was certified by the First Comptroller for payment to the judgment creditor, with direction that the draft issued in payment be delivered in care of the attorneys of record. J. F. Manning requested the First Comptroller to direct the draft issued in payment of said judgment to be delivered to him.

The decision by LAWRENCE, the Comptroller, is worth full quotation: The Secretary of the Treasury is authorized by statute to prescribe regulations not inconsistent with law, for the performance of the business of the Treasury Department. This statute is merely declara-

74 Fed. 207; United States v. Goodsell, 84 Fed. 155; Orne v. Barstow, 175 Mass. 193; Matter of Spangler, 11 Mich. 298; Monette v. Cratt, 7 Minn. 247; State v. Davis, 69 N. H. 350; Peters v. United States, 2 Okl. 123.

tory, since, without it, the power to prescribe such regulations is an incident of the general duties of the Secretary. In statutes incidents are always supplied by intendments. The payment of claims against the United States is a part of the business of the Treasury Department, and is, therefore, a proper subject for regulations. The Secretary has, by a regulation—which has been quoted in the argument in this case, and has the force of law—provided that, in cases certified for payment to the Treasury Department by any commission created by Congress, the persons certified by said Court or Commission as the attorneys of record shall be regarded as such by this Department, and be entitled to receive the drafts in such cases. A subsequent regulation declares that: The accounting of officers will decide what persons as attorneys or claimants are entitled to receive drafts under the rules of the Department. These regulations grow out of the mode of paying claims against the United States. The usage is, as to claims certified for payment by the First Comptroller, that he inserts in the Treasury warrant authorizing payment a direction to the Treasurer to deliver to the proper claimant, or his attorney specified, the Treasury draft issued to make payment. Thus, the question is now to be decided by the First Comptroller: to whom shall the Treasurer deliver the draft in this case? And it is clear that, if the general usage based on the regulations mentioned is to prevail, the draft must be delivered to the attorneys of record—C. T. and T. H. Russell.

This last case is no mere assertion by the Executive Department; the latest decision by the Judicial Department is to the same effect—Boske v. Comingore, 177 U.

S. 459 (1900). A collector of Internal Revenue was adjudged by a Court in Kentucky to be in contempt because he refused while giving his deposition in a suit pending in a state court, to file copies of certain reports made by distillers, which reports were in his custody as a subordinate officer in the Treasury Department. He based his refusal upon a regulation of that department which provided that no subordinate had any right to permit the use of papers in his custody for any purpose outside of the collection of revenue. The collector, imprisoned for this refusal, petitioned for a writ of habeas corpus upon the ground that his detention was in violation of the laws of the United States.

The federal court discharged the petitioner. Mr. Justice HARLAN explained: Congress may use any means appearing to it most eligible and appropriate which are adapted to the end to be accomplished. Can it be said that to invest the Secretary of the Treasury with authority to prescribe regulations not inconsistent with law for the conduct of the business of his Department was not a means appropriate and plainly adapted to the successful administration of the affairs of that Department? Manifestly not. This brings us to the question, whether it was inconsistent with law for the Secretary to adopt this regulation in this case. The Secretary deemed the regulation a wise and proper one, and we cannot perceive that his action went beyond his authority. In determining whether the regulations adopted by him are consistent with law, we must apply the rule of decision which controls when an act of Congress is assailed as not being within the powers conferred upon it by the Constitution; that is to say, a regulation should not be disregarded or annulled unless in the judgment of the court it is plainly and palpably inconsistent with law. Those who insist that such a regulation is invalid must make its invalidity so manifest that the court has no choice except to hold that the Secretary has exceeded his authority and employed means that are not at all appropriate to the end specified in the Act of Congress.

This regulation, it thus appears, is not legislation; it is administration. The authority for all regulation is to be found in the executive department itself. This is the part of the function of the administration to prescribe methods for the enforcement of the law. This is an inherent power, then, the employment of a method incidental to due administration. Statutes are by necessity couched in general terms, but these general terms carry with them by necessity all powers requisite to accomplish their object. This is so whether the law that goes before indicates that regulation is to follow after or whether the law is silent as to regulation. Often a body of regulations is framed by the head of an executive department upon no other basis than that the matter was given over to be administered under his direction. All of these regulations, if they are no more than administration, have the force of law.[77]

[77] SCOPE.—United States v. Eliason, 16 Pet. 291; Kurtz v. Moffitt, 115 U. S. 503; Real Estate Sav. Bank v. United States, 16 Ct. of Cl. 336; In re Smith, 23 Ct. of Cl. 455; United States v. Badeau, 31 Fed. 697; United States v. Ormsbee, 74 Fed. 209; Wilkins v. United States, 96 Fed. 840; United States v. Dastervignes, 118 Fed. 199; Monette v. Cratt, 7 Minn. 247; Peters v. United States, 2 Okl. 123.

§ 99. Extent.

Regulation is then but a method of administration. The consequences that follow upon this finding are of fundamental importance in the working out of the problem of the scope of the regulation. In administration, as has been seen, certain action is allowed, but certain action is forbidden. What is allowed to be done is anything within the law that is in execution of it; what is forbidden to be done is anything without the law that is in extension of it. In execution anything may be done that is administration, nothing may be done that is legislation—is the principal distinction. All this is restatement of the law governing the functions of the administration; but in this instance of regulation that law is more precise than in any other application of it.

There are two decisions upon two customs regulations decided at about the same time that help to get at the limitation upon the regulation. One is Morrill v. Jones, 106 U. S. 466 (1882). Section 2505, R. S., provided that certain animals ought to be admitted free of duty under proof satisfactory to the Secretary of the Treasury and under such regulations as he might prescribe. Article 383, treasury customs regulations, provided that the collector must be satisfied that the animals were of superior stock. The error assigned related to the instruction as to the effect of the treasury regulation.

The opinion of the Court was delivered by Mr. Justice WAITE: The Secretary of the Treasury cannot by his regulations alter or amend a revenue law. All he can do is to regulate the mode of proceedings to carry into effect what Congress has enacted. In the present case we are entirely satisfied that the regulation acted on by the Collector was in excess of the power of the Secretary. The statute plainly includes animals of all classes. The regulation seeks to confine its operation to animals of superior stock. This is manifestly an attempt to put into the body of the statute a limitation which Congress did not think it necessary to prescribe. Congress was willing to admit duty free all animals specially imported for breeding purposes; the Secretary thought this privilege should be confined to such animals as were adapted to the improvements of breeds already in the United States. In our opinion the object of the Seceretary could only be accomplished by an amendment of the law. That is not the office of a Treasury regulation.

The other is Merritt v. Welsh, 104 U. S. 694 (1881). This was an action brought to recover duties alleged to have been illegally exacted by the Collector of the Port of New York. On certain sugars imported by them the defendant, under general instructions from the Treasury Department, rated them at a higher grade than their standard in color, according to a chemical test applied under Treasury instructions. The issue was as to the validity of this regulation.

Mr. Justice BRADLEY said: The test described by the statute is Dutch standard in color. The first question that naturally arises is, if Congress desires the application of the chemical test in order to determine the saccharine strength of the sugar, why does not Congress say so? There are two very distinct modes of distinguishing sugar. One is determined by the color standard, the other by a chemical standard. Which of these did Congress adopt? We think, clearly, the former. If it be found by experience that the standard of the statute is a fallacious one, can the executive department supply the defects of legislation? Congress alone has the authority to levy duties. Its will alone is to be sought.

These decisions commend themselves, although the question was close enough in each case to justify litigation of it. The same fundamental principle is involved in each of them, that the sole external limitation upon the regulation is the law itself. It is the statute that gives the warrant for administration, so at that point where the legislation stops, the administration must stop also, for when the authority ceases, the exercise of it must cease. When a regulation is found with no positive law in support of it the regulation is thus held void; how much more will the regulation be held void when it is found that it is inconsistent with positive law. That the law is the limitation upon the regulation is in that case most evident.[78]

§ 100. Unwritten rules.

To note an analogy, it may be said that the administration has statute law of its own—its regulations—and that the administration has as well common law of its own—its customs. It is the obvious fact that the rules governing administration are both written and unwritten; and so long as administration proceeds by common consent in subjection with a body of rules, it makes no difference how many of those rules are written and how many of them are unwritten. It is more plain to de-

78 EXTENT.—Merritt v. Welsh, 104 U. S. 694; Morrill v. Jones, 106 U. S. 466; Boske v. Comingore, 177 U. S. 459; Landram v. United States, 16 Ct. of Cl. 74; Maddux v. United States, 20 Ct. of Cl. 193; In re Smith, 60 Fed. 599; United States v. Goodsell, 84 Fed. 155; Matter of Spangler, 11 Mich. 298; State v. Davis, 69 N. H. 350.

duce written rules than to induce unwritten rules. But the various acts in administration require for their validity an establishment of the unwritten usage of the departments in conformity with which they have been done.

The leading case is without doubt United States v. Macdaniel, 7 Peters, 1 (1833). This was an action brought by the government to recover a balance charged against an officer on the books of the Treasury. In defense the defendant pleaded as set-off a claim for services rendered to the government by orders of the heads of departments. There was an act of Congress providing for the same; and therefore the Auditor of the Treasury would not allow it. The claim arose under the custom as to a per cent upon appraisements.

The opinion of Mr. Justice DANIEL is worth extended quotation: The limitation is suggested on the power of the court that a claim which requires legislative sanction is not a proper offset, either before the treasury officers or the court. But there may be cases in which, the services having been rendered, a compensation may be made within the discretion of the head of the department; and in such cases the court and jury will do, not what the auditor was authorized to do, but what the head of the department should have done in sanctioning an equitable allowance. A practical knowledge af the actions of any one of the great departments of the government must convince every person that the head of a department in the distribution of its duties and responsibilities is often compelled to exercise his discretion. He is limited in the exercise of his powers by the law, but it does not follow that he must show a statutory provision for everything he does. No government could be administered on such principles. To attempt to regulate by law the minute movements of every part of the complicated machinery of government would evince a most unpardonable ignorance of the subject. Whilst the great outlines of these movements may be marked out and limitations imposed on the exercise of its powers, there are numberless things which must be done that can neither be anticipated nor defined, and which are essential to the proper action of the government. Hence usages have been established in every department of the government which have become a kind of common law, and regulate the rights and duties of those who act within their respective limits; and no change of such usages can have a retrospective effect, but must be limited to the future usage. It cannot alter, but it is evidence of the construction given to it and must be considered binding on past transactions.

The leading ruling by the departments upon this subject is without doubt the Lost Bond Case, 5 Lawrence, 197 (1884). On April 22, 1864, one Patterson, Secretary of said Fidelity Insurance, Trust and Safe Deposit Company, transmitted to the Secretary of the Treasury two bonds numbered 4225 and 31359 and coupons attached, with a letter saying they were enclosed for redemption, and adding "for which please remit principal and overdue interest." They were respectively endorsed as follows: "Pay to the Secretary of the Treasury for redemption. R. Patterson, Treasurer." The First Comptroller advised the Secretary of the Treasury that the claimant occupies simply the position of a finder, and as such has no lawful right to demand payment. Payment was therefore refused.

LAURENCE, the Comptroller, supported this: It is now well understood that there is a system of national executive common law, which, like the judicial common law of England, and of most of our States, adapts itself to conditions and circumstances, and is in constant process of development and growth. And it has been shown that the executive national common law is frequently different from the system of common law which prevails in courts even on similar questions. The difference rests on conditions and circumstances which fully justify it. In other words the rules of law applicable to private persons are not necessarily adapted to the government in the performance of its obligations, and in its relations to private persons. Hence, the question now to be decided must be determined on principles of national executive common law. This, like all common law, rests on reason. Law is the perfection of reason. The purpose of all common law is to secure justice. The real question, then, is, what does justice require? What does reason sanction? Reason furnishes the foundations of justice; and this is common law. The right of the government so to retain bonds is settled by long usage. The universal practice is, and always has been, for the Treasury Department to retain for the lawful purpose of paying the rightful owner all registered bonds presented for payment or transfer by a party having no right to either. And this is now, as it has generally been, the usage as to coupon bonds. This usage is founded on duty, policy, and justice.

The whole doctrine as to the force of usage is contained in these two opinions. In order to apply such a custom in any particular case it must be certain and defined. It must have the shape of law, a general rule recognized by common consent. The usage of a department consists of these rules under which action is done, upon which action is based, and by which action is justified. Such a usage is of the same force as law, as much as a regulation is of the same force as law. Indeed, it must be obvious that to a greater or lesser extent an administration involves a customary law of the service.[79]

§ 101. Validity.

A common case for the enforcement of this unwritten law is seen when the construction given to a statute by the administration is brought in question. The leading case is Edwards' Lessee v. Darby, 12 Wheaton 206 (1827). Under the North Carolina Act of 1782 for the relief of officers and soldiers in the Continental line, the commissioners determined that the French Lick was within the reservations of the statute as public property. The litigation in this case at last turned upon the construction of the statute made by these commissioners. The statute was ambiguous, to be sure; but the propriety of the construction as an original question was doubtful also.

Mr. Justice TRUMBLE said: In the construction of a doubtful and ambiguous law, the contemporaneous

[79] UNWRITTEN RULES.—United States v. Macdaniel, 7 Pet. 1; Five Per Cent Cases, 110 U. S. 485; Symonds v. United States, 21 Ct. of Cl. 148; Wilson v. United States, 26 Ct. of Cl. 187; Holbrook v. Wightman, 31 Minn. 168; Hilburn v. St. Paul, etc., R. R., 23 Mont. 245; Hewitt v. Schultz, 7 N. D. 611; Lockwood v. Bank, 9 R. I. 308; Keane v. Brygger, 3 Wash. 338.

construction of those who are called upon to act under the law, are bound to carry its provisions into effect, is entitled to very great respect. The law was not only thus construed by commissioners, but that construction seems to have received the sanction of the legislature. It was a public act done by a public authorized agent of the government, and afterwards recognized by the government itself. None but the government itself ought, therefore, to be permitted to call it in question.

This paragraph has been quoted with approval in repeated decisions. One of these from the many is United States v. Hill, 120 U. S. 169 (1887). It is the custom in the United States courts to charge $3 as fees in naturalization proceedings. The clerk of the courts never included those fees in his returns. The judges passed upon his returns without requiring him to include these fees. It was true that statute required a return to be made of all office fees, but the construction of the statute by those concerned in its enforcement had never regarded such returns to be made as within the contemplation of those statutes.

Mr. Justice BLATCHFORD said: This practice has had the approval of the Department of the Treasury, the Department of the Interior and the Department of Justice. Until this suit was brought it had never been called in question by any accounting officer of the government, nor has Congress seen fit to put a stop to it by legislation. This construction of the statute in practice, concurred in by all the departments of the government and continued for so many years, must be regarded as absolutely conclusive in its effect. If a change of the practice should be thought desirable, it is obvious that it should be made by Congress and not by the Courts. That this long practice, amounting to contemporaneous and continuous construction of the statute, in a case where it is doubtful whether the statute requires return of the disputed fees, and the heads of the departments have concurred in an interpretation in which those concerned are confided—in the construction of a doubtful and ambiguous law, contemporaneous construction by those who are called upon to act under the law is entitled to great respect.

This is a salutary rule it must be admitted. The department that is most concerned with the execution of law is thus given a prepondering position in the construction of the statute. That comes about, it is to be noted, by the recognition of the force of the unwritten usage of the administration as a law to be taken into the account. Of course this construction must be within the bounds of the discretion vested in the administration. The unwritten rule must be within that as well as the written rule. But within that sphere of influence the operation of the custom of the service as a law is recognized by this line of decisions.[80]

§ 102. Propriety.

The best evidence to be found of the existence of these unwritten rules is in the adjudications of the departments based upon them. Hatfield, 17 Land Dec., 79 (1893). The motion for rehearing in the matter of

[80] VALIDITY.—Edwards' Lessee v. Darby, 12 Wheat. 206; Robertson v. Downing, 127 U. S. 613; Arthur v. United States, 16 Ct. of Cl. 422; United States v. Union Pac. R. R., 37 Fed. 555; Holbrook v. Wightman, 31 Minn. 168; Keane v. Brygger, 3 Wash. 338.

Smith Hatfield et al. for certification of additional homestead rights involving the question as to the right of those who rendered service in what were termed Missouri Home Guards to the benefits of the provisions of sections 2304 and 2306 of the Revised Statutes of the United States. This question had repeatedly been before the department, and the decisions have uniformly been to the effect that those who were members of the Missouri Home Guards were not entitled to the benefits of the statutes above cited.

Secretary SMITH ruled: The legal principle involved seems so well settled by numerous decisions of the Department that I am not now called upon to determine its correctness. Thus, for a number of years, the rulings of the Department have uniformly been to the effect above indicated, and the principle has become so well established as to bring it within the rule of stare decisis, and as so settling a point by decision that it forms a precedent not to be departed from. I must therefore decline to disturb a ruling of so long standing as that which controls in this case, and the petition for re-review is overruled.

The theory that a previous decision is evidence of what the law is prevails in administration.—Eastridge, 8 Pen. Dec. 5 (1894). The rate of pension allowed in the invalid claim was $2 per month, and the amount so allowed from Oct. 2, 1862, date of soldier's discharge from the service, to date of death, January 8, 1881, was paid to his widow, the appellant herein. From this action an appeal was taken, wherein it was contended that the degree of disability shown in the invalid claim from discharge to August 15, 1880, was fully one-half as much as the total for loss of a hand or foot. The action of the bureau was affirmed January 15, 1889, whereupon claimant filed additional affidavits, which were merely cumulative, in which affiants gave it as their opinion that the soldier was disabled in a degree entitling him to a higher rating, and were not deemed sufficient to justify the bureau in again opening said claim and rerating the pension. This appeal involves the correctness of the action of the bureau refusing to reconsider the application for rerating, or to again rerate the appellant's husband's pension.

Secretary REYNOLDS ruled: Aside from the sufficiency of these affidavits it is the well-settled rule, established by a long line of departmental decisions, that in cases of non-specific disability, the ratings fixed at the date of the certificate and based upon contemporaneous medical examinations, will not be disturbed on account of differences of opinion that may subsequently arise upon an application for rerating. If the placing of the name of an applicant upon the roll is to be considered a judicial act it should only be considered a judgment nisi. The proceedings are largely ex parte and from the vast numbers of applicants the work must be performed and the roll made up for the most part by the clerks. The doctrine, when adopted by the Department in pension cases, simply becomes a rule which each administration prescribes for itself as a matter of policy or convenience, and may be waived, suspended, or ignored as justice, public policy, or convenience requires. The facts in the case under consideration, however, show no reason for deviating from the hitherto almost uniform practice of refusing to disturb decisions of former administration where neither fraud nor manifest error in law nor palpable mistake of fact is shown to exist.

The theory of stare decisis as it is understood in the courts of law is thus to a certain extent the rule in the offices of the executive departments. It would be an unsatisfactory administration indeed where the determination of each question was different as caprice might dictate. What is wished is an orderly administration, in which precedents are regarded, in which the principles involved in those precedents are respected, as the cases that are to govern in future administration. That is the recognition of an unwritten body of law. No administration that does not proceed in that way can succeed. At the same time no administration that does not reserve discretion can succeed either.[81]

§ 103. Conclusion.

The requirement as to regulations in general must be that they shall not be contrary to public duty. The officer owes a duty to all of the public who have any concern in his exercise of his duties. It is true that the officer may by regulation lay down general rules for the conduct of the business of his office; but these rules must be reasonable in their application. If these rules in effect abridge the rights of the public they are void; otherwise they will stand. In any particular case where the rule is applicable, that rule can be set up against that particular person. A rule that is must be in pursuance of public duty; it cannot be in denial of public right.

[81] PROPRIETY.—United States v. Pugh, 99 U. S. 269; Hahn v. United States, 107 U. S. 406; Minneapolis, etc., R. R. v. United States, 24 Ct. of Cl. 351; Hilburn v. St. Paul, etc., R. R., 23 Mont. 245; Lockwood v. Bank, 9 R. I. 308.

CHAPTER XII.

THE REGULATION OF THE ADMINISTRATION.

§ 104. Introduction.

A regulation is an order, in that it is like any act done in administration. Wherever a superior gives an order to the inferior, the simplest form in administration is seen—the specific order. Whenever a superior with two inferiors gives to each the same order, the simplest form of the regulation is seen, the general order. After that, between a general order spoken for two and the general order printed for two thousand no distinction exists. The power to issue a regulation over all the officers in an office is a consequence of the power to issue any single order to any single officer. All this results from the theory of administration which gives the superior full direction over his inferiors in any way that may seem to him fit.

This is indeed the line of reasoning in the case called Furloughs, 21 Opin. 318 (1896). This was a request by the Secretary of the Interior upon the Attorney-General for an opinion upon this question as the furloughing of microscopists: Whether it is necessary for me to give a notice of furlough over my official signature in each individual case, or will a general order signed by me directing inspectors in charge of assistant microscopists to furlough them without pay when their services are not required be sufficient? It would be almost impossible for me to give individual furloughs in each case.

HARMON, the Attorney-General, wrote in reply: Your right to furlough cannot be questioned. Inasmuch as the contingencies upon which it is desirable to furlough microscopists arise from time to time and upon conditions which you cannot foresee or control, the advantages to the government of this system would largely be sacrificed if you are compelled to act personally in each individual case, and after the occasion has arisen, I am of opinion that you can make general regulations under which your subordinates in charge of particular localities can, as circumstances call for such action, furlough microscopists to take effect at once, reporting their action to you.

The true office of the regulation is to bring method into the administration—to have a system in administration that shall be uniform in its application. It is therefore the duty of the inferior to obey in all cases the regulations of the superior; for this, indeed, is no more than the usual law governing in all administration. The inferior must obey his superior; the application of that rule in this particular case is that no inferior can waive a regulation made by a superior. To the extent to which discretion has been left to an inferior he may act; inside of the regulation, that is, not outside. And if discretion is left him, and it pleases him to enact, he may promulgate minor rules of his own to govern the actio of his subordinates. All this is a restatement of th law found in the discussion of the theory of the admir istration.

§ 105. Conflict with legislation.

The original source of regulations is then the admir istration itself. It must be possible, therefore, to stat the law governing regulation in the terms of the lav governing administration, when the matter is reduce to its lowest. And so it is; a regulation is no differen from any act in administration at bottom. It must b possible, moreover, to apply one law governing admir istration to the regulation in essentials when matter come to decision. And so it is; the regulation is no dif ferent in nature from any action in administration a bottom. All this must be so, if the proposition is ac cepted to its full extent that regulation is no more tha one method in administration. That is the conclusio in this paragraph—that regulation is administration i substance. If, then, the regulation is an act of adminis tration, it must not be in conflict with the law.

One case for that is Hoyt v. Sullivan, 2 Land Dec. 28 (1883). It appears that Luther B. Sanborn entered th above described tract under the timber-culture laws O tober 28, 1880, and that October 28, 1881, Sullivan init ated a contest against said entry on the ground of abar donment. Pending Sullivan's appeal from the decisio of the local office dismissing his first contest, Novembe 17, 1882, Sanborn filed a relinquishment of his timbe culture entry, Rowe withdrew his contest, and Melvi A. Hoyt made timber-culture entry for the same land.

Secretary TELLER ruled: Rule 53 of the Rules of Practice prescribed by your office and this Department provides, that after the papers in an appeal have been sent up by the local office, such office will thereafter take no further action affecting the disposal of the land in contest until instructed by the Commissioner. The reason for the adoption of this rule is obvious. In the absence of such a provision, a multiplicity of suits would frequently arise involving practically the same question, and thus encumber and obscure the record to no good purpose. But no rule formulated for the administration of the law will be permitted in its operation to defeat a statutory right. At the time that Hoyt applied to enter the land it was open to such entry. The original claimant, Sanborn, having forfeited his rights and relinquished his entry, the local office properly allowed Hoyt's application, subject to outstanding rights of other parties. The illegal contest of Sullivan, then pending, could not deprive Hoyt of his statutory right to enter the land nor operate to remove the land from a proper disposition by the district officers. You are not at all bound by your rule of practice therefore.

A case explicit to the point that the usage must not extend the law, as a regulation must not, is Ogden v. Maxwell, 3 Blatchf. 320 (1855). This was an action against the collector of New York to recover back money paid under the following circumstances: The plaintiff, owner of the ship Racer, had paid for 154 permits, being one permit for every 20 passengers. This was proved to have been the uniform practice at the port of New York. The statute only provided for one fee for one permit and one permit for one entry.

On this Mr. Justice Betts said: The statute gives no reward except for doing the individual act named; and no consideration of convenience to either or both parties, or saving of expense by substituting another practice in place of that directed by law, will authorize a collector colore officii to charge and receive compensation for a service differing from that appointed by positive law. The custom or usage alleged to prevail at this port to make constructive charges for granting permits, whatever may be its notoriety or continuance, is void, both because it contravenes the construction of the statute, and also because there is no warrant of law except under the statute, for imposing any charge or fee for that official act. The defendant would without aid of the statute, be guilty of extortion in levying fees of any kind for his official services.[82]

§ 106. Repugnancy.

An example of that evident case is Stone v. Greaves, 1880 Pat. Dec. 23 (1879). Priority of invention was awarded to Graves by the Examiner of Interferences and on appeal by the Examiners-in-Chief. Afterward at the request of the Primary Examiner the interference was suspended and the applications remanded. Upon consideration thereof, the Primary Examiner rejected the application of Stone and the reissue application of Graves. Stone now moved that the interference be dissolved upon the ground that the invention was not pat-

82 Conflict with Legislation.—Navy Regulations, 6 Opin. 10; Manning's Case, 6 Lawrence 13; Real Estate, 3 Int. Rev. Rec. 37; Hatfield, 17 Land Dec. 79; Stone v. Greaves, 1880 Pat. Dec. 23; Eastridge, 8 Pen. Dec. 5.

entable. This motion involved a clash between the statute and the regulation.

PAINE, the Commissioner, ruled: On one side of the question stands the rule authorizing the dissolution of an interference for want of patentability of the claim. On the other side stands the statute conferring upon the applicant the right of appeal. It is necessary to avoid, if possible, both Scylla and Charybdis; but it is necessary, in any event, to avoid a violation of the statute. If possible that course is to be taken which will harmonize the statute and the rule and give effect to both. If that is impossible the rule must be sacrificed to the law, in every case.

To the same effect, not quite so obvious, is Bennett, 7 Pen. Dec. 1 (1893). Charles T. Bennett, late private, Company F., Thirteenth Indiana Volunteers, filed his original application for an invalid pension under the provisions of the Revised Statutes, on July 5, 1886, alleging that while in the service and in line of duty at Raleigh, N. C., about June 1, 1865, he was prostrated by sunstroke, from which resulted a disease of the head and loss of hearing. The claim was rejected by the bureau February 18, 1892, upon the ground that the evidence failed to establish the existence of any disability due to the claimant's army service. The applicant was awarded for slight deafness not of service origin $12. The award was made under the act of 1890. It was given by the bureau for "slight deafness" because under an entirely different act, applicable to disabilities of service origin alone, $15 was the lowest rating for slight deafness. The inability of the applicant to perform manual labor was not taken into consideration. Yet the act of

1890, under which the applicant sought and was allowed a pension, made inability of the applicant to perform manual labor, in such a degree as to prevent him from earning a support, the foundation of his claim.

The Assistant Secretary, REYNOLDS, ruled adversely to the Commissioner in this matter: It is, therefore clear that the rating under the Revised Statutes for disabilities of service origin was substituted for the act of 1890. The order having resulted in one error, a second error naturally followed, and the inability of the applicant to perform manual labor was not taken into consideration. In a word, the act of June 27, 1890, was changed and superseded by Order No. 164, as construed by your Bureau, and by a practice that neglected to take into consideration the ability of the applicant to perform manual labor. It is hardly necessary to present argument or to support by authority the proposition that neither the Secretary nor the Commissioner can by order or practice supersede an act of Congress. The power of the department so far as orders are concerned is limited to an execution of the law; it ceases when an effort is made to supersede the law.

Upon the whole this seems too plain for discussion, that regulations must not contravene existing law. The position of the regulation of the statute is much like the position of the statute to the constitution—the position of an inferior law to a superior law. And as a new constitutional provision would overrule a pre-existing law inconsistent with it, so the Legislature by its express enactment would overrule any regulation upon the same subject matter which had been promulgated by the administration in so far as the regulation was inconsistent with the legislation. But in any case, as has been pointed out, just as no statute should be held to be overruled by a constitution unless the repugnancy is plain, so no regulation should be held to be inconsistent with the statute unless the repugnancy is plain also. It is only by such accommodation that government can go on without continual irritation.[83]

§ 107. **Limitation.**

There is the same limitation upon the usage of the administration as there is upon the regulation of the administration—the law. A usage cannot be allowed to contravene the law. A usage cannot be allowed to contradict the law, any more than a regulation can be allowed. Whatever scope there is for usage is within the law. Since the office of the usage is to aid in administration, the usage cannot by the hypothesis go further and become legislation. The same limitation is upon the usage of the administration as is upon every separate act which goes to make up the usage.

The leading case is United States v. Mann, 2 Brock. 11 (1882). This was a motion by a marshal of the United States to discharge an attachment against him levied on behalf of the United States because, as he said, the United States was indebted to him in a larger sum for fees due to him, which fees the Treasury Department refused to pay: The refusal of the Treasury Department it appears was based upon a practice in that department that the officer must make his fees out of the execution.

83 REPUGNANCY.—Forest Reservations, 22 Opin. 266; Hoyt v. Sullivan, 2 Land Dec. 283; Stone v. Graves, 1880 Pat. Dec. 23; Bennett, 7 Pen. Dec. 1; Re-enlistment in Navy, 6 Compt. Dec. 589.

Otherwise it had been ruled that no claim of his in that respect would be allowed by the accounting officers.

Upon the propriety of this practice, Chief Justice MARSHALL, then upon circuit, held: The Treasury Department may certainly have its own rules for the adjustment of such claims, and these rules will, if reasonable, be respected. The situation of the officers who claim, will in general secure their respect, and the desire for the preservation of that harmony which ought to exist between the departments, will secure that of the court. But when these rules go to a total denial of justice, to an absolute refusal to allow a just and legal claim, a court cannot, if it has jurisdiction of the subject, disregard the rights of the party. In this case the officer has a right for services rendered.

A square case for the law as against the usage is Merritt v. Cameron, 137 U. S. 542 (1890). This is an action at law by Cameron & Co., importers, against the collector of the port of New York to recover duties alleged to have been illegally exacted on a cargo of sugar and molasses. The defense of the collector was that no protest had been made within ten days from the ascertainment and liquidation of the duties, as was required by the statute. The suit turned upon a determination of what constituted ascertainment and liquidation. The statute required a long process weighing and gauging, inspection and appraisal, fixing and assessing dutiable value. These goods were put in a warehouse under bond and payment was made at a later time to get the goods out of bond. What was the time of ascertainment and liquidation? By the statute it would be the placing in bond, it would seem; but by the practice, it was the time of taking from bond.

The Court—Mr. Justice LAMAR speaking—held to the statute over the regulation: In arriving at this conclusion we are not unmindful of the fact that the defendants in error made their protest in accordance with the regulations of the Treasury Department in force at that time. A regulation of a department, however, cannot repeal a statute; neither is a construction of a statute by a department charged with its execution to be held conclusive and binding upon the courts of the country unless such construction has been continuously in force for a long time. In this case there has been no such long and uninterrupted acquiescence in the regulation by a department or departmental construction of the statute, as will bring the case within the rule announced at an early day in this court, and followed in very many cases, to-wit: that in a case of doubtful and ambiguous law the contemporaneous construction of those called upon to carry it into effect is entitled to great respect and should not be disregarded without the most cogent and persuasive reasons.

As this problem of the limitation upon usage is the same as the problem of the limitation upon regulation, there need be no discussion of these cases, since there has been elaborate discussion of these matters in this same chapter. The limitation is the same—positive law; and the reason for the limitation is the same—due administration.[84]

§ 108. Conflict with administration.

There remains this possibility, which must often arise: can an officer dispense with his own regulations which

[84] LIMITATION.—Settlement of Accounts, 19 Opin. 177; Furloughs, 21 Opin. 318; Bubb's Case, 4 Compt. Dec. 40; Hoyt v. Sullivan, 2 Land Dec. 283; Hook, 8 Pen. Dec. 367.

would otherwise govern in any particular case? If these regulations are no more than his rules for administration which he has laid down for his own guidance, he may take counsel with himself at any time, and issue a new set of regulations, which will abrogate the old set of regulations. And if he can do that, may he not in any particular case waive his regulations for that particular case? This will be the consequence if these regulations are, after all, no more nor less than his own methods in administration. His own rules may bind others; can it be that his own rules will bind him? This is a test question, for if this is all administration within his discretion, he may in his discretion do what he will in spite of his regulations.

This is the test question, then in Bubb's Case, 4 Compt. Dec. 40 (1897). The Auditor of the Interior Department made a decision July 26, 1897, in the claim of John W. Bubb for reimbursement of an amount refunded by him because of an overpayment to Indians, and submitted that decision to the Comptroller for his approval, disapproval or modification. The Auditor decided that this payment would be a diversion of the annuity funds not sanctioned by the treaty or express provision of law, which is prohibited by section 2097, Revised Statutes, and Indian Regulations, 1894, section 156.

Assistant Comptroller BOWERS ruled: So far as the Indian Regulations have any bearing on this case, it is sufficient to say that they were made by the Secretary of the Interior, and he has authority to revoke or waive them in a particular case, and an order subsequently issued by him in contravention of a regulation must be held to be a waiver of a regulation in that case. The decision of the Auditor is accordingly disapproved, and the claim may be allowed.

And further, this case may be considered in this connection: Settlement of Accounts, 19 Opin. 177 (1888). The inquiry was whether or not under existing practice the accounts of the officers of courts, United States attorneys, etc., can be settled through one bureau of the Treasury Department or not, and "whether the Secretary of the Treasury has authority under the statutes, by departmental order or regulations, to change the existing practice in this department with regard to the settlement of certain accounts." The First Auditor of the Treasury details the existing practice and recommends a change.

The Attorney-General, GARLAND, ruled: The First Auditor says that the change proposed can mostly be reached by departmental action. A change of statute can not be made by any departmental regulation. However "illogical" the practice under the laws may be, the laws authorize and enjoin such practice, and a deviation from a practice thus established cannot be justified under the decisions of the Supreme Court of the United States, which sustain the doctrine that a contemporaneous and uniform interpretation by executive officers, charged with a duty acting under a statute, is entitled to great weight, and ought not to be overturned, particularly in cases that have been settled by construction, by precedent, by continuous practice, and the decision of the court. I am of the opinion, therefore, that so far as the contemplated changes are inconsistent with existing law, the Secretary of the Treasury cannot legally by a departmental order change a practice or a course prescribed by practice.[85]

§ 109. Characteristic.

At the same time, if the regulation is valid and the action of the officer is outside of the regulation, that action is void unless confirmed by his superior, for that is action beyond his powers by the hypothesis. A case in point is the Militia Bureau, 10 Opin. 11 (1861). This was an inquiry as to the power to make an order to establish a militia bureau and to constitute a certain Lieutenant Ellsworth for special duty, with special pay, as chief of the bureau. There was no statute law to authorize it and the regulations of the army were opposed to such a change. The question was whether the Secretary of War could issue an order to make the change.

Attorney-General BATES said in part: The appointment of Lieutenant Ellsworth as Chief of the proposed bureau is forbidden by Article 7 of the Regulations of the Army, which provides that no officer shall fill any position, the duties of which will detach him from his regiment or corps until he has served three years in his regiment or corps; and further, that no officer of a mounted corps shall be separated from his regiment except for duty connected with his particular army. These regulations stand in the way of the appointment of this particular officer, and although they may not have the authority of law, it is yet quite obvious that until abolished, no sound principle would justify this violation.

To the same effect is United States v. Symonds, 120

[85] CONFLICT WITH ADMINISTRATION.—Militia Bureau, 10 Opin. 11; Interstate Commerce Commission, 4 Compt. Dec. 266; Crawford, 7 Pen. Dec. 357; Gilbert, Bowler 213; Lost Bond Case, 5 Lawrence 197.

U. S. 46 (1887). The question in this case was whether certain services of the appellee, a lieutenant in the navy, were performed "at sea" within the meaning of the Revised Statutes. The Navy Department issued orders making one period sea service, the other period shore service. Whether the regulation must not govern all cases was the final point made for the appellant.

Mr. Justice HARLAN held for the lieutenant: The Secretary of the Navy could fix by ordering conclusively what was and what was not sea service. The authority of the Secretary to issue orders, regulations and instructions with the approval of the President in reference to matters connected with the navy, would be subject to the condition necessarily implied, that they must be consistent with the statutes which have been enacted by Congress in reference to the navy. He may, with the approval of the President, establish regulations in execution of or supplementary to, but not in conflict with statutes defining his powers or conferring rights upon others. This has been the consistent doctrine of the court. In no case has it been upheld that the regulations when in conflict with Acts of Congress could be upheld.[86]

§ 110. Situation.

The argument is indeed an elementary one. The power to execute the law involves a power to make regulations of general application for the reasonable conduct of administration. It involves that power because to prescribe such regulations is no more than a right in

[86] CHARACTERISTIC.—Coast Survey, 2 Comp. Dec. 306; Lost Bond Case, 5 Lawrence 197; Hoyt v. Sullivan, 2 Land Dec. 283; Hawkins, 8 Pen. Dec. 22; Real Estate, 3 Int. Rev. Rec. 37.

administration to use such methods as may seem fit to be used. It is a little stronger than that; indeed the proper conduct of a wide administration requires the establishment of regular forms and modes for the usual case if there is to be success. But the unusual case shows that this is administration after all is done, for in such a case the regulation may be waived by the officer that made it in any case that seems to him fit. This is the secret of administration—usual methods for the ordinary case, unusual methods for the extraordinary case. That is always in the reserve—discretion.

An important case upon the nature of the regulation is Orne v. Barstow, 175 Mass. 193 (1900). This was a petition to enforce a mechanic's lien. At the trial the copy of the statement put in evidence by the petitioners bore the endorsement, Filed Feb. 14, 1898, at 8 h. o. m. A. M. It was agreed that this was not within the thirty days allowed for filing by the statute; but evidence was admitted which showed the following facts: The office hours of the registry on Saturdays were from 8 A. M. to 1 P. M. On Saturday, Feb. 12, 1898, which was within the thirty days, between 1 P. M. and 2 P. M., the attorney for the petitioner, having got into the office after it was closed, tendered the statement and the fee to the register of deeds, who was there, but who refused to receive it. By the Public Statutes the register was required to note the reception of every paper filed and to certify to it.

Mr. Justice HOLMES said: We are of opinion on the facts proved, the statement was filed on Saturday afternoon. We shall go no further in our decision than this case requires. We shall not undertake to decide whether the register had a right to close his office as early as he did, so far as to exonerate himself from liability had some one come to the office and found it empty. But he was there. He undertook to refuse to give legal effect to the deposit, it is true, but in our opinion that was beyond his power. It was the petitioners' right, if they found the register in his office, to insist on their statement being filed forthwith, and it is no answer to say that the register might have been absent without liability under the law. As the petitioners did all that they could, or were bound to do, the register's conduct did not affect their rights.

§ 111. Conclusion.

All these regulations therefore have the same validity. In the formulation of the law upon this subject there has been much hesitation. An examination of the various decisions results in some uncertainty. When a statute is enacted, either there is specific indication in much detail for its execution, or there is express delegation to the executive to make regulation, or there is in contemplation in the act a subsequent ratification of the regulations which shall be framed, or there is no provision whatever touching the methods for its administration. The truth of the matter seems to be that in all these four cases the executive promulgates such regulations as seem to it fit with entire equanimity.

CHAPTER XIII.

THE ADJUDICATION OF THE ADMINISTRATION.

§ 112. Introduction.

There are these three methods in administration, then: execution, legislation, and adjudication. This is their order in importance, their order in value, their order in time. No administration is fully formed unless it has within its power the exercise of each of these functions, each at the appropriate time. In all but one case in ten thousand the citizen obeys the direction of the administration in the course of its execution without question; in all but one of these cases out of ten thousand in turn, the citizen accepts the interpretation of the administration by its legislation; and, the last step, in all but one out of ten thousand cases, the citizen accepts the adjudication of the administration upon his contest without further action. In computation administration by adjudication is one case in millions.

Notice that this is all administration from beginning to end. Administration by adjudication is no more than the determination by the administration of the controversies that arise out of the action of the administration. This jurisdiction of the administration is new in countries where the common law system prevails, but it is old in countries where the civil law system prevails. Indeed, so new is this function in the administration to try its own controversies that no discussion of it is to be found in our law writers. It is still the doctrine that all controversies must be decided in the judicial courts; which must be so, it is said, because the theory of the law of the land involves supremacy of the ordinary judicial tribunals. In the face of such theories, the jurisdiction of the administration to determine its own controversies has been established to an extent not often appreciated.

§ 113. Jurisdiction for adjudication.

The first question that arises in the discussion of adjudication by the administration is whether it is possible under our constitutional system that such power can be given to the executive department. The leading case to establish that is Cary v. Curtis, 3 How. 236 (1845). A certificate of division of opinion was sent by the judges of the circuit court upon the question whether the act of 1839 was a bar to an action against a collector of customs for money illegally exacted by him as duties paid under protest, the collector having paid for them into the Treasury. The Act of 1839 provides that all money paid to any collector of customs under protest shall be placed to the credit of the Treasury of the United States and disposed of as all other money paid for duties, as required by law or by regulations of the Treasury Department. But whenever it shall be shown to the satisfaction of the Secretary of the Treasury that in any case of ascertained duties, more money has been paid to the collector, or to the person acting as such, than the law requires, it shall be his duty to direct the said Treasurer to refund the same. The question then went to an inquiry into the constitutionality of this statute; which by its terms provided that the decision was left to the administration.

The opinion of Mr. Justice DANIEL is an excellent statement of the situation: The plain intent of this statute is that if the money has been placed to the credit of the Treasury, that it is the Secretary of the Treasury alone by whom the rights of the government and of the claimant are to be decided; and whoever shall pay to the collector any money must do so subject to the consequences. Uniformity of imposts and excises is required by the Constitution. Regularity and certainty of the payment of revenues must be admitted by every one as of primary importance. Within the extended limits of this country are numerous districts. Many officers must be entrusted with the collection of revenue, and with the payments by the government. To permit the receipts on the customs to depend on constructions as numerous as those who might be interested, or to require that those receipts shall await a settlement of every dispute or objection that might spring from so many conflicting views, would greatly disturb, if not prevent, the uniformity required by the Constitution. The money shall be placed in the possession of the Treasury to await decision instead of in the hands of collectors.

These measures are taken expressly to secure uniformity of decision and practice in relation to the amount of duties imposed by law. In devising a scheme for imposing and collecting the public revenue it is competent for Congress to designate the officer of the United States in whom the rights of that government should be represented, and to prescribe the manner and trial. There is nothing arbitrary in such an arrangement; they are general in their character; they are the results of principles inherent in the government; they are defined and promulgated as public law. The courts of the United States can take no cognizance of matters that are not assigned them by law, or conversely. They can take no cognizance of matters that by law are either denied to them or expressly referred ad aliud examen.

This decision goes to the extent of allowing that the jurisdiction of the administration may be exclusive. That covers the whole situation if they may be exclusive; it is plain that they may be concurrent. Again, those decisions go to the extent of regarding the decision of the administration as final. That again covers the whole situation. And this is upon a plain ground that this is all administration from first to last. It is all based upon the independence of the administration.

Another plain case, People v. Dental Examiners, 110 Ill. 180 (1884). The statute at that time provided that the State Board of Dental Examiners should issue a license to any regular graduate of every reputable dental college. The petitioner stated that he was a graduate of an Indiana Dental College. In his petition he states elaborately the course of instruction in that institution. Wherefore, being without other legal remedy, the petitioner prayed a writ of mandamus to the Board of

Dental Examiners to compel them to issue him a license, which he claimed was withheld by them contrary to law. It all depended upon whether the ruling of the board that the institution was not reputable in their view should stand.

This is the same issue as before,—whether this is within the discretion of the board; and the COURT says again that it is: These questions are by the act submitted to the decision of the State Board of Dental Examiners. Their action is to be predicated upon the requisite facts, and no other tribunal is authorized to investigate them. The act of ascertaining and determining what are the facts is in its nature judicial, involving investigation, judgment, and discretion. So upon this refusal of the Illinois State Board of Dental Examiners to grant a license to a person whose application was based upon a diploma issued by a dental college, mandamus will not issue to compel the board to grant the license, because to entitle the applicant to a license, the diploma must have been issued by a "reputable" dental college, and whether the college is a "reputable" one is, under the statute, within the judgment and discretion of the board to determine. In accordance with this decision are all cases similar to it; for the principle is undoubted.[87]

[87] JURISDICTION IN ADJUDICATION.—Gidley v. Palmerston, 3 Brod. & B. 275; In re Boyes, 13 Ont. 3; Cary v. Curtis, 3 How. 236; Bartlett v. Kane, 16 How. 272; Murray's Lessee v. Hoboken L. & I. Land Co., 18 How. 272; Carrick v. Lamar, 116 U. S. 426; Noble v. Logging R. R., 147 U. S. 165; United States v. Lamont, 155 U. S. 308; Ex parte Selma R. R., 46 Ala. 423; Lee v. Huff, 61 Ark. 494; Downer v. Lent, 6 Cal. 94; Raymond v. Fish, 51 Conn. 80; United States v. Douglass, 19 D. C. 99; Pensacola R. R. v. State, 25 Fla. 310; State v. Thrasher,

§ 114. Exclusive.

The case of Dugan v. United States, 34 Ct. of Cl. 458 (1899), shows that this has the positive side. This was a decision by the Commissioner of Internal Revenue under R. S. sect. 3426, upon satisfactory evidence of the fact that the post exchanges or canteens were not subject to the internal tax upon liquor dealers as they were in fact governmental agencies. The Commissioner, acting upon the statute, thereupon made an allowance by his certificate for a refunding. The question was whether this award was final upon the government.

The opinion of PEELE is in substance: The Commissioner's functions with respect to the matter referred to under the statute are judicial in their nature; and his action concludes a claimant from taking to the courts for investigation the things designed to be finally settled by him. Whatever rights the claimants had rested upon the statute, which left to the revenue officer to determine whether the special tax was wrongfully collected and for that reason should be refunded. The Commissioner had jurisdiction in the matter, and his allowances or awards for the refund of the taxes so paid, being unim-

77 Ga. 671; People v. Dental Examiners, 110 Ill. 180; Spitznogle v. Ward, 64 Ind. 30; Chamberlain v. Clayton, 56 Iowa, 331; Gilmore v. Hentig, 33 Kan. 170; Construction Co. v. Police Jury, 44 La. Ann. 863; Donahoe v. Richards, 38 Me. 379; Ulman v. Baltimore, 72 Md. 592; Miller v. Horton, 152 Mass. 540; Highway Commissioners v. Ely, 54 Mich. 173; State v. Chicago, etc., R. R., 38 Minn. 281; State v. Chicago, etc., R. R., 29 Neb. 412; Edes v. Boardman, 58 N. H. 580; Williams v. Weaver, 75 N. Y. 30; Board of Education v. Bladen Com'rs, 113 N. C. 379; Thomas v. Wilton, 40 Oh. St. 516; Burton v. Fulton, 49 Pa. St. 151; Keenan v. Perry, 24 Tex. 260; Burdett v. Allen, 35 W. Va. 354.

peached, must stand. Judgment will be entered in his favor for both awards.

How final the decision of an officer of the administration may be is shown in the ruling cases concerning grants by a government. United States v. The Commissioner, 5 Wall. 563 (1866). The case in that court arose on a petition by McConnell for a mandamus to command the Commissioner to issue a land patent to him. The relator held a certificate, but the Commissioner had refused to grant him a patent. What reasons influenced the Commissioner in this refusal did not appear. The court refused to go into the question at all.

The court disposed of this mandamus in a very summary manner. NELSON said: Where the merit of the several objections and questions made in this case lie we do not undertake to determine, nor can they be determined understandingly upon this record. Many of the acts of the parties, and of the officer, the registers and the commissioners of the land office may be valid or void. We have referred to them for the purpose of showing that this case is not one to which the remedy by mandamus can be applied. It calls for the exercise of the judicial functions of the officer and those of no ordinary character. The duty is not merely ministerial, but involves judgment and discretion, which cannot be controlled by this writ. We have found no case in which this power has been exercised. Patents are to be signed by the President in person or in his name by a Secretary under his direction and countersigned by the recorder of the general land office. The phrase in this opinion that is worth emphasis is, the exercise of the judicial functions of an officer.

To what extent the decisions of the administration upon contests within its jurisdiction are final is the first question. This depends upon one fundamental distinction in this subject. The decision of the administration may either be preliminary or final. Two steps may be provided for or one. The scheme may be either that the claimant must first apply to the administration for its adjudication, and after this condition precedent may begin over again in the judicial courts if he is still aggrieved; or the arrangement may be that the claimant has only the administration as the tribunal to try his case against the government, the provision being that this decision of the administration shall be without recourse elsewhere. In either case it is to be noted there is adjudication by the administration; only in the first case there is another examination possible afterwards, in the other case there is none. An administration that has power to go so far as to decide the controversies that arise out of its own action is most effective in its action. That process may well be made a preliminary proceeding in all cases. An appeal to a superior from any inferior it is well to provide in first instance; indeed this is part of the normal processes of administration. But to make the decision of the administration final will give a power to the administration that in most cases will be apt to be arbitrary in its exercise. So the result is that exclusive jurisdiction for the administration is the unusual case and the concurrent jurisdiction is the usual case. In one view this is a question of jurisdiction; in another view it is a question of procedure.[88]

§ 115. Final.

Within the scope of its jurisdiction the adjudication of the administration is final unless there is provision to the contrary. An explicit opinion to this extent is in Litchfield v. Register & Receiver, 9 Wall. 575 (1869). This was a bill filed against the local officers of a United States land office, asking an injunction to restrain them from acting upon the application of another for land claimed by him. The superior court at the final stage dismissed the bill. The ground taken by the defendant thus prevailed that the department was final within the scope of its authority.

Mr. Justice MILLER delivered a comprehensive opinion: The principle has been so repeatedly decided in this court that the judiciary cannot interfere, either by mandamus or injunction, with executive officers, such as the respondents here, in the discharge of their official duties, unless those duties are of a character purely ministerial and involving no exercise of judgment and discretion, that it would seem to be useless to repeat it here. The lands

[88] EXCLUSIVE.—Gaines v. Thompson, 7 Wall. 352; Secretary v. McGarrahan, 9 Wall. 314; Shepley v. Cowan, 91 U. S. 340; Moore v. Robbins, 96 U. S. 536; Davidson v. New Orleans, 96 U. S. 97; Fong Yue Ting v. United States, 149 U. S. 715; Porter v. Haight, 45 Cal. 631; Parmalee v. Baldwin, 1 Conn. 317; State v. Trustees, 20 Fla. 405; People v. Bartels, 138 Ill. 322; Walker v. Hallock, 32 Ind. 239; Donahoe v. Richards, 38 Me. 379; Dillingham v. Snow, 5 Mass. 547; Meade v. Haines, 81 Mich. 261; State v. Medical Examiners, 34 Minn. 387; Stuart v. Palmer, 74 N. Y. 194; American Pavement Co. v. Wagner, 139 Pa. St. 623; Davis v. Strong, 31 Vt. 332; Henderson v. Smith, 26 W. Va. 829.

in question are situated within the land district over which these officers have authority to receive proof of pre-emption, and grant certificate of entry. The very first duty which the register is called on to perform, when application is made to him to enter a tract of land, is to ascertain whether it is subject to entry. Has there been a proclamation offering it for sale; has it been reserved by any action of Congress, or of the proper department; has it been granted by any Act of Congress; or has it been sold? These are all questions for him to decide and they require the exercise of judgment and discretion. He says that the court below erred because it did not require them to come in and answer to his claim of title, to put the court in possession of their views, to defend their instructions from the Commissioner, and to convert the contest before the land department into one before the court. This is precisely what this court has decided that no court can do.

It is perhaps necessary to reinforce these principles. Indeed the extent of the power of the administration in the adjudication of questions that arise in the course of the application of the law is not often apprehended. The truth of the matter is that the power of the administration in its adjudication is often final; that is, without appeal to any other tribunal. Whenever a matter is entrusted to the adjudication of the administration, the decision of that department is final unless other provision is made. The rule that the power of the administration is final within the scope of its authority goes to this extent.

An encyclopaedic case upon these issues is Foster v.

United States, 32 Ct. of Cl. 170 (1897). The facts were peculiar. Claimant alleges that he entered a quarter-section of land, which grant was later, by a combination of circumstances, avoided because certain conditions precedent had not happened. The foundation of the suit was that the United States ought to make reparation for the failure of the entry to take effect. There was a statutory process provided which more or less covered the case. The question was whether the claimant could get at the judicial courts. The court dismissed the complaint.

MOTT summarized the law: (1) Where Congress create a class of claims, such as customs cases, or national revenue cases, or pension cases, and provides a jurisdiction for their ascertainment, that jurisdiction is exclusive. (2) But where Congress refer claims to accounting officers for payment and they refuse to give effect, the accounting officers are held to have no more than auditing powers. (3) And so where a claimant entered land within the boundaries of a railroad grant and paid the price, a suit cannot be maintained, because Congress annulled the grant in consequence of the railroad's inaction.[89]

§ 116. Adjudication in controversies.

Hook, 8 Pen. Dec. 367 (1896), is a case that gives an

[89] FINAL.—Litchfield v. Register & Receiver, 9 Wall. 575; Meade v. United States, 9 Wall. 691; United States v. Johnston, 124 U. S. 236; French v. Fyan, 93 U. S. 173; Marquez v. Frisbie, 101 U. S. 475; Stewart v. McHarry, 159 U. S. 650; Grider v. Tally, 77 Ala. 422; New York, etc., R. Co.'s Appeal, 62 Conn. 535; McCord v. High, 24 Ia. 336; Attorney-General v. Northampton, 143 Mass. 589; Ham v. Toledo R. R., 29 Oh. St. 174; Hicks v. Dorn, 42 N. Y. 47; State v. Verner, 30 S. C. 280; Bledsoe v. International R. Co., 40 Tex. 568; Thurston v. Hudgins, 93 Va. 784; Empev v. Plugert, 64 Wis. 612.

insight into this adjudication. A motion for reconstruction was filed in this case on the following grounds, as stated by the attorney in his motion: The claimant was and is drawing $10 per month. His declaration for increase was first passed and then rejected in the face of the favorable report by a ruling of the Medical Referee that the present rate is commensurate with the degree of his disability. This opinion appears to me to be arbitrary and illegal in that he assumes a discretionary power that the law does not confer upon him. If by the strokes of his pen the Medical Referee can virtually annul and set aside the finding and report of two medical examinations—the actual conclusion of six physicians who are sworn officers of the Government—then why are such examinations made? I ask this not for the purpose of casting any reflections, but solely in the interest of the legal phase of the situation.

The Assistant Secretary, REYNOLDS, did not leave this attorney in any doubt as to the internal law on this subject of administration by adjudication: The question immediately arises, to what end are all these inferior officers, the Surgeons and the Referee, appointed? The Commissioner of Pensions cannot personally interview each applicant or inquire into his alleged disabilities, neither is it to be supposed that one official or any other one man can pass intelligently upon the multitudinous and various questions that arise in the adjudication of pension claims when such questions involve special and technical knowledge in the various sciences. It is necessary that the facts be laid before the Commissioner, and when medical and surgical facts are involved the clear intent of the law is that in justice to the claimant as well as to the Government medical facts shall be brought out by the skilled in that particular science which will serve as a guide to the Commissioner of Pensions in arriving at his conclusions; but the Commissioner of Pensions is not bound by this expert opinion. He renders his decision upon all the evidence in the case which touches upon the points in issue. That the Medical Referee should not be bound by ratings affixed by the Boards of Surgeons ought to be apparent upon the same course of reasoning. He is doubtless often aided by the opinion of the examining surgeons as to how much to use the words of the statute in their judgment, as he must and does arrive at his conclusion by reason of the facts shown. It should, however, be remembered that neither the opinion of the examining surgeons nor the Medical Referee's opinion is final. It is the Commissioner of Pensions who finally passes upon the question; and he reaches his conclusions upon all the evidence, using as means to that end all of the various agencies that are placed at his disposal, potent among which are the facts and opinions as set out in the certificate of the examining boards and the judgment of the Medical Referee.

This opinion is worth quotation at this length, because it sets forth in the clearest manner possible the view of the administration. Upon the whole this ruling is one of the most perspicuous statements of the situation in administration. In administration the officers at the bottom of the hierarchy decide the questions that arise in administration, and it is the usual practice that the officers at the top of the hierarchy do not act unless there is an appeal. That is the internal law of the administration—to facilitate the conduct of its business. But the fact remains that the officer at the top can always come down upon the officer at the bottom, set that officer aside and decide upon the matter himself. The key to this is that the internal law of administration is in last analysis the discretion of the superior reduced to rules for the ordinary case, free of these rules in the extraordinary case. Such is all administration.

It is needless to pile case on case for this fundamental principle: that if a matter in which the government is involved is given over to an officer for his determination, his decision is final. This is the familiar law of the functions of the administration: that if an officer is invested with a discretionary power to act in behalf of the government, all that he does in the exercise of that discretion is final. This is the foundation of this method of administration in last analysis, as indeed it is the foundation of all powers in administration—discretion. This is all that is meant when it is said that an officer has judicial powers in the premises and that his jurisdiction over that subject matter is therefore exclusive.

A case in the administrative law reports that is regarded as a leading authority is Pueblo Case, 5 Land Dec. 483 (1887). This was an application which involved inter alia the recall and cancellation of the patent of the United States to the city of San Francisco and for the issue of a new patent with different boundaries, to-wit, the boundaries of what is known as the Stratton Survey. It was insisted by counsel that the Secretary of Interior has not the power to reverse the action of the Commissioner upon the survey of a land claim pending before him. That involved passing upon the question. The decision, therefore, is a fundamental one: whether the Commissioner of the Land Office was in the determination of controversies independent of the Secretary of Interior.

The opinion of Secretary LAMAR establishes that in this manner: By various acts of Congress the powers of the Department are clearly defined. These acts are, so far as it is necessary for me at present to consider them, embodied in the Revised Statutes. Title XI treats of the Department of the Interior and makes the Secretary of the Interior the head thereof. The third Chapter provides as follows: The Commissioner of the General Land Office shall perform under the direction of the Secretary of Interior all executive duties appertaining to the surveying and sale of the Public Lands of the United States, and also such as relate to private claims of land and the issuing of patents for all grants of land under authority of the government. The position of the applicants against the authority of the Secretary to review the decision of the Commissioner of the General Land Office rests upon the ground that the action of the Commissioner is passing upon the correctness of surveys of private land claims is a quasi judicial proceeding, and therefore not subject to review, as no appeal to the Secretary in such cases is specifically provided. Passing upon correctness of private land claims made by subordinate officers necessarily involves the exercise of judgment and may properly be called a quasi judicial proceeding; but it is none the less a proceeding taken in the discharge of an executive duty of the Commissioner. There seems to be some misapprehension as to the meaning of the term "executive duty." The executive duties of any one of the departments are such as are required of its officers in the administration of the law upon the subjects under its jurisdiction. They are not the less executive duties because they require in their performance the examination of evidence and the exercise of judgment thereon. All executive duties which are anything beyond the performance of ministerial acts involve the exercise of judgment, such as examination, decision and final judgment, but they are not judicial acts. There is hardly an act of any moment performed in an executive department which would not, if such were the case, be taken from the supervision and control of its head. The statutes in placing the whole business of the Department under the supervision of the Secretary invest him with authority to review, reverse, amend, annul or affirm all proceedings in the Department having for their ultimate object to secure the alienation of any part of the public lands or the adjustment of claims to lands.

This leading ruling is quoted at such length because it sets forth in exact language the theory of the administration as to the nature of its adjudication and its function therein.[90]

[90] ADJUDICATION IN CONTROVERSIES.—Evans v. Eaton, 7 Wheat. 434; Murray's Lessee v. Hoboken L. & I. Co., 18 How. 272; United States v. Jordan, 113 U. S. 423; Arnson v. Murphy, 115 U. S. 586; Spencer v. Merchant, 125 U. S. 356; Auffmordt v. Hedden, 137 U. S. 323; Norwood v. Baker, 172 U. S. 269; French v. Barber Asphalt Pav. Co., 181 U. S. 324; Ex parte Bridge Co., 62 Ark. 461; Downer v. Lent, 6 Cal. 94; Raymond v. Fish, 51 Conn. 80; Bureau Co. Sup'rs v. Chicago, etc., R. Co., 44 Ill. 229; Chicago, etc., R. R. v. Atchison Co. Com'rs, 54 Kan. 781; Gatch v. Des Moines, 63 Ia. 718; Monticello, etc., Co. v. Baltimore, 90 Md. 417; Weimer v. Bunbury, 30 Mich. 201; Nelson Lumber Co. v. McKinnon, 61 Minn. 219; State v. Chicago, etc., R. R., 29 Neb. 412; Central R. R. Co. v. Assessors, 48 N. J. L. 1; Stuart v. Palmer, 74 N. Y. 183; King v. Portland, 38 Ore. 402; Harrisburg v. McPherran, 200 Pa. St. 343; Dietz v. Neenah, 91 Wis.

§ 117. Concurrent.

In the present paragraph the executive department is seen with a concurrent jurisdiction vested in it. The condition is that administrative adjudication must precede; but if another examination of the question is wished afterwards before the judicial department, that may be demanded. As the greater includes the less, so if it is constitutional to give an exclusive jurisdiction to the executive department over these contests, there can be, of course, no constitutional objection to the grant of a concurrent jurisdiction to it.

In this connection Cheatham v. United States, 92 U. S. 85 (1875), is worth discussion. A party against whom an assessment was made for an income tax in 1865 appealed therefrom to the Commissioner of Internal Revenue, who in 1867 set it aside and ordered a new one, which was made in 1868, and the tax was thereupon collected. In 1869 suit was begun to recover the money; the defense in that suit was that by the statute no suit could be brought against the collector unless begun within six months from the decision of the Commissioner upon the appeal. The question was whether this was a short statute of limitation which ought not to run until the payment, when action accrued, or whether this was an express condition upon the right to sue.

The opinion of the court was by Mr. Justice MILLER: All governments at all times have found it necessary to accept stringent methods for the collection of taxes, and to be rigid in the enforcement of them. These measures are not judicial nor does the government resort ex-

428; Bartlett v. Wilson, 59 Vt. 23; Violett v. Alexandria, 92 Va. 561; State v. Cheney, 45 W. Va. 478.

cept in extreme cases to the courts for that purpose. The revenue measures of every sovereign government constitute a system which provides for its enforcement by officers commissioned for that purpose. In this country this system provides safeguards of its own against mistake, injustice or oppression in the administration of the revenue laws. Such appeals are allowed to specified tribunals as the law-makers deem expedient. Such remedies also for recovering back taxes as may seem wise are provided. In these respects the United States have enacted a system of corrective justice as well as a system of taxation. In both these extremes of the internal revenue, that system is intended to be complete. The government has the right to prescribe the conditions on which it will subject itself to the judgment of the courts; while the free course of remonstrance and appeal may be allowed within the departments, that is all a statutory matter. The general government has wisely made the payment of the tax claim, whether customs or internal revenue, a condition precedent to access to the court. The objecting party can then take his appeal. We regard this as a condition on which alone the government consents to litigate the lawfulness of the original tax. It is not a hard condition. Few governments have conceded such a right on any condition.

This condition of the law is seen in Nichols v. United States, 7 Wall. 122 (1868). The statute provided in that case that no action could be maintained against any collector to recover the amount of duties paid under protest unless the said protest was made in writing and signed by the claimant at or before the payment of the duties, setting forth distinctly and specifically the grounds of objection to the payment thereof. Notwithstanding this, Nichols & Company, after having paid th duties with no protest in the matter, brought suit agains the United States for the over-payment in the Court o Claims. The question was then whether this protest wa a condition precedent, indispensable in bringing suit.

The court held that this was the exclusive method Mr. Justice DAVIS said: The prompt collection of th revenue and its faithful application is one of the mos vital duties of the government. Congress has from tim to time passed laws on the subject of revenue, which no only provide for the manner of its collection but als point out a way in which errors may be corrected. Thes laws constitute a system which Congress has provided for the benefit of those persons who complain of illega assessment of taxes and illegal exactions of duty. In the administration of the tariff laws, as we have seen the Secretary of Treasury decides what is due on a spe cific importation of goods; but if the importer is dissatis fied with this decision, he can contest the question in a suit against the Collector, if before he pays the duties he tells the officers of the law in writing why he objects to that payment. If the importer does not protest, his right of action is gone. The mischiefs that would re sult if the aggrieved party could disregard the provisions in the system devised for his security and benefit and sue at any time in the Court of Claims forbid the idea that Congress intended to allow any other mode to re dress a supposed wrong in the operation of the revenue laws than is given in them.[91]

§ 118. Alternative.

In certain cases the law stands that although the mat

[91] CONCURRENT.—Nichols v. United States, 7 Wall. 122; Averill v

ter may be brought before the administration for its adjudication, it need not be so. A suit may be brought against the officer in the ordinary courts of law at any time. That indeed is the situation unless there is statutory provision such as has been seen in the cases that have just been discussed. One of the best known cases upon that point is United States v. Harmon, 147 U. S. 268 (1893). This was a suit brought in the Circuit Court by a United States marshal to recover against the United States certain fees and disbursements which had been forwarded by him to the First Auditor of the Treasury and by him allowed, and then by him to the First Comptroller, and by him disallowed. The act which gave the Circuit Court jurisdiction withheld claims rejected by any department authorized to determine the same.

Whether this subject matter was one upon which a Comptroller had power of final determination was therefore the issue. Upon that Mr. Justice BLATCHFORD said: The action of the accounting officers has never been considered as a conclusive determination when the question has been brought before a Court of Justice. The laws themselves, after providing that the balances certified to the heads of Departments by the Comptroller upon

Smith, 17 Wall. 90; Cheatham v. United States, 92 U. S. 85; Snyder v. Marks, 109 U. S. 189; Oberteuffer v. Robertson, 116 U. S. 515; Auffmordt v. Hedden, 137 U. S. 324; Saltonstall v. Russell, 152 U. S. 633; Medbury v. United States, 173 U. S. 495; Eslava v. Jones, 83 Ala. 139; Woolfork v. Buckner, 60 Ark. 163; McCormick v. Burt, 95 Ill. 263; Spitznogle v. Ward, 64 Ind. 30; Ferry v. Campbell, 110 Ia. 290; Union Trust Co. v. Wayne Probate Judge, 125 Mich. 487; St. Joseph v. McCabe, 58 Mo. App. 542; McDaniel v. Tebbetts, 60 N. H. 497; Adams v. Ives, 63 N. Y. 650; American Pavement Co. v. Wagner. 139 Pa. St. 623; Heth v. Radford, 96 Va. 272; Hubbard v. Kelley, 8 W. Va. 49; Druecker v. Salomon, 21 Wis. 621.

the settlement of public accounts shall not be subject to be modified by the heads of the Departments but shall be conclusive upon the executive branch of the government, adds in unequivocal terms that the same shall be subject to revision only by proper courts. That is, the force of this adjudication is administrative only—internal; it has no judicial force—external.

An analogous situation is seen in Morgan v. Daniels, 153 U. S. 120 (1894). Daniels in his suit against Morgan asserted in his bill that he was the original inventor, but that the Commissioner of Patents had declared Daniels to be first inventor. The suit was brought under an express statute which gave a person aggrieved by a refusal of the Patent Office this remedy by injunction to establish his right. The contention of counsel was that the prior decision of the Patent Office should stand unless the testimony should show beyond any reasonable doubt that that decision had been erroneous.

Mr. Justice BREWER dealt with the case in this manner: This is something different from a mere appeal. It is an application to the Courts to set aside the action of one of the executive departments of the government. The determination of the Patent Office has given to the defendant the exclusive rights of a patentee. A new proceeding is now instituted in the Courts—a proceeding to set aside the conclusions reached by an administrative department, and to give to the plaintiff the rights there awarded to the defendant. Upon principal authority it must be laid down as a rule that the decision by the Patent Office must be accepted as controlling upon that question of fact, unless the contrary be established by testimony which in character and amount carries thorough conviction.

There are then these two classes of cases: The one holds the adjudication of the administration final upon all the world; the other holds the adjudication of the administration final only upon the administration. The solution of this puzzle is that this is all a question of statute, to what extent the adjudication of the administration shall be final. If the Legislature definitely enacts that the decision of the administration shall be final, that decision is not open to a collateral attack. But if the Legislature does not so provide, it will not be implied that the decision of the administration is beyond collateral attack.[92]

§ 119. Conclusion.

In all adjudication by the administration upon close examination there are signs of the administrative nature of the proceedings. Things are done in administrative adjudication which could never be done in judicial process. Principles are violated in administrative process which are fundamental in the courts. Oftentimes the whole solemn procedure is upset so that there may be prompt administration. All this can mean but one thing; and that is that this process is nothing more nor less than administration. This will be seen upon an analysis of the nature of the processes of the administration to which the discussion now proceeds.

92 ALTERNATIVE.—Collector v. Hubbard, 12 Wall. 15; Erskine v. Hohnbach, 14 Wall. 616; United States v. Harmon, 147 U. S. 268; Morgan v. Daniels, 153 U. S. 126; Wisconsin Cent. Ry. v. United States, 164 U. S. 205; McCord v. High, 24 Ia. 336; Strickfaden v. Zipprick, 49 Ill. 286; Bright v. Murphy, 105 La. 795; Thomas v. Owens, 4 Md. 189; Maxwell v. Pike, 2 Me. 8; Gage v. Currier, 4 Pick. 399; Williams v. Weaver, 75 N. Y. 32; Sexton v. Leliorne, 8 Heisk. 14; Milwaukee Iron Co. v. Schubel, 29 Wis. 444.

CHAPTER XIV.

THE PROCESSES OF THE ADMINISTRATION.

§ 120. Introduction.

The external law of administration governs the jurisdiction of the administration over controversies that arise in the course of the execution of the law. But the internal law of the administration governs the procedure in the controversies when the decision is made. It is to be remarked that while the rules of external law that have been discussed upon the whole are rigid, the rules of the internal law that are to be discussed, it will be found, are often discretionary. As this is quasi judicial work, upon the whole the judicial process is used, as that is best adapted in a large way to the determination of controversies. But in the course of adjudication by the administration there will often be a departure from the forms of judicial process. After all, in any emergencies the administration is impatient of forms.

The nature of the process in administration may best

be seen by the examination of some typical proceedings in various lines of administration. In the course of this chapter examples of ex parte proceedings will first be brought forward. There will be a description of a claim before the Pension Office. Next there will be a description of an allowance before the Comptroller's Office. Next there will be a description of a collection by the Customs branch. Then inter partes will be taken up. Next in order, a contest before the Patent Office. After that a protest before the Land Office. After that a remission before the Internal Revenue Office. It is hoped that from these diverse illustrations some idea can be gotten of the processes of the administrations.

§ 121. Ex parte proceedings.

That is because there is no necessity in law to use judicial form in the adjudication. The only requirement is that the decision shall be reached in some proper manner. A case upon that point is Earnshaw v. United States, 146 U. S. 60 (1892). In that case the importer had been given a day to appear before the appraiser. His clerk answered that he was absent in Cuba; whereupon he was given another day by telegram, to which no reply was made. The appraiser thereupon adjudicated upon the case ex parte. The complaint of the importer was that he had not had a proper opportunity to present his case according to due process.

Mr. Justice Brown gave the opinion: It is conceded in this case that the appraisement was binding provided that it was properly conducted. It is complained that due notice was not given. No provision is expressly made by statute for notice to the importer. The Board of Appraisers is invested with powers of a quasi judicial character; and the appraisers are bound by all reasonable ways and means to ascertain the appraisement. With respect to their method of procedure, they are vested with a certain discretion, which will be respected by the courts except where such discretion has been manifestly abused and the Board has proceeded in wanton disregard of justice. The general principle is too well established to admit of doubt that where the action of an inferior tribunal is discretionary its decision is final. The tribunal in this case was created as part of the machinery of the government for the collection of duties upon imports, and while its proceedings partake of a semi-judicial character it is not reasonable to expect that in notifying the importer it should proceed with the technical accuracy necessary to charge the defendant with liability in a court of law. The operations of the government in the collection of its revenue ought not to be embarrassed by requiring too strict an adherence to the forms and modes of proceedings recognized in the courts of law, so long as the rights of its taxpayers are not sacrificed.

A case upon this point from the administrative point of view is Dargie, 13 Land Dec. 277 (1892). This was a motion before the Secretary of the Interior to remand a certain contested case to the Commissioner. It was argued in support of this motion that no notice of the petition upon which the cases were transmitted to the department was ever served upon the contestant, that the transmission was therefore in violation of the rules which limit appeal from local officers. It was claimed therefore that the department could have no jurisdiction in the matter. The question was rather what should be done at this stage, than what might be done if the Secretary had seen fit to act.

Secretary NOBLE held: The fact that the law places the entire duty of its execution upon the Secretary of the Interior furnishes no reason for suspending the rules of practice and depriving parties of the rights given thereby; for the Secretary of the Interior is charged with the supervision of the public business relating to public land, and the Commissioner of the General Land Office is charged with the performance under the direction of the Secretary of the Interior of all executive duties. The duty of the Secretary under the act now in question is supervision. The usual and ordinary mode of seeking a decision from the Secretary upon questions of this character is by way of appeal pointed out in the rules which have been formulated and approved as best adapted to protect the interests of claimants for public lands and at the same time to expedite the transaction of business in relation to such lands. None of them shall be construed to deprive the Secretary of Interior of the exercise of the directory and supervisory powers conferred on him by the law; but it is also true that they are to be followed when there is no occasion made out for the invoking of these powers. The importance of having uniform rules in these matters and of enforcing them has often been recognized.[93]

[93] EX PARTE PROCEEDINGS.—United States v. Jones, 8 Pet. 375; Decatur v. Paulding, 14 Pet. 497; United States v. Tappan, 11 Wheat. 426; Lawrence v. Caswell, 13 How. 497; Vance v. Burbank, 101 U. S. 519; United States v. Teller, 107 U. S. 68; United States v. Black, 128 U. S. 40; Earnshaw v. United States, 146 U. S. 67; United States v. Harmon, 147 U. S. 268; Passavant v. United States,

§ 122. Claim.

The first illustration proposed is that of a claim for a pension through the Pension Bureau. The application for a pension which is filed by the claimant contains, like a declaration, the grounds upon which the pension is claimed, following its main point,—the provision of the act under which the application is made. For example, in an invalid pension the applicant must describe his military status, relate how he was disabled, state his medical record and set forth what rating he claims. Of course this matter is all covered by general forms.

The first stage in the proceedings in the Pension Office may be briefly described. The application is recorded in the Record Division. From the Record Division it is sent to the proper Adjudicating Division, according to the territory from which the claims come. It is there placed before the chief of that division, who assigns it to a subordinate examiner to determine in the first instance whether there is pensionable status. As pensionable status depends upon the disabilities of service in the case under consideration, the next reference will be to the Record Office of the War Department. Upon the answer of the War Department the case is reopened by the examiner. The point now is to determine whether the proof submitted is sufficient to establish the material facts made necessary by the law. It may be necessary to call for further proof.

If the claim is one that requires proof of present disability, the next step in the process is an official medical

148 U. S. 219; Ballew v. United States, 160 U. S. 187; Chorpenning v. United States, 11 Ct. of Cl. 625; McElrath v. United States, 12 Ct. of Cl. 201.

examination. For this purpose the applicant is directed to appear before a Board of Examining Surgeons which sits in his neighborhood. At Washington there is a Medical Division, which has power over all medical questions in review. The approval of this Medical Division must be had before the application is in shape for adjudication.

Meanwhile from the Adjudicating Division the claim has been forwarded to the Board of Review. This board is composed of reviewers and re-reviewers. There are thus two successive adjudications upon the whole proof submitted for each application. The sole function of these reviews is to treat the question judicially upon the law and the fact. It is therefore almost impossible that any point would be left unnoticed which is not covered by sufficient evidence.

The matter is now ready for the formal action of the Commissioner of Pensions. Not infrequently it is in this office that the application is rejected. The Commissioner, as has been repeatedly pointed out, has full power in the matter. The only act in the office which is of legal validity is this last act of his. If the application is rejected an appeal is allowed from the Commissioner to the Secretary of Interior. The business is done in that office by a Board of Pension Appeals,—a useful body of lawyers who have had a salutary influence upon pension adjudication. The regulations governing the procedure in claims for pensions are put in Appendix A for further consultation.[94]

[94] CLAIM.—Preston, 1 Pen. Dec. 41; Riordan, 1 Pen. Dec. 45; Ennis, 1 Pen. Dec. 127; Smith, 1 Pen. Dec. 201; Romine, 1 Pen. Dec. 299; Lauback, 1 Pen. Dec. 318; Morris, 2 Pen. Dec. 73; Mueller,

§ 123. Allowance.

The second illustration proposed was the process by which a claim against the government is allowed by the Treasury Department. As before, the claim must be made according to the regular form demanded by the department. Moreover it must be a liquidated claim. Each office of the government has a disbursing officer. The application in the first instance should be to that officer. The next step that must be taken is administration revision,—some approval of the disbursement by the officer who had charge of the administration. This is a preliminary stage simply.

The claim then goes to the office of the proper Auditor for allowance. If there has been administrative revision, the claim is examined there by one clerk and approved by the chief of division; if there has been no administrative revision, the claim is examined by two clerks before approval by the chief of division. Thus it will be seen that in the office of the Auditor there is a careful adjudication, so that the claim is only approved upon sufficient evidence.

An account is either settled as rendered or is disallowed in whole or in part. The party aggrieved has an appeal from the Auditor to the Comptroller. Moreover the Comptroller upon his own motion may take up any account. In either case the whole account is before the Comptroller and he may take any action thereupon which

2 Pen. Dec. 192; Hamilton, 2 Pen. Dec. 217; Gaskell, 3 Pen. Dec. 87; Tuttle, 3 Pen. Dec. 52; Sherer, 4 Pen. Dec. 5; Johnson, 4 Pen. Dec. 167; Cady, 5 Pen. Dec. 84; McElfatrick, 5 Pen. Dec. 278; Bennett, 7 Pen. Dec. 1; Ratliff, 7 Pen. Dec. 6; Cramer, 7 Pen. Dec. 459; Allen, 7 Pen. Dec. 568; Predmore, 8 Pen. Dec. 165; Green, 8 Pen. Dec. 444; Hook, 8 Pen. Dec. 367; Luther, 9 Pen. Dec. 72.

seems to him fit. The form of the appeal sets forth the reason of it; but there is no obligation that the decision of the Comptroller shall be responsive to the pleadings. It is well settled that the action of the Comptroller is final upon all the executive departments upon any matters of allowance which is within his jurisdiction. Certain provisions governing the allowance of claims are put in Appendix B for further illustration.[95]

§ 124. Collection.

The third illustration proposed is that of the process by which customs duties are collected. The general rule is that goods imported must be declared, the assessment be made, and the duty be paid at the port of entry. Of course each and every article imported cannot be examined by the Appraiser. The method is by the examination of a certain proportion of each entry. As customs acts lay duties according to two systems, specific and ad valorem, it follows that the appraiser must have in mind the classification of goods and the valuation of goods. When the appraisal has been made, if all is found in accordance with the entry which has been made by the importer, the matter is passed for liquidation by the importer of the duties imposed.

[95] ALLOWANCE.—Exporters' Case, 5 Laurence, 13; Gilbert, Bowler, 213; Exposition Case, 1 Compt. Dec. 13; Clerk of Court, 1 Compt. Dec. 31; Requisitions, 1 Compt. Dec. 409; Advance Decisions, 1 Compt. Dec. 431; In re Sugar Bounty, 2 Compt. Dec. 98; Claim of Scala, 3 Compt. Dec. 657; Heads of Departments, 4 Compt. Dec. 1; Interstate Commission, 4 Compt. Dec. 341; Maine Losses, 4 Compt. Dec. 622; Revision of Accounts, 4 Compt. Dec. 723; Revision of an Account, 5 Compt. Dec. 333; Unliquidated Damages, 5 Compt. Dec. 770; Professor's Claim, 5 Compt. Dec. 520; Advance Appeal, 6 Compt. Dec. 50; Liquidated Claims, 7 Compt. Dec. 517; Pending Suits, 8 Compt. Dec. 841.

If the importer feels aggrieved an appeal is provided for from the appraiser to the Board of General Appraisers. Moreover, if the collector feels aggrieved, he may institute an appeal before the Board of General Appraisers. The decision of this Board of General Appraisers may again be upon the whole matter of value without regard to the valuation which has been fixed upon the goods. The decision of the Board of General Appraisers upon dutiable value is final and conclusive. But upon questions of classification either the importer or the collector may have an appeal to the Judicial Courts. The administrative statute covering this is put in Appendix C for further use.[96]

§ 125. Inter partes proceedings.

Inter partes proceedings are abnormal in administration, while ex parte proceedings are normal in administration. The true function of the administration is only to determine upon matters between the government and citizens; to determine upon matters between citizens is the true function of the judiciary. Therefore it cannot be in the last analysis that in inter partes proceedings the administration is doing anything but administration. The truth of the matter seems to be that what seems inter partes proceedings is in reality two ex parte proceedings consolidated into one process for the pur-

[96] COLLECTION.—Liquidation, Treas. Dec. No. 7,047; Examination, Treas. Dec. No. 9,849; Protest, Treas. Dec. No. 10,400; Proceedings in rem, etc., Treas. Dec. No. 11,942; Reappraisements, Treas. Dec. No. 12,483; Free Entry, Treas. Dec. No. 13,677; Decisions, Treas. Dec. No. 16,908; Classification, Treas. Dec. No. 18,211; Rules for Transaction of Business, Treas. Dec. No. 18,488; Appeal, Treas. Dec. No. 18,595; Appraisement, Treas. Dec. No. 21,332.

pose of administration. At all events that is the hypothesis defended in this section.

That is seen in Fowler v. Dodge, 1898 Pat. Dec. 257 (1898). In this case there had been an issue in the Patent Office upon the question of priority between two applicants. Then it appeared that upon one of the applications there was a question of operativeness. Fowler thus had an interest in having the application of Dodge withheld; but the question had now become whether the Patent Office should allow the contest to proceed. The case, indeed, raised the very issue of the nature of these interference proceedings in the Patent Office.

GREELY, the Assistant Commissioner, said: Contests as to whether a patent shall issue to a particular applicant are permitted in this office, not because of the interest of the contestant, but because the circumstances are such that there is doubt as to whether the applicant is entitled to a patent; and this question cannot properly be decided without some further investigation. After the office become satisfied on this question it would not be justified in allowing the contest to continue.

Another important ruling along this same line is Saunders v. Baldwin, 9 Land Dec. 391 (1889). In this case a contest was instituted for the same land. By error in practice the contestant did not bring forward his evidence at the proper time set in the regulation. At a later time the contestant brought forward evidence which was in truth conclusive in favor of his contention. The occupant claimed, however, that the contestant could have no right to have the entry cancelled in these proceedings because he had not come forward within the requisite time demanded by the practice of the office.

CHANDLER, the Commissioner, ruled: The department can and may of its own motion, if necessary, direct the cancellation. The government is a real party in interest against both contesting parties; and it is entitled to judgment on the facts, however such facts may have been disclosed, and whatever the rights of the private parties as against one another. This is the object in all administration.[97]

§ 126. Contest.

The fourth illustration proposed was of a contest in the Patent Office between two applicants. The first prerequisite is that each application should be found good according to the regular process in point of patentability. This involves an examination of each application before the proper Primary Examiner and an allowance by him, according to the proper course of proceedings. It may then appear that two applications interfere; that is, that two claims have the same tenor and scope. If such an interference is found between two applications, either by discovery of the examiners or by indications of one of the applicants, the two claims are certified to another division of the Patent Office and there put in interference. The Examiner of Interferences then adjudicates upon the priority between the two applications upon the case as submitted to him.

[97] INTER PARTES PROCEEDINGS.—West v. Cochran, 17 How. 416; Commissioner v. Whiteley, 4 Wall. 532; Collector v. Beggs, 17 Wall. 182; Pahlman v. Collector, 20 Wall. 199; Clinkenbeard v. United States, 21 Wall. 65; Snyder v. Marks, 109 U. S. 193; Butterworth v. United States, 112 U. S. 50; Caha v. United States, 152 U. S. 217; Morgan v. Daniels, 153 U. S. 120; Orchard v. Alexander, 157 U. S. 383; Michigan L. & L. Co. v. Rust, 168 U. S. 602; United States v. Duell, 172 U. S. 582.

If either applicant is aggrieved the appeal lies in due course to the Board of Examiners-in-Chief. The process before the Examiners-in-Chief is more formal. A record is made up and submitted. The Examiners-in-Chief in usual confine their decision to the pleadings submitted to them. Their decision upon the interference in point of law and fact is then given in due form.

From the decision of the Examiners-in-Chief an appeal lies to the Commissioner himself. In an extraordinary case the Commissioner may require the matter to be brought before him on his own motion. It often happens that before the Commissioner or the Assistant Commissioner most important questions involving great property interests are argued with the same forms as in any court of law. If either party feel aggrieved by the decision of the Commissioner an appeal lies according to the provisions of the specific statute to the judicial courts. This statute has been criticized on an earlier page. The rules of practice in this matter are put in Appendix D for further detail.[98]

§ 127. Protest.

The fifth illustration proposed was that of a protest by a stranger, which is allowed by the process of the Land Office. A statute gives a right of preferential entry

[98] CONTEST.—Foster v. Fowle, 1869 Pat. Dec. 35; Krake, 1869 Pat. Dec. 100; Hull, 1869 Pat. Dec. 68; Eames v. McDougall, 1871 Pat. Dec. 206; Clymer's Appeal, 1874 Pat. Dec. 72; United States v. Thacher, 7 O. G. 603; Little v. Lillie, 10 O. G. 543; Whiteley v. McCormick, 10 O. G. 826; Wilson v. Yakel, 10 O. G. 944; Elbers, 1877 Pat. Dec. 123; Ex parte Rodgers, 1879 Pat. Dec. 207; Packard v. Sandford, 1879 Pat. Dec. 314; Hibbard v. Richmond, 17 O. G. 1155; Moore, 1881 Pat. Dec. 249; Sellers v. Walter, 37 O. G. 1001; Zeidler v. Leech, 1891 Pat. Dec. 9; Fowler v. Dodge, 1898 Pat. Dec. 257.

upon a tract of land to a contestant who has protested and procured the cancellation of any entry by any previous entryman. The policy of this act requires some explanation. It was remedial to keep lands which had been occupied unjustly still open for entry and to induce citizens to co-operate in unearthing frauds upon the government by giving to the successful contestants the premium of a preferential entry. Such a contestant may thus appear after any entry and file his protest against the occupants in the form required by the regulations of the department.

The matter is first adjudicated before the local land officers who decide the matter after a full hearing upon the law in fact involved. After the decision upon the contest by the local officers, the whole record of the case is forwarded to the General Land Office. An appeal from the decision of the Register and Receiver may be taken by either party. Moreover, as in all adjudication by the administration, the Commissioner may take the matter up upon his own motion in extraordinary circumstances. At all events the matter is in Washington referred to the Contest Division, where the whole merits of the controversy are reviewed and laid before the Commissioner for his action.

When a final adjudication has been made by the General Land Office, either party, if he still feels aggrieved, may take an appeal to the Secretary of the Interior. There the matter is decided by a trained body of experts who act under the direction of an Assistant Attorney-General assigned to the Interior Department for this purpose. This is the last stage possible in the proceeding and the adjudication is therefore adequate and thorough upon the points taken. The process necessary in such contests is put in Appendix E, if more information is wanted.[99]

§ 128. Remission.

The sixth illustration proposed was an account of the proceedings for an abatement of a tax which must be made before the office of the Commissioner of Internal Revenue. Upon the whole the complainant has no remedy until the tax has been paid by him to the collector. The rule in cases of collection is to pay first and litigate afterwards. It is true that after assessment it is not impossible that a motion for an abatement of the tax may be entertained by the Commissioner before payment of the tax to the Collector; but upon the whole no motion for remission will generally be entertained until the tax has been paid, when a motion for a refund is in order.

The claimant must, as in the usual administrative process, set forth his claim upon a form provided, which relates the essential facts and makes the points upon which he believed he should have refund. The motion is first passed upon by the Collector, who must make affidavit of his finding. The papers, together with all the evidence in the case, is then forwarded to the principal office, where a decision is made upon the matter. Upon the whole, the decision of the Commissioner is final upon

[99] PROTEST.—So. Minnesota Ry. v. Kufner, 2 Land Dec. 492; Field v. Black, 2 Land Dec. 581; Albion Mfg. Co., 4 Land Dec. 376; Stevens v. Robinson, 5 Land Dec. 111; Pueblo Case, 5 Land Dec. 483; Middle Grounds, 7 Land Dec. 255; Saunders v. Baldwin, 9 Land Dec. 391; Gray v. Whitehouse, 15 Land Dec. 352; Mott v. Coffman, 19 Land Dec. 106; Currency Min. Co., 20 Land Dec. 178; Trotter v. Yowell, 21 Land Dec. 54.

the executive department. The statutes governing such abatement are in Appendix F.[100]

§ 129. Conclusion.

It is not pretended that it would be safe to follow this outline in proceeding in any actual case before the office without a careful consultation of the regulations which are in the appendix. All that has been wished is to bring together a variety of illustrations of the sort of thing that is met in practice before the various offices of the administration. The appendix will be found more definite as to the steps necessary in procedure of a given department.

Moreover, it is hoped that a more definite idea of the methods employed in administration may be had even after the description of the proceedings is reduced to such general terms as to be vague. Upon the whole, one is impressed by the excellent balance maintained in administration between form and substance. The regulations indeed are explicit upon the forms to be observed in the practice; but whenever a case arises where these forms would obstruct the due execution of administrative justice they are not followed. This is the most characteristic thing in the processes of the administration.

100 REMISSION.—In re Brown, 3 Int. Rev. Rec. 134; In re Phillips, 10 Int. Rev. Rec. 107; Compromises, 12 Opin. 472; Taxes, 13 Opin. 439; Instructions, 22 Int. Rev. Rec. 109; Commissioner, Treas. Dec. No. 20,459.

CHAPTER XV.

THE JURISDICTION OF THE ADMINISTRATION.

§ 130. Introduction.

The last question of all is the jurisdiction of the administration. Throughout this extended discussion the administration has been seen in the exercise of various powers. Sometimes what was noted was administration by execution; sometimes what was found was administration by legislation; sometimes what was remarked was administration by adjudication. Upon the whole the point of view has been for the most part thus internal; in what way may the administration act? Now, by way of precaution, it will be well to take last of all the other point of view, external; beyond what limits may the administration not act? In a word, this last question is concerned with the extent of the jurisdiction of the administration over all these various questions which it takes upon itself to decide.

§ 131. Scope of jurisdiction.

A recent case contains the best general discussion of this problem—Rex v. Commissioners [1901] 2 K. B. 879 (1901). Kodak, Limited, an English company, had its principal place of business in London. The Eastman Kodak Company, a New York company, had its principal place of business in that state. It appeared that 98 per cent. of the capital stock of the American company was owned by the English company; and there was evidence tending to show that the direction over the whole business came from the London office, so that the American company was to all intents the agent of the English company. Upon that view of the matter, the Commissioners for the London district assessed the income tax not only upon all the profits of the English business, but upon all the profits of the American business as well. This was an application for a prohibition.

STERLING, Lord Justice, drew this important distinction: It appears to me that this section of the statutes conferred upon these Commissioners jurisdiction to charge any person carrying on a trade within that district in respect to the whole profits of his trade, whether that trade be wholly or partly carried on within the district; or, in other words, the only essential requisite to the existence of the jurisdiction to charge a trader in respect of the whole profits is that he be found within the district carrying on the trade in part. Having jurisdiction to charge in respect to all profits, they have jurisdiction to decide all questions of fact necessary for making the full assessment, and, therefore, to determine the true extent of the trade. In my opinion it is not true to say that the facts found by the Commissioners in the course of an inquiry properly entered upon are the facts which are necessary to give jurisdiction. In my judgment they have not exceeded their jurisdiction.

This same position is taken in an explicit manner upon

the case to be distinguished from the preceding case where there is no jurisdiction. In the Middle Grounds, 7 Land Dec. 255 (1888), there was a question as to the right to a certain tract of land which had been surveyed in a general way by the Land Department. This land in dispute had been patented by the United States to a pre-emption settler. The adverse claimant was the State of Michigan, which based its title under the Swamp Land Act. The department took the position in this case at the outset that it had no jurisdiction any longer, since at all events the title to the land in controversy was out of the United States.

To this effect Secretary VILAS wrote: Whatever alteration has come by accretion and the like is a matter between the parties. The Department seems clearly to have no jurisdiction over the matter or power to take action in any form. All these questions can far better be determined by a judicial tribunal than by this Department. Indeed, no action of the Department would be within its jurisdiction. No further action should be taken by the Department in this matter, but the parties should mutually be left to such proceedings in the courts as they may be advised to take in the maintenance of their respective claims. All action before the Department should be discontinued.[101]

§ 132. Administration by execution.

This brings the discussion to the general problem. Let it be supposed that some officer of the administration has extended power over a certain subject matter by the broad provision of some general statute. Then let it be

101 SCOPE OF JURISDICTION.—Gidley v. Palmerston, 3 Brod. & B. 275; Rex v. Commissioners [1901] 2 K. B. 879; Enterprise Ass'n v. Zums-

supposed that he does some action in the course of administration, which is close to the line of his authority. It may be granted that he has power to decide matters within his jurisdiction; but it may not be granted that he has power to decide what matters are within his jurisdiction. The distinction may often be a nice one, but its observance is an absolute necessity in point of law.

No law, that is, is to be construed to give to the administration authority to determine whether the jurisdiction exists; but that question is always open to collateral attack in the judicial courts. United States v. Burke, 99 Federal, 895 (1899), is a plain case upon that point. A statute gave to immigration officials power to exclude aliens under certain circumstances of this qualification. Have such officials thereby power to determine whether certain persons who demand admission are aliens or not? No. Have such officials power to determine whether certain aliens are within the disqualifications laid down? Yes. That is the distinction that the judge had in mind in this case.

TOULMIN, the District Judge, said: I am not unmindful of the provision of the statute that in every case where an alien is excluded from admission into the United States under any law or treaty now existing or hereafter made, decision of the appropriate Immigration or

tein, 64 Fed. 840; United States v. Burke, 99 Fed. 895; Lee v. Huff, 61 Ark. 494; Pacific Tel. Co. v. Dalton, 119 Cal. 604; State v. Staub, 61 Conn. 553; State v. Gamble, 13 Fla. 9; State v. Bell, 9 Ga. 334; Partlow v. Moore, 184 Ill. 119; Brown v. Porter, 37 Ind. 206; Miller v. Horton, 152 Mass. 540; Wall v. Trumbull, 16 Mich. 228; Newman v. Elam, 30 Miss. 507; McCutchen v. Windsor, 55 Mo. 149; State v. Commissioners, 12 Neb. 6; United Lines Tel. Co. v. Grant, 137 N. Y. 7; Long v. Commissioners, 76 N. C. 273; McKinney v. Robinson, 84 Tex. 489; Supervisors v. Catlett's Ex'rs, 86 Va. 158; Brown v. Mason, 40 Vt. 157; Milwaukee Iron Co. v. Schubel, 29 Wis. 444.

Customs Office, if adverse to the admission of such alien, shall be final unless reversed on appeal to the Secretary of the Treasury. Under the decisions the status of any alien and the question of his right to enter the United States is exclusively vested in the executive department of the government; and where it has been legitimately exercised, the courts cannot interfere in behalf of the aliens. But these complainants are not aliens coming into the country within the meaning of the statute; therefore, they are not of that class whose right to remain here can be finally determined by the executive department of the government.

Cases like Miller v. Horton, 152 Mass. 540 (1891), that are upon the line are difficult to deal with. This particular case was an action of tort for killing the plaintiff's horse. The defendants admit the killing, but justify as the members of a Board of Health under an order addressed to the Board by the Commissioners on Contagious Diseases of Animals. This order declared that it was adjudged that the horse had the glanders and that it was accordingly condemned to be killed. The judge before whom the case was tried found that the horse did not have the glanders; but he declined to rule that the defendants had not failed to make out their justification.

The opinion was by Mr. Justice HOLMES: We cannot admit that the legislature has an unlimited right to destroy property without compensation on the ground that destruction is not an appropriation to public use. Certainly the legislature could not declare that all animals are nuisances and order them to be killed outright without compensation. It does not attempt to do so. As we have said, it only declares diseased animals to be nuisances.

With all respect to so eminent a judge, it seems that the solution of this case should be that the legislature had left the determination of the question whether the animals were diseased or not to the fair discretion of the administration.[102]

§ 133. Administration by legislation.

As regulations depend upon a statute, they can never go to the extent of being independent of the statute. A regulation which is in effect legislation is in a just sense a regulation no longer. That is, as a regulation is derivative, it must keep within the scope of the statute under which it is framed. These are abstract distinctions; the truth of the matter is that it is very difficult, therefore, to apply them to particular cases. The course of adjudication upon the jurisdiction of the administration to promulgate regulations is proof of this.

If this line is passed it may be argued with justice that the administration has gone beyond its proper function. To show how perplexing the question is, a statement of two recent cases in the Supreme Court of the United States will be made. The first of these is United States v. Eaton, 144 U. S. 677 (1892). By the terms of the oleomargarine statute the Commissioner of Internal

102 ADMINISTRATION BY EXECUTION.—Kendall v. United States, 12 Pet. 524; United States v. Schurz, 102 U. S. 378; Eslava v. Jones, 83 Ala. 139; Danley v. Whiteley, 14 Ark. 687; Harpending v. Haight, 39 Cal. 189; Howell v. Cooper, 2 Colo. App. 531; State v. Gamble, 13 Fla. 9; Barksdale v. Cobb, 16 Ga. 13; McCord v. High, 24 Ia. 336; State v. Barker, 4 Kan. 379; Tardos v. Bozant, 1 La. Ann. 199; Baker v. Johnson, 41 Me. 15; Magruder v. Swann, 25 Md. 173; Nowell v. Wright, 3 Allen 166; Allor v. Wayne Co. Auditors, 43 Mich. 76; Riley v. James, 73 Miss. 1; McCulloch v. Stone, 64 Miss. 378; Kimball v. Lamprey, 19 N. H. 215; Citizens' Bank v. Wright, 6 Oh. St. 318; Commonwealth v. Martin, 170 Pa. St. 118; Peters v. Auditor, 33 Grat. 368; State v. Hastings, 15 Wis. 83.

Revenue was given the power to make regulations to carry the act into effect. The petitioner, a dealer in oleomargarine, failed to comply with these regulations. Prosecution was begun against him for the penalty for the failure to do anything required by the act. Upon the question whether the failure to obey the regulations came under this head the lower court divided.

In the Supreme Court of the United States the opinion was given by Mr. Justice BLATCHFORD: It would be a very dangerous principle to hold that the thing prescribed by the Commissioner of Internal Revenue as a need for regulation under the oleomargaine act for carrying it into effect should be considered as a thing required by law. Regulations prescribed by the President and by the heads of the Departments under authority granted by Congress may be regulations prescribed by law. They are lawful to support acts done under them and in accordance with them, and may thus in a proper sense have the force of law; but it does not follow that a thing required by them is a thing required by law so as to make the neglect to do it a criminal offense.

The principles employed in the last opinion are fair enough; for this is a delegation of legislative authority that makes the statute is void; but the application of these principles may well be questioned, for it seems that these regulations are not much more than the detail to a general statute. That is in effect the holding in the second case—In re Kollock, 165 U. S. 535 (1897)—which must now be regarded as the ruling case. The act in its then form required packages to be marked and branded; prohibited the sale of packages that were not; and set down the punishment for sales in violation of its provisions. It next authorized the Commissioner to make regulations describing the marks and brands to be used. This proceeding was a habeas corpus on the ground of the unconstitutionality of that provision.

Mr. Chief Justice FULLER supported this statute: Considered as a revenue act the designation of stamps, marks and brands is merely the discharge of an administrative function, and falls within the numerous instances of regulation needful to the operation of the machinery of particular laws, authority to make which has always been recognized as within the competency of the legislative power to confer. The identification of dealer, substance, quantity, &c., by marking and branding must be regarded as a means to effectuate the objects of the act. And we are of opinion that leaving the matter of designating the marks, brands and stamps to the Commissioner involved no unconstitutional legislation.[103]

§ 134. Administration by adjudication.

All that has been laid down as to the limitation of the administration to its jurisdiction applies with peculiar force in the judicial proceedings of the administration. Indeed, at that stage of the problem the situation is plain to any one used to the law governing the jurisdic-

103 ADMINISTRATION BY LEGISLATION.—United States v. 200 Barrels, 95 U. S. 571; Merritt v. Welsh, 104 U. S. 694; Morrill v. Jones, 106 U. S. 466; Campbell v. United States, 107 U. S. 410; United States v. Eaton, 144 U. S. 677; In re Kollock, 165 U. S. 535; Boske v. Comingore, 177 U. S. 459; United States v. Ormsbee, 74 Fed. 209; United States v. Dastervignes, 118 Fed. 199; Bloxham v. Consumers' St. R. Co., 36 Fla. 543; Orne v. Barstow, 175 Mass. 193; Matter of Spangler, 11 Mich. 323; Holbrook v. Wightman, 31 Minn. 172; Hilburn v. St. Paul R. R., 23 Mont. 249; State v. Davis, 69 N. H. 350; Hewitt v. Schultz, 7 N. D. 611; Lockwood v. Bank, 9 R. I. 333; Peters v. United States, 2 Okl. 123; McSorley v. Hill, 2 Wash. 651.

tion of courts of law. No tribunal can be final judge of its jurisdiction. At any subsequent time it may always be set up, even in collateral proceedings, that the court decides the question without jurisdiction. That, also, is the law in administration by adjudication.

A case which involves this issue is Noble v. Logging Railroad, 147 U. S. 171 (1893). This was a bill in equity by the railroad to enjoin the Secretary from revoking an approval of its maps. It appeared in the case that the grants had been duly made. Later there was an attempt to retake the land on the ground that the railroad was not a public carrier. The fundamental difficulty in the case, one sees, is that the grant had once been made; so that it was claimed that to adjudicate concerning it would not be action concerning public land, but action concerning private land.

The opinion of Mr. Justice Brown was in part as follows: In the present case it is charged that there are certain facts which are strictly jurisdictional, the existence of which is necessary to the validity of the proceeding, and without which the act of the court is a nullity. If the Land Department issues a patent for land which has already been granted to another person, the act is not voidable merely, but void. The proceeding is a nullity and its invalidity may be shown in a collateral attack. Upon the other hand, if the patent be for land which the department had authority to convey, but if it was imposed upon or induced by false representations to issue a patent, the finding of the department cannot be collaterally impeached.

A well known case on this same principle is In re Fassett, 142 U. S. 479 (1892). A Collector of Customs seized the yacht Conqueror, alleging that the vessel was liable to duty as an imported article. It was asserted by the owner that he had no intention of bringing the yacht within the United States. He claimed, therefore, that the Collector had no jurisdiction. Now the Collector may levy proper duties upon imported articles; may he, therefore, say what articles are imported articles?

The court by Chief Justice FULLER showed: This was not a question which the collector was to decide within his discretionary powers. Because this is a question of jurisdiction, no appeal is provided. That is no process to bring up for review the question of whether an article is imported merchandise or not. Nor is the ascertainment of that fact such a decision as has been provided for by any process of the administration.[104]

§ 135. Extent of jurisdiction.

One other case to enforce this principle of the extent of the jurisdiction of the administration is Marquez v. Frisbie, 101 U. S. 473 (1879). This bill was filed in the state court by the complainant, alleging that, having the requisite qualifications of a pre-emptor, he had settled upon a tract of the public land; but that the proper register had refused to receive the purchase money upon the ground that the Commissioners had ordered the sur-

[104] ADMINISTRATION BY ADJUDICATION.—Lawrence v. Caswell, 13 How. 497; Marquez v. Frisbie, 101 U. S. 473; Oelbermann v. Merritt, 123 U. S. 363; Wisconsin Cent. R. R. v. Forsythe, 159 U. S. 61; Clark v. Herington, 186 U. S. 210; Ex parte Selma R. R., 46 Ala. 423; Ex parte Bridge Co., 62 Ark. 461; United States v. Douglass, 19 D. C. 99; Pensacola R. R. v. State, 25 Fla. 310; Chicago, etc., R. R. v. Atchison Co. Com'rs, 54 Kan. 781; People v. Dental Examiners, 110 Ill. 180; Miller v. Horton, 152 Mass. 540; Merrill v. Humphrey, 24 Mich. 170; State v. Chicago, etc., R. R., 38 Minn. 281; State v. Chicago, etc., R. R., 29 Neb. 412; Stuart v. Palmer, 74 N. Y. 183; Bartlett v. Wilson, 59 Vt. 23; State v. Cheney, 45 W. Va. 478.

veys to be withheld. The defendant, who claimed a right to pre-empt under later proceedings, demurred. The question thus was raised whether the judicial courts would undertake to review the action of the administration.

Mr. Justice MILLER said: The grounds principally, if not conclusively, relied on by the plaintiff in this court are (1) that the Land Department mistook the law of the United States and thereby deprived the plaintiff of a vested right, and (2) that their decision was obtained by fraud, and, therefore, ought to be set aside. We have repeatedly held that the courts will not interfere with the officers of the government in the discharge of their duties in disposing of the public lands either by injunction or mandamus. The rule which governs the court in correcting errors has been fully stated. It is idle to suppose that the expensive machinery of a court of equity is to be put in operation for the purpose of reviewing and reversing the judgment of the tribunal by whom that question of law is to be decided.

The latest case goes almost to that extreme. Publication Company v. Payne, 30 Wash. Law Rep. 339 (1902). This was an application for a writ of mandamus against the Postmaster-General. The Postmaster-General had prescribed in a regulation that second class matter should include only such as consisted of current news or miscellaneous literature matter. Upon the strength of this regulation a collection of railway time tables was excluded from second class matter. The publishers claim that the regulation was invalid.

An extract from the opinion of Mr. Justice BRADLEY follows: Is this amendment of the postal regulations inconsistent with law? It is clearly beyond the power of the Postmaster-General to prescribe. Periodical publications by this regulation must not only conform to the statutory characteristic of second class mail matter, but further requisites are prescribed. Obviously "information of a public character" is much broader than "current news." It is then a narrowing and restricting of the terms of the statute. The court is bound to consider that the legislature never contemplated such an addition to the statute.[105]

§ 136. Conclusion.

These are the general principles: That neither in its executive processes, nor in its legislative processes, nor in its judicial processes can the administration act beyond its jurisdiction. Beyond jurisdiction every act done in the course of administration must be void. All that is allowed to the administration is action within the scope of its authority. The distinction is this: The internal law of the administration is concerned with the

105 EXTENT OF JURISDICTION.—Litchfield v. Register & Receiver, 9 Wall. 575; Johnson v. Towsley, 13 Wall. 72; In re Fassett, 142 U. S. 479; Nishimura Ekiu v. United States, 142 U. S. 660; Noble v. Logging R. R., 147 U. S. 171; McCormick v. Hayes, 159 U. S. 342; Menotti v. Dillon, 167 U. S. 721; Japanese Immigrant Case, 189 U. S. 86; United States v. Garlinger, 169 U. S. 321; United States v. Lee Huen, 118 Fed. 442; United States v. Three Barrels, 77 Fed. 964; Meads v. United States, 81 Fed. 684; Woolfork v. Buckner, 60 Ark. 163; New York, etc., R. Co.'s Appeal, 62 Conn. 535; Pensacola R. R. v. State, 25 Fla. 310; Brown v. Porter, 37 Ind. 206; McCormick v. Burt, 95 Ill. 263; Chicago, etc., R. R. v. Atchison Co. Com'rs, 54 Kan. 781; Lowell v. Commissioners, 152 Mass. 375; State v. Chicago, etc., R. R., 38 Minn. 281; Newman v. Elam, 30 Miss. 507; State v. Commissioners, 12 Neb. 6; United Lines Tel. Co. v. Grant, 137 N. Y. 7; Long v. Commissioners, 76 N. C. 273; Sproat v. Durland, 2 Okl. 52; American Pavement Co. v. Wagner, 139 Pa. 623.

action of the administration within its jurisdiction; the external law of the administration is concerned with the limitation upon the authority of the administration. These make up the whole of the law governing administration.

APPENDIX.

APPENDIX A.

REGULATIONS RELATING TO ARMY AND NAVY PENSIONS FOR THE GUIDANCE OF CLAIMANTS AND ATTORNEYS.

All declarations and evidence must be executed in accordance with the provisions of the act of Congress approved July 20, 1892.

INVALID.

Blank forms for a declaration will be furnished to claimants upon application therefor, but will not be furnished to attorneys and claim agents.

The declaration should set forth the company and regiment in which the applicant served, the name of the commanding officer of the company or organization, and the dates of enlistment and discharge. In Navy cases the vessel upon which claimant served should be stated. If the claim is made on account of a wound or injury, the declaration should set forth the nature and locality of the wound or injury, the time when, the place where, and the circumstances under which it was received, and the duty upon which the applicant was engaged.

If the wound or injury was accidental, the applicant should state whether it happened through his own agency or that of other persons, and he should minutely detail the circumstances under which it was received.

If the claim is made on account of disability from disease, the applicant should state in his declaration when the disease first appeared, the place where he was when it appeared, and the duty upon which he was at the time engaged. He should also detail the circumstances of exposure to the causes which, in his opinion, produced the disease. Whether the application be made on account of disability from injury or disease the claimant should state the names, numbers, and localities of all hospitals in which he received medical or surgical treatment, giving the dates of his admission thereto as correctly as he may be able.

The applicant should state whether he was in the military or naval service prior to or after the term of service in which his disability originated.

The applicant should state his postoffice address. In cities, the street and number of his residence should be given.

The identity of the applicant must be shown by the testimony of two credible witnesses, who must appear with him before the officer by whom the declaration may be taken.

NATURE OF THE EVIDENCE REQUIRED TO SUSTAIN A CLAIM FOR INVALID PENSION.

As soon as practicable after the receipt of a claim for pension, application will be made by this office, in Army cases, to the Adjutant-General and the Surgeon-General of the Army, for a report of the applicant's service and evidence in regard to the disability alleged which may appear upon the rolls and other records in the possession of those officers. In Navy cases application for such evidence will be made to the proper Bureaus of the Navy Department.

When the records of the War and Navy Departments do not furnish satisfactory evidence that the disability on account of which the claim is made originated in the service of the United States and in the line of duty, the claimant will be required to furnish such evidence, in accordance with the instructions hereinafter given, compliance with which must be full and definite; and if the disability results from a wound or other injury, the nature and location of the wound or injury, the time when, the place where, and the manner in which it was received, whether in battle or otherwise, should be shown by the affidavit of some one who was a commissioned officer and had personal knowledge of the facts.

If the person called upon to give evidence is still in the service as a commissioned officer, his certificate will be accepted in lieu of his affidavit.

If there is no record of the disability claimed, the applicant will be called on to furnish the testimony of the surgeon by whom he was treated, showing the location and nature of the wound or injury and the circumstances under which it was received. If the disability arises from disease, the testimony of the person who was surgeon or assistant surgeon of the regiment to which the applicant belonged, or the vessel on which he served, should, if possible, be furnished, showing the name or nature of the disease, the time when, the place where it was contracted, and the circumstances of exposure to the causes which, in his opinion, produced the same.

The surgeon should state whether, in his opinion, the habits of the applicant had any agency in the production of the disease.

In any claim, whether made on account of injury or disease, if it be shown that the testimony of a surgeon, assistant surgeon, or other commissioned officer cannot be produced as evidence of the origin of the disability alleged, the testimony of other persons having personal knowledge of the facts will be considered.

In a claim on account of disability from disease, he must furnish the testimony of the physicians who have attended him since the date of discharge, explicitly setting forth the history of the disease and disability since its first appearance. It is especially important that the physician who first attended the applicant after his discharge should state the date at which his attendance commenced and his condition at that time. If it should not be possible for the applicant to show the condition of his health during the whole period since the date of his discharge by the testimony of physicians, the cause of his inability to do so should be stated by him under oath. The testimony of other persons on this point may then be presented. The statement of the witnesses in regard to the manner in which the applicant was affected should be full and definite, and they should state how they obtained a knowledge of the facts stated by them.

A pensioner who may deem himself entitled to an increase of pension should file a declaration setting forth the ground upon which he claims such increase.

CLAIMS FOR RENEWAL OF PENSIONS.

Applications for renewal of pension must be made to the Commissioner by a declaration executed as in original claims, setting forth that the cause for which pension was allowed still continues.

In cases of unclaimed pensions, evidence must be filed satisfactorily accounting for the failure to claim such pension; and, in invalid claims, medical evidence showing the continuance of the disability.

Blank forms of declaration will be furnished by this office at the request of the claimant, but will not be furnished to agents or attorneys.

CLAIMS OF WIDOWS AND CHILDREN.

THE DECLARATION.

The blank form of declaration, with the accompanying notes, which is furnished by this office upon the request of a claimant, sufficiently indicates the facts which should be stated by the widow or guardian.

EVIDENCE.

The facts relating to the cause of the soldier's death on account of whom the pension is claimed, including his last illness and date and place of death, should be set forth fully and in detail, and should be proven by the physicians who attended him during his illness; but when that is impossible, the testimony of other persons who are acquainted with the circumstances may be furnished.

PROOF OF MARRIAGE IN WIDOWS' CLAIMS.

The marriage of the applicant to the person on account of whose service and death the claim is made should be shown—

(1) By a duly verified copy of a church or other public record; or

(2) By the affidavit of the clergyman or magistrate who officiated; or

(3) By the testimony of two or more eye witnesses to the ceremony; or

(4) By a duly verified copy of the church record of baptism of the children; or

(5) By the testimony of two or more witnesses who know that the parties lived together as husband and wife, and who will state how long, within their knowledge, such cohabitation continued.

Special provision, however, is made by section 4705 of the Revised Statutes in regard to the character of the evidence which shall be required in the claims of widows and children of colored and Indian soldiers and sailors.

PROOF OF THE DATES OF BIRTH OF CHILDREN.

The dates of birth of children should be proved—

(1) By a duly verified copy of the church record of baptism or other public record; or

(2) By the affidavit of the physician who attended the mother; or

(3) By the testimony of persons who were present at the births, who should state how they are able to testify to the precise dates.

If any child of the person on whose account the claim is made died after the date at which the widow's pension will commence, the date of the death must be shown.

CLAIMS ON BEHALF OE MINOR CHILDREN.

In claims on behalf of minor children the guardian must furnish proof upon the following points:

(1) A copy of his letters of guardianship, bearing the seal of the court making the appointment, together with the certificate of the court that such appointment has not been revoked; which certificate should also state the amount of the guardian's bond.

(2) The cause and date of the father's death, the marriage of the parents, and the dates of birth of the children must be proved. When, however, satisfactory

proof upon these points has been furnished in the claim of the widow, it will not again be required in the claim on behalf of the minors.

(3) If the mother of the children is dead, the date of her death must be proved. If she remarried, her remarriage must be proved in the same manner that her marriage to the father of the children is required to be proved. If the claim is made on account of the widow having abandoned the children, or on account of her unfitness to have custody of them, the abandonment or unfitness can be shown by the certificate of the court having probate jurisdiction or upon the presentation of satisfactory evidence thereof to the Commissioner of Pensions.

(4) If the mother of the children died before the father, it must be shown whether he again married.

(5) It must be shown whether the father left any other pensionable child than those for whose benefit the claim is made; and, if so, why such child is not embraced in the application. A guardian is not entitled on account of a child which died prior to the date of the application.

CLAIMS OF DEPENDENT RELATIVES.

DEPENDENT MOTHERS.

A mother must show her relationship, the date and cause of the son's death, and whether he left a widow or minor children surviving, and her dependence upon him for support at the time of his death.

In proof of dependence it must be shown that previous to the date of the said son's decease her husband had died, or that he had permanently abandoned her support, or that on account of disability from injury or disease he was unable to support her. If the husband is dead, the date of his death must be proved. If he abandoned the support of his family, the date of such abandonment and all the facts of the case, showing whether he ever returned or ever afterward contributed to the support of the claimant, must be fully set forth. If he was disabled, the nature and cause of the disability and when and to what extent it rendered him unable to support the claimant must be shown by the testimony of his physician. The extent of his disability during the period from the son's death to the present time should also be shown.

The value of the property of the claimant and her husband, the income which they derived therefrom, and the other means of support possessed by them while she was receiving the contributions of her said son, and from that time to the present, should be shown by the testimony of credible and disinterested witnesses, who must state how they know the facts. The value of property assessed for taxation may be shown by the testimony of the officer having possession of the records relating thereto. The true as compared with the assessed value should be stated.

It must be shown to what extent, for what period, and in what manner her said son contributed to her support, by the testimony of persons for whom the son labored, to whom he paid rent, of whom he purchased groceries, fuel, clothing, or other necessary articles for her use, or of those who otherwise had a knowledge of the contributions of the son, and who must state how they obtained such knowledge. Any letter from the son bearing upon the question of support should be filed. If the son, in any other manner than by actual contributions, acknowledged his obligation to support his mother, or was by law bound to such support, the facts should be shown.

DEPENDENT FATHERS.

A father claiming pension on account of the death of his son, upon whom he was dependent for support, must prove—

(1) The cause and date of his son's death; that said son left no widow or minor child surviving him; the cause and extent of his disability during the period in which the son contributed to his support, and from that time to the present; the amount of his property and all other means of support possessed by him during that period, and the extent of his dependence upon his son for support. The facts of the case in these respects should be shown by such testimony as is required in the claim of a mother.

(2) The date of his marriage, the date of the death of the mother, and the date of birth of the son must be proved.

In case the mother applied for pension, reference should be made to her application, and the number of the same or of her certificate should be given. Evidence upon any point established in her claim will not again be required.

MINOR BROTHERS AND SISTERS.

The claim on behalf of minor brothers and sisters should be made by a guardian duly appointed, who must furnish the evidence of his or her authority under the seal of the court from which the authority was obtained. He must prove the cause and date of the death of the brother on whose account the claim is made, his celibacy, the dates of death of the mother and father, his relationship to the persons on whose behalf the claim is made, the dates of their births, and their dependence upon the brother for support. If the mother or father applied for pension, the number of his or her application or of his or her certificate should be given. Evidence upon any point established in the claim of the mother or father will not again be required.

In the administration of the pension laws no distinction is made between brothers and sisters of the half blood and those of the whole blood.

WITNESSES AND TESTIMONY.

Evidence executed before the attorney of record in a claim or before any person who has a manifest interest therein will not be considered. All certificates of executing officers must certify that they have no interest in the claim.

It is desirable that the facts required to be proved in the prosecution of a claim for pension should, if possible, be shown by the testimony of other persons than near relatives of the claimant.

Every fact required to be proved should be shown by the best evidence obtainable. Every witness should state whether he has any interest, direct or indirect, in the prosecution of the claim in which he may be called to testify, and give his postoffice address.

Witnesses should not merely confirm the statements of other parties, but they should give a detailed statement of the facts known to them in regard to the matter concerning which they may testify, and they should state how they obtained a knowledge of such facts. The officer who may take the deposition must certify as to his knowledge of the credibility of the witnesses, and must state how such knowledge was obtained. If they sign by mark, he must certify that the contents of their depositions were fully made known to them before he administered the oath.

It is desirable that affidavits should be free from interlineations and erasures. When an alteration is made in an affidavit, or an addition is made thereto, it must appear by the certificate of the officer who administered the oath that such alteration or addition was made with the knowledge and sworn consent of the affiant.

In all affidavits from surgeons or physicians it is desirable that that portion detailing the nature of the disability, dates of treatment, and death, symptoms and opinions as to connection between diseases or injury and disease, should be in the handwriting of the party by whom it is signed. The testimony of any person as an expert should be drawn up by some one professionally competent to make such a statement.

The official certificates of judicial officers using a seal, or of commissioned officers of the Army and Navy in actual service, will be accepted without affidavit; but all other witnesses must testify under oath.

COPIES OR ORIGINALS OF PAPERS.

Private papers or personal mementos filed as evidence in claims for pension become a part of the record. Copies of same or originals can only be returned within the discretion of the Commissioner of Pensions, upon application by the parties properly entitled thereto.

Certified copies of declarations, affidavits, or certificates of medical examinations on file in claims for pension can only be furnished upon the call of a court or department wherein the same are to be used as evidence, under certain conditions.

PENSIONS TO THE SURVIVORS OF THE WARS PRIOR TO 1861, AND TO THEIR WIDOWS.

(1) War of the Revolution, Service Pensions.—(*a*) Widows of soldiers who served for fourteen days or more, or were in any battle during the war, are entitled, provided they have not remarried, to eight dollars per month from March 9, 1878, and twelve dollars per month from March 19, 1886. (*b*) Widows of Revolutionary soldiers who in their lifetime were granted pensions are entitled, under section 4743, Revised Statutes, to pension at the same rate as was paid the husband, notwithstanding remarriage, upon proof of present widowhood. (*c*) There is no law granting pensions to the daughters or other descendants of soldiers of the Revolution. The daughters of Revolutionary soldiers who are now drawing pensions were placed on the pension roll by special acts of Congress.

(2) War of 1812, Service Pensions.—(*a*) Under sections 4736 to 4740, Revised Statutes, soldiers and sailors who served for sixty days or more in this war and were honorably discharged, or who were personally named in any resolution of Congress for specific service therein, and the widows of such soldiers and sailors, are entitled to eight dollars per month from February 14, 1871, upon proof by all applicants, of loyalty to the United States Government during the war of the rebellion, and by widow applicants of their marriage to the soldier or sailor prior to the treaty of peace, February 17, 1815. (*b*) Under the act of March 9, 1878, soldiers and sailors who served fourteen days or more, or were in any battle during the war, and were honorably discharged, and the widows of such soldiers and sailors, irrespective of the date of marriage, are entitled to eight dollars per month from

March 9, 1878. Under the act of March 19, 1886, widow pensioners mentioned in this paragraph are entitled to twelve dollars per month from that date. (*c*) There is no law granting service pension to the descendants of soldiers or sailors of the War of 1812, nor increase to the soldier or sailor himself on account of disability, age, or infirmity. The rate of pension does not vary with the rank of the soldier or sailor, nor can it be increased for any cause.

(3) Indian Wars from 1832 to 1842, Service Pensions.—(*a*) The act of July 27, 1892, provides pensions for the surviving officers and enlisted men, including marines, militia, and volunteers, who were in the military or naval service of the United States for thirty days in the Black Hawk war, the Creek war, the Cherokee disturbances, or the Florida war with the Seminole Indians, and were honorably discharged; or who were personally named in any resolution of Congress for specific service therein; and for their widows, provided they have not remarried. All pensions under this act are fixed at eight dollars per month irrespective of rank; are not subject to increase for any cause; and are payable from July 27, 1892; but the pension of a widow whose husband was living on that date commences from the day of his death. (*b*) This act does not provide pension for any descendant of the soldier or sailor.

(4) Mexican War, Service Pensions.—(*a*) Under the act of January 29, 1887, officers and enlisted men who were in the military or naval service of the United States for sixty days in Mexico, or on the coasts or frontier thereof, or en route thereto, or who were in a battle, and were honorably discharged; or who were personally named in any resolution of Congress for specific service

therein, are entitled to pension if sixty-two years of age; or, if not, upon proof of pensionable disability or dependence. (*b*) Widows of officers and enlisted men who served as above are entitled to pension on the same conditions as to age or dependence as apply to the officer or soldier; but disability incurred while voluntarily aiding or abetting the late rebellion does not give title to pension, nor are any persons entitled thereto while under the political disabilities imposed by the fourteenth amendment to the Constitution. Pensions under this act commence on January 29, 1887, if a pensionable condition by reason of age or dependence then existed; if not, then on the date the applicant becomes sixty-two years of age or dependent within the meaning of the law. The rate of pension is eight dollars per month irrespective of rank; which rate, for survivors who were pensioners on January 5, 1893, may be increased to twelve dollars under the act of that date, on proof that the pensioner is wholly disabled for manual labor and in such destitute circumstances that eight dollars is a sum insufficient to provide him with the necessaries of life. (*c*) Widows' pensions are not subject to increase, nor are the descendants of survivors entitled to service pension.

(5) NAVY SERVICE PENSIONS.—(*a*) Under sections 4756 and 4757, Revised Statutes, pensions for twenty years' service and for ten years' service, are allowed by the Secretary of the Navy to enlisted men and appointed petty officers who have not been discharged for misconduct. Pension commences on the date of filing the claim therefor in the Navy Department, and, for twenty years' service, amounts to one-half the monthly pay of the applicant's rating at his discharge; for ten years' service, the pension cannot exceed the rate for total disability,

and is fixed, as is also its duration, by a board of naval officers. The application should be addressed to the Secretary of the Navy, and all subsequent communications to the Chief of the Bureau of Navigation, Navy Department, Washington, D. C. (*b*) Pensions are not granted for a service of less than ten years except as provided in paragraphs 2, 3, and 4.

(6) PENSIONS FOR DISABILITY OR DEATH DUE TO SERVICE PRIOR TO MARCH 4, 1861.—(*a*) Soldiers who were wounded or injured or who contracted disease in the line of duty are entitled to pension corresponding in rate to the degree of disability incurred in service. Persons in the naval service are entitled to a like pension under the same conditions, excepting that no pension may be granted to an engineer, a fireman, or a coal heaver for disability incurred prior to August 31, 1842. (*b*) The widows, or children under sixteen years of age, of soldiers who served prior to March 4, 1861, are entitled to pension if the soldier's death was due to causes originating in time of actual war, and not otherwise. (*c*) The widows, or children under sixteen, of sailors who served prior to March 4, 1861, are entitled to pension only when the death occurred in the service and in the line of duty. Pensions mentioned in this paragraph, if not applied for within three years from the discharge or death of the person on whose account the right to pension exists, or within three years of the termination of a pension previously granted on account of the service and death of such person, commence from the date of filing, by the person prosecuting the claim, the last paper requisite to establish it. (*d*) There is no provision of law allowing pensions to the parents, brothers, or sisters of persons who rendered military or naval service prior to March 4, 1861.

(7) BOUNTY LAND—(*a*) Service, to give title to bounty land, must have been for at least fourteen days or in a battle prior to March 3, 1855; and, if in the Navy or Regular Army, must have been in some war in which the United States Government was engaged. (*b*) Inquiries relative to the assignment of bounty land warrants and to homestead lands for services during the war of the rebellion should be addressed to the Commissioner of the General Land Office, Interior Department.

(8) MISCELLANEOUS.—(*a*) Applications for reimbursement should be filed with the Auditor for the Interior Department, Treasury Department. (*b*) Communications relative to back pay, extra pay, and bounty in money for military service should be addressed to the Auditor for the War Department; in regard to bounty, extra pay, or prize money for naval service, to the Auditor for the Navy Department. (*c*) When a certificate of service in lieu of a lost discharge is desired, application should be made to the Adjutant-General, U. S. Army, War Department, if the service was in the Regular Army; to the Chief of Record and Pension Office, War Department, if the service was in a volunteer organization, and to the Chief of the Bureau of Navigation, Navy Department, if the service was in the Navy. (*d*) Copies only of discharges are furnished by this Bureau when the originals were filed in claims made on account of service rendered prior to March 4, 1861, and no such copy will be furnished for use in claims against the Government. (*e*) Remarriage after the soldier's death (except in the case of certain widows referred to in (*b*) of paragraph 1) and prior to the passage of an act taking effect from the date of its approval deprives the widow of the benefits of such act. In the case of remarriage subsequent to the

approval of such act, pension may be paid from the date of approval, or from the date of the soldier's death if after approval, to the date of remarriage.

[ACT OF JUNE 27, 1890.]

All pensions under this act will commence from the date of filing the formal application (after the passage of the act) in the Pension Bureau.

No application for pension under this act will be good unless filed in the Pension Bureau on or after June 27, 1890 (date of the act), or if not in the form, substanly, prescribed by the Secretary.

Discharge certificate need not be filed until called for.

The rates of this law are not affected by the rank of the soldier.

This act provides the following rates: For dependent father or mother, $12. The widow, $8, and $2 additional for each child of soldier under sixteen years; and if the widow dies, the child or children can draw such pension. The soldier is entitled to any rate from $6 to $12, according to inability to earn a support.

A pensioner under existing laws may apply under this one, or a pensioner under this one may apply under other laws, but can draw only *one* pension at the same time.

This law requires in a soldier's case:

(1) An *honorable discharge.*

(2) That he served at least *ninety days.*

(3) A *permanent* physical or mental inability to earn a support, but not due to vicious habits. (It need not have originated in the service.)

In case of a widow:

(1) That the soldier served at least ninety days.

(2) That he was *honorably discharged.*

(3) Proof of death; but it need not have been the result of his army service.

(4) That the widow is "without other means of support than her daily labor."

(5) That she married soldier prior to June 27, 1890, date of the act.

In dependent parents' case:

(1) That the soldier died of a wound, injury, or disease which under prior laws would have given him a pension.

(2) That he left no wife or minor child.

(3) That mother or father is at present dependent on her or on his own manual labor, being "without other present means of support than their own manual labor or the contributions of others not legally bound for their support." The benefits of the first section of the act of June 27, 1890, are not confined to the parents of those who served in the war of the rebellion, but are extended to all parents where pensionable dependence has arisen on account of the death of a son who served since said war in behalf of the United States.

(4) That in case a minor child is insane, idiotic, or otherwise permanently helpless the pension shall continue during the life of said child or during the period of such disability, and this proviso shall apply to all pensions heretofore granted or hereafter to be granted under this or any former statute, and such pension shall commence from the date of application therefor after the passage of this act.

The rules and regulations of the Department will govern all applicants and attorneys.

No contract for attorney's fee shall provide for a sum

greater than $10, but in the absence of a contract the attorney's fee shall be $10.

H. CLAY EVANS,
Commissioner of Pensions.

The foregoing rules and regulations, with the forms here following, are adopted and approved.

E. A. HITCHCOCK,
Secretary of the Interior.

APPENDIX B.

RULES OF PRACTICE IN CASES BEFORE THE ACCOUNTING OFFICERS OF THE UNITED STATES IN THE DIVISION OF THE COMPTROLLER.

I. REGULATIONS GOVERNING ATTORNEYS AND AGENTS PRACTICING BEFORE THE TREASURY DEPARTMENT.

The act of July 7, 1884 (23 Stat., 258), making appropriations to supply deficiencies in appropriations for the fiscal year ending June thirtieth, eighteen hundred and eighty-four, and for prior years, *provides* "That the Secretary of the Treasury may prescribe rules and regulations governing the recognition of agents, attorneys, or other persons representing claimants before his Department, and may require of such persons, agents, and attorneys, before being recognized as representatives of claimants, that they shall show that they are of good character and in good repute, possessed of the necessary qualifications to enable them to render such claimants valuable service, and otherwise competent to advise and assist such claimants in the presentation of their cases. And such Secretary may, after due notice and opportunity for hearing, suspend and disbar from further practice before his Department any such person, agent, or attorney, shown to be incompetent, disreputable, or who refuses to comply with the said rules and regulations, or who shall with intent to defraud, in any manner willfully and knowingly deceive, mislead, or threaten any claimant or prospective claimant, by word, circular, letter, or by advertisement."

In accordance therewith, the following rules and regulations are established by the Secretary of the Treasury:

1. A list of all persons entitled to practice as attorneys or agents before the Treasury Department will be kept in the office of the Secretary of the Treasury. On this list may be placed the names of members of the bar in good standing, but the Secretary of the Treasury may require from any such member evidence that he is in good standing at the bar.

2. An agent before being enrolled may be required to file a certificate of a judge of a United States, State, or Territorial court, or a United States district attorney, that the agent is of good moral character, and competent to render claimants valuable service, and to advise and to assist them in the presentation of their claims.

3. No attorney or agent now debarred from practice in this department, or any other of the Executive Departments, will be placed upon said list until the charges upon which he was so debarred shall be removed or satisfactorily answered.

4. The head of any Bureau may require an attorney or agent to present satisfactory evidence that the claimant has authorized him to prosecute the claim, but no *draft* will be delivered to such attorney or agent, unless he files a power of attorney, duly witnessed and acknowledged, expressly authorizing him to receive it.

5. The revocation of a power of attorney, or other authority to prosecute a claim, by a claimant or his legal

representatives, will not be recognized, unless by decision to that effect by the proper accounting officer. But in cases of suspended claims, any agent or attorney who has failed, or shall hereafter fail, to take action thereon within three months after the suspension of the claim, shall be deemed to have abandoned such claim, and the right of the claimant to employ another attorney shall be absolute.

6. No agent or attorney who appears by substitution filed after these regulations go into force will be recognized, unless by written consent of the claimant thereto, dated after the date of the substitution, and naming the person substituted.

7. No power of attorney filed after the adjustment of a claim or account by the accounting officers will be recognized, unless it shows that the claimant was fully cognizant when he executed it of the adjustment and of the balance found due him.

8. When a firm engaged in prosecuting claims shall be dissolved, or when persons associated as attorneys in a power of attorney shall contest the right of either to receive a draft, the members or survivors of such firm, or the associates in such power of attorney, must file with the Secretary of the Treasury an agreement showing which of such members, survivors, or associates may continue to prosecute the claims, or may receive a draft; otherwise, only the claimant will be recognized; and in no case will a final settlement of the account, or any steps towards the transmission of a draft to the claimant, be delayed more than sixty days by reason of the nonfiling of such agreement.

9. If a head of a Bureau has reason to believe, or if complaint be made to him, that any attorney or agent

is guilty of any of the offenses set out in the above act, or of any violation of these rules, he shall report the case forthwith to the Secretary of the Treasury. The Secretary of the Treasury will then mail to the usual address of such attorney or agent notice of the charges preferred against him, informing him that they will be investigated at the time stated in the notice, which time in no case shall be less than thirty days from the date of the notice. If on the investigation it shall appear that the charge is sustained, the Secretary of the Treasury will disbar or suspend such attorney or agent, and, until reinstated, he will not be recognized as an attorney or agent before the Treasury Department or any Bureau thereof. Such investigation will be upon written or oral testimony, as the Secretary of the Treasury may direct.

10. These regulations shall go into force on and from the first day of March, eighteen hundred and eighty-six; and shall apply to all unsettled claims then pending in this Department, or which may thereafter be presented or referred to this Department for adjudication, but shall not be construed to abrogate any existing rules or orders of the accounting officers relating to the fees of attorneys or claim agents practicing before their respective offices.

DANIEL MANNING,
Secretary.

II. REGULATIONS GOVERNING THE REVISION, BY THE COMPTROLLER OF THE TREASURY, OF ACCOUNTS SETTLED BY THE AUDITORS.

The following regulations governing the matter of applications to the Comptroller of the Treasury, for a revision of accounts settled by the Auditors of the Treasury, are published for the information and guidance of all persons interested.

Section 8 of the Legislative, Executive, and Judicial Appropriation Act of July 31, 1894, which Act in so far as it provided for a reorganization of the accounting offices of the Treasury became effective October 1, 1894, contains the following:

"The balances which may from time to time be certified by the Auditors to the Division of Bookkeeping and Warrants, or to the Postmaster-General, upon the settlement of public accounts, shall be final and conclusive upon the Executive Branch of the Government, except that any person whose accounts may have been settled, the head of the Executive Department, or of the board, commission, or establishment not under the jurisdiction of an Executive Department, to which the account pertains, or the Comptroller of the Treasury, may, within a year, obtain a revision of said account by the Comptroller of the Treasury, whose decision upon such revision shall be final and conclusive upon the Executive Branch of the Government: *Provided,* That the Secretary of the Treasury may, when in his judgment the interests of the Government require it, suspend payment and direct the re-examination of any account."

* * * * * *

"Any person accepting payment under a settlement by an Auditor shall be thereby precluded from obtaining a revision of such settlement as to any items upon which payment is accepted; but nothing in this Act shall prevent an Auditor from suspending items in an account in order to obtain further evidence or explanations necessary to their settlement. When suspended items are finally settled a revision may be had as in the case of the original settlement. Action upon any account or business shall not be delayed awaiting applications for revision: *Provided,* That the Secretary of the Treasury shall make regulations fixing the time which shall expire before a warrant is issued in payment of an account certified as provided in sections seven and eight of this Act."

Any person authorized by the law above cited to apply for a revision of an account should address a communication in writing directed to the Comptroller of the Treasury. In addition to a specific request for a revision the communication should contain the following:

(1) The name and address of the person whose account is to be revised; and, if the application is by attorney, his address should be given, together with his authority to appear, or a reference to his power of attorney on file with the account or in the Department.

(2) The nature of the account or claim, by which Auditor it was settled, with the number and date of his certificate of settlement.

(3) The applicant should state the objections he has to the Auditor's settlement, and submit any reasons or arguments which he claims tend to show that such settlement was not in accordance with the law and facts.

(4) Claimants must state that the application is made in good faith, believing error to have been made in the settlement by the Auditor to their prejudice.

Attorneys wishing to present briefs should do so with the application for revision, but if not furnished at that time action will not be suspended unless notice is given that the attorney wishes to submit a brief, in which case a reasonable time will be given for that purpose.

Attorneys wishing to submit oral arguments should give notice, and a time will be fixed by the Comptroller to suit their convenience so far as the condition of the business of the office will permit. The Auditor who settled the account will be notified of the application for revision and opportunity given him to explain the reason for his action.

Attention is specially called to the fact that the law does not authorize the Comptroller to revise the settlement of an Auditor simply to the extent to which the applicant objects to such settlement, but upon a revision the whole account and every item of it is open for the consideration and final action of the Comptroller as if the account had not been theretofore audited. But one revision of an account will be made.

Attention is also called to that clause of the act above quoted which provides that: "Any person accepting payment under a settlement by an Auditor shall be thereby precluded from obtaining a revision of such settlement as to any items upon which payment is accepted." When an application for revision is upon an item or items part of which has been allowed by the Auditor the warrant in payment of the account must be transmitted to the Comptroller with the application.

The Comptroller has no authority, upon the revision of an account, to consider items which have been simply suspended by the Auditor and not disallowed. An applicant should not, in his application for the revision of his account, explain suspended items, for such explanations will necessarily have to be ignored. All explanations of suspended items must be made directly to the Auditor who settled the account. When suspended items are finally settled by the Auditor (either by allowing or disallowing them in whole or in part) a revision may be had as in the case of the original settlement.

When an account has been revised the differences as found by the Comptroller will be certified to the Auditor for the statement of an account as required by law, and the applicant will be promptly notified of the action taken by the Comptroller.

A compliance with the requirements of the law and these regulations will facilitate the revision of accounts.

R. B. BOWLER,
Comptroller.

Approved:
J. G. CARLISLE,
Secretary.

III. STATUTES GOVERNING POWERS AND DUTIES OF THE ACCOUNTING OFFICERS OF THE TREASURY DEPARTMENT.

The following provisions of the act of July 31, 1894 (28 Stat., 205-211), prescribe the powers and duties of the accounting officers of the Treasury Department as reorganized by that act.

To facilitate reference to particular provisions headings have been inserted briefly indicating the subject of each subdivision and in a few instances paragraphs have been subdivided.

THE AUDITORS.

SEC. 3. The Auditors of the Treasury shall hereafter be designated as follows: The First Auditor as Auditor for the Treasury Department; the Second Auditor as Auditor for the War Department; the Third Auditor as Auditor for the Interior Department; the Fourth Auditor as Auditor for the Navy Department; the Fifth Auditor as Auditor for the State and other Departments; the Sixth

Auditor as Auditor for the Post Office Department. The designations of the deputy auditors and other subordinates shall correspond with those of the Auditors. And each deputy auditor, in addition to the duties now required to be performed by him, shall sign, in the name of the Auditor, such letters and papers as the Auditor may direct. (Amended by act of March 2, 1895, 28 Stat. 777.)

THE COMPTROLLER.

SEC. 4. The offices of Commissioner of Customs, Deputy Commissioner of Customs, Second Comptroller, Deputy Second Comptroller and Deputy First Comptroller of the Treasury are abolished, and the First Comptroller of the Treasury shall hereafter be known as Comptroller of the Treasury. He shall perform the same duties and have the same powers and responsibilities (except as modified by this Act) as those now performed by or appertaining to the First and Second Comptrollers of the Treasury and the Commissioner of Customs; and all provisions of law not inconsistent with this Act, in any way relating to them or either of them, shall hereafter be construed and held as relating to the Comptroller of the Treasury. His salary shall be five thousand five hundred dollars per annum. There shall also be an Assistant Comptroller of the Treasury, to be appointed by the President, with the advice and consent of the Senate, who shall receive a salary of five thousand dollars per annum, and a chief clerk in the office of the Comptroller, who shall receive a salary of two thousand five hundred dollars per annum.

The Assistant Comptroller of the Treasury shall perform such duties as may be prescribed by the Comptroller of the Treasury and shall have the power, under the direction of the Comptroller of the Treasury, to countersign all warrants and sign all other papers.

The chief clerk shall perform such duties as may be assigned to him by the Comptroller of the Treasury, and shall have the power, in the name of the Comptroller of the Treasury, to countersign all warrants except accountable warrants. (Amended by act of March 2, 1895, 28 Stat., 776.)

RECOVERY OF DEBTS.

The Auditors, under the direction of the Comptroller of the Treasury, shall superintend the recovery of all debts finally certified by them, respectively to be due to the United States.

FAILURE TO RENDER ACCOUNTS.

Section thirty-six hundred and twenty-five of the Revised Statutes is amended by substituting the words "proper Auditor" for the words "First Comptroller of the Treasury (or the Commissioner of Customs as the case may be.)"

Section thirty-six hundred and thirty-three of the Revised Statutes is amended by substituting the words "proper Auditor" for the words "First or Second Comptroller of the Treasury."

FORM OF ACCOUNTS.

SEC. 5. The Comptroller of the Treasury shall, under the direction of the Secretary of the Treasury, prescribe the forms of keeping and rendering all public accounts, except those relating to the postal revenues and expenditures therefrom.

The returns of fees mentioned in section seventeen hundred and twenty-five of the Revised Statutes shall be made as prescribed by the Comptroller of the Treasury.

AN AUDITOR MAY BE DIRECTED TO SETTLE AN ACCOUNT.

SEC. 6. Section two hundred and seventy-one of the Revised Statutes is amended to read as follows:

"SEC. 271. The Comptroller of the Treasury, in any case where, in his opinion, the interests of the Government require it, shall direct any of the Auditors forthwith to audit and settle any particular account which such Auditor is authorized to audit and settle."

AUDITOR FOR THE TREASURY DEPARTMENT.

SEC. 7. Accounts shall be examined by the Auditors as follows:

First. The Auditor of the Treasury Department shall receive and examine all accounts of salaries and incidental expenses of the office of the Secretary of the Treasury, and all bureaus and offices under his direction, all accounts relating to the customs service, public debt, internal revenue, Treasurer and assistant treasurers, mints and assay offices, Bureau of Engraving and Printing, Coast and Geodetic Survey, Revenue Cutter Service, Life-Saving Service, Light-House Board, Marine-Hospital Service, public buildings, Steamboat-Inspection Service, immigration, navigation, Secret Service, Alaskan fur-seal fisheries, and to all other business within the jurisdiction of the Department of the Treasury, and certify the balances arising thereon to the Division of Bookkeeping and Warrants.

AUDITOR FOR THE WAR DEPARTMENT.

Second. The Auditor for the War Department shall receive and examine all accounts of salaries and incidental expenses of the office of the Secretary of War and all bureaus and offices under his direction, all accounts relating to the military establishment, armories and arsenals, national cemeteries, fortifications, public buildings and grounds under the Chief of Engineers, rivers and harbors, the Military Academy, and to all other business within the jurisdiction of the Department of War, and certify the balances arising thereon to the Division of Bookkeeping and Warrants, and send forthwith a copy of each certificate to the Secretary of War.

AUDITOR FOR THE INTERIOR DEPARTMENT.

Third. The Auditor for the Interior Department shall receive and examine all accounts of salaries and incidental expenses of the office of the Secretary of the Interior, and of all bureaus and offices under his direction, and all accounts relating to the Army and Navy pensions, Geological Survey, public lands, Indians, Architect of the Capitol, patents, census, and to all other business within the jurisdiction of the Department of the Interior, and certify the balances arising thereon to the Division of Bookkeeping and Warrants, and send forthwith a copy of each certificate to the Secretary of the Interior.

Sections two hundred and seventy-three and two hundred and seventy-five of the Revised Statutes are repealed.

Section four hundred and fifty-six of the Revised Statutes is amended to read as follows:

"SEC. 456. All returns relative to the public lands shall be made to the Commissioner of the General Land Office."

AUDITOR FOR THE NAVY DEPARTMENT.

Fourth. The Auditor for the Navy Department shall receive and examine all accounts of salaries and incidental expenses of the office of the Secretary of the Navy, and of all bureaus and offices under his direction, all accounts relating to the Naval Establishment Marine Corps, Naval Academy, and to all other business within the jurisdiction of the Department of the Navy, and certify the balances arising thereon to the Division of Bookkeeping and Warrants, and send forthwith a copy of each certificate to the Secretary of the Navy.

AUDITOR FOR THE STATE AND OTHER DEPARTMENTS.

Fifth. The Auditor for the State and other Departments shall receive and examine all accounts of salaries and incidental expenses of the offices of the Secretary of State, the Attorney General, and the Secretary of Agriculture, and of all bureaus and offices under their direction; all accounts relating to all other business within the jurisdiction of the Department of State, Justice and Agriculture; all accounts relating to the diplomatic and consular service, the judiciary, United States courts, judgments of United States courts, Executive Office, Civil Service Commission, Interstate Commerce Commission, Department of Labor, District of Columbia, Fish Commission, Court of Claims and its judgments, Smithsonian Institution, Territorial governments, the Senate, the House of Representatives, the Public Printer, Library of Congress, Botanic Garden, and accounts of all boards, commissions, and establishments of the Government not within the jurisdiction of any of the Executive Departments. He shall certify the balances arising thereon to the Division of Bookkeeping and Warrants, and send forthwith a copy of each certificate, according to the character of the account, to the Secretary of the Senate, Clerk of the House of Representatives, Sergeant at Arms of the House of Representatives, or the chief officer of the Executive Department, commission, board, or establishment concerned. (Amended by act of July 1, 1902, 32 Stat. 592.)

AUDITOR FOR THE POST-OFFICE DEPARTMENT.

Sixth. The Auditor for the Post-Office Department shall receive and examine all accounts of salaries and incidental expenses of the office of the Postmaster-General and of all bureaus and offices under his direction, all postal and money-order accounts of postmasters, all accounts relating to the transportation of the mails, and to all other business within the jurisdiction of the Post-Office Department, and certify the balances arising thereon to the Postmaster-General for accounts of the postal revenue and expenditures therefrom, and to the Division of Bookkeeping and Warrants for other accounts, and send forthwith copies of the certificates in the latter cases to the Postmaster-General.

The further duties of this Auditor shall continue as now defined by the law, except as the same are modified by the provisions of this Act.

REVISION OF ACCOUNTS BY THE COMPTROLLER.

SEC. 8. The balances which may from time to time be certified by the Auditors to the Division of Bookkeeping and Warrants, or to the Postmaster-General, upon the settlements of public accounts, shall be final and conclusive upon the Executive Branch of the Government, except that any person whose accounts may have been settled, the head of the Executive Department, or of the board, commission, or establishment not under the jurisdiction of an Executive Department, to which the account pertains or the Comptroller of the Treasury, may, within a year, obtain a revision of the said account by the Comptroller of the Treasury, whose decisions upon such revision shall be final and conclusive upon the Executive Branch of the Government:

RE-EXAMINATION OF ACCOUNTS.

Provided, That the Secretary of the Treasury may, when in his judgment the interests of the Government require it, suspend payment and direct the re-examination of any account.

AUDITORS TO STATE ACCOUNTS FOR DIFFERENCES.

Upon a certificate by the Comptroller of the Treasury of any differences ascertained by him upon revision the Auditor who shall have audited the account shall state an account of such differences, and certify it to the Division of Bookkeeping and Warrants, except that balances found and accounts stated as aforesaid by the Auditor for the Post-Office Department for postal revenues and expenditures therefrom shall be certified to the Postmaster-General.

ACCEPTANCE OF PAYMENT PRECLUDES REVISION.

Any person accepting payment under a settlement by an Auditor shall be thereby precluded from obtaining a revision of such settlement as to any items upon which payment is accepted.

SUSPENSION OF ITEMS BY AUDITORS.

But nothing in this Act shall prevent an Auditor from

suspending items in an account in order to obtain further evidence or explanations necessary to their settlement. When suspended items are finally settled, a revision may be had as in the case of the original settlement. Action upon any account or business shall not be delayed awaiting applications for revision:

DELAYING THE ISSUE OF WARRANTS.

Provided, That the Secretary of the Treasury shall make regulations fixing the time which shall expire before a warrant is issued in payment of an account certified as provided in sections seven and eight of this Act.

PRESERVATION OF ACCOUNTS.

The Auditors shall, under the direction of the Comptroller of the Treasury, preserve, with their vouchers and certificates, all accounts which have been finally adjusted.

CONSTRUCTION OF STATUTES BY THE AUDITORS.

All decisions by Auditors making an original construction or modifying an existing construction of statutes shall be forthwith reported to the Comptroller of the Treasury, and items in any account affected by such decisions shall be suspended and payment thereof withheld until the Comptroller of the Treasury shall approve, disapprove, or modify such decisions and certify his actions to the Auditor.

TRANSMISSION OF DECISIONS TO THE AUDITORS.

All decisions made by the Comptroller of the Treasury under this Act shall be forthwith transmitted to the Auditor or Auditors whose duties are affected thereby.

ADVANCE DECISIONS BY THE COMPTROLLER.

Disbursing officers, or the head of any Executive Department or other establishment not under any of the Executive Departments, may apply for and the Comptroller of the Treasury shall render his decision upon any question involving a payment to be made by them or under them, which decision, when rendered, shall govern the Auditor and the Comptroller of the Treasury in passing upon the account containing said disbursement.

GENERAL PROVISIONS.

Sections one hundred and ninety-one and two hundred and seventy of the Revised Statutes are repealed.

SEC. 9. This Act, so far as it relates to the First Comptroller of the Treasury and the several Auditors and Deputy Auditors of the Treasury, shall be held and construed to operate merely as changing their designations and as adding to and modifying their duties and powers, and not as creating new officers.

All laws not inconsistent with this Act, relating to the Auditors of the Treasury in connection with any matter, shall be understood in each case to relate to the Auditor to whom this Act assigns the business of the Executive Department or other establishment concerned in that matter.

SEC. 10. The Division of Warrants, Estimates, and Appropriations in the office of the Secretary of the Treasury is hereby recognized and established as the Division of Bookkeeping and Warrants. It shall be under the direction of the Secretary of the Treasury as heretofore. Upon the books of this Division shall be kept all accounts of receipts and expenditures therefrom; and section three hundred and thirteen and so much of sections two hundred and eighty-three and thirty-six hundred and seventy-five of the Revised Statutes as require those accounts to be kept by certain Auditors and the Register of the Treasury are repealed. The duties of the Register of the Treasury shall be such as are now required of him in connection with the public debt and such further duties as may be prescribed by the Secretary of the Treasury.

REQUISITIONS TO BE SENT TO THE AUDITORS.

SEC. 11. Every requisition for an advance of money, before being acted on by the Secretary of the Treasury, shall be sent to the proper Auditor for action thereon as required by section twelve of this Act.

WARRANTS TO BE COUNTERSIGNED BY THE COMPTROLLER, ETC.

All warrants, when authorized by law and signed by the Secretary of the Treasury, shall be countersigned by the Comptroller of the Treasury, and all warrants for the payment of money shall be accompanied either by the Auditor's certificate, mentioned in section seven of this Act, or by the requisition for advance of money, which certificate or requisition shall specify the particular appropriation to which the same should be charged, instead of being specified on the warrant, as now provided by section thirty-six hundred and seventy-five of the Revised Statutes; and shall also go with the warrant to the Treasurer, who shall return the certificate or requisition to the proper Auditor, with the date and amount of the draft issued indorsed thereon. Requisitions for the payment of money on all audited accounts, or for covering money into the Treasury, shall not hereafter be required. And requisitions for advances of money shall not be countersigned by the Comptroller of the Treasury.

Section two hundred and sixty-nine and so much of section three hundred and five of the Revised Statutes as requires the Register of the Treasury to record warrants, are repealed.

TRANSMISSION OF ACCOUNTS AND DISAPPROVAL OF REQUISITIONS.

SEC. 12. All monthly accounts shall be mailed or otherwise sent to the proper officer at Washington within ten days after the end of the month to which they relate, and quarterly and other accounts within twenty days after the period to which they relate, and shall be transmitted to and received by the Auditors within twenty days of their actual receipt at the proper office in Washington in the case of monthly, and sixty days in the case of quarterly and other accounts. Should there be any delinquency in this regard at the time of the receipt by the Auditor of a requisition for an advance of money, he shall disapprove the requisition, which he may also do for other reasons arising out of the condition of the officer's accounts for whom the advance is requested; but the Secretary of the Treasury may overrule the Auditor's decision as to the sufficiency of these latter reasons: Provided, That the Secretary of the Treasury shall prescribe suitable rules and regulations, and may make orders in particular cases, relaxing the requirement of mailing or otherwise sending accounts, as aforesaid, within ten or twenty days, or waiving delinquency, in such cases only in which there is, or is likely to be, a manifest physical difficulty in complying with same, it being the purpose of this provision to require the prompt rendition of accounts without regard to the mere convenience of the officers, and to forbid the advance of money to those delinquent in rendering them: Provided further, That should there be a delay by the administrative Departments beyond the aforesaid twenty or sixty days in transmitting accounts, an order of the President in the particular case shall be necessary to authorize the advance of money requested: And provided further, That this section shall not apply to accounts of the postal revenue and expenditures therefrom, which shall be rendered as now required by law. (Amended by acts of March 2, 1895, 23 Stat., 807; January 5, 1899, 30 Stat., 772; December 20, 1899, 31 Stat., 1; March 2, 1901, id., 910.)

DELINQUENT OFFICERS TO BE REPORTED TO CONGRESS.

The Secretary of the Treasury shall, on the first Monday of January in each year, make report to Congress of such officers as are then delinquent in the rendering of their accounts or in the payment of balances found due from them for the last preceding fiscal year. Sections two hundred and fifty and two hundred and seventy-two of the Revised Statutes are repealed.

Section thirty-six hundred and twenty-two of the Revised Statutes is amended by striking therefrom the following words: "The Secretary of the Treasury may, if in his opinion the circumstances of the case justify and require it, extend the time hereinbefore prescribed for the rendition of accounts."

JUDICIARY ACCOUNTS.

SEC. 13. Before transmission to the Department of the Treasury, the accounts of district attorneys, assistant attorneys, marshals, commissioners, clerks, and other officers of the courts of the United States, except consular courts, made out and approved as required by law, and accounts relating to prisoners convicted or held for trial in any court of the United States, and all other accounts relating to the business of the Department of Justice or of the courts of the United States other than consular courts, shall be sent with their vouchers to the Attorney-General and examined under his supervision.

Judges receiving salaries from the Treasury of the United States shall be paid monthly by the disbursing officer of the Department of Justice, and to him all certificates of nonabsence or of the cause of absence of judges in the Territories shall be sent. Interstate Commerce Commissioners and other officers, now paid as judges are, shall be paid monthly by the proper disbursing officer or officers.

CLAIMS, DOUBLE EXAMINATION OF.

SEC. 14. In case of claims presented to an Auditor which have not had an administrative examination, the Auditor shall cause them to be examined by two of his subordinates independently of each other.

RECEIPTS AND EXPENDITURES TO BE REPORTED TO CONGRESS.

SEC. 15. It shall be the duty of the Secretary of the Treasury annually to lay before Congress on the first day of the regular session thereof, an accurate, combined statement of the receipts and expenditures during the last preceding fiscal year of all public moneys, including those of the Post-Office Department, designating the amount of the receipts, whenever practicable, by ports, districts and States, and the expenditures, by each separate head of appropriation.

SEC. 16. In section three hundred and seven of the Revised Statutes the words "Secretary of the Treasury" are substituted for the words "Register of the Treasury."

CERTIFICATION OF TRANSCRIPTS.

SEC. 17. The transcripts from the books and proceedings of the Department of the Treasury, provided for in section eight hundred and eighty-six of the Revised Statutes, shall hereafter be certified by the Secretary or an Assistant Secretary of the Treasury, and the copies of the contracts and other papers, therein provided for, shall be certified by the Auditor having the custody of such papers. (Amended by act of March 2, 1895, 28 Stat., 809.)

CONTRACTS TO BE DEPOSITED WITH THE AUDITORS.

SEC. 18. Section thirty-seven hundred and forty-three of the Revised Statutes is amended to read as follows:

"SEC. 3743. All contracts to be made by virtue of any law, and requiring the advance of money, or in any manner connected with the settlement of public accounts, shall be deposited promptly in the offices of the Auditors of the Treasury, according to the nature of the contracts: Provided, That this section shall not apply to the existing laws in regard to the contingent fund of Congress."

SEC. 19. Section twenty-six hundred and thirty-nine of the Revised Statutes is amended by substituting the words "proper Auditor" for the words "Commissioner of Customs."

CUSTOMS OFFICERS TO TRANSMIT PAPERS.

SEC. 20. It shall be the duty of the collectors of customs and other officers of customs to transmit, with their accounts, to the officers charged with the settlement of their accounts, all such papers, records, or copies thereof relating to their transactions as officers of customs as the Secretary of the Treasury may direct.

ACCOUNTS PENDING FOR SETTLEMENT OCTOBER 1, 1894.

SEC. 21. All accounts stated by the Auditors before the first day of October, eighteen hundred and ninety-four, and then pending for settlement in the offices of the First or Second Comptroller, or the Commissioner of Customs, shall be revised by the Comptroller of the Treasury in the manner provided by existing law, and the balances arising thereon shall be certified to the Division of Bookkeeping and Warrants.

PRESERVATION OF PAPERS AND PROPERTY.

SEC. 22. It shall be the duty of the Secretary of the Treasury to make appropriate rules and regulations for carrying out the provisions of this Act, and for transferring or preserving books, papers or other property appertaining to any office or branch of business affected by it.

ADMINISTRATIVE EXAMINATION OF ACCOUNTS.

It shall also be the duty of the heads of the several Executive Departments and of the proper officers of other Government establishments, not within the jurisdiction of any Executive Department, to make appropriate rules and regulations to secure a proper administrative examination of all accounts sent to them, as required by section twelve of this Act, before their transmission to the Auditors, and for the execution of other requirements of this Act in so far as the same relate to the several Departments or establishments.

REOPENING ACCOUNTS.

SEC. 23. Nothing in this Act shall be construed to authorize the re-examination and payment of any claim or account which has heretofore been disallowed or settled.

SEC. 24. The provisions of sections three to twenty-three inclusive, of this Act shall be in force on and after the first day of October eighteen hundred and ninety-four.

SEC. 25. All laws or parts of laws inconsistent with this Act are repealed.

APPENDIX C.

CUSTOMS ADMINISTRATIVE ACT OF JUNE 10, 1890, AS AMENDED BY ACT OF JULY 24, 1897.

AN ACT TO SIMPLIFY THE LAWS IN RELATION TO THE COLLECTION OF THE REVENUES.

Be it enacted by the Senate and House of Representatives of the United States of America in Congress assembled, That all merchandise imported into the United States shall, for the purposes of this act, be deemed and held to be the property of the person to whom the merchandise may be consigned; but the holder of any bill of lading consigned to order and indorsed by the consignor shall be deemed the consignee thereof; and in case of the abandonment of any merchandise to the underwriters the latter may be recognized as the consignee.

SEC. 2. That all invoices of imported merchandise shall be made out in the currency of the place or country from whence the importations shall be made or if purchased in the currency actually paid therefor, shall contain a correct description of such merchandise, and shall be made in triplicate or in quadruplicate in case of merchandise intended for immediate transportation without appraisement, and signed by the person owning or shipping the same, if the merchandise has been actually purchased, or by the manufacturer or owner thereof, if the same has been procured otherwise than by purchase, or by the duly authorized agent of such purchaser, manufacturer, or owner.

SEC. 3. That all such invoices shall, at or before the shipment of the merchandise, be produced to the consul, vice consul, or commercial agent of the United States of the consular district in which the merchandise was manufactured or purchased as the case may be, for export to the United States, and shall have indorsed thereon, when so produced, a declaration signed by the purchaser, manufacturer, owner, or agent, setting forth that the invoice is in all respects correct and true, and was made at the place from which the merchandise is to be exported to the United States; that it contains, if the merchandise was obtained by purchase, a true and full statement of the time when, the place where, the person from whom the same was purchased, and the actual cost thereof and of all charges thereon, as provided by this act; and that no discounts, bounties, or drawbacks are contained in the invoice but such as have been actually allowed thereon; and when obtained in any other manner than by purchase, the actual market value or wholesale price thereof at the time of exportation to the United States in the principal markets of the country from whence exported; that such actual market value is the price at which the merchandise described in the invoice is freely offered for sale to all purchasers in said markets, and that it is the price which the manufacturer or owner making the declaration would have received, and was willing to receive, for such merchandise sold in the ordinary course of trade, in the usual wholesale quantities, and that it includes all charges thereon as provided by this act; and the actual quantity thereof; and that no different invoice of the merchandise mentioned in the invoice so produced has been or will be furnished to any one. If the merchandise was actually purchased, the declaration shall also contain a statement that the currency in which such invoice is made out is that which was actually paid for the merchandise by the purchaser.

SEC. 4. That, except in case of personal effects accompanying the passenger, no importation of any merchandise exceeding one hundred dollars in dutiable value shall be admitted to entry without the production of a duly-certified invoice thereof as required by law, or of an affidavit made by the owner, importer, or consignee, before the collector or his deputy, showing why it is impracticable to produce such invoice; and no entry shall be made in the absence of a certified invoice, upon affidavit as aforesaid, unless such affidavit be accompanied by a statement in the form of an invoice, or otherwise, showing the actual cost of such merchandise, if purchased, or if obtained otherwise than by purchase, the actual market value or wholesale price thereof at the time of exportation to the United States, in the principal markets of the country from which the same has been imported; which statement shall be verified by the oath of the owner, importer, consignee, or agent desiring to make entry of the merchandise, to be administered by the collector or his deputy, and it shall be lawful for the collector or his deputy to examine the deponent under oath touching the sources of his knowledge, information, or belief in the premises, and to require him to produce any letter, paper, or statement of account, in his possession, or under his control, which may assist the officers of customs in ascertaining the actual value of the importation or any part thereof; and in default of such production when so requested, such owner, importer, consignee, or agent shall be thereafter debarred from producing any such letter, paper, or statement for the purpose of avoiding any additional duty, penalty, or forfeiture incurred under this act, unless he shall show to the satisfaction of the court or the officers of the customs, as the case may be, that it was not in his power to produce the same when so demanded; and no merchandise shall be admitted to entry under the provisions of this section unless the collector shall be satisfied that the failure to produce a duly certified invoice is due to causes beyond the control of the owner, consignee, or agent thereof: *Provided,* That the Secretary of the Treasury may make regulations by which books, magazines, and other periodicals published and imported in successive parts, numbers, or volumes, and entitled to be imported free of duty, shall require but one declaration for the entire series. And when entry of merchandise exceeding one hundred dollars in value is made by a statement in the form of an invoice the collector shall require a bond for the production of a duly certified invoice.

SEC. 5. That whenever merchandise imported into the United States is entered by invoice, one of the following declarations, according to the nature of the case, shall be filed with the collector of the port, at the time of entry by the owner, importer, consignee, or agent; which declaration so filed shall be duly signed by the owner, importer, consignee, or agent, before the collector, or before a notary public or other officer duly authorized by law to administer oaths and take acknowledgments, who may be designated by the Secretary of the Treasury to receive such declarations and to certify to the identity of the persons making them, under regulations to be prescribed by the Secretary of the Treasury; and every officer so designated shall file with the collector of the port a copy of his official signature and seal: *Provided,* That if any of the invoices or bills of lading of any merchandise imported in any one vessel, which should otherwise be embraced in said entry, have not been received at the date of the entry, the declaration may state the fact, and thereupn such merchandise of which the invoices or bills of lading are not produced shall not be included in such entry, but may be entered subsequently.

DECLARATION OF CONSIGNEE, IMPORTER, OR AGENT.

I ——— ———, do solemnly and truly declare that I am the consignee [importer or agent] of the merchandise described in the annexed entry and invoice; that the invoice and bill of lading now presented by me to the collector of ——— —— are the true and only invoice and bill of lading by me received of all the goods, wares, and merchandise imported in the ——— whereof ——— ——— is master, from ——— ——, for account of any person whomsoever for whom I am authorized to enter the same; that the said invoice and bill of lading are in the state in which they were actually received by me, and that I do not know or believe in the existence of any other invoice or bill of lading of the said goods, wares, and merchandise; that the entry now delivered to the collector contains a just and true account of the said goods, wares, and merchandise, according to the said invoice and bill of lading; that nothing has been, on my part, nor to my knowledge on the part of any other person, concealed or suppressed, whereby the United States may be defrauded of any part of the duty lawfully due on the said goods, wares, and merchandise; that the said invoice and the declaration therein are in all respects true, and were made by the person by whom the same purports to have been made; and that if at any time hereafter I discover any error in the said invoice, or in the account now rendered of the said goods, wares, and merchandise, or receive any other invoice of the same, I will immediately make the same known to the collector of this district. And I do further solemnly and truly declare that to the best of my knowledge and belief [insert the name and residence of the owner or owners] is [or are] the owner [or owners] of the goods, wares, and merchandise mentioned in the annexed entry; that the invoice now produced by me exhibits the actual cost [if purchased] or the actual market value or wholesale price [if otherwise obtained] at the time of exportation to the United States in the principal markets of the country from whence imported of the said goods, wares, and merchandise, and includes and specifies the value of all cartons, cases, crates, boxes, sacks, and coverings of any kind, and all other costs, charges, and expenses incident to placing said goods, wares, and merchandise in condition, packed ready for shipment to the United States, and no other or different discount, bounty, or drawback but such as has been actually allowed on the same.

DECLARATION OF OWNER IN CASES WHERE MERCHANDISE HAS BEEN ACTUALLY PURCHASED.

I, ——— ——— do solemnly and truly declare that I am the owner of the merchandise described in the annexed entry and invoice; that the entry now delivered by me to the collector of ——— contains a just and true account of all the goods, wares, and merchandise imported by or consigned to me, in the ——— —— whereof ——— ——— is master, from ———; that the invoice and entry which I now produce contain a just and faithful account of the actual cost of the said goods, wares, and merchandise and include and specify the value of all cartons, cases, crates, boxes, sacks, and coverings of any kind, and all other costs, charges, and expenses incident to placing said goods, wares, and merchandise in condition, packed ready for shipment to the United States, and no other discount, drawback, or bounty but such as has been actually allowed on the same; that I do not know nor believe in the existence of any invoice or bill of lading other than those now produced by me, and that they are in the state in which I actually received them. And I further solemnly and truly declare that I have not in the said entry or invoice concealed or suppressed anything whereby the United States may be defrauded of any part of the duty lawfully due on the said goods, wares, and merchandise; that to the best of my knowledge and belief the said invoice and the declaration thereon are in all respects true, and were made by the person by whom the same purports to have been made; and that if at any time hereafter I discover any error in the said invoice or in the account now produced of the said goods, wares, and merchandise, or receive any other invoice of the same, I will immediately make the same known to the collector of this district.

DECLARATION OF MANUFACTURER OR OWNER IN CASES WHERE MERCHANDISE HAS NOT BEEN ACTUALLY PURCHASED.

I, ——— ———, do solemnly and truly declare that I am the owner (or manufacturer) of the merchandise described in the annexed entry and invoice; that the entry now delivered by me to the collector of ——— contains a just and true account of all the goods, wares, and merchandise imported by or consigned to me in the ———, whereof ——— ——— is master, from ———; that the said goods, wares, and merchandise were not actually bought by me, or by my agent, in the ordinary mode of bargain and sale, but that nevertheless the invoice which I now produce contains a just and faithful valuation of the same, at their actual market value or wholesale price, at the time of exportation to the United States, in the principal markets of the country from whence imported for my account (or for account of myself or partners); that such actual market value is the price at which the merchandise described in the invoice is freely offered for sale to all purchasers in said markets, and is the price which I would have received and was willing to receive for such merchandise sold in the ordinary course of trade in the usual wholesale quantities; that the said invoice contains also a just and faithful account of all the cost of finishing said goods, wares, and merchandise to their present condition, and includes and specifies, the value of all cartons, cases, crates, boxes, sacks, and coverings of any kind, and all other costs and charges incident to placing said goods, wares, and merchandise in condition packed ready for shipment to the United States, and no other discount, drawback, or bounty but such as has been actually allowed on the said goods, wares, and merchandise; that the said invoice and the declaration thereon are in all respects true, and were made by the person by whom the same purports to have been made; that I do not know nor believe in the existence of any invoice or bill of lading other than those now produced by me, and that they are in the state in which I actually received them. And I do further solemnly and truly declare that I have not in the said entry or invoice concealed or suppressed anything whereby the United States may be defrauded of any part of the duty lawfully due on the said goods, wares, and merchandise; and that if at any time hereafter I discover any error in the said invoice, or in the account now produced of the said goods, wares, and merchandise, or receive any other invoice of the same, I will immediately make the same known to the collector of this district.

SEC. 6. That any person who shall knowingly make any false statement in the declarations provided for in the preceding section, or shall aid or procure the making of any such false statement as to any matter material thereto, shall, on conviction thereof, be punished by a fine not exceeding five thousand dollars, or by imprisonment at hard labor not more than two years, or both, in the discretion of the court: *Provided,* That nothing in this section shall be construed to relieve imported merchandise from forfeiture by reason of such false statement or for any cause elsewhere provided by law.

SEC. 7. That the owner, consignee, or agent of any imported merchandise which has been actually purchased may, at the time when he shall make and verify his written entry of such merchandise, but not afterwards, make such addition in the entry to the cost or value given in the invoice or pro forma invoice or statement in form of an invoice, which he shall produce with his entry, as in his opinion may raise the same to the actual market value or wholesale price of such merchandise at the time of exportation to the United States, in the principal markets of the country from which the same has been imported; but no such addition shall be made upon entry to the invoice value of any imported merchandise obtained otherwise than by actual purchase; and the collector within whose district any merchandise may be imported or entered, whether the same has been actually purchased or procured otherwise than by purchase, shall cause the actual market value or wholesale price of such merchandise to be appraised; and if the appraised value of any article of imported merchandise subject to an ad valorem duty or to a duty based upon or regulated in any manner by the value thereof shall exceed the value declared in the entry, there shall be levied, collected, and paid, in addition to the duties imposed by law on such merchandise, an additional duty of one per centum of the total appraised value thereof for each one per centum that such appraised value exceeds the value declared in the entry, but the additional duties shall only apply to the particular article or articles in each invoice that are so undervalued, and shall be limited to fifty per centum of the appraised value of such article or articles. Such additional duties shall not be construed to be penal, and shall not be remitted, nor payment thereof in any way avoided, except in cases arising from a manifest clerical error, nor shall they be refunded in case of exportation of the merchandise, or on any other account, nor shall they be subject to the benefit of drawback: *Provided*, That if the appraised value of any merchandise shall exceed the value declared in the entry by more than fifty per centum, except when arising from a manifest clerical error, such entry shall be held to be presumptively fraudulent, and the collector of customs shall seize such merchandise and proceed as in case of forfeiture for violation of the customs laws, and in any legal proceeding that may result from such seizure, the undervaluation as shown by the appraisal shall be presumptive evidence of fraud, and the burden of proof shall be on the claimant to rebut the same and forfeiture shall be adjudged unless he shall rebut such presumption of fraudulent intent by sufficient evidence. The forfeiture provided for in this section shall apply to the whole of the merchandise or the value thereof in the case or package containing the particular article or articles in each invoice which are undervalued: *Provided, further*, That all additional duties, penalties or forfeitures applicable to merchandise entered by a duly certified invoice, shall be alike applicable to merchandise entered by a pro forma invoice or statement in the form of an invoice, and no forfeiture or disability of any kind, incurred under the provisions of this section shall be remitted or mitigated by the Secretary of the Treasury. The duty shall not, however, be assessed in any case upon an amount less than the invoice or entered value.

SEC. 8. That when merchandise entered for customs duty has been consigned for sale by or on account of the manufacturer thereof, to a person, agent, partner, or consignee in the United States, such person, agent, partner, or consignee shall, at the time of the entry of such merchandise, present to the collector of customs at the port where such entry is made, as a part of such entry, and in addition to the certified invoice or statement in the form of an invoice required by law, a statement signed by such manufacturer, declaring the cost of production of such merchandise, such cost to include all the elements of cost as stated in section eleven of this act. When merchandise entered for customs duty has been consigned for sale by or on account of a person other than the manufacturer of such merchandise, to a person, agent, partner, or consignee in the United States, such person, agent, partner, or consignee shall, at the time of the entry of such merchandise present to the collector of customs at the port where such entry is made, as a part of such entry, a statement signed by the consignor thereof, declaring that the merchandise was actually purchased by him or for his account, and showing the time when, the place where, and from whom he purchased the merchandise, and in detail the price he paid for the same: *Provided,* That the statements required by this section shall be made in triplicate, and shall bear the attestation of the consular officer of the United States resident within the consular district wherein the merchandise was manufactured, if consigned by the manufacturer or for his account, or from whence it was imported when consigned by a person other than the manufacturer, one copy thereof to be delivered to the person making the statement, one copy to be transmitted with the triplicate invoice of the merchandise to the collector of the port in the United States to which the merchandise is consigned, and the remaining copy to be filed in the consulate.

SEC. 9. That if any owner, importer, consignee, agent, or other person shall make or attempt to make any entry of imported merchandise by means of any fraudulent or false invoice, affidavit, letter, paper, or by means of any false statement, written or verbal, or by means of any false or fraudulent practice or appliance whatsoever, or shall be guilty of any willful act or omission by means whereof the United States shall be deprived of the lawful duties, or any portion thereof, accruing upon the merchandise, or any portion thereof, embraced or referred to in such invoice, affidavit, letter, paper, or statement, or affected by such act or omission, such merchandise, or the value thereof, to be recovered from the person making the entry, shall be forfeited, which forfeiture shall only apply to the whole of the merchandise or the value thereof in the case or package containing the particular article or articles of merchandise to which such fraud or false paper or statement relates; and such person shall, upon conviction, be fined for each offense a sum not exceeding five thousand dollars, or be imprisoned for a time not exceeding two years, or both, in the discretion of the court.

SEC. 10. That it shall be the duty of the appraisers of the United States, and every of them, and every person who shall act as such appraiser, or of the collector, as the case may be, by all reasonable ways and means in his or their power to ascertain, estimate, and appraise (any invoice or affidavit thereto or statement of cost, or of cost of production to the contrary notwithstanding) the actual market value and wholesale price of the merchandise at the time of exportation to the United States, in the principal markets of the country whence the same has been imported, and the number of yards, parcels, or quantities, and actual market value or wholesale price of every of them, as the case may require.

SEC. 11. That, when the actual market value as defined by law, of any article of imported merchandise, wholly or partly manufactured and subject to an ad valorem duty, or to a duty based in whole or in part on value, can not be otherwise ascertained to the satisfaction of the appraising officer, such officer shall use all available means in his power to ascertain the cost of production of such merchandise at the time of exportation to the United States, and at the place of manufacture; such cost of production to include the cost of materials and of fabrication, all general expenses covering each and every outlay of whatsoever nature incident to such production, together with the expense of preparing and putting up such merchandise ready for shipment, and an addition of not less than eight nor more than fifty per centum upon the total cost as thus ascertained; and in no case shall such merchandise be appraised upon original appraisal or reappraisement at less than the total cost of production as thus ascertained. It shall be lawful for appraising officers, in determining the dutiable value of such merchandise, to take into consideration the wholesale price at which such or similar merchandise is sold or offered for sale in the United States, due allowance being made for estimated duties thereon, the cost of transportation, insurance, and other necessary expenses from the place of shipment to the United States, and a reasonable commission, if any has been paid, not exceeding six per centum.

SEC. 12. That there shall be appointed by the President, by and with the advice and consent of the Senate, nine general appraisers of merchandise, each of whom shall receive a salary of seven thousand dollars a year. Not more than five of such general appraisers shall be appointed from the same political party. They shall not be engaged in any other business, avocation, or employment, and may be removed from office at any time by the President for inefficiency, neglect of duty, or malfeasance in office. They shall be employed at such ports and within such territorial limits, as the Secretary of the Treasury may from time to time prescribe, and are hereby authorized to exercise the powers, and duties devolved upon them by this act and to exercise, under the general direction of the Secretary of the Treasury, such other supervision over appraisements and classifications, for duty, of imported merchandise as may be needful to secure lawful and uniform appraisements and classifications at the several ports. Three of the general appraisers shall be on duty as a board of general appraisers daily (except Sunday and legal holidays) at the port of New York, during the business hours prescribed by the Secretary of the Treasury, at which port a place for samples shall be provided, under such rules and regulations as the Secretary of the Treasury may from time to time prescribe, which shall include rules as to the classes of articles to be deposited, the time of their retention, and as to their disposition, which place of samples shall be under the immediate control and direction of the board of general appraisers on duty at said port.

SEC. 13. That the appraiser shall revise and correct the reports of the assistant appraisers as he may judge proper, and the appraiser, or, at ports where there is no appraiser, the person acting as such, shall report to the collector his decision as to the value of the merchandise appraised. At ports where there is no appraiser, the certificate of the customs officer to whom is committed the estimating and collection of duties, of the dutiable value of any merchandise required to be appraised, shall be deemed and taken to be the appraisement of such merchandise. If the collector shall deem the appraisement of any imported merchandise too low he may order a reappraisement, which shall be made by one of the general appraisers, or, if the importer, owner, agent, or consignee of such merchandise shall be dissatisfied with the appraisement thereof, and shall have complied with the requirements of law with respect to the entry and appraisement of merchandise, he may, within two days thereafter give notice to the collector, in writing, of such dissatisfaction, on the receipt of which the collector shall at once direct a reappraisement of such merchandise by one of the general appraisers. The decision of the appraiser or the person acting as such (in cases where no objection is made thereto, either by the collector or by the importer, owner, consignee, or agent), or of the general appraiser in cases of re-appraisement, shall be final and conclusive as to the dutiable value of such merchandise against all parties interested therein, unless the importer, owner, consignee, or agent of the merchandise shall be dissatisfied with such decision, and shall, within two days thereafter give notice to the collector in writing of such dissatisfaction, or unless the collector shall deem the appraisement of the merchandise too low, in either case the collector shall transmit the invoice and all the papers appertaining thereto to the board of three general appraisers, which shall be on duty at the port of New York, or to a board of three general appraisers who may be designated by the Secretary of the Treasury for such duty at that port or at any other port, which board shall examine and decide the case thus submitted, and their decision, or that of a majority of them, shall be final and conclusive as to the dutiable value of such merchandise against all parties interested therein, and the collector or the person acting as such shall ascertain, fix, and liquidate the rate and amount of duties to be paid on such merchandise, and the dutiable costs and charges thereon, according to law.

SEC. 14. That the decision of the collector as to the rate and amount of duties chargeable upon imported merchandise, including all dutiable costs and charges, and as to all fees and exactions of whatever character (except duties on tonnage), shall be final and conclusive against all persons interested therein, unless the owner, importer, consignee, or agent of such merchandise, or the person paying such fees, charges, and exactions other than duties, shall, within ten days after "but not before" such ascertainment and liquidation of duties, as well in cases of merchandise entered in bond as for consumption, or within ten days after the payment of such fees, charges, and exactions, if dissatisfied with such decision give notice in writing to the collector, setting forth therein distinctly and specifically, and in respect to each entry or payment, the reasons for his objections thereto, and if the merchandise is entered for consumption shall pay the full amount of the duties and charges ascertained to be due thereon. Upon such notice and payment the collector shall transmit the invoice and all the papers and exhibits connected therewith to the board of three general appraisers, which shall be on duty at the port of New York, or to a board of three general appraisers who may be designated by the Secretary of the Treasury for such duty at that port or at any other port, which board shall examine and decide the case thus submitted, and their decision, or that of a majority of them, shall be final and conclusive upon all persons interested therein, and the record shall be transmitted to the proper collector or person acting as such who shall liquidate the entry accordingly, except in cases where an application shall be filed in the circuit court within the time and in the manner provided for in section fifteen of this act.

SEC. 15. That if the owner, importer, consignee, or agent of any imported merchandise, or the collector, or the Secretary of the Treasury, shall be dissatisfied with the decision of the board of general appraisers, as provided for in section fourteen of this act, as to the construction of the law and the facts respecting the classification of such merchandise and the rate of duty imposed thereon under such classification, they or either of them, may, within thirty days next after such decision, and not afterwards, apply to the circuit court of the United States within the district in which the matter arises, for a review of the questions of law and fact involved in such decision. Such application shall be made by filing in the office of the clerk of said circuit court a concise statement of the errors of law and fact complained of, and a copy of such statement shall be served on the collector, or on the importer, owner, consignee, or agent, as the case may be. Thereupon the court shall order the board of appraisers to return to said circuit court the record and the evidence taken by them, together with a certified statement of the facts involved in the case, and their decisions thereon; and all the evidence taken by and before said appraisers shall be competent evidence before said circuit court; and within twenty days after the aforesaid return is made the court may, upon the application of the Secretary of the Treasury, the collector of the port, or the importer, owner, consignee, or agent, as the case may be, refer it to one of said general appraisers, as an officer of the court, to take and return to the court such further evidence as may be offered by the Secretary of the Treasury, collector, importer, owner, consignee, or agent, within sixty days thereafter, in such order and under such rules as the court may prescribe; and such further evidence with the aforesaid returns shall constitute the record upon which said circuit court shall give priority to and proceed to hear and determine the questions of law and fact involved in such decision, respecting the classification of such merchandise and the rate of duty imposed thereon under such classification, and the decision of such court shall be final, and the proper collector, or person acting as such, shall liquidate the entry accordingly, unless such court shall be of opinion that the question involved is of such importance as to require a review of such decision by the Supreme Court of the United States, in which case said circuit court, or the judge making the decision may, within thirty days thereafter, allow an appeal to said Supreme Court; but an appeal shall be allowed on the part of the United States whenever the Attorney-General shall apply for it within thirty days after the rendition of such decision. On such original application, and on any such appeal, security for damages and costs shall be given as in the case of other appeals in cases in which the United States is a party. Said Supreme Court shall have jurisdiction and power to review such decision, and shall give priority to such cases, and may affirm, modify, or reverse such decision of such circuit court, and remand the case with such orders as may seem to it proper in the premises, which shall be executed accordingly. All final judgments, when in favor of the importer, shall be satisfied and paid by the Secretary of the Treasury from the permanent indefinite appropriation provided for in section twenty-three of this act. For the purposes of this section the circuit courts of the United States shall be deemed always open, and said circuit courts, respectively, may establish, and from time to time alter, rules and regulations not inconsistent herewith for the procedure in such cases as they shall deem proper.

SEC. 16. That the general appraisers, or any of them, are hereby authorized to administer oaths, and said general appraisers, the boards of general appraisers, the local appraisers or the collectors, as the case may be, may cite to appear before them, and examine upon oath any owner, importer, agent, consignee, or other person touching any matter or thing which they, or either of them, may deem material respecting any imported merchandise, in ascertaining the dutiable value or classification thereof; and they, or either of them, may require the production of any letters, accounts, or invoices relating to said merchandise, and may require such testimony to be reduced to writing, and when so taken it shall be filed in the office of the collector, and preserved for use or reference until the final decision of the collector or said board of appraisers shall be made respecting the valuation or classification of said merchandise, as the case may be.

SEC. 17. That if any person so cited to appear shall neglect or refuse to attend, or shall decline to answer, or shall refuse to answer in writing any interrogatories, and subscribe his name to his deposition, or to produce such papers, when so required by a general appraiser, or a board of general appraisers, or a local appraiser or a collector, he shall be liable to a penalty of one hundred dollars; and if such person be the owner, importer, or consignee, the appraisement which the general appraiser, or board of general appraisers, or local appraiser, or collector, where there is no appraiser, may make of the merchandise, shall be final and conclusive; and any person who shall willfully and corruptly swear falsely on an examination before any general appraiser, or board of general appraisers, or local appraiser, or collector, shall be deemed guilty of perjury; and if he is the owner, importer, or consignee, the merchandise shall be forfeited.

SEC. 18. That all decisions of the general appraisers and of the boards of general appraisers, respecting values and rates of duty, shall be preserved and filed, and shall be open to inspection under proper regulations to be prescribed by the Secretary of the Treasury. All decisions of the general appraisers shall be reported forthwith to the Secretary of the Treasury and to the board of general appraisers on duty at the port of New York, and the report to the board shall be accompanied, whenever practicable, by samples of the merchandise in question, and it shall be the duty of the said board, under the direction of the Secretary of the Treasury, to cause an abstract to be made and published of such decisions of the appraisers as they may deem important, and of the decisions of each of the general appraisers and boards of general appraisers, which abstract shall contain a general description of the merchandise in question, and of the value and rate of duty fixed in each case, with reference, whenever practicable, by number or other designation, to samples deposited in the place of samples at New York, and such abstract shall be issued from time to time, at least once in each week, for the information of customs officers and the public.

SEC. 19. That whenever imported merchandise is subject to an ad valorem rate of duty, or to a duty based upon or regulated in any manner by the value thereof, the duty shall be assessed upon the actual market value or wholesale price of such merchandise as bought and sold in usual wholesale quantities, at the time of exportation to the United States, in the principal markets of the country from whence imported, and in the condition in which such merchandise is there bought and sold for exportation to the United States, or consigned to the United States for sale, including the value of all cartons, cases, crates, boxes, sacks, and coverings of any kind, and all other costs, charges and expenses incident to placing the merchandise in condition, packed ready for shipment to the United States, and if there be used for covering or holding imported merchandise, whether dutiable or free, any unusual article or form designed for use otherwise than in the bona fide transportation of such merchandise to the United States, additional duty shall be levied and collected upon such material or article at the rate to which the same would be subject if separately imported. That the words "value" or "actual market value" whenever used in this act or in any law relating to the appraisement of imported merchandise shall be construed to mean the actual market value or wholesale price as defined in this section.

SEC. 20. Any merchandise deposited in any public or private bonded-warehouse may be withdrawn for consumption within three years from the date of original importation, on payment of the duties and charges to which it may be subject by law at the time of such withdrawal: *Provided,* That nothing herein shall affect or impair existing provisions of law in regard to the disposal of perishable or explosive articles.

SEC. 21. That in all suits or informations brought, where any seizure has been made pursuant to any act providing for or regulating the collection of duties on imports or tonnage, if the property is claimed by any person, the burden of proof shall lie upon such claimant: *Provided,* That probable cause is shown for such prosecution, to be judged of by the court.

SEC. 22. That all fees exacted and oaths administered by officers of the customs, except as provided in this act, under or by virtue of existing laws of the United States, upon the entry of imported goods and the passing thereof through the customs, and also upon all entries of domestic goods, wares, and merchandise for exportation, be, and the same are hereby, abolished; and in case of entry of merchandise for exportation, a declaration, in lieu of an oath, shall be filed, in such form and under such regulations as may be prescribed by the Secretary of the Treasury; and the penalties provided in the sixth section of this act for false statements in such declaration shall be applicable to declarations made under this section: *Provided,* That where such fees, under existing laws, constitute, in whole or in part, the compensation of any officer, such officer shall receive, from and after the passage of this act, a fixed sum for each year equal to the amount which he would have been entitled to receive as fees for such services during said year.

SEC. 23. That no allowance for damage to goods, wares, and merchandise imported into the United States shall hereafter be made in the estimation and liquidation of duties thereon; but the importer thereof may, within ten days after entry, abandon to the United States all or any portion of goods, wares, and merchandise included in any invoice, and be relieved from the payment of the duties on the portion so abandoned: *Provided,* That the portion so abandoned shall amount to ten per centum or over of the total value or quantity of the invoice; and the property so abandoned shall be sold by public auction or otherwise disposed of for the account and credit of the United States under such regulations as the Secretary of the Treasury may prescribe. All merchandise so abandoned by the importer thereof shall be delivered by such importer at such place within the port of arrival as the chief officer of customs may direct, and on the failure of the importer to comply with the directions of the collector in this respect the abandoned merchandise shall be disposed of by the collector at the expense of such importer.

SEC. 24. That whenever it shall be shown to the satisfaction of the Secretary of the Treasury that, in any case of unascertained or estimated duties, or payments made upon appeal, more money has been paid to or deposited with a collector of customs than, as has been ascertained by final liquidation thereof, the law required to be paid or deposited, the Secretary of the Treasury shall direct the Treasurer to refund and pay the same out of any money in the Treasury not otherwise appropriated. The necessary moneys therefor are hereby appropriated, and this appropriation shall be deemed a permanent indefinite appropriation; and the Secretary of the Treasury is hereby authorized to correct manifest clerical errors in any entry or liquidation, for or against the United States, at any time within one year of the date of such entry, but not afterwards: *Provided,* That the Secretary of the Treasury shall in his annual report to Congress, give a detailed statement of the various sums of money refunded under the provisions of this act or of any other act of Congress relating to the revenue, together with copies of the rulings under which repayments were made.

SEC. 25. That from and after the taking effect of this act no collector or other officers of the customs shall be in any way liable to any owner, importer, consignee, or agent of any merchandise, or any other person, for or on account of any rulings or decisions as to the classification of said merchandise or the duties charged thereon, or the collection of any dues, charges, or duties on or on account of said merchandise, or any other matter or thing as to which said owner, importer, consignee, or agent of such merchandise might, under this act, be entitled to appeal from the decision of said collector or other officer, or from any board of appraisers provided for in this act.

SEC. 26. That any person who shall give, or offer to give or promise to give any money or thing of value, directly or indirectly, to any officer or employee of the United States in consideration of or for any act or omission contrary to law in connection with or pertaining to the importation, appraisement, entry, examination, or inspection of goods, wares, or merchandise including herein any baggage, or of the liquidation of the entry thereof, or shall by threats or demands, or promises of any character attempt to improperly influence or control any such officer or employee of the United States as to the performance of his official duties shall, on conviction thereof, be fined not exceeding two thousand dollārs, or be imprisoned at hard labor not more than one year, or both, in the discretion of the court; and evidence of such giving, or offering, or promising to give, satisfactory to the court in which such trial is had, shall be regarded as prima facie evidence that such giving or offering or promising was contrary to law, and shall put upon the accused the burden of proving that such act was innocent, and not done with an unlawful intention.

SEC. 27. That any officer or employee of the United States who shall, excepting for lawful duties or fees, solicit, demand, exact or receive from any person, directly or indirectly, any money or thing of value, in connection with or pertaining to the importation, appraisment, entry, examination, or inspection of goods, wares, or merchandise, including herein any baggage, or liquidation of the entry thereof, on conviction thereof, shall be fined not exceeding five thousand dollars, or be imprisoned at hard labor not more than two years, or both, in the discretion of the court. And evidence of such soliciting, demanding, exacting, or receiving, satisfactory to the court in which such trial is had, shall be regarded as prima facie evidence that such soliciting, demanding, exacting, or receiving was contrary to law, and shall put upon the accused the burden of proving that such act was innocent and not with an unlawful intention.

SEC. 28. That any baggage or personal effects arriving in the United States in transit to any foreign country may be delivered by the parties having it in charge to the collector of the proper district, to be by him retained, without the payment or exaction of any import duty, or to be forwarded by such collector to the collector of the port of departure and to be delivered to such parties on their departure for their foreign destination, under such rules and regulations as the Secretary of the Treasury may prescribe.

SEC. 29. That sections twenty-six hundred and eight,

twenty-eight hundred and thirty-eight, twenty-eight hundred and thirty-nine, twenty-eight hundred and forty-one, twenty-eight hundred and forty-three, twenty-eight hundred and forty-five, twenty-eight hundred and fifty-three, twenty-eight hundred and fifty-four, twenty-eight hundred and fifty-six, twenty-eight hundred and fifty-eight, twenty-eight hundred and sixty, twenty-nine hundred, and twenty-nine hundred and two, twenty-nine hundred and five, twenty-nine hundred and seven, twenty-nine hundred and eight, twenty-nine hundred and nine, twenty-nine hundred and twenty-two, twenty-nine hundred and twenty-three, twenty-nine hundred and twenty-four, twenty-nine hundred and twenty-seven, twenty-nine hundred and twenty-nine, twenty-nine hundred and thirty, twenty-nine hundred and thirty-one, twenty-nine hundred and thirty-two, twenty-nine hundred and forty-three, twenty-nine hundred and forty-five, twenty-nine hundred and fifty-two, three thousand and eleven, three thousand and twelve, three thousand and twelve and one-half, three thousand and thirteen, of the Revised Statutes of the United States, be, and the same are hereby, repealed, and sections nine, ten, eleven, twelve, fourteen, and sixteen of an act entitled "An act to amend the customs-revenue laws and to repeal moieties," approved June twenty-second, eight hundred and seventy-four, and sections seven, eight, and nine of the act entitled "An act to reduce internal-revenue taxation, and for other purposes," approved March third, eighteen hundred and eighty-three, and all other acts and parts of acts inconsistent with the provisions of this act, are hereby repealed, but the repeal of existing laws or modifications thereof embraced in this act shall not affect any act done, or any right accruing or accrued, or any suit or proceeding had or commenced in any civil cause before the said repeal or modifications; but all rights and liabilities under said laws shall continue and may be enforced in the same manner as if said repeal or modifications had not been made. Any offenses committed, and all penalties or forfeitures or liabilities incurred prior to the passage of this act under any statute embraced in or changed, modified, or repealed by this act may be prosecuted and punished in the same manner and with the same effect as if this act had not been passed. All acts of limitation, whether applicable to civil causes and proceedings or to the prosecution of offenses or for the recovery of penalties or forfeitures embraced in or modified, changed, or repealed by this act, shall not be affected thereby; and all suits, proceedings, or prosecutions, whether civil or criminal, for causes arising or acts done or committed prior to the passage of this act, may be commenced and prosecuted within the same time and with the same effect as if this act had not been passed. *And provided further,* That nothing in this act shall be construed to repeal the provisions of section three thousand and fifty-eight of the Revised Statutes as amended by the act approved February twenty-third, eighteen hundred and eighty-seven, in respect to the abandonment of merchandise to underwriters or the salvors of property, and the ascertainment of duties thereon.

SEC. 30. That this act shall take effect on the first day of August, eighteen hundred and ninety, except so much of section twelve as provides for the appointment of nine general appraisers, which shall take effect immediately.

Approved, June 10, 1890.

APPENDIX D.

RULES OF PRACTICE IN THE UNITED STATES PATENT OFFICE.

CORRESPONDENCE.

1. All business with the office should be transacted in writing. Unless by the consent of all parties, the action of the office will be based exclusively on the written record. No attention will be paid to any alleged oral promise, stipulation, or understanding in relation to which there is a disagreement or doubt.

2. All office letters must be sent in the name of the "Commissioner of Patents." All letters and other communications intended for the office must be addressed to him; if addressed to any of the other officers, they will ordinarily be returned.

3. Express charges, freight, postage, and all other charges on matter sent to the Patent Office must be prepaid in full; otherwise it will not be received.

4. The personal attendance of applicants at the Patent Office is unnecessary. Their business can be transacted by correspondence.

5. The assignee of the entire interest of an invention is entitled to hold correspondence with the office to the exclusion of the inventor. (See Rule 20.)

6. When there has been an assignment of an undivided part of an invention, amendments and other actions requiring the signature of the inventor must also receive the written assent of the assignee; but official letters will

only be sent to the post-office address of the inventor, unless he shall otherwise direct.

7. When an attorney shall have filed his power of attorney, duly executed, the correspondence will be held with him.

8. A double correspondence with the inventor and an assignee, or with a principal and his attorney, or with two attorneys, cannot generally be allowed.

9. A separate letter should in every case be written in relation to each distinct subject of inquiry or application. Assignments for record, final fees, and orders for copies or abstracts must be sent to the office in separate letters.

Papers sent in violation of this rule will be returned.

10. When a letter concerns an application, it should state the name of the applicant, the title of the invention, the serial number of the application (see Rule 31), and the date of filing the same. (See Rule 32.)

11. When the letter concerns a patent it should state the name of the patentee, the title of the invention, and the number and date of the patent.

12. No attention will be paid to unverified *ex parte* statements or protests of persons concerning pending applications to which they are not parties, unless information of the pendency of such applications shall have been voluntarily communicated by the applicants.

13. Letters received at the office will be answered, and orders for printed copies filled, without unnecessary delay. Telegrams, if not received before 3 o'clock p. m., can not ordinarily be answered until the following day.

INFORMATION TO CORRESPONDENTS.

14. The office can not respond to inquiries as to the novelty of an alleged invention in advance of the filing

of an application for a patent, nor to inquiries propounded with a view to ascertaining whether any alleged improvements have been patented, and, if so, to whom; nor can it act as an expounder of the patent law, nor as counsellor for individuals, except as to questions arising within the office.

Of the propriety of making an application for a patent, the inventor must judge for himself. The office is open to him, and its records and models pertaining to all patents granted may be inspected either by himself or by any attorney or expert he may call to his aid, and its reports are widely distributed. (See Rule 210.) Further than this the office can render him no assistance until his case comes regularly before it in the manner prescribed by law. A copy of the rules, with this section marked, sent to the individual making an inquiry of the character referred to, is intended as a respectful answer by the office.

Examiners' digests are not open to public inspection.

15. Caveats and pending applications are preserved in secrecy. No information will be given, without authority, respecting the filing by any particular person of a caveat or of an application for a patent or for the reissue of a patent, the pendency of any particular case before the office, or the subject-matter of any particular application, unless it shall be necessary to the proper conduct of business before the office, as provided by Rules 97, 103, and 108.

16. After a patent has issued, the model, specification, drawings, and all documents relating to the case are subject to general inspection, and copies, except of the model, will be furnished at the rates specified in Rule 204.

ATTORNEYS.

17. An applicant or an assignee of the entire interest may prosecute his own case, but he is advised, unless familiar with such matters, to employ a competent attorney, as the value of patents depends largely upon the skillful preparation of the specification and claims. The office can not aid in the selection of an attorney.

A register of attorneys will be kept in this office, on which will be entered the names of all persons entitled to represent applicants before the Patent Office in the presentation and prosecution of applications for patent. The names of persons in the following classes will, upon their written request, be entered upon this register.

(*a*) Any person who on June 18, 1897, was engaged as attorney or agent in the active prosecution of applications for patent before this office, or had been so engaged at any time within five years prior thereto and is not disbarred, or is or was during such period a member of a firm so engaged and not disbarred, provided that such person shall, if required, furnish information as to one or more applications for patent so prosecuted by him.

(*b*) Any attorney at law who is in good standing in any court of record in the United States or any of the States or Territories thereof and shall furnish a certificate of the clerk of such United States, State or Territorial court, duly authenticated under the seal of the court, that he is an attorney in good standing.

(*c*) Any person who has been regularly recognized as an attorney or agent to represent claimants before the Department of the Interior or any bureau thereof and is in good standing, provided that such person shall furnish a statement of the date of his admission to practice as such attorney or agent, and shall further show, if required by the Commissioner, that he is possessed of the necessary qualifications to render applicants for patents valuable service and is otherwise competent to advise and assist them in the presentation and prosecution of their applications before the Patent Office.

(*d*) Any person not an attorney at law who shall file a certificate from a judge of a United States, State, or Territorial court, duly authenticated under the seal of the court, that such person is of good moral character and of good repute and possessed of the necessary qualifications to enable him to render applicants for patents valuable service, and is otherwise competent to advise and assist them in the presentation and prosecution of their applications before the Patent Office.

(*e*) Any firm which on June 18, 1897, was engaged in the active prosecution as attorneys or agents of applications for patents before the Patent Office, or had been so engaged at any time within five years prior thereto, provided such firm or any member thereof is not disbarred, provided the names of the individuals composing the firm are stated, and provided, also, that such firm shall, if required, furnish information as to one or more applications prosecuted before the Patent Office by them.

(*f*) Any firm not entitled to registration under the preceding sections which shall show that the individuals composing the firm are each and all recognized as patent attorneys or agents or are each and all entitled to be so recognized under the preceding sections of this rule.

The Commissioner may demand additional proof of qualifications and reserves the right to decline to recognize any attorney, agent, or other person applying for registration under this rule.

Any person or firm not registered and not entitled to

be recognized under this rule as an attorney or agent to represent applicants generally may, upon a showing of circumstances which render it necessary or justifiable, be recognized by the Commissioner to prosecute as attorney or agent certain specified application or applications, but this limited recognition shall not extend further than the application or applications named.

No person not registered as above provided will be permitted to prosecute applications before the Patent Office.

18. Before any attorney, original or associate, will be allowed to inspect papers or take action of any kind, his power of attorney must be filed. But general powers given by a principal to an associate can not be considered. In each application the written authorization must be filed. A power of attorney purporting to have been given to a firm or copartnership will not be recognized, either in favor of the firm or of any of its members, unless all its members shall be named in such power of attorney.

* * * * * * * *

19. Substitution or association can be made by an attorney upon the written authorization of his principal; but such authorization will not empower the second agent to appoint a third.

20. Powers of attorney may be revoked at any stage in the proceedings of a case upon application to and approval by the Commissioner; and when so revoked the office will communicate directly with the applicant, or such other attorney as he may appoint. An attorney will be promptly notified by the docket clerk of the revocation of his power of attorney. An assignment of an undivided interest will not operate as a revocation of the

power previously given; but the assignee of the entire interest may be represented by an attorney of his own selection.

21. Parties or their attorneys will be permitted to examine their cases in the attorney's room, but not in the rooms of the examiners. Personal interviews with examiners will be permitted only as hereinafter provided. (See Rule 152.)

22. (*a*) Applicants and attorneys will be required to conduct their business with the office with decorum and courtesy. Papers presented in violation of this requirement will be returned. But all such papers will first be submitted to the Commissioner, and only returned by his direct order.

(*b*) Complaints against examiners and other officers must be made in separate communications, and will be promptly investigated.

(*c*) For gross misconduct the Commissioner may refuse to recognize any person as a patent agent, either generally or in any particular case; but the reasons for such refusal will be duly recorded and be subject to the approval of the Secretary of the Interior.

23. Inasmuch as applications can not be examined out of their regular order, except in accordance with the provisions of Rule 63, and members of Congress can neither examine nor act in patent cases without written powers of attorney, applicants are advised not to impose upon Senators or Representatives labor which will consume their time without any advantageous results.

APPLICANTS.

24. A patent may be obtained by any person who has invented or discovered any new and useful art, machine,

manufacture, or composition of matter, or any new and useful improvement thereof, not known or used by others in this country before his invention or discovery thereof, and not patented or described in any printed publication in this or any foreign country before his invention or discovery thereof, *or more than two years prior to his application,* and not patented in a country foreign to the United States on an application filed more than twelve months before his application, and not in public use or on sale in the United States for more than two years prior to his application, unless the same is proved to have been abandoned, upon payment of the fees required by law and other due proceedings had. (For designs, see Rule 79.)

25. In case of the death of the inventor, the application will be made by and the patent will issue to his executor or administrator. In such case the oath required by Rule 46 will be made by the executor or administrator. In case of the death of the inventor during the time intervening between the filing of his application and the granting of a patent thereon, the letters patent will issue to the executor or administrator upon proper intervention by him.

In case an inventor becomes insane, the application may be made by and the patent issued to his legally appointed guardian, conservator, or representative, who will make the oath required by Rule 46.

26. In case of an assignment of the whole interest in the invention, or of the whole interest in the patent to be granted, the patent will, upon request of the applicant embodied in the assignment, issue to the assignee; and if the assignee hold an undivided part interest, the patent will, upon like request, issue jointly to the inventor and

the assignee; but the assignment in either case must first have been entered of record, and at a day not later than the date of the payment of the final fee (see Rule 201); and if it be dated subsequently to the execution of the application, it must give the date of execution of the application, or the date of filing, or the serial number, so that there can be no mistake as to the particular invention intended. The application and oath must be signed by the actual inventor, if alive, even if the patent is to issue to an assignee (see Rules 30, 40); if the inventor be dead, the application may be made by the executor or administrator.

27. If it appear that the inventor, at the time of making his application, believed himself to be the first inventor or discoverer, a patent will not be refused on account of the invention or discovery, or any part thereof, having been known or used in any foreign country before his invention or discovery thereof, if it had not been before patented or described in any printed publication.

28. Joint inventors are entitled to a joint patent; neither of them can obtain a patent for an invention jointly invented by them. Independent inventors of distinct and independent improvements in the same machine can not obtain a joint patent for their separate inventions. The fact that one person furnishes the capital and another makes the invention does not entitle them to make an application as joint inventors; but in such case they may become joint patentees, upon the conditions prescribed in Rule 26.

29. The receipt of letters patent from a foreign government will not prevent the inventor from obtaining a patent in the United States, unless *the application on which the foreign patent was granted was filed more than*

twelve months prior to the filing of the application in this country, in which case no patent shall be granted in this country.

THE APPLICATION.

30. Applications for letters patent of the United States must be made to the Commissioner of Patents, and must be signed by the inventor, if alive. (See Rules 26, 33, 40, 46.) A complete application comprises the first fee of $15, a petition, specification, and oath; and drawings, model, or specimen when required. (See Rules 49, 56, 62.) The petition, specification, and oath must be in the English language. All papers which are to become a part of the permanent records of the office must be legibly written or printed in permanent ink.

31. An application for a patent will not be placed upon the files for examination until all its parts, except the model or specimen, are received.

Every application signed or sworn to in blank, or without actual inspection by the applicant of the petition and specification, and every application altered or partly filled up after being signed or sworn to, will be stricken from the files.

Completed applications are numbered in regular order, the present series having been commenced on the 1st of January, 1900.

The applicant will be informed of the serial number of his application.

The application must be completed and prepared for examination within *one year* after the filing of the petition; and in default thereof, or upon failure of the applicant to prosecute the same within *one year* after any action thereon (Rule 77), of which notice shall have been duly mailed to him or his agent, the application will be regarded as abandoned, unless it shall be shown to the satisfaction of the Commissioner that such delay was unavoidable. (See Rules 171 and 172.)

32. It is desirable that all parts of the complete application should be deposited in the office at the same time, and that all the papers embraced in the application should be attached together; otherwise a letter must accompany each part, accurately and clearly connecting it with the other parts of the application. (See Rule 10.)

THE PETITION.

33. The petition must be addressed to the Commissioner of Patents, and must state the name, residence, *and postoffice address* of the petitioner requesting the grant of a patent, designate by title the invention sought to be patented, contain a reference to the specifications for a full disclosure of such invention, and must be signed by the applicant.

THE SPECIFICATION.

34. The specification is a written description of the invention or discovery and of the manner and process of making, constructing, compounding, and using the same, and is required to be in such full, clear, concise, and exact terms as to enable any person skilled in the art or science to which the invention or discovery appertains, or with which it is most nearly connected, to make, construct, compound, and use the same.

35. The specification must set forth the precise invention for which a patent is solicited, and explain the principle thereof, and the best mode in which the applicant has contemplated applying that principle, in such manner as to distinguish it from other inventions.

36. In case of a mere improvement, the specification must particularly point out the parts to which the improvement relates, and must by explicit language distinguish between what is old and what is claimed as new; and the description and the drawings, as well as the claims, should be confined to the specific improvement and such parts as necessarily co-operate with it.

37. The specification must conclude with a specific and distinct claim or claims of the part, improvement, or combination which the applicant regards as his invention or discovery.

38. When there are drawings the description will refer to the different views by figures and to the different parts by letters or numerals (preferably the latter).

39. The following order of arrangement should be observed in framing the specification:

(1) Preamble stating the name and residence of the applicant and the title of the invention.
(2) General statement of the object and nature of the invention.
(3) Brief description of the several views of the drawings (if the invention admits of such illustration).
(4) Detailed description.
(5) Claim or claims.
(6) Signature of inventor.
(7) Signatures of two witnesses.

40. The specification must be signed by the inventor or by his executor or administrator, and the signature must be attested by two witnesses. Full names must be given, and all names, whether of applicants or witnesses, must be legibly written.

41. Two or more independent inventions can not be

claimed in one application; but where several distinct inventions are dependent upon each other and mutually contribute to produce a single result they may be claimed in one application.

CLAIMS FOR A MACHINE AND ITS PRODUCT MUST BE PRESENTED IN SEPARATE APPLICATIONS.

CLAIMS FOR A MACHINE AND THE PROCESS IN THE PERFORMANCE OF WHICH THE MACHINE IS USED MUST BE PRESENTED IN SEPARATE APPLICATIONS.

CLAIMS FOR A PROCESS AND ITS PRODUCT MAY BE PRESENTED IN THE SAME APPLICATION.

42. If several inventions, claimed in a single application, be of such a nature that a single patent may not be issued to cover them, the inventor will be required to limit the description, drawing, and claim of the pending application to whichever invention he may elect. The other inventions may be made the subjects of separate applications, which must conform to the rules applicable to original applications. If the independence of the inventions be clear, such limitation will be made before any action upon the merits; otherwise it may be made at any time before final action thereon, in the discretion of the examiner.

43. When an applicant files two or more applications relating to the same subject-matter of invention, all showing but only one claiming the same thing, the applications not claiming it must contain references to the application claiming it.

44. A reservation for a future application of subject-matter disclosed but not claimed in a pending application, but which subject-matter might be claimed therein, will not be permitted in the pending application.

45. The specification and claims must be plainly writ-

ten or printed on but one side of the paper. All interlineations and erasures must be clearly referred to in marginal or foot notes on the same sheet of paper. Legal-cap paper with the lines numbered is deemed preferable, and a wide margin must always be reserved upon the left-hand side of the page.

THE OATH.

46. The applicant, if the inventor, must make oath or affirmation that he does verily believe himself to be the original and first inventor or discoverer of the art, machine, manufacture, composition, or improvement for which he solicits a patent; that he does not know and does not believe that the same was ever before known or used, and shall state of what country he is a citizen and where he resides. In every original application the applicant must distinctly state under oath that the invention has not been *patented to himself or to others with his knowledge or consent in this or any foreign country for more than two years prior to his application, or on an application for a patent filed in any foreign country by himself or his legal representatives or assigns more than twelve months prior to his application. If any application for patent has been filed in any foreign country by the applicant in this country, or by his legal representatives or assigns, prior to his application in this country, he shall state the country or countries in which such application has been filed, giving the date of such application, and shall also state that no application has been filed in any other country or countries than those mentioned;* that to the best of his knowledge and belief the invention has not been in public use or on sale in the United States, *nor described in any printed publication*

or patent in this or in any foreign country, for more than two years prior to his application in this country. This oath must be subscribed to by the affiant.

The Commissioner may require an additional oath in cases where the applications have not been filed in the Patent Office within a reasonable time after the execution of the original oath.

47. If the application be made by an executor or administrator of a deceased person or the guardian, conservator, or representative of an insane person, the form of the oath will be correspondingly changed.

The oath or affirmation may be made before any person within the United States authorized by law to administer oaths, or, when the applicant resides in a foreign country, before any minister, charge d'affaires, consul, or commercial agent holding commission under the government of the United States, or before any notary public, *judge, or magistrate having an official seal and authorized to administer oaths in the foreign country in which the applicant may be, whose authority shall be proved by a certificate of a diplomatic or consular officer of the United States*, the oath being attested in all cases, in this and other countries, by the proper official seal of the officer before whom the oath or affirmation is made. When the person before whom the oath or affirmation is made is not provided with a seal, his official character shall be established by competent evidence, as by a certificate from a clerk of a court of record or other proper officer having a seal.

When the oath is taken before an officer in a country foreign to the United States, all the application papers must be attached together and a ribbon passed one or more times through all the sheets of the application, and the ends of said ribbon brought together under the seal before the latter is affixed and impressed, or each sheet must be impressed with the official seal of the officer before whom the oath was taken, or, if he is not provided with a seal, then each sheet must be initialed by him.

48. When an applicant presents a claim for matter originally shown or described but not substantially embraced in the statement of invention or claim originally presented, he will file a supplemental oath to the effect that the subject-matter of the proposed amendment was part of his invention, was invented before he filed his original application, was not known or used before his invention, was not patented or described in a printed publication in any country more than two years before his application, was not patented to himself or to others with his knowledge or consent in this or any foreign country on an application filed more than twelve months prior to his application, was not in public use or on sale in this country for more than two years before the date of his application, and has not been abandoned. Such supplemental oath must be attached to and properly identify the proposed amendment.

THE DRAWINGS.

49. The applicant for a patent is required by law to furnish a drawing of his invention whenever the nature of the case admits of it.

50. The drawing may be signed by the inventor, or the name of the inventor may be signed on the drawing by his attorney in fact, and must be attested by two witnesses. The drawing must show every feature of the invention covered by the claims, and the figures should be consecutively numbered if possible. When the invention

consists of an improvement on an old machine the drawing must exhibit, in one or more views, the invention itself, disconnected from the old structure, and also in another view so much only of the old structure as will suffice to show the connection of the invention therewith.

51. Three several editions of patent drawings are printed and published—one for office use, certified copies, etc., of the size and character of those attached to patents, the work being about 6 by 9½ inches; one reduced to half that scale, or one-fourth the surface, of which four are printed on a page to illustrate the volumes, distributed to the courts; and one reduction—to about the same scale —of a selected portion of each drawing for the Official Gazette.

This work is done by the photolithographic process, and therefore the character of each original drawing must be brought as nearly as possible to a uniform standard of excellence, suited to the requirements of the process, and calculated to give the best results, in the interests of inventors, of the office, and of the public. The following rules will therefore be rigidly enforced, and any departure from them will be certain to cause delay in the examination of an application for letters patent:

(1) Drawings must be made upon pure white paper of a thickness corresponding to three-sheet Bristol-board. The surface of the paper must be calendered and smooth. India ink alone must be used, to secure perfectly black and solid lines.

(2) The size of a sheet on which a drawing is made must be exactly 10 by 15 inches. One inch from its edges a single marginal line is to be drawn, leaving the "sight" precisely 8 by 13

inches. Within this margin all work and signatures must be included. One of the shorter sides of the sheet is regarded as its top, and, measuring downwardly from the marginal line, a space of not less than 1¼ inches is to be left blank for the heading of title, name, number, and date.

(3) All drawings must be made with the pen only. Every line and letter (signatures included) must be absolutely black. This direction applies to all lines, however fine, to shading, and to lines representing cut surfaces in sectional views. All lines must be clean, sharp, and solid, and they must not be too fine or crowded. Surface shading, when used, should be open. Sectional shading should be made by oblique parallel lines, which may be about one-twentieth of an inch apart. Solid black should not be used for sectional or surface shading.

(4) Drawings should be made with the fewest lines possible consistent with clearness. By the observance of this rule the effectiveness of the work after reduction will be much increased. Shading (except on sectional views) should be used only on convex and concave surfaces, where it should be used sparingly, and may even there be dispensed with if the drawing is otherwise well executed. The plane upon which a sectional view is taken should be indicated on the general view by a broken or dotted line. Heavy lines on the shade sides of objects should be used, except where they tend to thicken the work and obscure letters of reference.

The light is always supposed to come from the upper left-hand corner at an angle of forty-five degrees. Imitations of wood or surface graining should not be attempted.

(5) The scale to which a drawing is made ought to be large enough to show the mechanism without crowding, and two or more sheets should be used if one does not give sufficient room to accomplish this end; but the number of sheets must never be more than is absolutely necessary.

(6) The different views should be consecutively numbered. Letters and figures of reference must be carefully formed. They should, if possible, measure at least one-eighth of an inch in height, so that they may bear reduction to one twenty-fourth of an inch; and they may be much larger when there is sufficient room. They must be so placed in the close and complex parts of drawings as not to interfere with a thorough comprehension of the same, and therefore should rarely cross or mingle with the lines. When necessarily grouped around a certain part, they should be placed at a little distance, where there is available space, and connected by short broken lines with the parts to which they refer. They must never appear upon shaded surfaces, and when it is difficult to avoid this, a blank space must be left in the shading where the letter occurs, so that it shall appear perfectly distinct and separate from the work. If the same part of an invention appear

in more than one view of the drawing it must always be represented by the same character, and the same character must never be used to designate different parts.

(7) The signature of the inventor should be placed at the lower right-hand corner of each sheet, and the signatures of the witnesses at the lower left-hand corner, all within the marginal line, but in no instance should they trespass upon the drawings. The title should be written with pencil on the back of the sheet. The permanent names and title will be supplied subsequently by the office in uniform style.

When views are longer that the width of the sheet, the sheet should be turned on its side and the heading will be placed at the right and the signatures at the left, occupying the same space and position as in the upright views, and being horizontal when the sheet is held in an upright position; and all views on the same sheet must stand in the same direction. One figure must not be placed upon another or within the outline of another.

(8) As a rule, one view only of each invention can be shown in the Gazette illustrations. The selection of that portion of a drawing best calculated to explain the nature of the specific improvement would be facilitated and the final result improved by the judicious execution of a figure with express reference to the Gazette, but which might at the same time serve as one of the figures referred to in the specification. For this

purpose the figure may be a plan, elevation, section, or perspective view, according to the judgment of the draftsman. It must not cover a space exceeding 16 square inches. All its parts should be especially open and distinct, with very little or no shading, and it must illustrate the invention claimed only, to the exclusion of all other details. When well executed, it will be used without curtailment or change, but any excessive fineness, or crowding, or unnecessary elaborateness of detail will necessitate its exclusion from the Gazette.

(9) Drawings should be rolled for transmission to the office, not folded.

An agent's or attorney's stamp, or advertisement, or written address will not be permitted upon the face of a drawing, within or without the marginal line.

52. In certain cases these rules may be modified as to drawings for designs. (See rules for designs, 83 and 84.)

53. All reissue applications must be accompanied by new drawings, of the character required in original applications, and the inventor's name must appear upon the same in all cases; and such drawings shall be made upon the same scale as the original drawing, or upon a larger scale, unless a reduction of scale shall be authorized by the Commissioner.

54. The foregoing rules relating to drawings will be rigidly enforced. Every drawing not artistically executed in conformity thereto may be admitted for purposes

of examination if it sufficiently illustrates the invention, but in such cases a new drawing must be furnished before the application can be allowed. The office will make the necessary corrections at the applicant's option and cost.

55. Applicants are advised to employ competent artists to make their drawings.

The office will furnish the drawings at cost, as promptly as its draftsmen can make them, for applicants who can not otherwise conveniently procure them.

THE MODEL.

56. Preliminary examinations will not be made for the purpose of determining whether models are required in particular cases. Applications complete in all other respects will be sent to the examining divisions, whether models are or are not furnished. A model will only be required or admitted as a part of the application when on examination of the case in its regular order the primary examiner shall find it to be necessary or useful. In such case, if a model has not been furnished, the examiner shall notify the applicant of such requirement, which will constitute an official action in the case. When a model is received in compliance with the official requirement, the date of its filing shall be entered on the file wrapper. Models not required nor admitted will be returned to the applicants. When a model is required, the examination will be suspended until it shall have been filed. From a decision of the primary examiner overruling a motion to dispense with a model an appeal may be taken to the Commissioner in person, under the provisions of Rule 145.

57. The model must clearly exhibit every feature of the machine which forms the subject of a claim of invention, but should not include other matter than that covered by the actual invention or improvement, unless it be necessary to the exhibition of the invention in a working model.

58. The model must be neatly and substantially made of durable material, metal being deemed preferable; but when the material forms an essential feature of the invention, the model should be constructed of that material. The model must not be more than one foot in length, width, or height, except in cases in which the Commissioner shall admit working models of complicated machines of larger dimensions. If made of wood, it must be painted or varnished. Glue must not be used; but the parts should be so connected as to resist the action of heat and moisture. When practicable, to prevent loss, the model or specimen should have the name of the inventor permanently fixed thereon. In cases where models are not made strong and substantial as here directed, the application will not be examined until a proper model is furnished.

59. A working model is often desirable, in order to enable the office fully and readily to understand the precise operation of the machine.

60. In all applications which have remained rejected for more than *one year* the model, unless it is deemed necessary that it should be preserved in the office, may be returned to the applicant upon demand and at his expense; and the model in any pending case of less than *one year's* standing may be returned to the applicant upon the filing of a formal abandonment of the applica-

tion, signed by the applicant in person and any assignee. (See Rule 171.)

Models belonging to patented cases shall not be taken from the office except in the custody of some sworn employe of the office specially authorized by the Commissioner.

61. Models filed as exhibits in contested cases may be returned to the parties at their expense. If not claimed within a reasonable time, they may be disposed of at the discretion of the Commissioner.

SPECIMENS.

62. When the invention or discovery is a composition of matter, the applicant, if required by the Commissioner, shall furnish specimens of the composition, and of its ingredients, sufficient in quantity for the purpose of experiment. In all cases where the article is not perishable, a specimen of the composition claimed, put up in proper form to be preserved by the office, must be furnished. (Rules 56, 60, and 61 apply to specimens also.)

THE EXAMINATION.

63. Applications filed in the Patent Office are classified according to the various arts, and are taken up for examination in regular order of filing, those in the same class of invention being examined and disposed of, as far as practicable, in the order in which the respective applications are completed.

The following new applications have preference over all other new cases at every period of their examination in the order enumerated:

(1) Applications wherein the inventions are deemed of peculiar importance to some branch of

the public service, and when for that reason the head of some Department of the Government requests immediate action and the Commissioner so orders; *but in such case it shall be the duty of such head of a Department to be represented before the Commissioner in order to prevent the improper issue of a patent.*

(2) Applications for reissues.

(3) Applications which appear to interfere with other applications previously considered and found to be allowable, or which it is demanded shall be placed in interference with an unexpired patent or patents.

The following applications, previously acted upon, will have preference over other business:

(1) Cases remanded by an appellate tribunal for further action, and statements of grounds of decisions provided for in Rules 135 and 145.

(2) Applications which have been put into condition for further action by the examiner shall be entitled to precedence over new applications in the same class of invention.

(3) Applications which have been renewed or revived but the subject-matter not changed.

(4) When the inventor dies and his executor or administrator files a new application for the same invention, the new application may be given the same status in the order of examination as the original by order of the Commissioner.

64. Where the specification and claims are such that the invention may be readily understood, the examination of a complete application and the action thereon will be

directed throughout to the merits; but in each letter the examiner shall state or refer to all his objections.

Only in applications found by the examiner to present patentable subject-matter and in applications on which appeal is taken to the examiners-in-chief will requirements in matters of form be insisted on. (See Rules 95 and 134.)

REJECTIONS AND REFERENCES.

65. Whenever, on examination, any claim of an application is rejected for any reason whatever, the applicant will be notified thereof. The reasons for such rejection will be fully and precisely stated, and such information and references will be given as may be useful in aiding the applicant to judge of the propriety of prosecuting his application or of altering his specification; and if, after receiving such notice, he shall persist in his claim, with or without altering his specification, the application will be re-examined. If upon re-examination the claim shall be again rejected, the reasons therefor will be fully and precisely stated.

66. Upon the rejection of an application for want of novelty, the examiner must cite the best references at his command. When the reference shows or describes inventions other than that claimed by the applicant, the particular part relied on will be designated as nearly as practicable. The pertinence of the reference, if not obvious, must be clearly explained and the anticipated claim specified.

If domestic patents be cited, their dates and numbers, the names of the patentees, and the classes of invention must be stated. If foreign patents be cited, their dates and numbers, the names of the patentees, titles of the inventions, and the classes of inventions must be stated, and such other data must be furnished as will enable the applicant to identify the patents cited. If printed publications be cited, the title, date, page or plate, author, and place of publication, or place where a copy can be found, will be given. When reference is made to facts within the personal knowledge of an employe of the office, the data will be as specific as possible, and the reference must be supported, when called for, by the affidavit of such employe (Rule 76); such affidavit shall be subject to contradiction, explanation, or corroboration by the affidavits of the applicant and other persons. If the patent, printed matter, plates, or drawings so referred to are in the possession of the office, copies will be furnished at the rate specified in Rule 204, upon the order of the applicant.

67. Whenever, in the treatment of an *ex parte* application, an adverse decision is made upon any preliminary or intermediate question, without the rejection of any claim, notice thereof, together with the reasons therefor, will be given to the applicant, in order that he may judge of the propriety of the action. If, after receiving such notice, he traverse the propriety of the action, the matter will be reconsidered.

AMENDMENTS AND ACTIONS BY APPLICANTS.

68. The applicant has a right to amend before or after the first rejection or action; and he may amend as often as the examiner presents new references or reasons for rejection. In so amending, the applicant must clearly point out all the patentable novelty which he thinks the case presents in view of the state of the art disclosed by the references cited or the objections made. He must

also show how the amendments avoid such references or objections.

After such action upon an application as will entitle the applicant to an appeal to the examiners-in-chief (Rule 134), or after such appeal has been taken, amendments canceling claims or presenting those rejected in better form for consideration on appeal may be admitted; but the admission of such an amendment or its refusal, and any proceedings relative thereto, shall not operate to relieve the application from its condition as subject to appeal, or to save it from abandonment under Rule 171. If amendments touching the merits of the application are presented after the case is in condition for appeal, or after appeal has been taken, they may be admitted upon a showing duly verified of good and sufficient reasons why they were not earlier presented. From the refusal of the primary examiner to admit an amendment a petition will lie to the Commissioner under Rule 145. No amendment can be made in appealed cases between the filing of the examiner's statement of the grounds of his decision (Rule 135) and the decision of the appellate tribunal. After decision on appeal amendments can only be made as provided in Rule 142, or to carry into effect a recommendation under Rule 139.

69. In order to be entitled to the reconsideration provided for in Rules 65 and 67, the applicant must make request therefor in writing, and he must distinctly and specifically point out the supposed errors in the examiner's action. The mere allegation that the examiner has erred will not be received as a proper reason for such reconsideration.

70. In original applications which are capable of illustration by drawing or model all amendments of the mod-

el, drawings, or specifications, and all additions thereto, must conform to at least one of them as it was at the time of the filing of the application. Matter not found in either, involving a departure from the original invention, can be shown or claimed only in a separate application.

71. The specification and drawing must be amended and revised when required, to correct inaccuracies of description or unnecessary prolixity and to secure correspondence between the claim, the specification, and the drawing. But no change in the drawing may be made except by written permission of the office and after a photographic copy of the drawing as originally presented has been filed.

72. After the completion of the application the office will not return the specification for any purpose whatever. If applicants have not preserved copies of the papers which they wish to amend, the office will furnish them on the usual terms.

The model or drawing, but not both at the same time, may be withdrawn for correction; but a drawing can not be withdrawn unless a model has been filed and accepted by the examiner as a part of the application.

73. In every amendment the exact word or words to be stricken out or inserted in the application must be specified and the precise point indicated where the erasure or insertion is to be made. All such amendments must be on sheets of paper separate from the papers previously filed, and written on but one side of the paper. Erasures, additions, insertions, or mutilations of the papers and records must not be made by the applicant.

Amendments and papers requiring the signature of the applicant must also, in case of assignment of an undivided part of the invention, be signed by the assignee. (Rules 6, 107.)

74. When an amendatory clause is amended, it must be wholly rewritten, so that no interlineation or erasure shall appear in the clause, as finally amended, when the application is passed to issue. If the number or nature of the amendments shall render it otherwise difficult to consider the case or to arrange the papers for printing or copying, the examiner or Commissioner may require the entire specification to be rewritten.

75. When an original or reissue application is rejected on reference to an expired or unexpired domestic patent which substantially shows or describes but does not claim the rejected invention, or on reference to a foreign patent or to a printed publication, and the applicant shall make oath to facts showing a completion of the invention in this country before the filing of the application on which the domestic patent issued, or before the date of the foreign patent, or before the date of the printed publication, and shall also make oath that he does not know and does not believe that the invention has been in public use or on sale in this country, *or patented or described in a printed publication in this or any foreign country* for more than two years prior to his application, and that he has never abandoned the invention, then the patent or publication cited will not bar the grant of a patent to the applicant, *unless the date of such patent or printed publication is more than two years prior to the date on which application was filed in this country.*

76. When an application is rejected on reference to an expired or unexpired domestic patent which shows or describes but does not claim the invention, or on reference

to a foreign patent, or to a printed publication, or to facts within the personal knowledge of an employe of the office, set forth in an affidavit (when requested) of such employe (Rule 66), or when rejected on the ground of public use or sale, or upon a mode or capability of operation attributed to a reference, or because the alleged invention is held to be inoperative or frivolous or injurious to public health or morals, affidavits or depositions supporting or traversing these references or objections may be received, but affidavits will not be received in other cases without special permission of the Commissioner. (See Rule 141.)

77. If an applicant neglect to prosecute his application for *one year* after the date when the last official notice of any action by the office was mailed to him, the application will be held to be abandoned, as set forth in Rule 171.

Whenever action upon an application is suspended upon request of an applicant, and whenever an applicant has been called upon to put his application in condition for interference, the period of *one year* running against such application shall be considered as beginning at the date of the last official action preceding such actions.

Acknowledgment of the filing of an application is an official action. Suspensions will only be granted for good and sufficient cause, and for a reasonable time specified.

Only one suspension will be granted by the primary examiner; any further suspension must be approved by the Commissioner.

78. Amendments will not be permitted after the notice of allowance of an application, and the examiner will exercise jurisdiction over such an application only by special authority from the Commissioner.

Amendments may be made after the allowance of an application, and after payment of the final fee, if the specification has not been printed, on the recommendation of the primary examiner, approved by the Commissioner, without withdrawing the case from issue. (See Rule 135.)

DESIGNS.

79. A design patent may be obtained by any person who has invented any new, original, and ornamental design for an article of manufacture, not known or used by others in this country before his invention thereof, and not patented or described in any printed publication in this or any foreign country before his invention thereof, or more than two years prior to his application, *and not caused to be patented by him in a foreign country on an application filed more than four months before his application in this country,* and not in public use or on sale in this country for more than two years prior to his application, unless the same is proved to have been abandoned, upon payment of the fees required by law and other due proceedings had, the same as in cases of inventions or discoveries.

80. Patents for designs are granted for the term of three and one-half years, or for seven years, or for fourteen years, as the applicant may, in his application, elect.

81. The proceedings in applications for patents for designs are substantially the same as in applications for other patents. The specification must distinctly describe the article in its aspect of shape or configuration and ornamentation. This having been done, as every design must be new, original, and ornamental, the claim may properly be, in the broadest form, for the ornamental

design, substantially as shown and described. The following order of arrangement should be observed in framing the specifications:

(1) Preamble, stating name and residence of the applicant, title of the design, and the name of the article for which the design has been invented.
(2) Detailed description of the design, as it appears in the drawing.
(3) Claim.
(4) Signature of inventor.
(5) Signatures of two witnesses.

82. When the design can be sufficiently represented by drawings a model will not be required.

83. The design must be represented by a drawing made to conform to the rules laid down for drawings of mechanical inventions.

84. Reference to the materials used or the mode of their utilization or the mechanical construction of the design can not properly enter into the description of the design.

(For forms to be used in applications for design patents, see Appendix.)

REISSUES.

85. A reissue is granted to the original patentee, his legal representatives, or the assignees of the entire interest, when the original patent is inoperative or invalid by reason of a defective or insufficient specification, or by reason of the patentee claiming as his invention or discovery more than he had a right to claim as new, provided the error has arisen through inadvertence, accident, or mistake, and without any fraudulent or deceptive intention.

Reissue applications must be made and the specifications sworn to by the inventors, if they be living.

86. The petition for a reissue must be accompanied by a certified copy of the abstract of title, giving the names of all assignees owning any undivided interest in the patent. In case the application be made by the inventor it must be accompanied by the written assent of such assignees.

87. Applicants for reissue, in addition to the requirements of Rule 46, must also file with their petitions a statement on oath as follows:

(1) That applicant verily believes the original patent to be inoperative or invalid, and the reason why.

(2) When it is claimed that such patent is so inoperative or invalid "by reason of a defective or insufficient specification," particularly specifying such defects or insufficiencies.

(3) When it is claimed that such patent is inoperative or invalid "by reason of the patentee claiming as his own invention or discovery more than he had a right to claim as new," distinctly specifying the part or parts so alleged to have been improperly claimed as new.

(4) Particularly specifying the errors which it is claimed constitute the inadvertence, accident, or mistake relied upon, and how they rose or occurred.

(5) That said errors arose "without any fraudulent or deceptive intention" on the part of the applicant.

88. New matter shall not be allowed to be introduced into the reissue specification, nor in the case of a machine

shall the model or drawings be amended except each by the other.

89. The Commissioner may, in his discretion, cause several patents to be issued for distinct and separate parts of the thing patented, upon demand of the applicant, and upon payment of the required fee for each division of such reissued letters patent. Each division of a reissue constitutes the subject of a separate specification descriptive of the part or parts of the invention claimed in such division; and the drawing may represent only such part or parts, subject to the provisions of Rule 50. Unless otherwise ordered by the Commissioner, all the divisions of a reissue will issue simultaneously; if there be any controversy as to one division, the others will be withheld from issue until the controversy is ended, unless the Commissioner shall otherwise order.

90. An original claim, if reproduced in the reissue specification, is subject to re-examination, and the entire application will be revised and restricted in the same manner as original applications.

91. *The application for a reissue must be accompanied by the original patent and an offer to surrender the same, or, if the original be lost, by an affidavit to that effect, and a certified copy of the patent. If a reissue be refused, the original patent will be returned to applicant upon his request.*

92. Matter shown and described in an unexpired patent, and which might have been lawfully claimed therein, but which was not claimed by reason of a defect or insufficiency in the specification, arising from inadvertence, accident, or mistake, and without fraud or deceptive intent, can not be subsequently claimed by the patentee in a separate patent, but only in a reissue of the original patent.

INTERFERENCES.

93. An interference is a proceeding instituted for the purpose of determining the question of priority of invention between two or more parties claiming substantially the same patentable invention. The fact that one of the parties has already obtained a patent will not prevent an interference, for, although the Commissioner has no power to cancel a patent, he may grant another patent for the same invention to a person who proves to be the prior inventor.

94. Interferences will be declared in the following cases, when all the parties claim substantially the same patentable invention:

(1) Between two or more original applications containing conflicting claims.

(2) Between an original application and an unexpired patent containing conflicting claims, when the applicant, having been rejected on the patent, shall file an affidavit that he made the invention before the patentee's application was filed.

(3) Between an original application and an application for the reissue of a patent granted during the pendency of such original application.

(4) Between an original application and a reissue application, when the original applicant shall file an affidavit showing that he made the invention before the patentee's original application was filed.

(5) Between two or more applications for the reissue of patents granted on applications pending at the same time.

(6) Between two or more applications for the reissue of patents granted on applications not pending at the same time, when the applicant for reissue of the later patent shall file an affidavit showing that he made the invention before the application was filed on which the earlier patent was granted.

(7) Between a reissue application and an unexpired patent, if the original applications were pending at the same time, and the reissue applicant shall file an affidavit showing that he made the invention before the original application of the other patentee was filed.

(8) Between an application for reissue of a later unexpired patent and an earlier unexpired patent granted before the original application of the later patent was filed, if the reissue applicant shall file an affidavit showing that he made the invention before the original application of the earlier patent was filed.

(9) *An interference will not be declared between an original application filed subsequently to December 31, 1897, and a patent issued more than two years prior to the date of filing such application or an application for a reissue of such a patent.*

95. Before the declaration of interference all preliminary questions must be settled by the primary examiner, and the issue must be clearly defined; the invention which is to form the subject of the controversy must be decided to be patentable, and the claims of the respective parties must be put in such condition that they will not require alteration after the interference shall have

been finally decided, unless the testimony adduced upon the trial shall necessitate or justify such change.

96. *Whenever two or more applications disclose the same invention, and one of said applications is ready for allowance and contains a claim to said invention, the primary examiner will notify the other applicant of such fact, furnish him with a copy of the patentable claim, and require him to make such claim and put his case in condition for allowance within a specified time, so that an interference can be declared. Upon the failure of any applicant to make the claim suggested within the time specified, such failure or refusal shall be taken without further action as a disclaimer of the invention covered by the claim, and the issue of the patent to the applicant whose application is in condition for allowance will not be delayed unless the time for making the claim and putting the application in condition for allowance be extended upon a proper showing. If a party make the claim without putting his application in condition for allowance, the declaration of the interference will not be delayed, but after judgment of priority the application of such party will be held for revision and restriction, subject to interference with other applications.*

97. When an interference is found to exist and the applications are prepared therefor, the primary examiner will forward to the examiner of interferences the files and drawings; notices of interference for all the parties (as specified in Rule 103) disclosing the name and residence of each party and that of his attorney, and of any assignee, and, if any party be a patentee, the date and number of the patent; the ordinals of the conflicting claims and the title of the invention claimed; and the issue, which shall be clearly and concisely defined in so

many counts or branches as may be necessary in order to include all interfering claims. Where the issue is stated in more than one count the respective claims involved in each count should be specified. The primary examiner shall also forward to the examiner of interferences for his use a statement disclosing the applications involved in interference, fully identified, the name and residence of any assignee, and the names and residences of all attorneys, both principal and associate, and arranged in the inverse chronological order of their filing as completed applications, and also disclosing the issue or issues and the ordinals of the conflicting claims.

Whenever it shall be found that two or more parties whose interests are in conflict are represented by the same attorney, the examiner will notify each of said principal parties, and also the attorney, of this fact.

98. Upon receipt of the notices of interference, the examiner of interferences will make an examination thereof, in order to ascertain whether the issue between the parties has been clearly defined, and whether they are otherwise correct. If he be of the opinion that the notices are ambiguous or are defective in any material point, he will transmit his objections to the primary examiner, who will promptly notify the examiner of interferences of his decision to amend or not to amend them.

99. In case of a material disagreement between the examiner of interferences and the primary examiner, the points of difference shall be referred to the Commissioner for decision.

100. The primary examiner will retain jurisdiction of the case until the declaration of interference is made.

101. Upon the institution and declaration of the in-

terference, as provided in Rule 102, the examiner of interferences will take jurisdiction of the same, which will then become a contested case; but the primary examiner will determine the motions mentioned in Rule 122, as therein provided.

102. When the notices of interference are in proper form, the examiner of interferences will add thereto a designation of the time within which the preliminary statements required by Rule 110 must be filed, and will, *pro forma,* institute and declare the interference by forwarding the notices to the several parties to the proceeding.

103. The notices of interference will be forwarded by the examiner of interferences to all the parties, in care of their attorneys, if they have attorneys, and, if the application or patent in interference has been assigned, to the assignees. When one of the parties has received a patent, a notice will be sent to the patentee and to his attorney of record.

When the notices sent in the interest of a patent are returned to the office undelivered, or when one of the parties resides abroad and his agent in the United States is unknown, additional notice may be given by publication in the Official Gazette for such period of time as the Commissioner may direct.

104. If either party require a postponement of the time for filing his preliminary statement, he will present his motion, duly served on the other parties, with his reasons therefor, supported by affidavit, and such motion should be made, if possible, prior to the day previously fixed upon. But the examiner of interferences may, in his discretion, dispense with service of notice of such motion.

105. When an application is involved in an interference in which a part only of the invention is included in the issue, the applicant may file certified copies of the part or parts of the specification, claims, and drawings which cover the interfering matter, and such copies may be used in the proceeding in place of the original application.

106. When a part only of an application is involved in an interference, the applicant may withdraw from his application the subject-matter adjudged not to interfere, and file a new application therefor, or he may file a divisional application for the subject-matter involved, if the invention can be legitimately divided: *Provided,* That no claim shall be made in either application broad enough to include matter claimed in the other.

107. An applicant involved in an interference may, with the written consent of the assignee, when there has been an assignment, before the date fixed for the filing of his preliminary statement (see Rule 110), in order to avoid the continuance of the interference, disclaim under his own signature, attested by two witnesses, the invention of the particular matter in issue, and upon such disclaimer and the cancellation of any claims involving such interfering matter judgment shall be rendered against him, and a copy of the disclaimer shall be embodied in and form part of his specification. (See Rule 182.)

108. When applications are declared to be in interference, the interfering parties will be permitted to see or obtain copies of each other's file-wrappers, and so much of their contents as relate to the interference, after the preliminary statements referred to in Rule 110 have been received and approved; but information of an application

will not be furnished by the office to an opposing party, except as provided in Rules 97 and 103, until after the approval of such statement.

109. When an application is involved in an interference in part and shows and describes, without claiming a patentable invention claimed by another party thereto, the applicant may, at any time within twenty days after the preliminary statements (referred to in Rule 110) of the parties have been received and approved, on motion duly made, as provided in Rule 153, file an amendment of his application duly claiming such invention, and on the admission of such amendment the invention shall be included in the interference. Such motion must be accompanied by the proposed amendment, and when in proper form will be transmitted by the examiner of interferences to the primary examiner for his determination. In case the amendment shall be admitted, the primary examiner will redeclare the interference, prepare new notices, and forward the papers and files to the examiner of interferences, who will proceed in accordance with Rule 103. The decision of the primary examiner will be binding upon the examiner of interferences, unless reversed or modified on appeal, as provided in Rule 124.

110. Each party to the interference will be required to file a concise preliminary statement, under oath, on or before a date to be fixed by the office, showing the following facts:

(1) The date of original conception of the invention set forth in the declaration of interference.

(2) The date upon which a drawing of the invention was made.

(3) The date upon which a model of the invention was made.

(4) The date upon which the invention was first disclosed to others.

(5) The date of the reduction to practice of the invention.

(6) A statement showing the extent of use of the invention.

If a drawing or model has not been made, or if the invention has not been reduced to practice or disclosed to others, or used to any extent, the statement must specifically disclose these facts.

When the invention was made abroad the statement should set forth:

(1) That applicant made the invention set forth in the declaration of interference.

(2) Whether or not the invention was ever patented; if so, when and where, giving the date and number of each patent, the date of publication, and the date of sealing thereof.

(3) Whether or not the invention was ever described in a printed publication; if so, when and where, giving the title, place, and date of such publication.

(4) Whether or not the invention was ever introduced into this country; if so, giving the circumstances, with the dates connected therewith, which are relied upon to establish the fact.

(5) *If the applicant is a citizen of a foreign country adhering to the International Convention for the Protection of Industrial Property, or a*

country having similar treaty relations with the United States, he shall state the date and number of any application for the same invention filed in his own country within twelve months of the filing date in the United States.

The preliminary statements should be carefully prepared, as the parties will be strictly held in their proofs to the dates set up therein.

If a party prove any date earlier than alleged in his preliminary statement, such proof will be held to establish the date alleged and none other.

The statement must be sealed up before filing (to be opened only by the examiner of interferences; see Rule 111), and the name of the party filing it, the title of the case, and the subject of the invention indicated on the envelope. The envelope should contain nothing but this statement.

111. The preliminary statements shall not be opened to the inspection of the opposing parties until each one shall have been filed, or the time for such filing, with any extension thereof, shall have expired, and not then unless they have been examined by the proper officer and found to be satisfactory.

Any party in default in filing his preliminary statement shall not have access to the preliminary statement or statements of his opponent or opponents until he has either filed his statement or waived his right thereto, and agreed to stand upon his record date.

112. If, on examination, a statement is found to be defective in any particular, the party shall be notified of the defect and wherein it consists, and a time assigned within which he must cure the same by an amended state-

ment; but in no case will the original or amended statement be returned to the party after it has been filed. *Unopened statements will be removed from interference files and preserved by the office, and in no case will such statements be open to the inspection of the opposing party without authority from the Commissioner.* If a party shall refuse to file an amended statement, he will be restricted to his record date in the further proceedings in the interference.

113. In case of material error arising through inadvertence or mistake, the statement may be corrected on motion (see Rule 153), upon showing to the satisfaction of the Commissioner that the correction is essential to the ends of justice. The motion to correct the statement must be made, if possible, before the taking of any testimony, and as soon as practicable after the discovery of the error.

114. If the junior party to an interference, or if any party thereto other than the senior party, fails to file a statement, or if his statement fails to overcome the *prima facie* case made by the respective dates of application, such party will be notified by the examiner of interferences that judgment upon the record will be rendered against him at the expiration of twenty days. Within this period of twenty days any of the motions permitted by the rules may be brought. Motions brought after judgment on the record has been rendered will not be entertained unless sufficient reasons appear for the delay.

115. If a party to an interference fails to file a statement, testimony will not be received subsequently from him to prove that he made the invention at a date prior to his application.

116. In original proceedings in cases of interference the several parties will be presumed to have made the invention in the chronological order in which they filed their completed applications for patents clearly illustrating and describing the invention; and the burden of proof will rest upon the party who shall seek to establish a different state of facts.

117. The preliminary statement can in no case be used as evidence in behalf of the party making it.

118. Times will be assigned in which the junior applicant shall complete his testimony in chief, and in which the other party shall complete the testimony on his side, and a further time in which the junior applicant may take rebutting testimony; but he shall take no other testimony. If there be more than two parties to the interference, the times for taking testimony will be so arranged that each shall have an opportunity to prove his case against prior applicants and to rebut their evidence, and also to meet the evidence of junior applicants.

119. Whenever the time for taking the testimony of a party to an interference shall have expired, and no testimony shall have been taken by such party, any senior party may, by motion based on a showing properly verified and served on such party in default, have an order entering judgment against such defaulting party, unless the latter shall, at a day set and not less than ten days after the hearing of the motion, show good and sufficient cause why the judgment shall not be entered.

120. If either party desire to have the hearing continued, he will make application for such postponement by motion (see Rule 153), and will show sufficient reason therefor by affidavit.

121. If either party desire an extension of the time assigned to him for taking testimony, he will make application therefor, as provided in Rule 154 (4).

122. Motions to dissolve an interference upon the ground that no interference in fact exists, or that there has been such irregularity in declaring the same as will preclude a proper determination of the question of priority, or which deny the patentability of an applicant's claim, or his right to make the claim, should, if possible, be made not later than the twentieth day after the statements of the parties have been received and approved. Such motions, and all motions of a similar character, should be accompanied by a motion to transmit the same to the primary examiner, and such motion to transmit should be noticed for hearing upon a day certain before the examiner of interferences. When in proper form the motion presented will be transmitted by the examiner of interferences, with the files and papers, to the proper primary examiner for his determination, who will thereupon fix a day certain when the said motion will be heard before him upon the merits, and give notice thereof to all the parties. If a stay of proceedings be desired, a motion therefor should accompany the motion for transmission.

When the motion has been decided by the primary examiner, if no appeal has been taken therefrom, at the expiration of the time limited for appeal the examiner will return the files and papers, with his decision, to the examiner of interferences. Such decision will be binding on the examiner of interferences unless reversed or modified on appeal. (Rule 124.)

123. All lawful motions, except those mentioned in Rule 122, will be made before and determined by the tri-

bunal having jurisdiction at the time. The filing of motions will not operate as a stay of proceedings in any case. To effect this, motion should be made before the tribunal having jurisdiction of the interference, who will, sufficient grounds appearing therefor, order a suspension of the interference pending the determination of such motion.

124. Appeal may be taken directly to the Commissioner from decisions on all motions except the following: (1) On motions to dissolve which deny the patentability of applicant's claim; (2) on motions to dissolve which deny the right of an applicant to make the claim; (3) on motions involving the merits of the invention. Decisions on these motions, when appealable, go to the examiners-in-chief, *in the first instance,* and upon such appeals the questions *shall* be heard *inter partes.*

From a decision of the primary examiner affirming the patentability of the claim or the applicant's right to make the same no appeal can be taken.

125. After the interference is finally declared, it will not, except as herein otherwise provided, be determined without judgment of priority founded either upon the testimony, or upon a written concession of priority by one of the parties, signed by the inventor himself (and by the assignee, if any), or upon a written declaration of abandonment of the invention.

126. The examiner of interferences or the examiners-in-chief may, either before or in their decision on the question of priority, direct the attention of the Commissioner to any matter not relating to priority which may have come to their notice, and which, in their opinion, establishes the fact that no interference exists, or that there has been irregularity in declaring the same (Rule

122), or which amounts to a statutory bar to the grant of a patent to either of the parties for the claim or claims in interference. The Commissioner may, before judgment on the question of priority, suspend the interference and remand the case to the primary examiner for his consideration of the matters to which attention has been directed. From the decision of the examiner appeal may be taken as in other cases. If the case shall not be so remanded, the primary examiner will, after judgment, consider any matter affecting the rights of either party to a patent which may have been called to his attention, unless the same shall have been previously disposed of by the Commissioner.

127. A second interference will not be declared upon a new application for the same invention filed by either party.

128. If, during the pendency of an interference, a reference be found, the interference may be suspended at the request of the primary examiner until the final determination of the pertinency and effect of the reference and the interference shall then be dissolved or continued as the result of such determination. The consideration of such reference *shall* be *inter partes.*

129. If, during the pendency of an interference, another case appear, claiming substantially the subject-matter in issue, the primary examiner shall request the suspension of the interference for the purpose of adding said case. Such suspension will be granted as a matter of course by the examiner of interferences if no testimony has been taken. If, however, any testimony has been taken, a notice for the proposed new party, disclosing the issue in interference and the names and addresses of the interferants and of their attorneys, and notices for the

interferants disclosing the name and address of the said party and his attorney, shall be prepared by the primary examiner and forwarded to the examiner of interferences, who shall mail said notices and set a time of hearing on the question of the admission of the new party. If the examiner of interferences be of the opinion that the interference should be suspended and the new party added, he shall prescribe the terms for such suspension. The decision of the examiner of interferences as to the addition of a party shall be final.

130. Amendments to the specification will not be received during the pendency of an interference, except as provided in Rules 106, 107, 109.

131. When, on motion duly made and upon satisfactory proof, it shall be shown that, by reason of the inability or refusal of the inventor to prosecute or defend an interference, or from other cause, the ends of justice require that an assignee of an undivided interest in the invention should be permitted to prosecute or defend the same, the Commissioner may so order.

132. Whenever an award of priority has been rendered in an interference proceeding by any tribunal and the limit of appeal from such decision has expired, and whenever an interference has been terminated by reason of the written concession, signed by the applicant in person, of priority of invention in favor of his opponent or opponents, the primary examiner shall advise the defeated or unsuccessful party or parties to the interference that their claim or claims which were so involved in the issue stand finally rejected.

APPEALS.

133. Every applicant for a patent, any of the claims of

whose application have been twice rejected for the same reasons, upon grounds involving the merits of the invention, such as lack of invention, novelty, or utility, or on the ground of abandonment, public use or sale, inoperativeness of invention, aggregation of elements, incomplete combination of elements, or, when amended, for want of identity with the invention originally disclosed, or because the amendment involves a departure from the invention originally presented; and every applicant for the reissue of a patent whose claims have been twice rejected for any of the reasons above enumerated, or on the ground that the original patent is not inoperative or invalid, or if so inoperative or invalid that the errors which rendered it so did not arise from inadvertence, accident, or mistake, may, upon payment of a fee of $10, appeal from the decision of the primary examiner to the examiners-in-chief. The appeal must set forth in writing the points of the decision upon which it is taken, and must be signed by the applicant or his duly authorized attorney or agent.

134. There must have been two rejections of the claims as originally filed, or, if amended in matter of substance, of the amended claims, and all the claims must have been passed upon, and all preliminary and intermediate questions relating to matters not affecting the merits of the invention settled, before the case can be appealed to the examiners-in-chief.

135. Upon the filing of the appeal the same shall be submitted to the primary examiner, who, if he find it to be regular in form, shall, within *five* days from the filing thereof, furnish the examiners-in-chief with a written statement of the grounds of his decision on all the points involved in the appeal, with copies of the rejected

claims and with the references applicable thereto. The examiner shall at the time of making such statement furnish a copy of the same to the appellant. If the primary examiner shall decide that the appeal is not regular in form, a petition from such decision may be taken directly to the Commissioner, as provided in Rule 145.

136. The appellant shall, before the day of hearing, file a brief of the authorities and arguments on which he will rely to maintain his appeal.

137. If the appellant desire to be heard orally before the examiners-in-chief, he will so indicate when he files his appeal; a day of hearing will then be fixed, and due notice of the same given him.

138. In contested cases the appellant shall have the right to make the opening and closing arguments, unless it shall be otherwise ordered by the tribunal having jurisdiction of the case.

139. (*a*) The examiners-in-chief in their decision will affirm or reverse the decision of the primary examiner only on the points on which appeal shall have been taken. (See Rule 133.) Should they discover any apparent grounds not involved in the appeal for granting or refusing letters patent in the form claimed, or any other form, they will annex to their decision a statement to that effect, with such recommendation as they shall deem proper.

(*b*) From an adverse judgment of the primary examiner on points embraced in the recommendation annexed to the decision, appeal may be taken on questions involving the merits to the board of examiners-in-chief and on other questions to the Commissioner as in other cases.

(*c*) The Commissioner may, when an appeal from the decision of the examiners-in-chief is taken to him, remand the case to the primary examiner, either before or after final judgment, for consideration of any amendment or action which may be based on the recommendation annexed to the decision of the examiners-in-chief.

(*d*) If the Commissioner, in reviewing the decision of the examiners-in-chief, discovers any apparent grounds for granting or refusing letters patent not involved in the appeal, he will, before or after final judgment, and whenever in his opinion substantial justice shall require it, give reasonable notice thereof to the parties; and if any amendment or action based thereon be proposed, he will remand the case to the primary examiner for consideration.

(*e*) From the decisions of the primary examiner, in cases remanded as herein provided, appeal will lie to the board of examiners-in-chief, or directly to the Commissioner, as in other cases.

140. From the adverse decision of the board of examiners-in-chief appeal may be taken to the Commissioner in person, upon payment of the fee of $20 required by law.

141. If affidavits be received after the case has been appealed, the application will be remanded to the primary examiner for reconsideration.

142. Cases which have been heard and decided by the Commissioner on appeal will not be reopened except by his order; cases which have been decided by the examiners-in-chief will not be reheard by them, when no longer pending before them, without the written authority of the Commissioner; and cases which have been decided by either the Commissioner or the examiners-in-chief will not be reopened by the primary examiner without like authority, and then only for the consideration of matters

not already adjudicated upon, sufficient cause being shown. (See Rule 68.)

143. Contested cases will be regarded as pending before a tribunal until the limit of appeal, which must be fixed, has expired, or until some action has been had which waives the appeal or carries into effect the decision from which appeal might have been taken.

Ex parte cases decided by an appellate tribunal will, after decision, be remanded at once to the primary examiner, subject to the applicant's right of appeal, or such action as will carry into effect the decision, or for such further action as the applicant is entitled to demand.

144. Cases which have been deliberately decided by one Commissioner will not be reconsidered by his successor except in accordance with the principles which govern the granting of new trials.

145. Upon receiving a petition stating concisely and clearly any proper question which has been twice acted upon by the examiner, and which does not involve the merits of the invention claimed, or the rejection of a claim, and also stating the facts involved and the point or points to be reviewed, an order will be made fixing a time for hearing such petition by the Commissioner, and directing the examiner to furnish a written statement of the grounds of his decision upon the matters averred in such petition within *five days after being notified of the order fixing* the day of hearing. The examiner shall at the time of making such statement furnish a copy thereof to the petitioner. No fee is required for such a petition.

146. In interference cases parties have the same remedy by appeal to the examiners-in-chief, to the Commis-

sioner, and to the court of appeals of the District of Columbia, as in *ex parte* cases.

147. Appeals in interference cases must be accompanied by brief statements of the reasons therefor. Parties will be required to file six copies of printed briefs of their arguments, the appellant five days before the hearing and the appellee one day.

148. From the adverse decision of the Commissioner upon the claims of an application and in interference cases, an appeal may be taken to the court of appeals of the District of Columbia in the manner prescribed by the rules of that court.

149. When an appeal is taken to the court of appeals of the District of Columbia, the appellant will give notice thereof to the Commissioner, and file in the Patent Office within forty days, *exclusive of Sundays and holidays*, from the date of the decision appealed from, his reasons of appeal specifically set forth in writing.

150. *Pro forma* proceedings will not be had in the Patent Office for the purpose of securing to applicants an appeal to the court of appeals of the District of Columbia.

(See Rules of the Court of Appeals of the District of Columbia.)

HEARINGS AND INTERVIEWS.

151. Hearings will be had by the Commissioner at 10 o'clock a. m., and by the board of examiners-in-chief at 1 o'clock p. m., and by the examiner of interferences at 11 o'clock a. m., on the day appointed, unless some other hour be specially designated. If either party in a contested case, or the appellant in an *ex parte* case, appear

at the proper time, he will be heard. After the day of hearing, a contested case will not be taken up for oral argument except by consent of all parties. If the engagements of the tribunal having jurisdiction are such as to prevent the case from being taken up on the day of hearing, a new assignment will be made, or the case will be continued from day to day until heard. Unless it shall be otherwise ordered before the hearing begins, oral arguments will be limited to one hour for each party in contested cases, and to one-half hour in other cases. After a contested case has been argued, nothing further relating thereto will be heard unless upon request of the tribunal having jurisdiction of the case; and all interviews for this purpose with parties in interest or their attorneys will be invariably denied.

152. Interviews with examiners concerning applications and other matters pending before the office must be had in the examiners' rooms at such times, within office hours, as the respective examiners may designate; in the absence of the primary examiners, with the assistant in charge. Interviews will not be permitted at any other time or place without the written authority of the Commissioner. Interviews for the discussion of pending applications will not be had prior to the first official action thereon.

MOTIONS.

153. In contested cases reasonable notice of all motions, and copies of motion-papers and affidavits, must be served, as provided in Rule 154 (2). Proof of such service must be made before the motion will be entertained by the office. Motions will not be heard in the absence of either party except upon default after due notice.

Motions will be heard in the first instance by the officer or tribunal before whom the particular case may be pending; but an appeal from the decision rendered may be taken on questions involving the merits of the case to the board of examiners-in-chief; on other questions, directly to the Commissioner. In original hearings on motions the moving parties shall have the right to make the opening and closing arguments. In contested cases the practice on points to which the rules shall not be applicable will conform, as nearly as possible, to that of the United States courts in equity proceedings.

TESTIMONY IN INTERFERENCES AND OTHER CONTESTED CASES.

154. The following rules have been established for taking and transmitting testimony in interferences and other contested cases:

(1) Before the depositions of witnesses are taken by either party due notice shall be given to the opposing party, as hereinafter provided, of the time when and place where the depositions will be taken, of the cause or matter in which they are to be used, and of the names and residences of the witnesses to be examined, and the opposing party shall have full opportunity, either in person or by attorney, to cross-examine the witnesses. If the opposing party shall attend the examination of witnesses not named in the notice, and shall either cross-examine such witnesses or fail to object to their examination, he shall be deemed to have waived his right to object to such examination for want of notice. Neither party shall take testimony in more

than one place at the same time, nor so nearly at the same time that reasonable opportunity for travel from one place of examination to the other can not be had.

(2) The notice for taking testimony or for motions must be served (unless otherwise stipulated in an instrument in writing filed in the case) upon the attorney of record, if there be one, or, if there be no attorney of record, upon the adverse party. Reasonable time must be given therein for such adverse party to reach the place of examination. Service of such notice may be made in either of the following ways: (1) By delivering a copy of the notice to the adverse party or his attorney; (2) by leaving a copy at the usual place of business of the adverse party or his attorney with some one in his employment; (3) when such adverse party or his attorney has no usual place of business, by leaving a copy at his residence, with a member of his family over fourteen years of age and of discretion; (4) transmission by registered letter; (5) by express. Whenever it shall be satisfactorily shown to the Commissioner that neither of the above modes of obtaining or reserving notice is practicable, the notice may be published in the Official Gazette. Such notice shall, with sworn proof of the fact, time, and mode of service thereof, be attached to the deposition or depositions whether the opposing party shall have cross-examined or not.

(3) Each witness before testifying shall be duly sworn according to law by the officer before

whom his deposition shall be taken. The deposition shall be carefully read over by the witness, or by the officer to him, and shall then be subscribed by the witness in the presence of the officer. The officer shall annex to the deposition his certificate showing (1) the due administration of the oath by the officer to the witness before the commencement of his testimony; (2) the name of the person by whom the testimony was written out, and the fact that, if not written by the officer, it was written in his presence; (3) the presence or absence of the adverse party; (4) the place, day, and hour of commencing and taking the deposition; (5) the reading by, or to, each witness of his deposition before he signs the same; and (6) the fact that the officer was not connected by blood or marriage with either of the parties, nor interested, directly or indirectly, in the matter in controversy. The officer shall sign the certificate and affix thereto his seal of office, if he have such seal. He shall then, without delay, securely seal up all the evidence, notices, and paper exhibits, inscribe upon the envelope a certificate giving the title of the case, the name of each witness, and the date of sealing, address the package, and forward the same to the Commissioner of Patents. If the weight or bulk of an exhibit shall exclude it from the envelope, it shall be authenticated by the officer and transmitted in a separate package, marked and addressed as above provided.

(4) If a party shall be unable to take any testimony within the time limited, and desires an extension for such purpose, he must file a motion, accompanied by a statement under oath setting forth specifically the reason why such testimony has not been taken, and distinctly averring that such motion is made in good faith, and not for the purpose of delay. If either party shall be unable to procure the testimony of a witness or witnesses within the time limited, and desires an extension for such purpose, he must file a motion, accompanied by a statement under oath setting forth the cause of such inability, the name or names of such witness or witnesses, the facts expected to be proved by such witness or witnesses, the steps which have been taken to procure such testimony, and the dates on which efforts have been made to procure it. (See Rule 153.)

(5) When a party relies upon a caveat to establish the date of his invention, the caveat itself, or a certified copy thereof, must be filed in evidence, with due notice to the opposite party.

(6) Upon notice given to the opposite party before the closing of the testimony, any official record, and any special matter contained in a printed publication, if competent evidence and pertinent to the issue, may be used as evidence at the hearing.

(7) All depositions which are taken must be duly filed in the Patent Office. On refusal to file, the office at its discretion will not further hear

or consider the contestant with whom the refusal lies; and the office may, at its discretion, receive and consider a copy of the withheld deposition, attested by such evidence as is procurable.

155. The pages of each deposition must be numbered consecutively, and the name of the witness plainly and conspicuously written at the top of each page. The testimony must be written upon legal-cap or foolscap paper, with a wide margin on the left-hand side of the page, and with the writing on one side only of the sheet.

156. The testimony will be taken in answer to interrogatories, with the questions and answers committed to writing in their regular order by the officer, or, in his presence, by some person not interested in the case, either as a party thereto or as attorney. *But with the written consent of the parties the testimony may be taken stenographically, and the deposition may be written out by other persons in the presence of the officer.*

Where testimony is taken stenographically, a longhand or typewritten copy shall be read to the witness, or read over by him, as soon as it can be made, and shall be signed by him as provided in paragraph 3 of Rule 154. No officer who is connected by blood or marriage with either of the parties, or interested, directly or indirectly, in the matter in controversy, either as counsel, attorney, agent, or otherwise, is competent to take depositions, unless with the written consent of all the parties.

157. By leave of the Commissioner, first obtained, testimony taken in an interference proceeding may be used in any other or subsequent interference proceeding, so far as relevant and material, subject, however, to the right of any contesting party to recall witnesses whose

depositions have been taken, and to take other testimony in rebuttal of the depositions.

158. By leave of the Commissioner, first obtained, testimony may be taken in foreign countries, upon complying with the following requirements:

(1) Such permission will be granted only upon motion duly made. (See Rule 153.) The motion must designate a place for the examination of the witnesses at which an officer duly qualified to take testimony under the laws of the United States in a foreign country shall reside, and it must be accompanied by a statement under oath that the motion is made in good faith, and not for purposes of delay or of vexing or harassing any party to the case; it must also set forth the names of the witnesses, the particular facts to which it is expected each will testify, and the grounds on which is based the belief that each will so testify.

(2) It must appear that the testimony desired is material and competent, and that it can not be taken in this country at all, or can not be taken here without hardship and injury to the moving party greatly exceeding that to which the opposite party will be exposed by the taking of such testimony abroad.

(3) Upon the granting of such motion, a time will be set within which the moving party shall file in duplicate the interrogatories to be propounded to each witness, and serve a copy of the same upon each adverse party, who may, within a designated time, file, in duplicate, cross-interrogatories. Objections to any of the

interrogatories or cross-interrogatories may be filed at any time before the depositions are taken, and such objections will be considered and determined upon the hearing of the case.

(4) As soon as the interrogatories and cross-interrogatories are decided to be in proper form, the Commissioner will cause them to be forwarded to the proper officer, with the request that, upon payment of, or satisfactory security for, his official fees, he notify the witnesses named to appear before him within a designated time and make answer thereto under oath; and that he reduce their answers to writing, and transmit the same, under his official seal and signature, to the Commissioner of Patents, with the certificate prescribed in Rule 154 (3).

(5) By stipulation of the parties the requirements of paragraph 3 as to written interrogatories and cross-interrogatories may be dispensed with, and the testimony may be taken before the proper officer upon oral interrogatories by the parties or their agents.

(6) Unless false swearing in the giving of such testimony before the officer taking it shall be punishable as perjury under the laws of the foreign state where it shall be taken, it will not stand on the same footing in the Patent Office as testimony duly taken in the United States; but its weight in each case will be determined by the tribunal having jurisdiction of such case.

159. Evidence touching the matter at issue will not be considered on the hearing which shall not have been taken and filed in compliance with these rules. But no-

tice will not be taken of merely formal or technical objections which shall not appear to have wrought a substantial injury to the party raising them; and in case of such injury it must be made to appear that, as soon as the party became aware of the ground of objection, he gave notice thereof to the office, and also to the opposite party, informing him at the same time that, unless it should be removed, he (the objector) should urge his objection at the hearing. This rule is not to be so construed as to modify established rules of evidence, which will be applied strictly in all practice before the office.

160. The law requires the clerks of the various courts of the United States to issue subpoenas to secure the attendance of witnesses whose depositions are desired as evidence in contested cases in the Patent Office.

161. After testimony is filed in the office it may be inspected by any party to the case, but it can not be withdrawn for the purpose of printing. It may be printed by someone specially designated by the office for that purpose, under proper restrictions.

162. *Thirty-one* or more printed copies of the testimony must be furnished, five for the use of the office, one for each of the opposing parties, *and twenty-five for the court of appeals of the District of Columbia, should appeal be taken. If no appeal be taken, the twenty-five copies will be returned to the party filing them.* The preliminary statement required by Rule 110 must be printed as a part of the record. These copies must be filed not less than ten days before the day of hearing. They will be of the same size, both page and print, as the Rules of Practice, with the names of the witnesses at the top of the pages over their testimony, and will contain indexes

with the names of all witnesses and reference to the pages where copies of papers and documents introduced as exhibits are shown.

When but one of the contestants takes testimony, he may furnish six or more bound type-written copies of the required size.

When it shall appear, on motion duly made and by satisfactory proof, that a party, by reason of poverty, is unable to print his testimony, the printing may be dispensed with; but in such case typewritten copies must be furnished—one for the office and one for each adverse party. Printing of the testimony can not be dispensed with upon the stipulation of the parties.

163. Briefs in all contested cases shall be submitted in printed form, and shall be of the same size and the same as to page and print as the printed copies of testimony. But in case satisfactory reason therefor is shown to the office, typewritten briefs may be submitted. Briefs shall be filed three days before the hearing, except as provided in Rule 147. By consent of the parties they may be filed later, but in any case must be filed before the hearing. If either party fail to comply with this regulation, no extension of time will be granted for the purpose, except upon consent of the adverse parties.

ISSUE.

164. If, on examination, it shall appear that the applicant is justly entitled to a patent under the law, a notice of allowance will be sent him or his attorney, calling for the payment of the final fee within six months from the date of such notice of allowance, upon the receipt of which within the time fixed by law the patent will be prepared for issue. (See Rules 207, 208.)

165. After notice of the allowance of an application is given, the case will not be withdrawn from issue except by approval of the Commissioner, and if withdrawn for further action on the part of the office a new notice of allowance will be given. When the final fee has been paid upon an application for letters patent, and the case has received its date and number, it will not be withdrawn or suspended from issue on account of any mistake or change of purpose of the applicant or his attorney, nor for the purpose of enabling the inventor to procure a foreign patent, nor for any other reasons except mistake on the part of the office, or because of fraud, or illegality in the application, or for interference. (See Rule 78.)

166. Whenever the Commissioner shall direct the withdrawal of an application from issue on request of an applicant for reasons not prohibited by Rule 165, such withdrawal shall not operate to stay the period of *one year* running against the application, which begins to attach from the date of the notice of allowance.

DATE, DURATION, AND FORM OF PATENTS.

167. Every patent will bear date as of a day not later than six months from the time the application was passed and allowed and notice thereof was mailed to the applicant or his attorney, if within that period the final fee be paid to the Commissioner of Patents, or if it be paid to the Treasurer or any of the assistant treasurers or designated depositaries of the United States, and the certificate promptly forwarded to the Commissioner of Patents; and if the final fee be not paid within that period, the patent will be withheld. (See Rule 175.)

A patent will not be antedated.

168. Every patent will contain a short title of the invention or discovery indicating its nature and object, and a grant to the patentee, his heirs and assigns, for the term of seventeen years, of the exclusive right to make, use, and vend the invention or discovery throughout the United States and the Territories thereof. The duration of a design patent may be for the term of three and a half, seven, or fourteen years, as provided in Rule 80. A copy of the specifications and drawings will be annexed to the patent and form part thereof.

DELIVERY.

169. The patent will be delivered or mailed on the day of its date to the attorney of record, if there be one; if not, to the patentee; or, if the attorney so request, to the patentee or assignee of an interest therein.

CORRECTION OF ERRORS IN LETTERS PATENT.

170. Whenever a mistake, incurred through the fault of the office, is clearly disclosed by the records or files of the office, a certificate, stating the fact and nature of such mistake, signed by the Commissioner of Patents, and sealed with the seal of the Patent Office, will, at the request of the patentee or his assignee, be indorsed without charge upon the letters patent, and recorded in the records of patents, and a printed copy thereof attached to each printed copy of the specification and drawing.

Whenever a mistake, incurred through the fault of the office, constitutes a sufficient legal ground for a reissue, such reissue will be made, for the correction of such mistake only, without charge of office fees, at the request of the patentee.

Mistakes not incurred through the fault of the office, and not affording legal grounds for reissues, will not be corrected after the delivery of the letters patent to the patentee or his agent.

Changes or corrections will not be made in letters patent after the delivery thereof to the patentee or his attorney, except as above provided.

ABANDONED, FORFEITED, REVIVED, AND RENEWED APPLICATIONS.

171. An abandoned application is one which has not been completed and prepared for examination within *one year* after the filing of the petition, or which the applicant has failed to prosecute within *one year* after any action therein of which notice has been duly given (see Rules 31 and 77), or which the applicant has expressly abandoned by filing in the office a written declaration of abandonment, signed by himself and assignee, if any, identifying his application by title of invention, serial number, and date of filing. (See Rule 60.)

Prosecution of an application to save it from abandonment must include such proper action as the condition of the case may require. The admission of an amendment not responsive to the last official action, or refusal to admit the same, and any proceedings relative thereto, shall not operate to save the application from abandonment under section 4894 of the Revised Statutes.

172. Before an application abandoned by failure to complete or prosecute can be revived as a pending application, it must be shown to the satisfaction of the Commissioner that the delay in the prosecution of the same was unavoidable.

173. When a new application is filed in place of an abandoned or rejected application, a new petition, specification, oath, drawing, and fee will be required; but the old model, if suitable, may be used.

174. A forfeited application is one upon which a patent has been withheld for failure to pay the final fee within the prescribed time. (See Rule 167.)

175. When the patent has been withheld by reason of nonpayment of the final fee, any person, whether inventor or assignee, who has an interest in the invention for which such patent was ordered to issue may file a renewal of the application for the same invention; but such second application must be made within two years after the allowance of the original application. Upon the hearing of such new application abandonment will be considered as a question of fact.

176. In such renewal the oath, petition, specification, drawing, and model of the original application may be used for the second application; but a new fee will be required. The second application will not be regarded for all purposes as a continuation of the original one, but must bear date from the time of renewal and be subject to examination like an original application.

177. Forfeited and abandoned applications will not be cited as references.

178. Notice of the filing of subsequent applications will not be given to applicants while their cases remain forfeited.

179. Copies of the files of forfeited and abandoned applications may be furnished when ordered by the Commissioner. The requests for such copies must be presented in the form of a petition properly verified as

to all matters not appearing of record in the Patent Office. (See Form 34.)

EXTENSIONS.

180. Patents can not be extended except by act of Congress.

DISCLAIMERS.

181. Whenever, through inadvertence, accident, or mistake, and without any fraudulent or deceptive intention, a patentee has claimed as his invention or discovery more than he had a right to claim as new, his patent shall be valid for all that part which is truly and justly his own, provided the same is a material or substantial part of the thing patented; and any such patentee, his heirs or assigns, whether of the whole or any sectional interest therein, may, on payment of the fee required by law (ten dollars), make disclaimer of such parts of the thing patented as he or they shall not choose to claim or to hold by virtue of the patent or assignment, stating therein the extent of his interest in such patent. Such disclaimer shall be in writing, attested by one or more witnesses, and recorded in the Patent Office; and it shall thereafter be considered as part of the original specification to the extent of the interest possessed by the claimant and by those claiming under him after the record thereof. But no such disclaimer shall affect any action pending at the time of filing the same, except as to the question of unreasonable neglect or delay in filing it.

182. Such disclaimer must be distinguished from those which are embodied in original or reissue applications as first filed or subsequently amended, referring

to matter shown or described, but to which the disclaimant does not choose to claim title, and also from those made to avoid the continuance of an interference. Such disclaimers must be signed by the applicant in person and must be duly witnessed, and require no fee. (See Rule 107.)

CAVEATS.

183. A caveat, under the patent law, is a notice given to the Patent Office of the caveator's claim as inventor, in order to prevent the grant of a patent to another person for the same alleged invention upon an application filed during the life of the caveat without notice to the caveator.

184. Any person who has made a new invention or discovery and desires further time to mature the same may, on payment of a fee of ten dollars, file in the Patent Office a caveat setting forth the object and the distinguishing characteristics of the invention, and praying protection of his right until he shall have matured his invention. Such caveat shall be filed in the confidential archives of the office and preserved in secrecy, and shall be operative for the term of one year from the filing thereof.

185. The caveat may be renewed, on request in writing, by the payment of a second caveat fee of ten dollars, and it will continue in force for one year from the date of the payment of such second fee. Subsequent renewals may be made with like effect. If a caveat be not renewed, it will still be preserved in the secret archives of the office.

186. The caveat must comprise a specification, oath, and, when the nature of the case admits of it, a drawing, and, like an application for a patent, must be limited to a single invention or improvement.

187. The same particularity of description is not required in a caveat as in an application for a patent; but the caveat must set forth the object of the invention and the distinguishing characteristics thereof, and it should be sufficiently precise to enable the office to judge whether there is a probable interference when a subsequent application is filed for a similar invention. If, upon examination, a caveat be found defective in this respect, amendment will be required. Without compliance with Rules 184, 186, 187, and 189, the caveator will not be entitled to the notice provided for in Rule 190.

188. The oath of the caveator must set forth that he believes himself the original and first inventor of the art, machine, or improvement set forth in his caveat. (See Rule 47.)

189. The caveat should be accompanied, when practicable, by full and accurate drawings, separate from the specification, well executed on tracing muslin or paper that may be folded. (See Rule 51.)

190. If at any time within one year after the filing or renewal of a caveat another person shall file an application for an invention which would in any manner interfere with the invention set forth in such caveat, then such application will be suspended and notice thereof will be sent to the person filing the caveat.

If the caveator shall file a complete application within the time prescribed, and if the invention be found patentable, he will be entitled to an interference with the previous application, for the purpose of proving priority of invention and obtaining the patent if he be adjudged the prior inventor. The caveator, if he would avail himself of his caveat, must file his application within three months from the expiration of the time regularly required for the transmission to him of the notice deposited in the post-office at Washington. The day on which the time for filing expires will be mentioned in the notice or indorsement thereon.

191. The caveator will not be entitled to notice of any application pending at the time of filing his caveat, nor of any application filed after the expiration of one year from the date of the filing or renewal thereof.

192. A caveat confers no rights and affords no protection except as to notice of an interfering application filed during its life, giving the caveator the opportunity of proving priority of invention if he so desires. It may be used as evidence in contests, as provided in Rule 154 (5).

193. There is no provision of law making the caveat assignable, although the alleged invention therein set forth is assignable, and the caveat may be used as means of identifying the invention transferred in an assignment.

194. Caveat papers cannot be withdrawn from the office after they have been filed; but copies of the papers may be obtained at the usual rates by the caveator or any person duly authorized by him. Additional papers, if containing new matter, must be filed as a separate caveat, with another fee.

ASSIGNMENTS.

195. Every patent or any interest therein shall be assignable in law by an instrument in writing; and the patentee or his assigns or legal representatives may, in like manner, grant and convey an exclusive right under the patent to the whole or any specified part of the United States.

196. Interests in patents may be vested in assignees, in grantees of exclusive sectional rights, in mortgagees, and in licensees.

(1) An assignee is a transferee of the whole interest of the original patent or of an undivided part of such whole interest, extending to every portion of the United States. The assignment must be written or printed and duly signed.

(2) A grantee acquires by the grant the exclusive right, under the patent, to make, use, and vend, and to grant to others the right to make, use, and vend, the thing patented within and throughout some specified part of the United States, excluding the patentee therefrom. The grant must be written or printed and be duly signed.

(3) A mortgage must be written or printed and be duly signed.

(4) A licensee takes an interest less than or different from either of the others. A license may be oral, written, or printed, and if written or printed, must be duly signed.

197. An assignment, grant, or conveyance of a patent will be void as against any subsequent purchaser

or mortgagee for a valuable consideration without notice unless recorded in the Patent Office within three months from the date thereof.

If any such assignment, grant, or conveyance of any patent shall be acknowledged before any notary public of the several States or Territories or the District of Columbia, or any commissioner of the United States circuit court, or before any secretary of legation or consular officer authorized to administer oaths or perform notarial acts under section seventeen hundred and fifty of the Revised Statutes, the certificate of such acknowledgment, under the hand and official seal of such notary or other officer, shall be prima facie evidence of the execution of such assignment, or conveyance.

198. No instrument will be recorded *which is not in the English language and* which does not, in the judgment of the Commissioner, amount to an assignment, grant, mortgage, lien, incumbrance, or license, or which does not affect the title of the patent or invention to which it relates. Such instrument should identify the patent by date and number; or, if the invention be unpatented, the name of the inventor, the serial number, and date of the application should be stated.

199. Assignments which are made conditional on the performance of certain stipulations, as the payment of money if recorded in the office, are regarded as absolute assignments until canceled with the written consent of both parties or by the decree of a competent court. The office has no means for determining whether such conditions have been fulfilled.

200. In every case where it is desired that the patents shall issue to an assignee, the assignment must be recorded in the Patent Office at a date not later than the

day on which the final fee is paid. (See Rule 26.) The date of the record is the date of the receipt of the assignment at the office.

201. The receipt of assignments is generally acknowledged by the office. They are recorded in regular order as promptly as possible, and then transmitted to the persons entitled to them.

OFFICE FEES.

202. Nearly all the fees payable to the Patent Office are positively required by law to be paid in advance—that is, upon making application for any action by the office for which a fee is payable. For the sake of uniformity and convenience, the remaining fees will be required to be paid in the same manner.

203. The following is the schedule of fees and of prices of publications of the Patent Office: (See Circulars.)

204. An order for a copy of an assignment must give the liber and page of the record, as well as the name of the inventor; otherwise an extra charge will be made for the time consumed in making any search for such assignment.

205. Persons will not be allowed to make copies or tracings from the files or records of the office. Such copies will be furnished, when ordered, at the rates already specified.

206. All payments of money required for office fees must be made in specie, Treasury notes, national-bank notes, certificates of deposit, post-office money orders, or certified checks. Money orders and checks should be made payable to the "Commissioner of Patents." Payment may also be made to the Treasurer, or to any of

the assistant treasurers of the United States, or to any of the depositaries, national banks, or receivers of public money, designated by the Secretary of the Treasury for that purpose, who shall give the depositor a receipt or certificate of deposit therefor. This receipt or certificate of deposit shall, in case of payment of final fees, be deposited in the mail for transmission to the Patent Office, within six months from the allowance of the application. Money sent by mail to the Patent Office will be at the risk of the sender. Letters containing money should be registered. In no case should money be sent with models.

207. The weekly issue closes on Thursday, and the patents of that issue bear date as of the third Tuesday thereafter. If the final fee in any application is not paid on or before Thursday, the patent will not go to issue until the following week.

REPAYMENT OF MONEY.

208. Money paid by actual mistake, such as a payment in excess, or when not required by law, or by neglect, or misinformation on the part of the office, will be refunded; but a mere change of purpose after the payment of money, as when a party desires to withdraw his application for a patent or for the registration of a trade-mark, or to withdraw an appeal, will not entitle a party to demand such a return.

PUBLICATIONS.

209. The Official Gazette, a weekly publication which has been issued since 1872, takes the place of the old Patent Office Report. It contains the claims of all patents issued, including reissues, with portions of the

drawings selected to illustrate the inventions claimed. It also contains decisions rendered by the courts in patent cases and by the Commissioner of Patents, and other special matters of interest to inventors.

The Gazette is furnished to subscribers at the rate of $5 per annum. When sent abroad, an additional charge of $5 is made for the payment of postage. Representatives and Senators are each entitled to a copy, and each is entitled to designate eight public libraries to which the Gazette will be sent without charge. Single copies are furnished for ten cents each.

An index is published annually, which is sent to all subscribers and designated libraries without additional cost.

Printed volumes are issued monthly, containing the entire specifications and drawings of all patents issued during the previous month. These are authenticated by the seal of the office, and may be used as evidence throughout the United States. One copy is deposited in the Library of Congress and in each State and Territorial library, and one copy in the custody of the clerk of each United States district court, for general reference.

LIBRARY REGULATIONS.

210. Officers of the bureau and members of the examining corps, only, are allowed to enter the alcoves or take books from the scientific library.

Books taken from this library must be entered in a register kept for the purpose, and returned on the call of the librarian. They must not be taken from the building except by permission of the Commissioner.

Any book lost or defaced must be replaced by a new copy.

Patentees and others doing business with the office can examine the books only in the library hall.

Translations will be made only for official use.

Copies or tracings from works in the library will be furnished by the office at the usual rates.

AMENDMENTS OF THE RULES.

211. All amendments of the foregoing rules will be published in the Official Gazette.

QUESTIONS NOT SPECIFICALLY PROVIDED FOR.

212. All cases not specifically defined and provided for in these rules will be decided in accordance with the merits of each case under the authority of the Commissioner, and such decision will be communicated to the interested parties in writing.

213. *Questions arising in applications filed prior to January 1, 1898, where these rules do not apply, shall be governed by the rules of June 18, 1897.*

FREDERICK I. ALLEN,
Commissioner of Patents.

DEPARTMENT OF THE INTERIOR,
December 17, 1902.

Approved, to take effect January 1, 1903.

E. A. HITCHCOCK,
Secretary of the Interior.

APPENDIX E.

RULES OF PRACTICE IN CASES BEFORE THE UNITED STATES DISTRICT LAND OFFICES, THE GENERAL LAND OFFICE, AND THE DEPARTMENT OF THE INTERIOR.

I. PROCEEDINGS BEFORE REGISTERS AND RECEIVERS.

INITIATION OF CONTESTS.

RULE 1.—Contests may be initiated by an adverse party or other person against a party to any entry, filing, or other claim under laws of Congress relating to the public lands, for any sufficient cause affecting the legality or validity of the claim.

RULE 2.—In every case of application for a hearing an affidavit must be filed by the contestant with the register and receiver, fully setting forth the facts which constitute the grounds of contest. When the contest is against the heirs of a deceased entryman, the affidavit shall state the names of all the heirs. If the heirs are nonresident or unknown, the affidavit shall set forth the fact and be corroborated with respect thereto by the affidavit of one or more persons.

RULE 3.—Where an entry has been allowed and remains of record the affidavit of the contestant must be accompanied by the affidavits of one or more witnesses in support of the allegations made.

HEARINGS IN CONTESTED CASES.

RULE 4.—Registers and receivers may order hearings in all cases wherein entry has not been perfected and no certificate has been issued as a basis for patent.

RULE 5.—In case of an entry or location on which final certificate has been issued the hearing will be ordered only by direction of the Commissioner of the General Land Office.

RULE 6.—Applications for hearings under Rule 5 must be transmitted by the register and receiver, with special report and recommendation, to the Commissioner for his determination and instructions.

NOTICE OF CONTEST.

RULE 7.—At least thirty days' notice shall be given of all hearings before the register and receiver unless by written consent an earlier day shall be agreed upon.

RULE 8.—The notice of contest and hearing must conform to the following requirements:

1. It must be written or printed.

2. It must be signed by the register and receiver, or by one of them.

3. It must state the time and place of hearing.

4. It must describe the land involved.

5. It must state the register and receiver's number of the entry and the land office where and the date when made, and the name of the party making the same.

6. It must give the name of the contestant and briefly state the grounds and purpose of the contest.

7. It may contain any other information pertinent to the contest.

SERVICE OF NOTICE.

RULE 9.—Personal service shall be made in all cases when possible if the party to be served is resident in the State or Territory in which the land is situated, and shall consist in the delivery of a copy of the notice to each person to be served. When the contest is against the heirs of a deceased entryman, the notice shall be served on each heir. If the heirs of the entryman are nonresident or unknown, notice may be served upon them by publication as hereinafter provided. If the person to be personally served is an infant under fourteen years of age or a person who has been legally adjudged of unsound mind, service of notice shall be made by delivering a copy of the notice to the statutory guardian or committee of such infant or person of unsound mind, if there be one; if there be none, then by delivering a copy of the notice to the person having the infant or person of unsound mind in charge.

RULE 10.—Personal service may be executed by any officer or person.

RULE 11.—Notice may be given by publication only when it is shown by affidavit presented on behalf of the contestant and by such other evidence as the register and receiver may require that due diligence has been used and that personal service can not be made. The affidavit must also state the present post-office address of the person intended to be served, if it is known to the affiant, and must show what effort has been made to obtain personal service.

RULE 12.—When it is found that the prescribed service can not be had, either personally or by publication, in time for the hearing provided for in the notice, the notice may be returned prior to the time fixed for the hearing, and a new notice issued fixing another time of hearing, for the proper service thereof, an affidavit being filed by the contestant showing due diligence and inability to serve the notice in time.

NOTICE BY PUBLICATION.

RULE 13.—Notice by publication shall be made by advertising the notice at least once a week for four successive weeks in some newspaper published in the county wherein the land in contest lies; and if no newspaper be published in such county, then in the newspaper published in the county nearest to such land. The first insertion shall be at least thirty days prior to the day fixed for the hearing.

RULE 14.—Where notice is given by publication a copy thereof shall, at least thirty days before the date for the hearing, be mailed, by registered letter, to each person to be so notified at the last address, if any, given by him as shown by the record, and to him at his present address named in the affidavit for publication required by Rule 11, if such present address is stated in such affidavit and is different from his record address. If there be no such record address and if no present address is named in the affidavit for publication, then a copy of the notice shall be so mailed to him at the post-office nearest to the land. A copy of the notice shall also be posted in the register's office for a period of at least thirty days before the date for the hearing and still another copy thereof shall be posted in a conspicuous place upon the land for at least two weeks prior to the date set for the hearing. When notice of proceedings commenced by the Government against timber and stone entries is given by publication the posting of notices upon the land will not be required.

PROOF OF SERVICE OF NOTICE.

RULE 15.—Proof of personal service shall be the written acknowledgment of the person served or the affidavit of the person who served the notice attached thereto, stating the time, place, and manner of service.

RULE 16.—When service is by publication, the proof of service shall be a copy of the advertisement, with the affidavit of the publisher or foreman attached thereto, showing that the same was successively inserted the requisite number of times, and the date thereof.

NOTICE OF PROCEEDINGS.

RULE 17.—Notice of motions, proceedings, orders, and decisions shall be in writing, and may be served personally or by registered letter mailed to the last address, if any, given by or on behalf of the party to be notified, as shown by the record, and if there be no such record address, then to the post-office nearest to the land; and in all those contest cases where notice of contest is given by registered mail under Rule 14, and the return of the registry receipt shows such notice to have been received by the contestee, the address at which the notice was so received shall be considered as an address given by the contestee, within the meaning of this rule.

RULE 18.—Proof of service by mail shall be the affidavit of the person who mailed the notice, attached to the post-office receipt for the registered letter.

REHEARINGS.

RULE 19.—Orders for rehearing must be brought to

the notice of the parties in the same manner as in case of original proceedings.

CONTINUANCES.

RULE 20.—A postponement of a hearing to a day to be fixed by the register and receiver may be allowed on the day of trial on account of the absence of material witnesses, when the party asking for the continuance makes an affidavit before the register and receiver showing—

1. That one or more of the witnesses in his behalf is absent without his procurement or consent;
2. The name and residence of each witness;
3. The facts to which they would testify if present;
4. The materiality of the evidence;
5. The exercise of proper diligence to procure the attendance of the absent witnesses; and
6. That affiant believes said witnesses can be had at the time to which it is sought to have the trial postponed.

Where hearings are ordered by the Commissioner of the General Land Office in cases to which the United States is a party, continuances will be granted in accordance with the usual practice in United States cases in the courts, without requiring an affidavit on the part of the Government.

RULE 21.—One continuance only shall be allowed to either party on account of absent witnesses, unless the party applying for a further continuance shall at the same time apply for an order to take the depositions of the alleged absent witnesses.

RULE 22.—No continuance shall be granted when the opposite party shall admit that the witnesses would, if present, testify to the statement set out in the application for continuance.

DEPOSITIONS ON INTERROGATORIES.

RULE 23.—Testimony may be taken by deposition in the following cases:

1. Where the witness is unable, from age, infirmity, or sickness, or shall refuse, to attend the hearing at the local land office.

2. Where the witness resides more than fifty miles from the place of trial, computing distance by the usually traveled route.

3. Where the witness resides out of or is about to leave the State or Territory, or is absent therefrom.

4. Where from any cause it is apprehended that the witness may be unable or will refuse to attend, in which case the deposition will be used only in event that the personal attendance of the witness cannot be obtained.

RULE 24.—The party desiring to take a deposition under Rule 23 must comply with the following regulations:

1. He must make affidavit before the register or receiver, setting forth one or more of the above-named causes for taking such deposition, and that the witness is material.

2. He must file with the register and receiver the interrogatories to be propounded to the witness.

3. He must state the name and residence of the witness.

4. He must serve a copy of the interrogatories on the opposing party or his attorney.

RULE 25.—The opposing party will be allowed ten days in which to file cross-interrogatories.

RULE 26.—After the expiration of the ten days allowed for filing cross-interrogatories, a commission to take the deposition shall be issued by the register and receiver, which commission shall be accompanied by a copy of all the interrogatories filed.

RULE 27.—The register and receiver may designate any officer, authorized to administer oaths within the county or district where the witness resides, to take such deposition.

RULE 28.—It is the duty of the officer before whom the deposition is taken to cause the interrogatories appended to the commission to be written out and the answers thereto to be inserted immediately underneath the respective questions, and the whole, when completed, is to be read over to the witness, and must be by him subscribed and sworn to in the usual manner before the witness is discharged.

RULE 29.—The officer must attach his certificate to the deposition, stating that the same was subscribed and sworn to by the deponent at the time and place therein mentioned.

RULE 30.—The deposition and certificate, together with the commission and interrogatories, must then be sealed up, the title of the cause indorsed on the envelope, and the whole returned by mail or express to the register and receiver.

RULE 31.—Upon receipt of the package at the local land office, the date when the same is opened must be indorsed on the envelope and body of the deposition by the local land officers.

RULE 32.—If the officer designated to take the deposition has no official seal, a proper certificate of his official character, under seal, must accompany his return.

RULE 33.—The parties in any case may stipulate in writing to take depositions before any qualified officer, and in any manner.

RULE 34.—All stipulations by parties or counsel must be in writing, and be filed with the register and receiver.

ORAL TESTIMONY BEFORE OFFICERS OTHER THAN REGISTERS AND RECEIVERS.

RULE 35.—In the discretion of registers and receivers testimony may be taken near the land in controversy before a United States commissioner, or other officer authorized to administer oaths, at a time and place to be fixed by them and stated in the notice of hearing.

2. Officers taking testimony under the foregoing rule will be governed by the rules applicable to trials before registers and receivers. (See Rules 36 to 42, inclusive.)

3. Testimony so taken must be certified to, sealed up, and transmitted by mail or express to the register and receiver, and the receipt thereof at the local office noted on the papers, in the same manner as provided in case of depositions by Rules 29 to 32, inclusive.

4. On the day set for hearing at the local office the register and receiver will examine the testimony taken by the officer designated, and render a decision thereon in the same manner as if the testimony had been taken before themselves. (See Rules 50 to 53, inclusive.)

5. No charge for examining testimony in such cases will be made by the register and receiver.

6. Officers designated to take testimony under this rule will be allowed to charge such fees as are properly authorized by the tariff of fees existing in the local courts

of their respective districts, to be taxed in the same or equivalent manner as costs are taxed by registers and receivers under Rules 54 to 58, inclusive.

7. When an officer designated to take testimony under this rule, or when an officer designated to take depositions under Rule 27, cannot act on the day fixed for taking the testimony or deposition, the testimony or deposition, as the case may be, will be deemed properly taken before any other qualified officer, at the same place and time, who may be authorized by the officer originally designated, or by agreement of parties, to act in the place of the officer first named.

TRIALS.

RULE 36.—Upon the trial of a cause, the register and receiver may in any case, and should in all cases when necessary, personally direct the examination of the witnesses, in order to draw from them all the facts within their knowledge requisite to a correct conclusion by the officers upon any point connected with the case.

RULE 37.—The register and receiver will be careful to reach, if possible, the exact condition and status of the land involved by any contest, and will ascertain all the facts having any bearing upon the rights of parties in interest.

RULE 38.—In pre-emption cases they will particularly ascertain the nature, extent, and value of alleged improvements; by whom made, and when; the true date of the settlement of persons claiming; the steps taken to mark and secure the claim, and the exact status of the land at that date as shown upon the records of their office.

Rule 39.—In like manner, under the homestead and other laws, the conditions affecting the inception of the alleged right, as well as the subsequent acts of the respective claimants, must be fully and specifically examined.

Rule 40.—Due opportunity will be allowed opposing claimants to confront and cross-examine the witnesses introduced by either party.

Rule 41.—No testimony will be excluded from the record by the register and receiver on the ground of any objection thereto; but when objection is made to testimony offered, the exceptions will be noted, and the testimony, with the exceptions, will come up with the case for the consideration of the Commissioner. Officers taking testimony will, however, summarily put a stop to obviously irrelevant questioning.

Rule 42.—Upon the day originally set for hearing, and upon any day to which the trial may be continued, the testimony of all the witnesses present shall be taken and reduced to writing. When testimony is taken in shorthand, the stenographer's notes must be written out and the written testimony then and there subscribed by the witness and attested by the officer before whom the same is taken, unless the parties shall by proper stipulation in writing, filed with the record, mutually agree to the contrary, in which event the transcribed stenographic notes shall in all cases be accompanied by a certificate of the officer or officers before whom the testimony was taken showing that the witnesses were each duly sworn before testifying, and also by the affidavit of the stenographer who took the testimony in shorthand that the purported transcription thereof is a true and correct statement of the testimony actually given by the witnesses after being duly sworn at the hearing.

APPEALS.

RULE 43.—Appeals from the final action or decisions of registers and receivers lie in every case to the Commissioner of the General Land Office. (Revised Statutes, sections 453, 2478.)

In cases dismissed for want of prosecution the register and receiver will by registered letter notify the parties in interest of the action taken, and that unless within thirty days a motion for reinstatement shall be made, the default of the plaintiff will be final, and that no appeal will be allowed; which notice shall be given as provided in circular of October 28, 1886 (5 L. D., 204).

If such motion for reinstatement be made within the time limited, the local officers shall take action thereon, and grant or deny it, as they deem proper. If granted, no appeal shall lie. If overruled, the plaintiff shall have the right of appeal, the time for which shall be thirty days, and run from the date of written notice to the plaintiff.

RULE 44.—After hearing in a contest case has been had and closed, the register and receiver will, in writing, notify the parties in interest of the conclusions to which they have arrived, and that thirty days are allowed for appeal from their decision to the Commissioner, the notice to be served personally or by registered letter, as provided in Rule 17.

RULE 45.—The appeal must be in writing or in print, and should set forth in brief and clear terms the specific points of exception to the ruling appealed from.

RULE 46.—Notice of appeal and copy of specification of errors shall be served on appellee within the time allowed for appeal, and appellee shall be allowed ten days for reply before transmittal of the record to the General Land Office.

RULE 47.—No appeal from the action or decisions of the register and receiver will be received at the General Land Office unless forwarded through the local officers.

RULE 48.—In case of a failure to appeal from the decision of the local officers, their decision will be considered final as to the facts in the case and will be disturbed by the Commissioner only as follows:

1. Where fraud or gross irregularity is suggested on the face of the papers.

2. Where the decision is contrary to existing laws or regulations.

3. In event of disagreeing decisions by the local officers.

4. Where it is not shown that the party against whom the decision was rendered was duly notified of the decision and of his right of appeal.

RULE 49.—In any of the foregoing cases the Commissioner will reverse or modify the decision of the local officers or remand the case, at his discretion.

RULE 50.—All documents once received by the local officers must be kept on file with the cases, and the date of filing must be noted thereon; and no papers will be allowed under any circumstances to be removed from the files or taken from the custody of the register and receiver, but access to the same, under proper rules, so as not to interfere with necessary public business, will be permitted to the parties in interest, or their attorneys, under the supervision of those officers.

REPORTS AND OPINIONS.

RULE 51.—Upon the termination of a contest, the register and receiver will render a joint report and opinion in the case, making full and specific reference to the postings and annotations upon their records.

RULE 52.—The register and receiver will promptly forward their report, together with the testimony and all the papers in the case, to the Commissioner of the General Land Office, with a brief letter of transmittal, describing the case by its title, the nature of the contest, and the tract involved.

RULE 53.—The local officers will thereafter take no further action affecting the disposal of the land in contest until instructed by the Commissioner.

In all cases, however, where a contest has been brought against any entry or filing on the public lands, and trial has taken place, the entryman may, if he so desires, in accordance with the provisions of the law under which he claims and the rules of the Department, submit final proof and complete the same, with the exception of the payment, and final certificate will issue, without any further action on the part of the entryman, except the furnishing of a nonalienation affidavit by the entryman, or, in case of his death, by his legal representatives.

In such cases the party making the proof, at the time of submitting the same, will be required to pay the fees for reducing the testimony to writing.

TAXATION OF COSTS.

RULE 54.—Parties contesting pre-emption, homestead, or timber-culture entries and claiming preference rights of entry under the second section of the act of May 14, 1880 (21 Stat., 140), must pay the costs of contest.

RULE 55.—In other contested cases each party must pay the costs of taking testimony upon his own direct and cross-examination.

RULE 56.—The accumulation of excessive costs under Rule 54 will not be permitted; but when the officer taking testimony shall rule that a course of examination is irrelevant and checks the same, under Rule 41, he may, nevertheless, in his discretion, allow the same to proceed at the sole cost of the party making such examination. This rule will apply also to cross-examination in contests covered by the provisions of Rule 55.

RULE 57.—Where parties contesting pre-emption, homestead, or timber-culture entries establish their right of entry under the pre-emption or homestead laws of the land in contest by virtue of actual settlement and improvement, without reference to the act of May 14, 1880, the cost of contest will be adjudged under Rule 55.

RULE 58.—Registers and receivers will apportion the cost of contest in accordance with the foregoing rules, and may require the party liable thereto to give security in advance of trial, by deposit or otherwise, in a reasonable sum or sums, for payment of the cost of transcribing the testimony.

RULE 59.—The cost of contest chargeable by registers and receivers are the legal fees for reducing testimony to writing. No other contest fees or costs will be allowed to or charged by those officers directly or indirectly.

RULE 60.—Contestants must give their own notices and pay the expenses thereof.

RULE 61.—Upon the termination of a trial, any excess in the sum deposited as security for the costs of transcribing the testimony will be returned to the proper party.

Rule 62.—When hearings are ordered by the Commissioner or by the Secretary of the Interior, upon the discovery of reasons for suspension in the usual course of examination of entries, the preliminary costs will be provided from the contingent fund for the expenses of local land offices.

Rule 63.—The preliminary costs provided for by the preceding section will be collected by the register and receiver when the parties are brought before them in obedience to the order of hearing.

Rule 64.—The register and receiver will then require proper provision to be made for such further notification as may become necessary in the usual progress of the case to final decision.

Rule 65.—The register and receiver will append to their report in each case a statement of costs and the amount actually paid by each of the contestants, and also a statement of the amount deposited to secure the payment of the costs, how said sum was apportioned, and the amount returned, if any, and to whom.

APPEALS FROM DECISIONS REJECTING APPLICATIONS TO ENTER PUBLIC LANDS.

Rule 66.—For the purpose of enabling appeals to be taken from the rulings or action of the local officers relative to applications to file upon, enter, or locate the public lands the following rules will be observed:

1. The register and receiver will indorse upon every rejected application the date when presented and their reasons for rejecting it.

2. They will promptly advise the party in interest of their action and of his right of appeal to the Commissioner.

3. They will note upon their records a memorandum of the transaction.

RULE 67.—The party aggrieved will be allowed thirty days from receipt of notice in which to file his appeal in the local land office. Where the notice is sent by mail, five days additional will be allowed for the transmission of notice and five for the return of the appeal.

RULE 68.—The register and receiver will promptly forward the appeal to the General Land Office, together with a full report upon the case.

RULE 69.—This report should recite all the facts and the proceedings had, and must embrace the following particulars:

1. A statement of the application and rejection, with the reasons for the rejection.

2. A description of the tract involved and a statement of its status, as shown by the records of the local land office.

3. References to all entries, filings, annotations, memoranda, and correspondence shown by the record relating to said tract and to the proceedings had.

RULE 70.—Rules 43 to 48, inclusive, and Rule 93 are applicable to all appeals from decisions of registers and receivers.

II. PROCEEDINGS BEFORE SURVEYORS-GENERAL.

RULE 71.—The proceedings in hearings and contests before surveyors-general shall, as to notices, depositions, and other matters, be governed as nearly as may be by the rules prescribed for proceedings before registers and receivers, unless otherwise provided by law.

III. PROCEEDINGS BEFORE THE COMMISSIONER OF THE GENERAL LAND OFFICE AND SECRETARY OF THE INTERIOR.

EXAMINATION AND ARGUMENT.

RULE 72.—When a contest has been closed before the local land officers and their report forwarded to the General Land Office, no additional evidence will be admitted in the case, unless offered under stipulation of the parties to the record, except where such evidence is presented as the basis of a motion for a new trial or in support of a mineral application or protest; but this rule will not prevent the Commissioner, in the exercise of his discretion, from ordering further investigation when necessary.

RULE 73.—After the Commissioner shall have received a record of testimony in a contested case, thirty days will be allowed to expire before any action thereon is taken, unless, in the judgment of the Commissioner, public policy or private necessity shall demand summary action, in which case he will proceed at his discretion, first notifying the attorneys of record of his proposed action.

RULE 74.—When a case is pending on appeal from the decision of the register and receiver or surveyor-general, and argument is not filed before the same is reached in its order for examination, the argument will be considered closed, and thereafter no further arguments or motions of any kind will be entertained except upon written stipulation duly filed or good cause shown to the Commissioner.

RULE 75.—If before decision by the Commissioner either party should desire to discuss a case orally, reasonable opportunity therefor will be given in the discretion of the Commissioner, but only at a time to be fixed by him upon notice to the opposing counsel, stating time and specific points upon which discussion is desired; and except as herein provided, no oral hearings or suggestions will be allowed.

REHEARING AND REVIEW.

RULE 76.—Motions for rehearing before registers and receivers, or for review or reconsideration of the decisions of the Commissioner or Secretary, will be allowed, in accordance with legal principles applicable to motions for new trials at law, after due notice to the opposing party.

RULE 77.—Motions for rehearing and review, except as provided in Rule 114, must be filed in the office wherein the decision to be affected by such rehearing or review was made or in the local land office, for transmittal to the General Land Office; and, except when based upon newly discovered evidence, must be filed within thirty days from notice of such decision.

RULE 78.—Motions for rehearing and review must be accompanied by an affidavit of the party, or his attorney, that the motion is made in good faith, and not for the purpose of delay.

RULE 79.—The time between the filing of a motion for rehearing or review and the notice of the decision upon such motion shall be excluded in computing the time allowed for appeal.

RULE 80.—No officer shall entertain a motion in a case after an appeal from his decision has been taken.

APPEALS FROM THE COMMISSIONER TO THE SECRETARY.

RULE 81.—No appeal shall be had from the action of the Commissioner of the General Land Office affirming the decision of the local officers in any case where the party or parties adversely affected thereby shall have failed, after due notice, to appeal from such decision of said local officers.

Subject to this provision, an appeal may be taken from the decision of the Commissioner of the General Land Office to the Secretary of the Interior upon any question relating to the disposal of the public lands and to private land claims, except in case of interlocutory orders and decisions and orders for hearing or other matter resting in the discretion of the Commissioner. Decisions and orders forming the above exception will be noted in the record, and will be considered by the Secretary on review in case an appeal upon the merits be finally allowed.

RULE 82.—When the Commissioner considers an appeal defective, he will notify the party of the defect, and if not amended within fifteen days from the date of the service of such notice the appeal may be dismissed by the Secretary of the Interior and the case closed.

RULE 83.—In proceedings before the Commissioner in which he shall formally decide that a party has no right of appeal to the Secretary, the party against whom such decision is rendered may apply to the Secretary for an order directing the Commissioner to certify said proceedings to the Secretary and to suspend further action until the Secretary shall pass upon the same.

RULE 84.—Applications to the Secretary under the preceding rule shall be made in writing, under oath, and shall fully and specifically set forth the grounds upon which the application is made.

RULE 85.—When the Commissioner shall formally decide against the right of an appeal, he shall suspend action on the case at issue for twenty days from service of notice of his decision, to enable the party against whom the decision is rendered to apply to the Secretary for an order, in accordance with Rules 83 and 84.

RULE 86.—Notice of an appeal from the Commissioner's decision must be filed in the General Land Office and served on the appellee or his counsel within sixty days from the date of the service of notice of such decision.

RULE 87.—When notice of the decision is given through the mails by the register and receiver or surveyor-general, five days additional will be allowed by those officers for the transmission of the letter and five days for the return of the appeal through the same channel before reporting to the General Land Office.

RULE 88.—Within the time allowed for giving notice of appeal the appellant shall also file in the General Land Office a specification of errors, which specification shall clearly and concisely designate the errors of which he complains.

RULE 89.—He may also, within the same time, file a written argument, with citation of authorities, in support of his appeal.

RULE 90.—A failure to file a specification of errors within the time required will be treated as a waiver of the right of appeal, and the case will be considered closed.

RULE 91.—The appellee may file a written argument in his behalf within thirty days from service of the argument of the appellant, when the latter files an argument within the time allotted by Rule 89; otherwise, within thirty days from the expiration of the time so allotted to appellant.

This rule (91) as thus amended will take effect September 1, 1901.

RULE 92.—The appellant shall be allowed thirty days from service of argument of appellee in which to file argument strictly in reply, and no other or further arguments or motions of any kind shall be filed without permission of the Commissioner or Secretary and notice to the opposite party.

RULE 93.—A copy of the notice of appeal, specification of errors, and all arguments of either party shall be served on the opposite party within the time allowed for filing the same.

RULE 94.—Such service shall be made personally or by registered letter.

RULE 95.—Proof of personal service shall be the written acknowledgment of the party served or the affidavit of the person making the service attached to the papers served, and stating time, place, and manner of service.

RULE 96.—Proof of service by registered letter shall be the affidavit of the person mailing the letter, attached to a copy of the post-office receipt.

RULE 97.—Fifteen days, exclusive of the day of mailing, will be allowed for the transmission of notices and papers by mail, except in case of notice to resident attorneys, when one day will be allowed.

RULE 98.—Notice of interlocutory motions and proceedings before the Commissioner and Secretary shall be served personally or by registered letter, and service proved as provided in Rules 94 and 95.

RULE 99.—No motion affecting the merits of the case

or the regular order of proceedings will be entertained except on due proof of service of notice.

RULE 100.—*Ex parte* cases and cases in which the adverse party does not appear will be governed by the foregoing rules as to notices of decisions, time for appeal, and filing of exceptions and arguments, as far as applicable. In such cases, however, the right to file additional evidence at any stage of the proceedings to cure defects in the proof or record will be allowed.

RULE 101.—No person hereafter appearing as a party or attorney in any case shall be entitled to a notice of the proceedings who does not at the time of his appearance file in the office in which the case is pending a statement in writing, giving his name and post-office address and the name of the party whom he represents; nor shall any person who has heretofore appeared in a case be entitled to a notice unless within fifteen days after being requested to file such statement he shall comply with said requirement.

RULE 102.—No person not a party to the record shall intervene in a case without first disclosing on oath the nature of his interest.

RULE 103.—When the Commissioner makes an order or decision affecting the merits of a case or the regular order of proceedings therein, he will cause notice to be given to each party in interest whose address is known.

ATTORNEYS.

RULE 104.—In all cases, contested or *ex parte*, where the parties in interest are represented by attorneys, such attorneys will be recognized as fully controlling the cases of their respective clients.

RULE 105.—All notices will be served upon the attorneys of record.

RULE 106.—Notice to one attorney in a case shall constitute notice to all counsel appearing for the party represented by him, and notice to the attorney will be deemed notice to the party in interest.

RULE 107.—All attorneys practicing before the General Land Office and Department of the Interior must first file the oath of office prescribed by section 3478, United States Revised Statutes.

RULE 108.—In the examination of any case, whether contested or *ex parte,* the attorneys employed in said case, when in good standing in the Department, for the preparation of arguments, will be allowed full opportunity to consult the records of the case, the abstracts, field notes, and tract books, and the correspondence of the General Land Office or of the Department not deemed *privileged* and *confidential;* and whenever, in the judgment of the Commissioner, it would not jeopardize any public or official interest, may make verbal inquiries of chiefs of divisions at their respective desks in respect to the papers or status of said case; but such inquiries will not be made to said chiefs or other clerks of division except upon consent of the Commissioner, Assistant Commissioner, or chief clerk, and will be restricted to hours between 11 a. m. and 2 p. m.

RULE 109.—Any attorney detected in any abuse of the above privileges, or of gross misconduct, upon satisfactory proof thereof, after due notice and hearing, shall be prohibited from further practicing before the Department.

RULE 110.—Should either party desire to discuss a case orally before the Secretary, opportunity will be afforded at the discretion of the Department, but only at a time specified by the Secretary or fixed by stipulation of the parties, with the consent of the Secretary, and in the absence of such stipulation or written notice to opposing counsel, with like consent, specifying the time when argument will be heard.

RULE 111.—The examination of cases on appeal to the Commissioner or Secretary will be facilitated by filing in printed form such arguments as it is desired to have considered.

DECISIONS.

RULE 112.—Decisions of the Commissioner not appealed from within the period prescribed become final, and the case will be regularly closed.

RULE 113.—The decision of the Secretary, so far as respects the action of the Executive, is final.

RULE 114.—Motions for review or rehearing before the Secretary must be filed with the Commissioner of the General Land Office within thirty days after notice of the decision complained of, and will act as a supersedeas of the decision until otherwise directed by the Secretary.

Any such motion must state concisely and specifically the grounds for review or rehearing, one or both as the case may be, upon which it is based, and may be accompanied by an argument in support thereof.

Upon its receipt, the Commissioner of the General Land Office will forward the motion immediately to this Department, where it will be treated as "special." If the motion does not show proper grounds for review or rehearing, it will be denied and sent to the files of the General Land Office, whereupon the Commissioner will remove the suspension and proceed to execute the decision before rendered. But if, upon examination, proper grounds are shown, the motion will be entertained and the moving party notified, whereupon he will be allowed thirty days within which to serve the same, together with all argument in support thereof, on the opposite party, who will be allowed thirty days thereafter in which to file and serve an answer, but consideration of the motion will not be deferred for further argument.

RULE 115.—None of these rules shall be construed to deprive the Secretary of the Interior of either the directory or supervisory power conferred upon him by law.

IV. REGULATIONS GOVERNING THE RECOGNITION OF AGENTS AND ATTORNEYS BEFORE DISTRICT LAND OFFICERS.

1. An attorney at law who desires to represent claimants or contestants before a district land office must file a certificate, under the seal of a United States, State, or Territorial court for the judicial district in which he resides or the local land office is situated, that he is an attorney in good standing.

2. Any person (not an attorney at law) who desires to appear as an agent for claimants or contestants before a district land office must file a certificate from a judge of a United States court, or of a State or Territorial court having common-law jurisdiction, except probate courts, in the county wherein he resides or the local office is situated, duly authenticated under the seal of the court, that such person is of good moral character and in good repute, possessed of the necessary qualifications to enable him to render clients valuable service, and otherwise competent to advise and assist them in the presentation of their claims or contests.

3. The oath of allegiance required by section 3478 of the United States Revised Statutes must also be filed by applicants. In case of a firm, the names of the individuals composing the firm must be given, and a certificate and oath as to each member of the firm will be required.

4. An applicant to practice under the above regulations must address a letter to the register and receiver, inclosing the certificate and oath above required, in which letter his full name and post-office address must be given. He must state whether or not he has ever been recognized as an attorney or agent before this Department or any bureau thereof, or any of the local land offices, and, if so, whether he has ever been suspended or disbarred from practice. He must also state whether he holds any office under the Government of the United States.

After an application to practice has been filed in due form, the register and receiver will recognize the applicant as an attorney or agent, as the case may be, unless they have good reason to believe that the person making the application is unfit to practice before their offices, or unless otherwise instructed by the Commissioner or Secretary.

Registers and receivers must keep a record of the names and residences of all attorneys and agents recognized as entitled to represent clients in their several offices.

Every attorney must, either at the time of entering his appearance for a claimant or contestant or within thirty days thereafter, file the written authority for such appearance, signed by said claimant or contestant, and setting forth his or her present residence, occupation, and post-office address. Upon a failure to file such written authority within the time limited, it is the duty of the register and receiver to no longer recognize him as attorney in the case.

An attorney in fact will be required to file a power of attorney of his principal, duty executed, specifying the power granted and stating the party's present residence, occupation, and post-office address.

When the appearance is for a person other than a claimant or contestant of record, the attorney or agent will be required to state the name of the person for whom he appears, his post-office address, the character and extent of his interest in the matter involved, and when and from what source it was acquired. Authorizations and powers signed or executed in blank will not be recognized.

If any attorney or agent shall knowingly commit any of the following acts, viz.: Represent fictitious or fraudulent entrymen; prosecute collusive contests; speculate in relinquishments of entries; assist in procuring illegal or fraudulent entries or filings; represent himself as the attorney or agent of entrymen when he is only attorney or agent for a transferee or mortgagee; conceal the name or interest of his client; give pernicious advice to parties seeking to obtain title to public land; attempt to prevent a qualified person from settling upon, entering, or filing for a tract of public land properly subject to such entry or filing, or be otherwise guilty of dishonest or unprofessional conduct, or who, in connection with business pending in local land offices or in this Department, shall knowingly employ as subagent, clerk, or correspondent a person who has been guilty of any one of these acts, or who has been prohibited from practicing before the register and receiver or this Department, it will be sufficient reason for his disbarment from practice, and registers and receivers are authorized to refuse to further recognize any person as agent or attorney who shall be known to them or be proven before them to be guilty of improper and unprofessional conduct as above stated.

An attorney or agent who has been admitted to practice in any particular land district may be enrolled and authorized to practice in any other district upon filing with the register and receiver of such district a certificate of the register or receiver before whom he was admitted to practice that he is an attorney or agent in good standing.

Any unprofessional conduct on the part of an attorney or agent should be reported to the Commissioner at once, together with the action of the local land officers in the premises.

Appeals from the action of the register and receiver in refusing to admit to practice or in refusing to further recognize an agent or attorney will lie to the Commissioner and Secretary, as in other appealable cases. (Circular approved March 19, 1887, 5 L. D., 508.)

V. LAWS AND REGULATIONS GOVERNING THE RECOGNITION OF AGENTS, ATTORNEYS, AND OTHER PERSONS TO REPRESENT CLAIMANTS BEFORE THE DEPARTMENT OF THE INTERIOR AND THE BUREAUS THEREOF.

LAWS.

The following statutes relate to the recognition of attorneys and agents for claimants before this Department:

"That the Secretary of the Interior may prescribe rules and regulations governing the recognition of agents, attorneys, or other persons representing claimants before his Department, and may require of such persons, agents, or attorneys, before being recognized as representatives of claimants, that they shall show that they are of good moral character and in good repute, possessed of the necessary qualifications to enable them to render such claimants valuable service, and otherwise competent to advise and assist such claimants in the presentation of their claims; and such Secretary may, after notice and opportunity for a hearing, suspend or exclude from further practice before his Department any such person, agent, or attorney shown to be incompetent, disreputable, or who refuses to comply with the said rules and regulations, or who shall with intent to defraud in any manner deceive, mislead, or threaten any claimant or prospective claimant by word, circular, letter or by advertisement." (Act July 4, 1884, sec. 5; 23 Stats., 101.)

"Every officer of the United States, or person holding any place of trust or profit, or discharging any official function under, or in connection with, any Executive Department of the Government of the United States, or under the Senate or House of Representatives of the United States, who acts as an agent or attorney for prosecuting any claim against the United States, or in any manner, or by any means, otherwise than in discharge of his proper official duties, aids or assists in the prosecution or support of any such claim, or receives any gratuity, or any share of or interest in any claim from any claimant against the United States, with intent to aid or assist, or in consideration of having aided or assisted, in the prosecution of such claim, shall pay a fine of not more than five thousand dollars, or suffer imprisonment not more than one year, or both." (Section 5498, Revised Statutes.)

"It shall not be lawful for any person appointed after the first day of June, one thousand eight hundred and seventy-two, as an officer, clerk, or employe in any of the departments, to act as counsel, attorney, or agent for prosecuting any claim against the United States, which was pending in either of said departments while he was such officer, clerk, or employe, nor in any manner, nor by any means, to aid in the prosecution of any such claim, within two years next after he shall have ceased to be such officer, clerk, or employe." (Section 190, Revised Statutes.)

"Any person prosecuting claims, either as attorney or on his own account, before any of the departments or bureaus of the United States, shall be required to take the oath of allegiance, and to support the Constitution of the United States, as required of persons in the civil service." (Section 3478, Revised Statutes.)

"The oath provided for in the preceding section may be taken before any justice of the peace, notary public, or other person who is legally authorized to administer an oath in the State or district where the same may be administered." (Section 3479, Revised Statutes.)

The act of May 13, 1884, sec. 2, (23 Stats., 22), provides that the oath above required shall be that prescribed by section 1757, Revised Statutes, which is as follows:

"I, A B, do solemnly swear (or affirm) that I will support and defend the Constitution of the United States against all enemies, foreign and domestic; that I will bear true faith and allegiance to the same; that I take this obligation freely, without any mental reservation or purpose of evasion; and that I will well and faithfully discharge the duties of the office on which I am about to enter. So help me God."

REGULATIONS.

"1. Under the authority conferred on the Secretary of the Interior by the fifth section of the act of July 4, 1884, it is hereby prescribed that an attorney at law who desires to represent claimants before the Department or one of its bureaus shall file a certificate of the clerk of the United States, State, or Territorial court, duly authenticated under the seal of the court, that he is an attorney *in good standing.*

"2. Any person (not an attorney at law) who desires to appear as agent for claimants before the Department or one of its bureaus must file a *certificate from a judge* of a United States, State, or Territorial court, *duly authenticated under the seal of the court,* that such person is of good moral character and in good repute, possessed of the necessary qualifications to enable him to render claimants valuable service, and otherwise competent to advise and assist them in the presentation of their claims.

"3. The Secretary may demand additional proof of qualifications, and reserves the right to decline to recognize any attorney, agent, or other person applying to represent claimants under this rule.

"4. The oath of allegiance required by section 3478 of the United States Revised Statutes must also be filed.

"5. In the case of a firm, the names of the individuals composing the firm must be given, and a certificate and oath as to each member of the firm will be required.

"6. Unless specially called for, the certificate above referred to will not be required of any attorney or agent heretofore recognized and now in good standing before the Department.

"7. An applicant for admission to practice under the above regulations must address a letter to the Secretary of the Interior, inclosing the certificate and oath above required, in which letter his full name and post-office address must be given. He must state whether or not he has ever been recognized as attorney or agent before this Department or any bureau thereof, and, if so, whether he has ever been suspended or disbarred from practice. *He must also state whether he holds any office of trust or profit under the Government of the United States.*

"8. No person who has been an officer, clerk, or employee of this Department within two years prior to his application to appear in any case pending herein shall be recognized or permitted to appear as an attorney or agent in any such case as shall have been pending in the Department at or before the date he left the service: *Provided,* This rule shall not apply to officers, clerks, or employees of the Patent Office, nor to cases therein.

"9. Whenever an attorney or agent is charged with improper practices in connection with any matter before a bureau of this Department, the head of such bureau shall investigate the charge, giving the attorney or agent due notice, together with a statement of the charge against him, and allow him an opportunity to be heard in the premises. When the investigation shall have been concluded, all the papers shall be forwarded to the Department, with a statement of the facts and such recommendations as to disbarment from practice as the head of the bureau may deem proper, for the consideration of the Secretary of the Interior. During the investigation the attorney or agent will be recognized as such, unless for special reasons the Secretary shall order his suspension from practice.

"10. If any attorney or agent in good standing before the Department shall knowingly employ as subagent or correspondent a person who has been prohibited from practice before the Department, it will be sufficient reason for the disbarment of the former from practice.

"11. Upon the disbarment of an attorney or agent, notice thereof will be given to the heads of bureaus of this Department, and to the other Executive Departments; and thereafter, until otherwise ordered, such disbarred person will not be recognized as attorney or agent in any claim or other matter before this Department or any bureau thereof."

APPENDIX F.

LAWS APPLICABLE TO THE ADMINISTRATION OF THE INTERNAL REVENUE LAWS.

SUPERVISION.

SEC. 3172, *as amended by section 34, act of August 28, 1894. (28 Stat., 509.)* Every collector shall, from time to time, cause his deputies to proceed through every part of his district and inquire after and concerning all persons therein who are liable to pay *any internal revenue tax*, and all persons owning or having the care and management of any objects liable to pay any tax, and to make a list of such persons and enumerate said objects.

SEC. 3173, *as amended by section 34, act of August 28, 1894. (28 Stat., 509.)* That it shall be the duty of any person, partnership, firm, association, or corporation, made liable to any duty, special tax, or *other* tax imposed by law, when not otherwise provided for, in case of a special tax on or before the thirty-first day of July in each year, in case of income tax on or before the first Monday of March in each year, and in other cases before the day on which the taxes accrue, to make a list or return, verified by oath or affirmation, to the collector or a deputy collector of the district where located, of the articles or objects, including the amount of annual income, charged with a duty or tax, the quantity of goods, wares, and merchandise made or sold, and charged with a tax, the several rates and aggregate amount, according to the forms and regulations to be prescribed by the Commissioner of Internal Revenue, with the approval of the Secretary of the Treasury, for which such person, partnership, firm, association, or corporation is liable: *Provided*, That if any person liable to pay any duty or tax, or owning, possessing, or having the care or management of property, goods, wares, and merchandise, articles or objects liable to pay any duty, tax, or license, shall fail to make and exhibit a list or return required by law, but shall consent to disclose the particulars of any and all the property, goods, wares, and merchandise, articles and objects liable to pay any duty or tax, or any business or occupation liable to pay any tax as aforesaid, then, and in that case, it shall be the duty of the collector or deputy collector to make such list or return, which, being distinctly read, consented to, and signed and verified by oath or affirmation by the person so owning, possessing, or having the care and management as aforesaid, may be received as the list of such person: *Provided further*, That in case no annual list or return has been rendered by such person to the collector or deputy collector as required by law, and the person shall be absent from his or her residence or place of business at the time the collector or a deputy collector shall call for the annual list or return, it shall be the duty of such collector or deputy collector to leave at such place of residence or business, with some one of suitable age and discretion, if such be present, otherwise to deposit in the nearest post-office a note or memorandum addressed to such person, requiring him or her to render to such collector or deputy collector the list or return required by law, within ten days from the date of such note or memorandum, verified by oath or affirmation. And if any person on being notified or required as aforesaid shall refuse or neglect to render such list or return within the time required as aforesaid, or whenever any person who is required to deliver a monthly or other return of objects subject to tax fails to do so at the time required, or delivers any return which, in the opinion of the collector, is false or fraudulent, or contains any undervaluation or understatement, it shall be lawful for the collector to summon such person, or any other person having possession, custody, or care of books of account containing entries relating to the business of such person, or any other person he may deem proper, to appear before him and produce such books, at a time and place named in the summons, and to give testimony or answer interrogatories, under oath, respecting any objects liable to tax or the returns thereof. The collector may summon any person residing or found within the State in which his district lies; and when the person intended to be summoned does not reside and can not be found within such State, he may enter any collection district where such person may be found, and there make the examination herein authorized. And to this end he may there exercise all the authority which he might lawfully exercise in the district for which he was commissioned.

SUMMONS.

SEC. 3174. Such summons shall in all cases be served by a deputy collector of the district where the person to whom it is directed may be found, by an attested copy delivered to such person in hand, or left at his last and usual place of abode, allowing such person one day for each twenty-five miles he may be required to travel, computed from the place of service to the place of examination; and the certificate of service signed by such deputy shall be evidence of the facts it states on the hearing of an application for an attachment. When the summons requires the production of books, it shall be sufficient if such books are described with reasonable certainty.

SEC. 3175. Whenever any person summoned under the two preceding sections neglects or refuses to obey such summons, or to give testimony, or to answer interrogatories as required, the collectors may apply to the judge of the district court or to a commissioner of the circuit court of the United States for the district within which the person so summoned resides for an attachment against him as for a contempt. It shall be the duty of the judge or commissioner to hear the application, and, if satisfactory proof is made, to issue an attachment, directed to some proper officer, for the arrest of such person, and upon his being brought before him to proceed to a hearing of the case; and upon such hearing the judge or commissioner shall have power to make such order as he shall deem proper not inconsistent with existing laws for the punishment of contempts, to enforce obedience to the requirements of the summons and to punish such person for his default or disobedience.

RETURNS.

SEC. 3176, *as amended by section 34, act of August 28, 1894* (28 Stat., 509). When any person, corporation, company, or association refuses or neglects to render any return or list required by law, or renders a false or fraudulent return or list, the collector or any deputy collector shall make, according to the best information which he can obtain, including that derived from the evidence elicited by the examination of the collector, and on his own view and information, such list or return, according to the form prescribed, of the income, property, and objects liable to tax owned or possessed or under the care or management of such person, or corporation, company, or association and the Commissioner of Internal Revenue shall assess all taxes not paid by stamps, including the amount, if any, due for special tax, income or other tax, and in case of any return of a false or fraudulent list or valuation intentionally he shall add one hundred per centum to such tax; and in case of a refusal or neglect, except in cases of sickness or absence, to make a list or return, or to verify the same as aforesaid, he shall add fifty per centum to such tax. In case of neglect occasioned by sickness or absence as aforesaid the collector may allow such further time for making and delivering such list or return as he may deem necessary, not exceeding thirty days. The amount so added to the tax shall be collected at the same time and in the same manner as the tax unless the neglect or falsity is discovered after the tax has been paid, in which case the amount so added shall be collected in the same manner as the tax; and the list or return so made and subscribed by such collector or deputy collector shall be held *prima facie* good and sufficient for all legal purposes.

SEC. 3177. Any collector, deputy collector, or inspector may enter, in the daytime, any building or place where any articles or objects subject to tax are made, produced, or kept, within his district, so far as it may be necessary, for the purpose of examining said articles or objects. And any owner of such building or place, or person having the agency or superintendence of the same, who refuses to admit such officer, or to suffer him to examine such article or articles, shall, for every such refusal, forfeit five hundred dollars. And when such premises are open at night, such officers may enter them while so open, in the performance of their official duties. And if any person shall forcibly obstruct or hinder any collector, deputy collector, or inspector, in the execution of any power and authority vested in him by law, or shall forcibly rescue or cause to be rescued any property, articles, or objects after the same shall have been seized by him, or shall attempt or endeavor so to do, the person so offending, excepting in cases otherwise provided for, shall, for every such offense, forfeit and pay the sum of five hundred dollars, or double the value of the property so rescued, or be imprisoned for a term not exceeding two years, at the discretion of the court.

SEC. 3179. Whenever any person delivers or discloses to the collector or deputy any false or fraudulent list, return, account, or statement, with intent to defeat or evade the valuation, enumeration, or assessment intended to be made, or, being duly summoned to appear to testify, or to appear and produce such books as aforesaid, neglects to appear or to produce said books, he shall be fined not exceeding one thousand dollars, or be imprisoned not exceeding one year, or both, at the discretion of the court, with costs of prosecution.

SEC. 3180. Whenever there are in any district any articles not owned or possessed by or under the care or control of any person within such district, and liable to be taxed, and of which no list has been transmitted to the collector, as required by law, the collector or one of his deputies shall enter the premises where such articles are situated and shall take such view thereof as may be necessary, and make lists of the same, according to the form prescribed. Said lists, being subscribed by such collector or deputy, shall be taken as sufficient lists of such articles for all purposes.

SEC. 3181. The lists or returns aforesaid shall, where not otherwise especially provided for, be taken with reference to the day fixed for that purpose by this Title as aforesaid; and where duties accrue at other and different times, the *list* shall be taken with reference to the time when said taxes become due, and shall be denominated annual, monthly, and special lists or returns.

ASSESSMENTS.

SEC. 3182. The Commissioner of Internal Revenue is hereby authorized and required to make the inquiries, determinations, and assessments of all taxes and penalties imposed by this Title, or accruing under any former internal-revenue act, where such taxes had not been duly paid by stamp at the time and in the manner provided by law, and shall certify a list of such assessments when made to the proper collectors respectively, who shall proceed to collect and account for the taxes and penalties so certified. Whenever it is ascertained that any list which has been or shall be delivered to any collector, is imperfect or incomplete in consequence of the omission of the name of any person liable to tax, or in consequence of any omission, or understatement, or undervaluation, or false or fraudulent statement contained in any return made by any person liable to tax, the Commissioner of Internal Revenue may, at any time within fifteen months from the time of the delivery of the list to the collector as aforesaid, enter on any monthly or special list the name of such person so omitted, together with the amount of tax for which he may have been or shall become liable, and also the name of any such person in respect to whose return, as aforesaid, there has been or shall be any omission, undervaluation, understatement, or false or fraudulent statement, together with the amount for which such person may be liable, above the amount for which he may have been or shall be assessed upon any return made as aforesaid; and he shall certify and return such list to the collector as required by law. And all provisions of law for the ascertainment of liability to any tax, or the assessment or collection thereof, shall be held to apply, so far as may be necessary, to the proceedings herein authorized and directed.

COLLECTION.

SEC. 3183, *as amended by section 3, act of March 1, 1879 (20 Stat., 327).* It shall be the duty of the collectors, or their deputies, in their respective districts, and they are authorized, to collect all the taxes imposed by law, however the same may be designated. And every collector and deputy collector shall give receipts for all sums collected by him, *excepting only when the same are in payment for stamps sold and delivered; but no collector or deputy collector shall issue a receipt in lieu of a stamp representing a tax.*

[SEC. 3183*a*.] *Section 37, act of August 28, 1894 (28 Stat., 509).* That it shall be the duty of every collector of internal revenue, to whom any payment of any taxes other than the tax represented by an adhesive stamp or other engraved stamp is made under the provisions of this Act, to give to the person making such payment a full written or printed receipt, expressing the amount paid and the particular account for which such payment was made; and whenever such payment is made such collector shall, if required, give a separate receipt for each tax paid by any debtor, on account of payments made to or to be made by him to separate creditors in such form that such debtor can conveniently produce the same separately to his several creditors in satisfaction of their respective demands to the amounts specified in such receipts; and such receipts shall be sufficient evidence in favor of such debtor, to justify him in withholding the amount therein expressed from his next payment to his creditor; but such creditor may, upon giving to his debtor a full written receipt, acknowledging the payment to him of whatever sum may be actually paid, and accepting the amount of tax paid as aforesaid (specifying the same) as a further satisfaction of the debt to that amount, require the surrender to him of such collector's receipt.

SEC. 3184. Where it is not otherwise provided, the collector shall in person or by deputy, within ten days after receiving any list of taxes from the Commissioner of Internal Revenue, give notice to each person liable to pay any taxes stated therein, to be left at his dwelling or usual place of business, or to be sent by mail, stating the amount of such taxes and demanding payment thereof. If such person does not pay the taxes within ten days after the service or the sending by mail of such notice, it shall be the duty of the collector or his deputy to collect the said taxes with a penalty of five per centum additional upon the amount of taxes, and interest at the rate of one per centum a month.

SEC. 3185. All returns required to be made monthly by any person liable to tax shall be made on or before the tenth day of each month, and the tax assessed or due thereon shall be returned by the Commissioner of Internal Revenue to the collector on or before the last day of each month. All returns for which no provision is otherwise made shall be made on or before the tenth day of the month succeeding the time when the tax is due and liable to be assessed, and the tax thereon shall be returned as herein provided for monthly returns, and shall be due and payable on or before the last day of the month in which the assessment is so made. When the said tax is not paid on or before the last day of the month, as aforesaid, the collector shall add a penalty of five per centum, together with interest at the rate of one per centum per month, upon such tax from the time the same became due; but no interest for a fraction of a month shall be demanded: *Provided,* That notice of the time when such tax becomes due and payable is given in such manner as may be prescribed by the Commissioner of Internal Revenue. It shall then be the duty of the collector, in case of the non-payment of said tax on or before the last day of the month, as aforesaid, to demand payment thereof, with five per centum added thereto, and interest at the rate of one per centum per month, as aforesaid, in the manner prescribed by law; and if said tax, penalty, and interest, are not paid within ten days after such demand, it shall be lawful for the collector or his deputy to make distraint therefor, as provided by law.

ENFORCEMENT.

SEC. 3186, *as amended by section 3, act of March 1, 1879 (20 Stat., 327).* If any person liable to pay any tax neglects or refuses to pay the same after demand, the amount shall be a lien in favor of the United States from the time when the assessment-list was received by the collector, except when otherwise provided, until paid, with the interest, penalties, and costs that may accrue in addition thereto, upon all property and rights to property belonging to such person.

SEC. 3187. If any person liable to pay any taxes neglects or refuses to pay the same within ten days after notice and demand, it shall be lawful for the collector or his deputy to collect the said taxes, with five per centum additional thereto, and interest as aforesaid, by distraint and sale, in the manner hereafter provided, of the goods, chattels, or effects, including stocks, securities, and evidences of debt, of the person delinquent as aforesaid: *Provided,* That there shall be exempt from distraint and sale, if belonging to the head of a family, the school-books and wearing apparel necessary for such family; also arms for personal use, one cow, two hogs, five sheep and the wool thereof, provided the aggregate market-value of said sheep shall not exceed fifty dollars; the necessary food for such cow, hogs, and sheep, for a period not exceeding thirty days; fuel to an amount not greater in value than twenty-five dollars; provisions to an amount not greater than fifty dollars; household furniture kept for use to an amount not greater than three hundred dollars; and the books, tools, or implements, of a trade or profession, to an amount not greater than one hundred dollars shall also be exempt; and the officer making the distraint shall summon three disinterested householders of the vicinity, who shall appraise and set apart to the owner the amount of property herein declared to be exempt.

SEC. 3188. In such case of neglect or refusal, the collector may levy, or by warrant may authorize a deputy collector to levy, upon all property and rights to property, except such as are exempt by the preceding section, belonging to such person, or on which the said lien exists, for the payment of the sum due as aforesaid, with interest and penalty for non-payment, and also of such further sum as shall be sufficient for the fees, costs, and expenses of such levy.

SEC. 3189. All persons, and officers of companies or corporations, are required, on demand of a collector or deputy collector about to distrain or having distrained on any property, or rights of property, to exhibit all books containing evidence or statements relating to the subject of distraint, or the property or rights of property liable to distraint for the tax due as aforesaid.

DISTRAINT.

SEC. 3190. When distraint is made, as aforesaid, the officer charged with the collection shall make or cause to be made an account of the goods or effects distrained, a copy of which, signed by the officer making such distraint, shall be left with the owner or possessor of such goods or effects, or at his dwelling or usual place of business, with some person of suitable age and discretion, if any such can be found, with a note of the sum demanded, and the time and place of sale; and the said officer shall forthwith cause a notification to be published in some newspaper within the county wherein said distraint is made, if a newspaper is published in said county, or to be publicly posted at the post-office, if there be one within five miles, nearest to the residence of the person whose property shall be distrained, and in not less than two other public places. Such notice shall specify the articles distrained, and the time and place for the sale thereof. Such time shall not be less than ten nor more than twenty days from the date of such notification to the owner or possessor of the property and the publication or posting of such notice as herein provided, and the place proposed for the sale shall not be more than five miles distant from the place of making such distraint. Said sale may be adjourned from time to time by said officer, if he deems it advisable, but not for a time to exceed in all thirty days.

SEC. 3191. When property subject to tax, but upon which the tax has not been paid, is seized upon distraint and sold, the amount of such tax shall, after deducting the expenses of such sale, be first appropriated out of the proceeds thereof to the payment of the tax. And if no assessment of such tax has been made upon such property, the collector shall make a return thereof in the form required by law, and the Commissioner of Internal Revenue shall assess the tax thereon.

SEC. 3192. When any property advertised for sale under distraint, as aforesaid, is of a kind subject to tax, and the tax has not been paid, and the amount bid for such property is not equal to the amount of the tax, the collector may purchase the same in behalf of the United States for an amount not exceeding the said tax. All property so purchased may be sold by the collector, under such regulations as may be prescribed by the Commissioner of Internal Revenue. The collector shall render to the Commissioner a distinct account of all charges incurred in such sales, and, in case of sale, shall pay into the Treasury the surplus, if any there be, after defraying all lawful charges and fees.

SEC. 3193. In any case of distraint for the payment of the taxes aforesaid, the goods, chattels, or effects so distrained shall be restored to the owner or possessor, if, prior to the sale, payment of the amount due is made to the proper officer charged with the collection, together with the fees and other charges; but in case of nonpayment as aforesaid, the said officer shall proceed to sell the said goods, chattels, or effects at public auction, and shall retain from the proceeds of such sale the amount demandable for the use of the United States, and a commission of five per centum thereon for his own use, with the fees and charges for distraint and sale, rendering the overplus, if any there be, to the person who may be entitled to receive the same.

SALE.

SEC. 3194. In all cases of sale, as aforesaid, the certificate of such sale shall be *prima facie* evidence of the right of the officer to make such sale, and conclusive evidence of the regularity of his proceedings in making the sale, and shall transfer to the purchaser all right, title, and interest of such delinquent in and to the property sold; and where such property consists of stocks, said certificate shall be notice, when received, to any corporation, company, or association of said transfer, and shall be authority to such corporation, company, or association to record the same on their books and records in the same manner as if transferred or assigned by the party holding the same, in lieu of any original or prior certificates, which shall be void, whether canceled or not. And said certificates, where the subject of sale is securities or other evidences of debt, shall be good and valid receipts to the person holding the same, as against any person holding, or claiming to hold, possession of such securities or other evidences of debt.

Sec. 3195. When any property liable to distraint for taxes is not divisible, so as to enable the collector by a sale of part thereof to raise the whole amount of the tax, with all costs, charges, and commissions, the whole of such property shall be sold, and the surplus of the proceeds of the sale, after satisfying the tax, costs, and charges, shall be paid to the person legally entitled to receive the same; or, if he can not be found, or refuses to receive the same, shall be deposited in the Treasury of the United States, to be there held for his use until he makes application therefor to the Secretary of the Treasury, who, upon such application and satisfactory proofs in support thereof, shall, by warrant on the Treasury, cause the same to be paid to the applicant.

Sec. 3196. When goods, chattels, or effects sufficient to satisfy the taxes imposed upon any person are not found by the collector or deputy collector, he is authorized to collect the same by seizure and sale of real estate.

Sec. 3197, *as amended by section 3, act of March 1, 1879 (20 Stat., 327).* The officer making the seizure mentioned in the preceding section shall give notice to the person whose estate it is proposed to sell by giving him in hand, or leaving at his last or usual place of abode, if he has any such within the collection-district where said estate is situated, a notice, in writing, stating what particular estate is to be sold, describing the same with reasonable certainty, and the time when and place where said officer proposes to sell the same; which time shall not be less than twenty nor more than forty days from the time of giving said notice. The said officer shall also cause a notification to the same effect to be published in some newspaper within the county where such seizure is made, if any such there be, and shall also cause a like notice to be posted at the post-office nearest to the estate seized, and in two other public places within the county; and the place of said sale shall not be more than five miles distant from the estate seized, except by special order of the Commissioner of Internal Revenue. At the time and place appointed, the officer making such seizure shall proceed to sell the said estate at public auction, offering the same at a minimum price, including the expense of making such levy, and all charges for advertising and an officer's fee of ten dollars. When the real estate so seized consists of several distinct tracts or parcels, the officer making sale thereof shall offer each tract or parcel for sale separately, and shall, if he deem it advisable, apportion the expenses, charges, and fees aforesaid to such several tracts or parcels, or to any of them, in estimating the minimum price aforesaid. If no person offers for said estate the amount of said minimum price, the officer shall declare the same to be purchased by him for the United States; otherwise the same shall be declared to be sold to the highest bidder.

And in case the same shall be declared to be purchased for the United States, the officer shall immediately transmit a certificate of the purchase to the Commissioner of Internal Revenue, and, at the proper time, as hereafter provided, shall execute a deed therefor, after its preparation and the indorsement of approval as to its form by the United States district attorney for the district in which the property is situate, and shall without delay cause the same to be duly recorded in the proper registry of deeds, and immediately thereafter shall transmit such deed to the Commissioner of Internal Revenue.

And said sale may be adjourned from time to time by said officer for not exceeding thirty days in all, if he shall think it advisable so to do. If the amount bid shall not be then and there paid, the officer shall forthwith proceed to again sell said estate in the same manner.

And it is hereby provided, That all certificates of purchase, and deeds of property purchased by the United States under the internal-revenue laws, on sales for taxes, or under executions issued from United States courts, which now are, or hereafter may be, found in the office of any collector, United States marshal, or United States district attorney, shall be immediately transmitted by such officers respectively to the Commissioner of Internal Revenue.

And it is hereby further provided, That for the preparation and approval by the United States district attorney of each deed as above required, a fee of five dollars shall be allowed to that officer, to be paid by the United States, and which he shall account for in his emolument returns.

SEC. 3198. Upon any sale of real estate, as provided in the preceding section, and the payment of the purchase money, the officer making the seizure and sale shall give to the purchaser a certificate of purchase, which shall set forth the real estate purchased, for whose taxes the same was sold, the name of the purchaser, and the price paid therefor; and if the said real estate be not redeemed in the manner and within the time hereafter provided, the said collector or deputy collector shall execute to the said purchaser, upon his surrender of said certificate, a deed of the real estate purchased by him as aforesaid, reciting the facts set forth in said certificate, and in accordance with the laws of the State in which such real estate is situate upon the subject of sales of real estate under execution.

SEC. 3199. The deed of sale given in pursuance of the preceding section shall be *prima facie* evidence of the facts therein stated; and if the proceedings of the officer as set forth have been substantially in accordance with the provisions of law, shall be considered and operate as a conveyance of all the right, title, and interest the party delinquent had in and to the real estate thus sold at the time the lien of the United States attached thereto.

SEC. 3200. Any collector or deputy collector may, for the collection of taxes imposed upon any person, and committed to him for collection, seize and sell the lands of such person situated in any other collection district within the State in which such officer resides; and his proceedings in relation thereto shall have the same effect as if the same were had in his proper collection district.

SEC. 3201. Any person whose estate may be proceeded against as aforesaid shall have the right to pay the amount due, together with the costs and charges thereon, to the collector or deputy collector at any time prior to the sale thereof, and all further proceedings shall cease from the time of such payment.

SEC. 3202. The owners of any real estate sold as aforesaid, their heirs, executors, or administrators, or any person having any interest therein, or a lien thereon, or any person in their behalf, shall be permitted to redeem the land sold, or any particular tract thereof, at any time within one year after the sale thereof, upon payment to the purchaser, or, in case he can not be found in the county in which the land to be redeemed is situate, then to the collector of the district in which the land is situate, for the use of the purchaser, his heirs or assigns, the amount paid by the said purchaser and interest thereon at the rate of twenty per centum per annum.

SEC. 3203, *as amended by section 3, act of March 1, 1879 (20 Stat., 327).* It shall be the duty of every collector to keep a record of all sales of land made in his collection district, whether by himself or his deputies, or by another collector, in which shall be set forth the tax for which any such sale was made, the dates of seizure and sale, the name of the party assessed, and all proceedings in making said sale, amount of fees and expenses, the name of the purchaser and the date of the deed; and said record shall be certified by the officer making the sale. And on or before the fifth day of each succeeding month he shall transmit a copy of such record of the preceding month to the Commissioner of Internal Revenue.

And it shall be the duty of every deputy making sale, as aforesaid, to return a statement of all his proceedings to the collector, and to certify the record thereof. In case of the death or removal of the collector, or the expiration of his term of office from any other cause, said record shall be delivered to his successor in office; and a copy of every such record, certified by the collector, shall be evidence in any court of the truth of the facts therein stated.

SEC. 3204. When any lands sold, as aforesaid, are redeemed as heretofore provided, the collector shall make entry of the fact upon the record mentioned in the preceding section, and the said entry shall be evidence of such redemption.

SEC. 3205. Whenever any property, personal or real, which is seized and sold by virtue of the foregoing provisions, is not sufficient to satisfy the claim of the United States for which distraint or seizure is made, the collector may, thereafter, and as often as the same may be necessary, proceed to seize and sell, in like manner, any other property liable to seizure of the person against whom such claim exists, until the amount due from him, together with all expenses, is fully paid.

SEC. 3206. The Commissioner of Internal Revenue shall by regulation determine the fees and charges to be allowed in all cases of distraint and other seizures; and shall have power to determine whether any expense incurred in making any distraint or seizure was necessary.

JUDICIAL PROCESS.

SEC. 3207. In any case where there has been a refusal or neglect to pay any tax, and it has become necessary to seize and sell real estate to satisfy the same, the Commissioner of Internal Revenue may direct a bill in chancery to be filed, in a district or circuit court of the United States, to enforce the lien of the United States for tax upon any real estate, or to subject any real estate owned by the delinquent, or in which he has any right, title, or interest, to the payment of such tax. All persons having liens upon or claiming any interest in the real estate sought to be subjected as aforesaid, shall be made parties to such proceedings, and be brought into court as provided in other suits in chancery therein. And the said court shall, at the term next after the parties have been duly notified of the proceedings, unless otherwise ordered by the court, proceed to adjudicate all matters involved therein, and finally determine the merits of all claims to and liens upon the real estate in question, and, in all cases where a claim or interest of the United States therein is established, shall decree a sale of such real estate, by the proper officer of the court, and a distribution of the proceeds of such sale according to the findings of the court in respect to the interests of the parties and of the United States.

SEC. 3208, *as amended by section 3, act of March 1, 1879 (20 Stat., 327).*

The Commissioner of Internal Revenue shall have charge of all real estate which is now or shall become the property of the United States by judgment of forfeiture under the internal-revenue laws, or which has been or shall be assigned, set off, or conveyed by purchase or otherwise to the United States in payment of debts or penalties arising under the laws relating to internal revenue, or which has been or shall be vested in the United States by mortgage or other security for the payment of such debts, and of all trusts created for the use of the United States in payment of such debts due them; and, with the approval of the Secretary of the Treasury, may at public vendue, and upon not less than twenty days' notice, sell and dispose of all real estate owned or held by the United States as aforesaid; and until such sale the Commissioner of Internal Revenue, with the approval of the Secretary of the Treasury, may lease such real estate owned as aforesaid on such terms and for such period as they shall deem expedient.

And in cases where real estate has or may become the property of the United States by conveyance or otherwise, in payment of or as security for a debt arising under the laws relating to internal revenue, and such debt shall have been paid, together with the interest thereon, at the rate of one per centum per month, to the United States, within two years from the date of the acquisition of such real estate, it shall be lawful for the Commissioner of Internal Revenue, with the approval of the Secretary of the Treasury, to release by deed, or otherwise convey such real estate to the debtor from whom it was taken, or to his heirs or other legal representatives.

SEC. 3209. Whenever a collector has on any list duly returned to him the name of any person not within his collection district who is liable to tax, or of any person so liable who has, in the collection district in which he resides, no sufficient property subject to seizure or distraint, from which the money due for tax can be collected, such collector shall transmit a statement containing the name of the person liable to such tax, with the amount and nature thereof, duly certified under his hand, to the collector of any district to which said person shall have removed, or in which he shall have property, real or personal, liable to be seized and sold for tax. And the collector to whom the said certified statement is transmitted shall proceed to collect the said tax in the same way as if the name of the person and objects of tax contained in the said certified statement were on any list of his own collection district; and he shall, upon receiving said certified statement as aforesaid, transmit his receipt for it to the collector sending the same to him.

PAYMENT.

SEC. 3210. The gross amount of all taxes and revenues received or collected by virtue of this title, or of any law hereafter enacted providing internal revenue, shall be paid, by the officers receiving or collecting the same, daily into the Treasury of the United States, under the instructions of the Secretary of the Treasury, without any abatement or deduction on account of salary, compensation, fees, costs, charges, expenses, or claims of any description; and a certificate of such payment, stating the name of the depositor and the specific account on which the deposit was made, signed by the Treasurer, Assistant Treasurer, designated depositary, or proper officer of a deposit bank, shall be transmitted to the Commissioner of Internal Revenue: *Provided,* That in districts where, from the distance of the officer, collector, or agent receiving or collecting such taxes and revenues from a proper Government depository, the Secretary of the Treasury may deem it proper, he may extend the time for making such payment, not exceeding, however, in any case a period of one month.

SEC. 3211. The Secretary of the Treasury is authorized to designate one or more depositories in each State, for the deposit and safe-keeping of the money collected by virtue of the internal-revenue laws; and the receipt of the proper officer of such depository to a collector for the money deposited by him shall be a sufficient voucher for such collector in the settlement of his accounts at the Treasury Department.

SEC. 3212. Every collector shall, at the expiration of each month after he commences his collections, transmit to the Commissioner of Internal Revenue a statement of the collections made by him within the month. And every collector shall complete the collection of all sums assigned to him for collection, and shall pay over the same into the Treasury, and shall render his accounts to the Treasury Department as often as he may be required.

FORFEITURES.

SEC. 3213. It shall be the duty of the collectors, in their respective districts, subject to the provisions of this title, to prosecute for the recovery of any sums which may be forfeited by law. All suits for fines, penalties, and forfeitures, where not otherwise provided for, shall be brought in the name of the United States, in any proper form of action, or by any appropriate form of proceedings, *qui tam* or otherwise, before any circuit or district court of the United States for the district within which said fine, penalty, or forfeiture may have been incurred, or before any other court of competent jurisdiction; and taxes may be sued for and recovered in the name of the United States, in any proper form of action, before any circuit or district court of the United States for the district within which the liability to such tax is incurred, or where the party from whom such tax is due resides at the time of the commencement of the said action.

SEC. 3214. No suit for the recovery of taxes, or of any fine, penalty, or forfeiture, shall be commenced unless the Commissioner of Internal Revenue authorizes or sanctions the proceedings: *Provided,* That in case of any suit for penalties or forfeitures brought upon information received from any person, other than a collector or deputy collector, the United States shall not be subject to any costs of suit.

SEC. 3215. It shall be the duty of the Commissioner of Internal Revenue, with the approval of the Secretary of the Treasury, to establish such regulations, not inconsistent with law, for the observance of revenue officers, district attorneys, and marshals, respecting suits arising under the internal-revenue laws in which the United States is a party, as may be deemed necessary for the just responsibility of those officers and the prompt collection of all revenues and debts due and accruing to the United States under such laws.

SEC. 3216. All judgments and moneys recovered or received for taxes, costs, forfeitures, and penalties, shall be paid to collectors as internal taxes are required to be paid.

DELINQUENCY.

SEC. 3217. When any collector fails either to collect or to render his account, or to pay over in the manner or within the times provided by law, the (First) Comptroller of the Treasury shall, immediately after evidence of such delinquency, report the same to the Solicitor of the Treasury, who shall issue a warrant of distress against such delinquent collector, directed to the marshal of the district, expressing therein the amount with which the said collector is chargeable, and the sums, if any, which have been paid over by him, so far as the same are ascertainable. And the said marshal shall, himself, or by his deputy, immediately proceed to levy and collect the sum which may remain due, with five per centum thereon, and all the expenses and charges of collection, by distress and sale of the goods and chattels, or any personal effects of the delinquent collector, giving at least five days' notice of the time and place of sale, in the manner provided by law for advertising sales of personal property on execution in the State wherein such collector resides. And the bill of sale of the officer of any goods, chattels, or other personal property, distrained and sold as aforesaid, shall be conclusive evidence of title to the purchaser, and *prima facie* evidence of the right of the officer to make such sale, and of the correctness of his proceedings in selling the same. And for want of goods and chattels, or other personal effects of such collector, sufficient to satisfy any warrant of distress, issued as aforesaid, the real estate of such collector, or so much thereof as may be necessary for satisfying the said warrant, after being advertised for at least three weeks next before the time of sale, in not less than three public places in the collection district, and in one newspaper printed in the county or district, if any there be, shall be sold at public auction by the marshal or his deputy. Upon such sale, the marshal shall make and deliver to the purchaser of the premises sold a deed of conveyance thereof, to be executed and acknowledged in the manner and form prescribed by the laws of the State in which said lands are situated, and said deed so made shall invest the purchaser with all the title and interest of the defendant named in said warrant, existing at the time of the seizure thereof. And all moneys that may remain of the proceeds of such sale of personal or real property, after satisfying the said warrant of distress, and paying the reasonable costs and charges of sale, shall be returned to the proprietor of the property sold as aforesaid.

SEC. 3218. Every collector shall be charged with the whole amount of taxes, whether contained in lists transmitted to him by the Commissioner of Internal Revenue, or by other collectors, or delivered to him by his predecessor in office, and with the additions thereto, with the par value of all stamps deposited with him, and with all moneys collected for penalties, forfeitures, fees, or costs; and he shall be credited with all payments into the Treasury made as provided by law, with all stamps returned by him uncanceled to the Treasury, and with the amount of taxes contained in the lists transmitted in the manner heretofore provided to other collectors, and by them receipted as aforesaid; also with the amount of the taxes of such persons as may have absconded, or become insolvent, prior to the day when the tax ought, according to the provisions of law, to have been collected, and with all uncollected taxes transferred by him or by his deputy acting as collector to his successor in office: *Provided,* That it shall be proved to the satisfaction of the Commissioner of Internal Revenue, who shall certify the facts to the (First) Comptroller of the Treasury, that due diligence was used by the collector. And each collector shall also be credited with the amount of all property purchased by him for the use of the United States, provided he faithfully account for and pay over the proceeds thereof upon a resale of the same as required by law.

SEC. 3219. In case of the death, resignation, or removal of any collector, all lists and accounts of taxes uncollected shall be transferred to his successor in office as soon as such successor is appointed and qualified, and it shall be the duty of such successor to collect the same.

REFUND.

SEC. 3220. The Commissioner of Internal Revenue, subject to regulations prescribed by the Secretary of the Treasury, is authorized, on appeal to him made, to remit, refund, and pay back all taxes erroneously or illegally assessed or collected, all penalties collected without authority, and all taxes that appear to be unjustly assessed or excessive in amount, or in any manner wrongfully collected; also to repay to any collector or deputy collector the full amount of such sums of money as may be recovered against him.

SEC. 3221, *as amended by section 6, act of March 1, 1879 (20 Stat., 327).* The Secretary of the Treasury, upon the production to him of satisfactory proof of the actual destruction by accidental fire or other casualty, and without any fraud, collusion, or negligence of the owner thereof, of any distilled spirits, while the same remained in the custody of any officer of internal revenue in any distillery warehouse, or bonded warehouse of the United States and before the tax thereon has been paid, may abate the amount of internal taxes accruing thereon, and may cancel any warehouse bond, or enter satisfaction thereon, in whole or in part, as the case may be. And if such taxes have been collected since the destruction of said spirits, the said Secretary shall refund the same to the owners thereof out of any moneys in the Treasury not otherwise appropriated. *And when any distilled spirits are hereafter destroyed by accidental fire or other casualty, without any fraud, collusion, or negligence of the owner thereof, after the time when the same should have been drawn off by the gauger and placed in the distillery warehouse provided by law, no tax shall be collected on such spirits so destroyed, or if collected, it shall be refunded upon the production of satisfactory proof that the spirits were destroyed as herein specified.*

SEC. 3222. The preceding section shall take effect in all cases of loss or destruction of distilled spirits as aforesaid which have occurred since January one, eighteen hundred and sixty-eight.

SEC. 3223, *as amended by section 3, act of March 1, 1879 (20 Stat., 327).* When the owners of distilled spirits in the cases provided for by the two preceding sections may be indemnified against such tax by a valid claim of insurance *for a sum greater than the actual value of the distilled spirits before and without the tax being paid,* the tax shall not be remitted to the extent of such insurance.

SEC. 3224. No suit for the purpose of restraining the assessment or collection of any tax shall be maintained in any court.

SEC. 3225. When a second assessment is made in case of any list, statement, or return, which in the opinion of the collector or deputy collector was false or fraudulent, or contained any understatement or undervaluation, no taxes collected under such assessment shall be recovered by any suit, unless it is proved that the said list, statement, or return was not false nor fraudulent, and did not contain any understatement or undervaluation.

REVISION.

SEC. 3226. No suit shall be maintained in any court for the recovery of any internal tax alleged to have been erroneously or illegally assessed or collected, or of any penalty claimed to have been collected without authority, or of any sum alleged to have been excessive or in any manner wrongfully collected, until appeal shall have been duly made to the Commissioner of Internal Revenue, according to the provisions of law in that regard, and the regulations of the Secretary of the Treasury established in pursuance thereof, and a decision of the Commissioner has been had therein: *Provided,* That if such decision is delayed more than six months from the date of such appeal, then the said suit may be brought, without first having a decision of the Commissioner at any time within the period limited in the next section.

SEC. 3227. No suit or proceeding for the recovery of

any internal tax alleged to have been erroneously or illegally assessed or collected, or of any penalty alleged to have been collected without authority, or of any sum alleged to have been excessive or in any manner wrongfully collected, shall be maintained in any court unless the same is brought within two years next after the cause of action accrued: *Provided,* That actions for such claims which accrued prior to June six, eighteen hundred and seventy-two, may be brought within one year from said date; and that where any such claim was pending before the Commissioner, as provided in the preceding section, an action thereon may be brought within one year after such decision and not after. But no right of action which was already barred by any statute on the said date shall be revived by this section.

SEC. 3228. All claims for the refunding of any internal tax alleged to have been erroneously or illegally assessed or collected, or of any penalty alleged to have been collected without authority, or of any sum alleged to have been excessive or in any manner wrongfully collected, must be presented to the Commissioner of Internal Revenue within two years next after the cause of action accrued: *Provided,* That claims which accrued prior to June six, eighteen hundred and seventy-two, may be presented to the Commissioner at any time within one year from said date. But nothing in this section shall be construed to revive any right of action which was already barred by any statute on that date.

SEC. 3229. The Commissioner of Internal Revenue, with the advice and consent of the Secretary of the Treasury, may compromise any civil or criminal case arising under the internal-revenue laws instead of commencing suit thereon; and, with the advice and consent of the said Secretary and the recommendation of the Attorney-General, he may compromise any such case after a suit thereon has been commenced. Whenever a compromise is made in any case there shall be placed on file in the office of the Commissioner the opinion of the Solicitor of Internal Revenue, or of the officer acting as such, with his reasons therefor, with a statement of the amount of tax assessed, the amount of additional tax or penalty imposed by law in consequence of the neglect or delinquency of the person against whom the tax is assessed, and the amount actually paid in accordance with the terms of the compromise.

SEC. 3230. No discontinuance or *nolle prosequi* of any prosecution under section three thousand two hundred and fifty-seven shall be allowed without the permission in writing of the Secretary of the Treasury and the Attorney-General.

SEC. 3231. It shall be lawful for any court in which any suit or criminal proceeding arising under the internal-revenue laws may be pending, to continue the same at any stage thereof, for good cause shown on motion by the district attorney.

SEC. 31. *Act June 13, 1898 (30 Stat., 448).* That all administrative, special, or stamp provisions of law, including the laws in relation to the assessment of taxes, not heretofore specifically repealed are hereby made applicable to this Act.

TABLE OF CASES.

[REFERENCES ARE TO SECTIONS.]

A.

[REFERENCES ARE TO SECTIONS.]

[REFERENCES ARE TO SECTIONS.]

[REFERENCES ARE TO SECTIONS.]

[REFERENCES ARE TO SECTIONS.]

[REFERENCES ARE TO SECTIONS.]

D.

E.

[REFERENCES ARE TO SECTIONS.]

F.

[REFERENCES ARE TO SECTIONS.]

G.

H.

[REFERENCES ARE TO SECTIONS.]

I.

[REFERENCES ARE TO SECTIONS.]

J.

K.

L.

[REFERENCES ARE TO SECTIONS.]

M.

[REFERENCES ARE TO SECTIONS.]

[REFERENCES ARE TO SECTIONS.]

[REFERENCES ARE TO SECTIONS.]

N.

O.

[REFERENCES ARE TO SECTIONS.]

P.

[REFERENCES ARE TO SECTIONS.]

[REFERENCES ARE TO SECTIONS.]

Q.

R.

[REFERENCES ARE TO SECTIONS.]

[REFERENCES ARE TO SECTIONS.]

[REFERENCES ARE TO SECTIONS.]

[REFERENCES ARE TO SECTIONS.]

[REFERENCES ARE TO SECTIONS.]

[REFERENCES ARE TO SECTIONS.]

[REFERENCES ARE TO SECTIONS.]

T.

U.

[REFERENCES ARE TO SECTIONS.]

[REFERENCES ARE TO SECTIONS.]

V.

W.

[REFERENCES ARE TO SECTIONS.]

Y.

Z.

INDEX.

[REFERENCES ARE TO SECTIONS.]

A.

[REFERENCES ARE TO SECTIONS.]

[REFERENCES ARE TO SECTIONS.]

B.

C.

[REFERENCES ARE TO SECTIONS.]

D.

[REFERENCES ARE TO SECTIONS.]

[REFERENCES ARE TO SECTIONS.]

[REFERENCES ARE TO SECTIONS.]

E.

[REFERENCES ARE TO SECTIONS.]

G.

[REFERENCES ARE TO SECTIONS.]

[REFERENCES ARE TO SECTIONS.]

M.

N.

O.

[REFERENCES ARE TO SECTIONS.]

[REFERENCES ARE TO SECTIONS.]

[REFERENCES ARE TO SECTIONS.]

[REFERENCES ARE TO SECTIONS.]

R.

[REFERENCES ARE TO SECTIONS.]

S.

[REFERENCES ARE TO SECTIONS.]

www.ingramcontent.com/pod-product-compliance
Lightning Source LLC
Chambersburg PA
CBHW051255200926
51612CB00002B/56
* 9 7 8 1 6 1 6 1 9 4 2 6 0 *